THE IMAGE OF LAW

*Cultural Memory
in
the
Present*

Mieke Bal and Hent de Vries, Editors

THE IMAGE OF LAW

Deleuze, Bergson, Spinoza

Alexandre Lefebvre

STANFORD UNIVERSITY PRESS
STANFORD, CALIFORNIA

Stanford University Press
Stanford, California
© 2008 by the Board of Trustees of the Leland Stanford Junior University.
All rights reserved.
No part of this book may be reproduced or transmitted in any form or by any means, electronic or mechanical, including photocopying and recording, or in any information storage or retrieval system without the prior written permission of Stanford University Press.
Printed in the United States of America on acid-free, archival-quality paper

Library of Congress Cataloging-in-Publication Data
Lefebvre, Alexandre, 1979-
   The image of law : Deleuze, Bergson, Spinoza / Alexandre Lefebvre.
      p. cm. -- (Cultural memory in the present)
   Includes bibliographical references and index.
   ISBN 978-0-8047-5984-7 (cloth : alk. paper) -- ISBN 978-0-8047-5985-4 (pbk. : alk. paper)
   1. Deleuze, Gilles, 1925-1995. 2. Bergson, Henri, 1859-1941. 3. Spinoza, Benedictus de, 1632-1677. 4. Law--Philosophy. 5. Judicial process. I. Title.
   B2430.D454L44 2009
   340'.1--dc22

2008014772

Typeset by Bruce Lundquist in 11/13.5 Adobe Garamond

*To Georges and Joanne
and to Melanie*

Contents

Preface xi
Abbreviations xvii

PART 1 THE DOGMATIC IMAGE OF LAW   1

1 The Judge as Schema: Hart   5
   How Does Law Work? Hart's Critique of Austin 8—Subsumption in the Critique of Pure Reason 12—Schematism and Choice in Adjudication 14

2 Reflective Judgment and the Law with Organs: Dworkin   22
   The Principle of Principle 22—Purposive Interpretation 26— Elegantia Juris: Integrity and the Lawfulness of the Contingent 29— Natural Purposes: The Law with Organs 33

3 Communication, Judgment, Retrospection: Habermas   37
   Habermas: Communicative Kantian 37—A Deleuzian Reply 41— Reply: Application Discourses 42

PART 2 THE IMAGE OF LAW: BERGSON AND TIME   51

4 Deleuze and the Critique of Law   53
   Jurisprudence vs. Law 53—Critique of Dogmatism in Law and Judgment 59— The Transcendental Encounter (Transcendental Empiricism) 72—Critique of Communication 77—Critique of Human Rights 82

5 The Time of Law I: Evolution in Holmes and Bergson   88
   Bergson: Time as Invention (Internal Difference and Differentiation) 91—Holmes: Evolution and the Time of Law 96— All Is Given: The Possible in Dworkin and Habermas 107

6 The Time of Law II: Bergson, Perception, and Memory   114
Pure Perception: Image and the Case as Image 117—The Pure Past and the Four Paradoxes of Time 126—Two Weak Points of Legal Pragmatism 137

7 The Time of Law III: Judgment *sub specie durationis*   143
The Pure Past of the Law and the Law without Organs 144—Actualizing the Pure Past of Law 152—Inattentive Judgment 162—Attentive Judgment 173— Griswold *and Attentive Judgment 190*

PART 3 SPINOZA AND PRACTICE   197

8 Three Spinozist Themes in a Deleuzian Jurisprudence   201
Spinoza's Physics in Deleuze's Philosophy of the Concept 201— Delgamuukw *I: Creation of a Legal Concept (Aboriginal Title) 207—Duration in Spinoza 218—* Delgamuukw *II: The Creation of Problems as the Power of Adjudication 226—Immanence and Expression 238—Summation: The Image of Law 251*

Notes   259
Cases Cited   287
Bibliography   289
Index   301

Preface: Why Deleuze and Law?

On first impression, it might seem inappropriate or futile to use Gilles Deleuze's philosophy in a theory of law and judgment. In due course I will explain why that may be so, but for now let's say that few philosophers have so systematically criticized and rejected the concepts of law and judgment as Deleuze has. In fact, by means of conventional textual commentary on his remarks on the subject, Deleuze would appear to be a dead-end from which to work out a philosophy of law: All that we would likely get is a sterile doubling of his critical, sometimes abusive, observations.

How then, or rather, why then proceed? A passage from *What Is Philosophy* gives a rationale for why it might be plausible to attempt a philosophy of law and judgment using Deleuze:

If one can still be a Platonist, Cartesian, or Kantian today, it is because one is justified in thinking that their concepts can be reactivated in our problems and inspire those concepts that need to be created. What is the best way to follow the great philosophers? Is it to repeat what they said or *to do what they did*, that is, create concepts for the problems that necessarily change? (*WP*, 28)

I began this book with a hunch that certain concepts central to Deleuze were promising resources from which to theorize law, keeping in mind his injunction that to read and think with a philosopher means extending thought to new problems. Accordingly, I have tried to activate some of Deleuze's key themes and concepts—such as his critique of recognition and dogmatic thought, his theory of time and repetition, and his concept of the encounter—within problems specific to the institutional operation of law and especially adjudication. This has nothing to do with "applying" concepts to a field as yet unconsidered; rather, it is to use Deleuze's thought in coordination with law toward the creation of new problems and new concepts. Extension to, and creation of, problems is the only way to remain faithful to Deleuze and to undertake a Deleuzian philosophy of law.

Although this notion of creating problems requires explanation, for the time being it can help elucidate two of my principal objectives: first, to contribute a Deleuzian concept of judgment, and, second, to engage Deleuze's thought with an analysis of institutions, namely, adjudication.

My first objective in turning Deleuze toward law is to develop more sophisticated ways of stating the problem of creativity in adjudication than is often the case. Today, the problem of innovation introduced into law by judges—what I call creativity in adjudication, which can be preliminarily understood as the introduction of the new into law by means of adjudication—is at the heart of jurisprudential and public debate. Questions concerning the creation of law by judges have become of interest not just to academics and legal scholars but also, as the recent U.S. Supreme Court nomination process shows, to the public, the media, and even the president. For the most part, and this holds for academic and public contexts, the problem of creativity in adjudication is stated as one of either *activism* or *accident* on the part of the judge: either that, in creating law, the judge appeals to extralegal considerations, such as policy or personal preference; or that the creation of law happens only by mistake, that the judge suffers a lapse of judgment. Either way, and regardless of whether it is commended or condemned, creativity is viewed as extrinsic to the law, as something that could, if perhaps only in principle, be eliminated from it.

For reasons I will explore, these two poles of activism and accident seem inadequate to state the problem of creativity in law. The turn to Deleuze, therefore, is motivated by an attempt to develop a concept of judgment and adjudication as inherently creative. I attempt to pose the problem of creativity as intrinsic to law, as a fundamental, necessary capacity of judgment. The point is neither to recommend nor to disparage creativity; it is instead to analyze how, within certain conditions, it is an inescapable aspect of judgment, one we must come to terms with if we are to understand law and adjudication.

Granted, "Judges create law" is a well-worn idea. It has even inspired entire schools of legal thought. And in that sense my claim that adjudication is creative is hardly news. However, my statement "Judges create law" takes its sense only through the problems and theory that inspire it; it remains abstract until we inquire how and in what precise sense that is the case. This is where Deleuze's contribution comes in. He helps us to state problems and concepts that can explain what it means for judges to create law, that is, to formulate and make sense of that claim. In this book I do not propose anything new about the law per se, nor do I advance practical (moral or pragmatic) recommendations. What I try to do is introduce ways of seeing how judges create law, why it is necessary, and how, given this necessity, it must be affirmed. This is a report of what adjudication is and does. The justification of the project, therefore, is to create new perspectives with which to understand and accept (and therefore practice—but again, not in any advocatory sense) creativity as inherent to adjudication.

My second objective is to show the value of Deleuze for the analysis of institutions. On the one hand, I try to elaborate in a systematic fashion the value of Deleuzian concepts and problems for legal analysis; on the other hand, I use the field of law and adjudication to interrogate Deleuze's own political philosophy. I suggest not only that Deleuze clarifies the operation of adjudication, but, vice versa, that significant features of adjudication—such as the encounter with the case or the repetition of rules—exemplify what is at stake in Deleuze's political philosophy. This reciprocal illumination (or better, actualization) of Deleuze and adjudication should not come as a surprise if thinking means extension to new problems—one should not expect that the only thing affected is that to which a philosophy is extended.

A special motivation with respect to my second objective is to achieve a certain tone with Deleuze by bringing him to everyday institutional concerns and giving his concepts more sober application than is often the case. On the one hand, I want to use Deleuze to explicate decidedly unexceptional things: the legal interest in a case, rule application, prudence, and so on. On the other hand, I want to take some of his more wild-sounding concepts (such as the encounter, the Body without Organs, and the virtual) into the context of law and its everyday operation. To my mind, much Deleuze scholarship focuses on the extreme, either by using him to explore limit situations such as nomadism, war, or schizophrenia, or by giving emphasis to the flashy nonidentitarian, deterritorializing strains in his (and especially his and Guattari's) thought. I do not object to this work per se but only suggest that Deleuze also provides underexplored resources to describe and understand everyday institutions, such as adjudication, that can put him in touch with a broader range of social, political, and legal thought and practice. A sober, more mundane use of Deleuze might prove rewarding.

To achieve this tone and to formulate a productive relation between Deleuze and law, I needed to adopt a peculiar organization for this book. Of the three parts, none is dedicated to Deleuze. Instead, I have taken three of his major interlocutors and designed sections around them together with his commentaries. Why? Because this is not a work *on* Deleuze but rather a work *with* Deleuze. As I have suggested, to simply expand on Deleuze's remarks *on* law (say, in *A Thousand Plateaus*, "Coldness and Cruelty," or in his interviews) is impracticable for developing a theory of adjudication: They are an arid (critical, sometimes polemical) ground that does not give a chance for a concept of law or judgment to grow. No doubt these remarks are valuable and no doubt they require and deserve elaboration, but to base a project solely on them would fail to create something positive with respect to law, and, if taken without precaution, might commit us to a pitch of thought and writing hostile to law as such, whatever that might mean.

If, however, our primary objective is not to see what Deleuze said about law but to develop a theory of adjudication *with* Deleuze, then we need a way to make his broader philosophy available to us. Happily, his career provides the precedent. What is particular about Deleuze's thought, almost unique in the history of philosophy, is the extent to which it develops in commentaries devoted to specific thinkers. The procedure, then, of having Deleuze emerge through sections devoted to other thinkers faithfully follows his own example. Each part of the book is focused on a philosopher to whom Deleuze is deeply indebted in order to draw from them a constitutive insight for a theory of adjudication. The reasons for this structure are twofold. First, I want to expand the range of Deleuze's thought germane to law and increase his points of contact with contemporary political and legal theory. Second, I use writers less allergic to law than Deleuze to develop positive concepts of law and judgment from him. In Part 1 I argue that contemporary Kantian-inspired legal theory sees judgment as a subsumptive activity, with the consequence that our understanding of and our sincerity toward creativity are inhibited. In Part 2 I use Bergson to develop a concept of judgment that is able to comprehend (but not recommend) how and why adjudication is creative. And in Part 3 I take Spinoza to suggest a practice that is appropriate to understand, evaluate, and affirm creativity in adjudication.

*

Two chapters of this book incorporate works that have been previously published. Chapter 2 contains selections from my "Critique of Teleology in Kant and Dworkin: The Law Without Organs (LwO)," and Chapter 3 contains selections from my "Habermas and Deleuze on Law and Adjudication." I am grateful to Sage Publications and Springer Science and Business Media, respectively, for their kind permission to reprint this material. I would also like to acknowledge the support of the Social Science and Humanities Research Council of Canada.

Two early and important influences on this project, even if they do not know it yet, are Lorraine Weir and Barbara Godard: the first for her exciting and embattled course, "From Derrida to Delgamuukw," which opened my eyes to the intersection of philosophy and law; and the second for hosting a summer seminar that introduced me, along with others, to Deleuze. From Toronto, I would like also to acknowledge Engin Isin for his energetic support, intellectual and material; and Peter Scrutton, who went over and above his court clerkship to help explain, find, and reference relevant points of law.

This book was written between the Department of Political Science and the Humanities Center at the Johns Hopkins University. From Political Science I give my fond gratitude to Jennifer Culbert, who not only made time to lead two reading groups directly formative of Part 1 but also read my text with such attention and scrutiny that, I admit, I came to anticipate our discussions with trepidation. I have her to thank for shaping my critique of legal theory as a critique of subsumption. I would also like to acknowledge conversations with Bill Connolly around the question of habit and memory in Bergson. His suggestions (he called them emphases, but I take it they were more) were decisive to my discussion in Part 2.

From the Humanities Center I thank its two directors, Michael Fried and Ruth Leys, for setting up and running a program with the right mix of positive and negative liberty. I would like to thank Hent de Vries and Paola Marrati for everything it is that good teachers do, and add two specific acknowledgments. First, to Hent, who by example and encouragement tried to impart to me a temperament (I worry imperfectly realized here) of intellectual generosity and of the avoidance of polemic. Of course, this is a lesson I always knew, but until it was put into continual practice, in every seminar and criticism he offered, it remained unlearned. Second, I want to express my quite immeasurable debt to Paola's seminars, especially those on Bergson and Deleuze. These seminars are known at Hopkins for their wonderful, clarifying simplicity (she calls them "plain"), and, for me, they remain a model of what teaching, not to mention writing, should do. Finally, although not exactly "of" Hopkins, I would like to warmly thank Paul Patton, who twice read through my manuscript and proposed several important improvements.

I reserve my deepest gratitude for last. To my parents, Georges and Joanne, to whose devotion, encouragement, and dinner table I owe so very much. And to Melanie White, who not only provided an ideal writing retreat and greatly improved three full drafts but also cheers not just this work but all our time together. I dedicate this book to the three of them.

Abbreviations

Bergson

CE   *Creative Evolution*, translated by Arthur Mitchell. New York: Dover, 1998 [1907].
CM   *The Creative Mind: An Introduction to Metaphysics*, translated by Mabelle L. Andison. New York: Citadel Press, 1974 [1938].
MM   *Matter and Memory*, translated by N. M. Paul and W. S. Palmer. New York: Zone Books, 1988 [1896].

Deleuze

ABC   *L'Abécédaire de Gilles Deleuze, avec Claire Parnet.* Paris: DVD Editions Montparnasse, 2004 [1995]. (Reference to chapter letter.)
B   *Bergsonism*, translated by Hugh Tomlinson and Barbara Habberjam. New York: Zone Books, 1991 [1966].
C_1 *Cinema 1: The Movement-Image*, translated by Hugh Tomlinson and Barbara Habberjam. Minneapolis: University of Minnesota Press, 1986 [1983].
C_2 *Cinema 2: The Time-Image*, translated by Hugh Tomlinson and Robert Galeta. Minneapolis: University of Minnesota Press, 1989 [1985].
CC   *Essays Critical and Clinical*, translated by Daniel W. Smith and Michael A. Greco. Minneapolis: University of Minnesota Press, 1997 [1993].
DR   *Difference and Repetition*, translated by Paul Patton. New York: Columbia University Press, 1994 [1968].
EPS   *Expressionism in Philosophy: Spinoza*, translated by Martin Joughin. New York: Zone Books, 1992 [1968].
N   *Negotiations, 1972–1990*, translated by Martin Joughin. New York: Columbia University Press, 1995 [1990].

xviii *Abbreviations*

PS *Proust and Signs*, translated by Richard Howard. Minneapolis: University of Minnesota Press, 2000 [1970].
SPP *Spinoza: Practical Philosophy*, translated by Robert Hurley. San Francisco: City Lights Books, 1988 [1970].

Deleuze and Guattari

TP *A Thousand Plateaus: Capitalism and Schizophrenia*, translated by Brian Massumi. Minneapolis: University of Minnesota Press, 1987 [1980].
WP *What Is Philosophy?* translated by Hugh Tomlinson and Graham Burchell. New York: Columbia University Press, 1994 [1991].

Kant

A/B *Critique of Pure Reason*, translated by Paul Guyer and Allan Wood. Cambridge, U.K.: Cambridge University Press, 1998 [1787]. (Reference to the A and/or B edition.)
CJ *Critique of Judgment*, translated by Werner S. Pluhar. Indianapolis, IN: Hackett, 1987 [1790].

Spinoza

E *The Ethics*, translated by Samuel Shirley. Indianapolis, IN: Hackett, 2002 [1677]. (Reference is as follows: E for *Ethics*, Roman numeral for Book, P for Proposition, S for Scholium, D for Definition, C for Corollary, L for Lemma, Ax for Axiom, Pos for Postulate.)
Letter *The Letters*, translated by Samuel Shirley. Indianapolis, IN: Hackett, 2002. (Reference to the letter number.)

Legal Theory

BFN Habermas, Jürgen. *Between Facts and Norms: Contributions to a Discourse Theory of Law and Democracy*, translated by William Rehg. Cambridge, MA: MIT Press, 1998 [1992].
CL Holmes, Oliver Wendell. *The Common Law*. New York: Dover, 1991 [1881].
COL Hart, H. L. A. *The Concept of Law*. Oxford, U.K.: Oxford University Press, 1961.

LE	Dworkin, Ronald. *Law's Empire*. Cambridge, MA: Belknap Harvard, 1986.
NJP	Cardozo, Benjamin N. *The Nature of the Judicial Process*. New York: Fallon, 1947 [1921].

THE IMAGE OF LAW

PART ONE

THE DOGMATIC IMAGE OF LAW

> The question "against whom" itself calls for several replies.
>
> DELEUZE, *Nietzsche and Philosophy*

A repeated difficulty admitted by English-language commentators on Deleuze with respect to political questions is that he "does not speak the familiar languages of politics or political theory."[1] This same difficulty is encountered, if not aggravated, in an exploration of jurisprudence and adjudication with Deleuzian concepts. It is true, on the one hand, that Deleuze left us tantalizing occasional observations on the value of jurisprudence and provocative, if polemical, remarks on human rights. On the other hand, he did not specifically elaborate these insights, nor did he engage with either the philosophy of law or its institutional practice (and especially not in an Anglo-American context). Narrowly understood, Deleuze's discussion of law is negligible.

But if we broaden our criteria, Deleuze's work does, in fact, treat themes of law and judgment. If we include his critiques of moral law and natural law and if we consider his relentless critique of judgment (distributive, determinative, reflective), we discover that the theme of law has never ceased to occupy Deleuze. Our problem is to find a way to fruitfully join his critique with our narrower investigation of the institution of adjudication. To this end, as a bridge, I introduce the concept of the dogmatic image of law.

Coordinating Part 1 is Kant. Kant is the great philosophico-jurist who framed each of his *Critiques* as a problem of law. As Deleuze comments in the *Abécédaire*, Kant is like an "examining magistrate [*un enquêteur*]" obsessed with judgment, with tribunals, and with establishing a system based on judgment, self-examination, and magistracy (*ABC*, K; also *WP*, 72; *CC*, 126). Beyond this simple characterization, however, Kant is significant for two reasons. First, Deleuze's discussion of law and judgment consistently addresses Kant and uses him as a reference point, and so any elaboration of a Deleuzian philosophy of law must pass through Kant and be coordinated with the specific problems he poses. Second, a Kantian interface relates Deleuze to contemporary theorists of law from whom he is several times removed.

I have selected three prominent theorists of law and adjudication—H. L. A. Hart, Ronald Dworkin, and Jürgen Habermas—as three modes, or expressions, of an underlying Kantianism. Sometimes the characterization is obvious (Habermas), and sometimes I must make an argument for it (Hart and Dworkin). Each theorist, I claim, adapts a different part of Kant's critical philosophy toward their own theory of adjudication: subsumption from the *Critique of Pure Reason* in Hart, reflective teleological judgment from the *Critique of Judgment* in Dworkin, and the philosophy of law from the *Metaphysics of Morals* (and the practical philosophy) in Habermas. In developing these theorists through their Kantianism, I hope to channel Kant's conceptions of law (whether categorical, moral, empirico-natural, or juridical) and of judgment (determinative and reflective) into contemporary problems of adjudication. This organization will allow me to bring Deleuze's discussions of law and judgment both to these theorists and to adjudication in general.

The dogmatic image of thought is a key concept in Deleuze's *Difference and Repetition*.[2] In that text, it signifies a set of implicit presuppositions operative throughout the history of philosophy about what it means to think and that compromise the true exercise of thought. Deleuze calls these presuppositions an *image* of thought because they are not concepts and have not been discursively secured; instead, they are opinions about what it means to think; they are what we imagine when we prephilosophically (or we could say precritically, if it didn't have a too Kantian ring) think about thought. As Deleuze says in an interview, "We live with a particular image of thought, that is to say, before we begin to think, we have a vague idea of what it means to think, its means and ends."[3] In short, philosophy and common sense alike (or rather, philosophy as compromised by its unexamined common sense) have assumed certain things about thought, what it is and what it does. Deleuze calls this image of thought *dogmatic*—first, because it has been drawn from the very realm of opinion and common sense from which philosophy has classically pretended to break and get its start and, second, because it assumes that *recognition* is the vocation of thought. As I will explain, this second point is the foremost assumption or image of dogmatic thought: thought equals recognition. With recognition as its aim, thought is reduced to a task of identification. And, as a consequence of its drive to recognize, dogmatic thought threatens to assimilate all its potential encounters (with things, others, texts, etc.) into the concepts and categories used to recognize them.

Extending this concept to adjudication, I have called this part of the book the dogmatic image of law. What unifies Hart, Dworkin, and Habermas—indeed, why their respective contributions can be characterized as a dogmatic image—is that they base adjudication on the image of judgment as subsumption. For them, the task of adjudication is to subsume cases under rules. I call this an *image* of law because subsumption is rarely, if ever, directly thematized by these theorists. Although developed according to three different constructions, each theorist assumes that the point of adjudication is to subsume cases under rules. I call this image *dogmatic* because it is based on a model of recognition that purports to identify cases as instances of rules. Cases, consequently, are reduced to the rules and categories used to subsume them. Most important, as we will see, in the dogmatic image we lose all perspective on creativity in the law. If adjudication is premised on the recognition of the existing rule appropriate for each case, then creativity is reduced to either willfulness or accident (a *lapsus judici*).

I have four goals in Part 1. First, to propose original readings of Hart and Dworkin as deeply, but tacitly, Kantian. (Habermas too is Kantian, but this comes as no surprise.) Second, to characterize a coherent image of judgment as subsumption effective in these three theories of adjudication. Third, to claim that these theories either ignore or repress creativity in law. And fourth, to prepare Deleuze's critique. In this last respect, I develop consequences specific to each theory that I revisit in Part 2: choice in Hart, teleological totality in Dworkin, and retrospective illusion in Habermas. Each of these consequences results from attempts to preclude creativity in adjudication.

1

The Judge as Schema: Hart

In his lecture "American Jurisprudence Through English Eyes: The Nightmare and the Noble Dream," H. L. A. Hart observes that American jurisprudence, whatever its internal controversies, preoccupies itself "almost to the point of obsession" with the judicial process.[1] As befits this obsession, in Part 1 I concentrate on the judicial process (what I call adjudication) to the point of exclusion, asking whether it is in the nature of judgment to be subsumptive and whether contemporary jurisprudence (implicitly, as an image of thought) takes adjudication to be a matter of subsuming cases under rules. In what follows I argue that, yes, there is such an (implicit) agreement or coherence within contemporary jurisprudence. But we must take care, for all three of our theorists—Hart, Dworkin, and Habermas—start out by criticizing an unsophisticated notion of subsumption, one that takes the judge's work to be a straightforward process of applying rules to cases. At this point, however, I cannot more fully specify what it is that these theorists oppose, for what requires criticism in a certain conception of subsumption is, of course, internal to the characterization of the theory that rejects it.

I have claimed that each of our three theorists borrows from Kant his respective vision of adjudication: Hart from the *Critique of Pure Reason*, Dworkin from the *Critique of Judgment*, and Habermas from the *Metaphysics of Morals* and the practical philosophy. Let's start by asking how the fundamental problems of Kant's *Critique of Pure Reason* are relevant to problems of adjudication, and, from there, observe how Hart adapts them.

A truism, shared by layman and jurist alike, is that the judge stands somehow between law and case and that the judge's job is to bring cases under law. A commonplace, perhaps, but one evocative of the animating problem of schematism from the *Critique of Pure Reason*: How are the pure concepts (or laws) of the understanding applied to the sensible phenomena (or cases) subject to them? The problem, as Kant sees it, is that something is required to bridge the distance between intelligible concepts and sensible phenomena, to make sure that the one fits and can be applied to the other. As Kant puts it in the first sentence of the Schematism chapter, "In all subsumptions of an object under a concept the representations of the former must be *homogeneous* [*gleichartig*] with the latter" (A137/B176). Or, to spell out the problem another way, given that *intelligible* concepts of the understanding are heterogeneous to *sensible* appearances, there must be a "third thing, which must stand in homogeneity with the category [or concept] on the one hand and the [sensible] appearance on the other, and makes possible the application of the former to the latter" (A138/B176). In brief, if judgment is to relate concepts to intuitions, laws to cases, a mediating figure at once sensible *and* intelligible—the schema, as Kant calls it—is required. As such, the schema must do two things at once: It must prepare the intuition to be determined by the concept, and it must adapt the concept for application to the intuition.

If we turn to the judge, it is possible to suggest that he or she operates as such a schematizing third thing. Laws are unable to apply by themselves to cases—as Hart puts it, "Rules cannot provide for their own application, and even in the clearest case a human being must apply them"[2]—and require a mediator who can partake of both laws and cases, someone competent to establish a correspondence between the two. As Kant's schematism would suggest, the judge allows the case to be determined by the law and adapts the law for application to the case.

In this chapter, I explore Hart's *Concept of Law* (1961)—the most influential contribution to Anglo-American jurisprudence of the last fifty years—to see how it advances a theory of the judge as schema. Now this is not an uncontroversial identification, for if we are to uncover the philosophical antecedents of *The Concept of Law*, a much surer bet than

Kant (mentioned only once and in passing in that text) would be to focus on Hart's indebtedness to ordinary language philosophy in J. L. Austin and the later Wittgenstein.[3] The reason for this potentially risky claim is that, to my mind, Hart's writings on adjudication share the fundamental insight or spirit of Kant's theory of judgment (encapsulated in the concept of schematism) in the *Critique of Pure Reason*: to internalize the relationship between objects and representations *within* representation itself.

What do I mean by this? According to Kant, for an object to appear before us, that is, in order for it to appear and be experiencable as an object, it must be conceptually mediated. An object of experience is possible, it stands for us, only insofar as it has been synthesized by the concepts of the understanding. This makes for a peculiar and interesting conception of subsumption. It is not as if objects are out there, external to us, waiting for concepts to be applied to them; rather, it is only insofar as a concept is applied to them that they can stand as objects in the first place. Subsumption in Kant does not stand for the application of a concept to an indifferent sensible object but is rather the act whereby an object is able to present and announce itself.

Following this Kantian thread, I argue that for Hart an analogous kind of subsumption is effective in adjudication: For the *case* to appear before a judge, it must be informed by, or mediated through, concepts of law. In other words, cases do not stand externally or indifferently before a judge but appear as cases (*legal* cases, cases at law) only insofar as they have always already been subsumed by the law. It is in this sense that I focus on the judge as the schematizing figure that constitutes the case in and through concepts of law. As we shall see, this theory of subsumption (one that challenges a conventional, externalist notion of subsumption at every point) agrees with a Deleuzian jurisprudence, but with two important exceptions: noncreativity and choice. The consequences of seeing the judge as schema are twofold. First, the rules by which a case is adjudicated are modeled along the lines of the categories of the understanding and are, as such, *unchanging*. Second, as a function of the last point, a fundamental feature of Hart's theory of adjudication is that in difficult cases where the applicable rule is not self-evident, the judge must *choose* between rules to subsume the case. I conclude this chapter by describing these two features, and in Chapter 7 I show why they are problematic from the standpoint of a Deleuzian jurisprudence.

How Does Law Work? Hart's Critique of Austin

In his preparatory notebooks for the *Concept of Law*, Hart writes, "My ambition in its most grandiose form is to dispel forever the definitional will o' the wisps—the search for 'definitions' of law—by showing that all that can be done and is important to do is to characterize the *Concept* of law by identifying the main elements and organization of elements which constitute a *standard* legal *system*."[4] In these lines we can recognize something of a Kantian impulse, one deepened and systematized by Wittgenstein: that certain of the questions and problems we set for ourselves are idle and deceptive, what Kant calls dialectical. According to Hart, the question "What is law?" represents this kind of threat to jurisprudence. It is a question bound to solicit empty answers unable to provide either a definition to the field or peace to jurists so occupied. That is why in the opening pages of the *Concept of Law*, Hart moves to replace the question "What is law?" with the problem "How does law work?" As he explains, all attempts to reveal the essence of law through a single covering definition (and his examples include Austin's command theory that laws are orders backed by threats of a sovereign, Holmes's idea that law is a prediction or prophecy as to what judges will do, and Llewellyn's claim that the law is what officials decide it is) have been revealing in parts but remain "great exaggerations" and are, on the whole, falsifications (*COL*, 1–2). At root, this inadequacy has less to do with the particular definition proposed but is endemic to the nature of the badly stated, dialectical question.[5]

Hart takes John Austin (not to be confused with J. L. Austin) as representative of the misguided attempt to provide a single definition for law. It is instructive to examine his critique, for it introduces two very different understandings of subsumption.

For Austin, law is an order backed by a threat of a sovereign. A sovereign is an extralegal authority who issues commands to political inferiors, who habitually obey these orders. This is the essence of law and "everywhere the existence of law implies the existence of such a sovereign" (*COL*, 65). The theory underpinning this definition has the following characteristics: The sovereign is external to the laws that bind his or her subjects; legality is a habit of obedience to the sovereign; and laws always impose duties backed by threats.[6] According to Hart, such a definition may have merits—it cuts through the metaphysical obfuscation of rationalist theories of natural right (*COL*, 60)[7]—but on the whole it is deeply inadequate. His criticism is twofold. First, Austin seems unaware of a whole domain of law essential to its operation, namely, secondary rules. Second, Austin misunderstands the relation that subjects have with law: Rules are not primarily threats but guides.

The first objection brings us directly to Hart's orienting problem: How does law work? For Hart, law consists of two irreducible kinds of legal rules: primary rules that impose duties and secondary rules that confer powers. The "key to the science of jurisprudence" is sought in the working combination of these two types of rule (*COL*, 79). The essence of law is not a definition, as in Austin; it is, instead, an operation between two types of rules. Take contracts. Contracts provide means to realize the wishes of the contracting parties; they are not commands. Contracts furnish us with power-conferring rules (secondary rules) able to produce a legal obligation (primary rules). Secondary power-conferring rules enable us to make legally binding promises: "When we promise, we shall make use of specified procedures to change our own moral situation by imposing obligations on ourselves and conferring rights on others . . . we exercise 'a power' conferred by rules to do this" (*COL*, 42–43). Contracts are an example of private power-conferring rules, but public power-conferring rules also exist. In direct contradiction to Austin's extralegal sovereign, law-producing agencies (legislature and judiciary) are granted their powers through secondary rules (electoral rules, constitutional rules, etc.) (*COL*, 74–75). Using a markedly Kantian term, we might say that secondary rules are properly transcendental; they are the condition of possibility for private relationships (such as contracts) and for public institutions (such as parliaments and courts).[8]

Hart's first criticism of Austin, then, is that he is unaware of secondary rules and cannot understand how law works. In theological terms, we can say that for Austin's transcendent conception of an external lawgiver, Hart substitutes secondary rules that, in combination with primary rules, function *immanently* to produce law. No longer is law issued from an extralegal sovereign source. Instead, secondary rules underlie both civil relationships and public institutions. Gone is the extralegal sovereign in favor of a legal immanence of rules enabling rules.

Hart's second objection to Austin is that he fails to adequately explain the relationship subjects have to law. This point is worth dwelling on, for it contains the seed of my characterization of Hart's theory of adjudication.

For Austin, subjects habitually obey orders issued by a sovereign; but for Hart this misses the fact that people "in one situation after another" use law as a *guide* for the conduct of social life, that is, as a "*basis for* claims, demands, admissions, criticism, or punishment, viz., in all the familiar transaction of life according to rules. For them the violation of a rule is not merely a basis for the prediction that a hostile reaction will follow but a *reason for* hostility" (*COL*, 88, emphasis added). For Hart, rules are not just (not even principally)[9] commands but are also guides irreducible to the threat of sanction. We do not obey rules merely because of implied threats. Instead, rules are adopted as the basis for conduct; they are, as Hart puts it, guides to the familiar transactions of life. In a formula: For Austin, conduct must conform to rules; for Hart, rules are formative of conduct.

Here again, we have recourse to the language of transcendence and immanence. For Austin, law is an external and transcendent force that compels obedience at the price of punishment. For Hart, law is internalized within (is immanent to) the subject's conduct. Rules do not primarily compel actions under threat; subjects instead adopt rules as constitutive standards for their own behavior. Rules are incorporated into behavior as standards and guides that serve to evaluate, identify, and provide reasons for right and wrong conduct.

Compared with Austin, Hart proposes a new perspective on the relation subjects have with law: It is not that our conduct merely conforms to law, but, by using law as a guide, our conduct is itself legal. Hart terms this new perspective on law and conduct "internal" (*COL*, 86). The external point of view occurs when subjects orient themselves to law with a strictly consequentialist attitude: Rules are abided by, lest unpleasant consequences follow (*COL*, 88).[10] For Hart, the external perspective cannot appreciate the sensibility of the internal; it "cannot properly understand the whole distinctive style of human thought, speech, and action which is involved in the existence of rules and which constitutes the normative structure of society" (*COL*, 86). According to the internal perspective, we do not follow rules merely because it is prudent to do so; instead, we *constitutively* incorporate legal standards to guide conduct, evaluate practices, and formulate standards of obligation and duty. I stress that Hart's critique is not cognitivist or practically motivated; in this sense, his jurisprudence is analytical. He is not recommending anything. He focuses on the descriptive problem. Externalist theories neglect the fact that rules are internalized into conduct and thus fail to comprehend what is distinctive about law and how it actually works.

In the internal perspective, law informs conduct and is the constitutive reference point for behavior and notions of right, duty, and obligation. The internal perspective is not merely a tool with which to analyze law; it is a new approach that describes how subjects relate to themselves through law.

What is necessary is that there should be a *critical reflective attitude* to certain patterns of behavior as a common standard, and that this should display itself in criticism (including self-criticism), demands for conformity, and in acknowledgements that such criticism and demands are justified, all of which find their characteristic expression in the normative terminology of "ought," "must" and "should," "right" and "wrong." (*COL*, 56, emphasis added)

Without yet analyzing the Kantian undertones of this short phrase, we can identify three distinct yet simultaneous functions of the critical reflective attitude: It generates conduct according to rules; it evaluates conduct according to these rules; and it establishes rules as common, shared standards. Most important for us is that the internal perspective combines conduct and a critical reflective attitude toward that conduct. According to this perspective, rules are constitutive of conduct and we use rules to reflect on the conduct of oneself and others. Rules are effective in both the formation and the evaluation of conduct. In other words, we use rules to evaluate conduct that is itself produced by rules.

But what is implied in this evaluation of the legality of conduct? As Hart explains, to say that a person has an obligation "is to apply [a] general rule to a particular person by *calling attention to the fact that his case falls under it*" (*COL*, 83, emphasis added). This statement is not as simple as it seems, for it *cannot* mean that we have rules on the one hand and conduct to which we apply these rules on the other hand. We cannot, in other words, understand this statement according to a commonsense kind of subsumption where rules are simply brought to cases. The internal perspective denies this possibility; it insists that conduct is generated through rules, that conduct is not external to rules. The rules used to apprehend conduct are already effective in the formation of it.

It is clarifying to restate the opposition between Austin and Hart on this point. For Austin, a sovereign hands down the law according to which a subject's conduct may or may not conform. Law and conduct are external to one another, with rules on one hand and conduct on the other. In cases of conflict, a judge must determine the conformity of the conduct to the rules.[11] Things are entirely different for Hart: Conduct is constituted *and* judged by rules. Conduct is never presented to us in an unmediated state and judged by rules brought to it; it is constituted and appears for judgment only insofar as it has already been mediated by rules. According to the internal perspective, we apprehend the legality of conduct insofar as it has always already been legalized through its very formation.

Although not raised in these terms, Hart's critique of Austin can be seen to turn on the question of subsumption: Can cases of conduct and rules of law remain external to one another? Or must they be shown to be mediated in their genesis? It appears that for Hart, Austin's concept of subsumption—bound as it is to a separation between conduct and rule, between case and law—can account neither for the relationship between subjects and law nor, as I will argue, for the process of adjudication itself. Restating my opening pragmatist question, this conventional concept of subsumption proves an impediment to understanding how law and adjudication work. If there is to be progress in this inquiry, a new concept of subsumption must be developed.

Subsumption in the *Critique of Pure Reason*

In what follows I suggest that Hart's concept of subsumption takes the central insight of Kant's *Critique of Pure Reason* into the field of adjudication; that is, it internalizes the relationship between objects and representations *within* representation itself. This means that we do not represent objects as external to our powers of representation but instead establish the object from within representations. In the *Critique* this process of establishing objects of experience within our representational capacities is twofold. First, phenomena appear to us only insofar as they are intuited through the pure forms of sensibility. (As Heidegger observes, in Kant we see for the first time a theory of the senses that is not sensualistic but ontological: Objects can appear only on condition that they are received and synthesized by our sensibility.)[12] Second, the categories of the understanding synthesize and make discursive sense of intuited phenomena. Thus in the *Critique* objects of experience are (conceptual) representations of (intuited) representations (A68/B93). Perhaps we can already see the outline of Hart: Conduct is not apprehended in and of itself but only insofar as it has been represented through rules.

Before moving back to Hart, let's look more closely at the relationship between these two levels of representation in which objects of experience are established. In the *Critique of Pure Reason*, Kant emphasizes that, in order to make sense, every concept must be given a correlate intuition; otherwise it remains "entirely empty of content, even though it may still contain the logical function" (A239/B298). Without an intuition, concepts and categories remain "mere play" and "blind," and so it is necessary "for one *to make* an abstract [*abgesondert*] concept *sensible*, i.e., to display the object that corresponds to it in intuition, since without this the concept would remain (as one says) without *sense*, i.e., without significance" (A239/B298, A51/B75, A240/B299). Far from being trivial or marginal for Kant, cases of intuition enable discovery not just of the laws of nature, but, even more important, of the pure concepts and of the transcendental conditions of judgment itself. For example, the concept of magnitude finds its expression and sense in numbers and fingers or in the beads of an abacus. In this manner, we can say that any *law* of the understanding requires its *case* of intuition; the concept requires the intuition to gain instantiation and existence. In order for the concept to manifest itself, it must undergo a sensible actualization in the object. In a way, law exists only through the case alone.

However, although it is true that for Kant concepts require cases for their instantiation and sense, intuited cases require concepts to stand as cases in the first place. Putting the problem in this way, we can see how critique internalizes the relation between the representation and the object within representation itself. At this point of our analysis, a brief turn to Jean-Luc Nancy's interpretation of Kant is helpful, for not only does Nancy speak directly to the question of how judgment is constitutive of (the very being of) a case, but he does so in language appropriate to our investigation: "A case only *falls* under the law once the law speaks of it [*que la loi soit dite de lui*]."[13] Here, Nancy indicates that Kant's insight that law can be announced only through its case is accompanied by the corollary claim that the case is itself modeled on and fashioned by the representation of the law. Continuing with Nancy's words, the enunciation of the law "states the right of the case, thereby making it a case: it *subsumes* it, suppresses its accidental character; picks it up [*relève*] after its fall."[14] This is the peculiar nature of Kantian subsumption: It is not that an existing case is subsumed under a concept as might occur in a judgment of traditional logic (union of subject, predicate, copula); rather, keeping these terms, the subject is itself formed as an object for judgment through its predication. As Nancy suggests, in being stated through the law, the case's accidentality is itself suppressed; however, this accidentality is itself unknowable given that the (phenomenal) case—the only one we can know given the conditions of knowledge and experience—is itself "made" by subsumption and is strictly immanent to the law that represents it.

We may now ask, If Kantian subsumption establishes the case as a case, is it still appropriate to use the term *subsumption*, given its implication of a separation or externality between concept and intuition, law and case? Heidegger, for one, railed against the language of subsumption, arguing that it was a "superficial" and preliminary entrance into a problem of a different nature.[15] He chose, however, to preserve it, casting it as a "peculiar, i.e., an *ontological*, 'subsumption.'"[16] This is the kind of subsumption that actualizes its subject as something judgable in the act of subsumption. I want to retain this term *ontological subsumption* not because I think that only Heidegger enables us to speak the truth of Hart but because it is helpful to characterize Hart's preservation of the problem of subsumption and rule application, along with his crucial modification of it along Kantian lines. Ontological subsumption serves as an economical expression for an innovative concept of subsumption whereby the case can be subsumed by a rule only if it is simultaneously constituted by it.

Schematism and Choice in Adjudication

In my introductory remarks on Hart, I identified the judge as a kind of schema. To recall, in the Schematism chapter Kant articulates the problem of correspondence between intelligible concepts and sensible intuitions and proposes the transcendental schema as a mediating representation that is at once intellectual and sensible. The schema performs two tasks simultaneously: It prepares intuition to be determined by the concept, and it "sensibilizes" the concept for application to intuition.

We saw that in the Hart's *Concept of Law* rules are used both to form and to judge conduct. Here we can identify a peculiar Kantian (or ontological) subsumption at work: The fact that rules are used to constitute and to judge conduct (and not externally applied to conduct that does or does not match its criteria) is definitive of Kant. In this sense, Hart's notion of conduct performs a kind of schematization. It makes the rule sensible by illustrating it in the case, and it forms the case in the application of the rule. In other words, conduct and rules are mediated; conduct is constitutively legal insofar as the law embodies itself within it.

Now we can extend this argument to Hart's understanding of adjudication. We start with a basic formulation.

The judge, in punishing, takes the rule as his *guide* and the breach of the rule as his *reason* and *justification* for punishing the offender. He does not look upon the rule as a statement that he and others are likely to punish deviations. . . . So we say that we reprove or punish a man *because* he has broken the rule: and not merely that it was probable that we would reprove or punish him. (*COL*, 10–11)

To examine this passage, as a way of making it available to us, I must remark on a significant difference between Kant's subsumption and the interpretation I am attempting with Hart. With respect to the *Critique*, the possibility that our experiences might be out of step or discrepant with our rules of judgment is out of the question. Experience (human, ordered, and regular experience) is possible on condition that it is informed by rules. That there is a priori agreement (with ourselves, with others) between judgment and experience is what, I take it, Kant is getting at when he proposes the alternative—for example, if cinnabar "were now red, now black, now light, now heavy," that is, if our experiences failed to align themselves with the rules of judgment (A100). In the subsumption Kant describes, our experience is universal and regular because it is constitutively rule governed.

In the world of law, however, it is a common and standing threat that the agreement between conduct and rules may come unstuck. This is at risk every time a case goes to trial. Let us consider this possibility in light of Hart's theory of conduct. We start with the claim that an offense and an offender can be judged only if their conduct should have been rule informed. That is the condition for a judge to judge; it is that which gives judgment purchase on conduct. The grammar or logic of judgments of law is such that known, public, common rules could and should have informed conduct in the first place.[17] It is not that the offender must have been actually aware of the appropriate rule but that the rule must have, in principle at least, been knowable in advance, that is, been given as a standard for conduct. It would be a dangerous, arbitrary, and heteronomous world if we were judged by rules without the prior possibility of having already implied them in our conduct. In applying the rule, the judge not only says that this particular case falls under it, but, moreover, that it should have constituted the conduct now under examination—that is the "reason," the "because," as Hart puts it, of punishing. What happens, then, when conduct goes awry from the rule that should have been internal to it? The judge uses the rule as a reason or guide to assess the points of departure of the conduct.

Read through a Kantian lens, the case before the judge is a curious kind of phenomenon: It does and it does not conform to the rules. It does not conform to the rule insofar as it finds itself reproved in court; but it does conform to the rule insofar as the rule is the standard under which it is to be judged, under which it can be made sense of and hence punished. The conduct might not conform to the rule, but *that* fact can be made sense of, judged, only in light of the rule. Such is the nature of subsumption wherein a case appears only in and through judgment, only in a rule application. The judge must repeat or double the subsumption or rule application that should have gone into the formation of conduct but, for some reason or another, did not. Or, another Kantian way of putting it is that the judge must reschematize the relationship between conduct and rule, an activity that *is* the judgment: A judgment is nothing other than the working-out of how the rule should have been embodied in the conduct and how the conduct should have been formed by the rule.

What I am describing is as simple (or complex) as saying that the conduct in question is a case *at* or *of* law. Conduct appears as a justiciable object (a case) insofar as it has had rules applied to it, that is, insofar as it has been constituted (judged) in and through its subsumption by rules. The point I want to make of Hart's reworking of subsumption is that a case appears only once it is represented by a rule. Considered as a schema, the judge's job is to make cases appear.

[The judge] chooses to add to a line of cases a new case because of resemblances which can reasonably be defended as both legally relevant and sufficiently close.

In the case of legal rules, the criteria of relevance and closeness of resemblance depend on many complex factors *running through the legal system* and on the aims or purposes which may be attributed to the rule. To characterize these would be to characterize whatever is specific in legal reasoning. (*COL*, 124, emphasis added)

I presume from his repeated use of *resemblance* that Hart is adapting Wittgenstein's caution that things called by the same name do not necessarily have something in common, such as an essence or universal, but bear a family resemblance to one another. And so cases would be defined not by a universal term designated by a rule but by their own overlapping imbrications. But what if, once again, we took this passage with a Kantian interpretation?[18] What Hart reveals as specific to legal reasoning is something like transcendental logic: The application of rules to a fact-situation makes it appear as, or turns it into, a case.

A judge identifies a rule (here, through a series of cases) and adds to it a new case on the basis of resemblance. Now, although it may seem an obvious point, the case is said to resemble the rule on the basis of criteria designated by the law; it is on this basis that the judge determines similarity between the case at hand and the tradition. What this means is that the points of the case emerge in and through the application of a rule said to resemble it. Just like a schema, the judge prepares the rule to be applied to the case by establishing points of resemblance between case and rule (or, better, between fact-situation not yet formed and rules not yet actualized—the case being the unity of the two). The fact-situation becomes a case by virtue of an identification of resemblances that can reasonably be defended as both legally relevant and sufficiently close. As Hart writes, "Particular fact-situations do not await us already marked off from each other, and labeled as instances of the general rule, the application of which is in question; nor can the rule itself step forward to claim its own instances" (*COL*, 123). What we need is a judge to, first, prepare the rule to be applied to the fact-situation and, second, to subsume the fact-situation with a rule and make it into a case.

At this point we can raise a question crucial to our project: Can laws be modified in application to the case? This question reveals another productive discrepancy between Kant and Hart. For Kant, insofar as he is concerned with the laws of the understanding, the answer is no. The laws of the understanding belong to us a priori, and the point of *Critique*, if I can put it this way, is to show how these laws apply to and enable experience without undergoing an empirical determination that might make them nonnecessary and nonuniversal (i.e., of doubtful objectivity).

Hart is not dealing with pure laws of the understanding but with the decidedly a posteriori laws of human society. Can cases, then, create law? Can application modify law? Is it plainly, as Hart seems to say at one point, that adjudication must only identify "circumstances *as instances* of the general classifications which the law makes" (*COL*, 121, emphasis added)? There is no direct answer in Hart to these questions; rather, it is possible to sketch two different and equally present lines of possible solution.

1. In the *Concept of Law*, Hart vigorously attacks legal formalism and its ambition to "freeze the meaning of the rule so that its general terms must have the same meaning in every case where its application is in question" (*COL*, 126).[19] Legal formalism tries to underplay any suggestion that judges create rather than find law and thus tries to fix the meaning of its rules "at the cost of blindly prejudging what is to be done in a range of future cases" (*COL*, 126). This "mechanical jurisprudence" would be possible only in a world characterized by a limited number of features whose combination could be known in advance (*COL*, 125). However—and this is a strikingly Kantian gesture insofar as the *Critique of Pure Reason* seeks to determine the conditions of human knowledge—Hart rejects formalism by virtue of a commitment to jurisprudential finitude.

It is a feature of the human predicament (and so of the legislative one) that we labor under two connected handicaps whenever we seek to regulate, unambiguously and in advance, some sphere of conduct by means of general standards.... The first handicap is our relative ignorance of fact: the second is our relative indeterminacy of aim. (*COL*, 125)

Given that our legislative aims are indeterminate and given that fact-situations are constantly "thrown up by nature or human invention," it is both impossible and undesirable to have rules so set that their application is automatic (*COL*, 123). In other words, given our finitude, rules must be able to adapt themselves to unforeseen cases. To prove his point, Hart cites the field of due care in the tort of negligence (too many unforeseeable fact-situations) and the regulation of industry standards for injury (indeterminate aim with respect to the balance between compensation and public good) (*COL*, 127–129). In these areas of law there exist vast open textures as to aim and foreseeable fact; as such, adjudication is granted freedom to make more determinate the criteria and purpose of rules vis-à-vis the case at hand. It might be said, therefore, that the judge who adjudicates in these (and other) so-called open textures of law should be sensitive to new cases and the possibility that they might call for adapted rules, for new schemata. It is not as if Hart admits this possibility for adjudication in general; but within the special open textures of law, adjudication elaborates indeterminate rules in such a way that the line between (mere) determination and creation is no longer placeable.[20]

2. In a few dense pages of the *Concept of Law*, Hart dismantles the received opposition of the difference between adjudicating by precedent and by statute. On first impression, rules based on precedent seem indistinct, for it is often difficult to extricate the general rule embedded in the case. Statutes, by contrast, "seem clear, dependable, and certain" insofar as they announce a rule on their own (*COL*, 122). The judge has, apparently, only "to 'subsume' particular facts under general classificatory heads and draw a simple syllogistic conclusion" (*COL*, 122). Yet, just as we saw with Kant, Hart explains that, for the rule to take on sense, it must be related to a concrete case, one that plainly satisfies its requirements. The statutory rule, therefore, also depends on a concrete case in order to signify (*COL*, 123).[21]

Given that the statute now marks out only a plain or authoritative example and given that it must be "used in much the same way as a precedent," the judge must confront the question of whether the unforeseen new case *resembles* the plain case sufficiently and in the relevant respects. The judge must ask, Does the plain case apply to this new fact-situation? Is this situation an example of the plain case? These questions lead Hart to characterize the juridical process as one of choosing between rules to apply to cases.

[The judge] consider[s] whether the present case *resembles* the plain case "sufficiently" in "relevant" respects. The *discretion* thus left to him by language may be very wide; so that if he applies the rule, the conclusion, even though it may not be arbitrary or irrational, *is in effect a choice. He chooses to add to a line of cases a new case because of resemblances which can be defended as both legally relevant and sufficiently close.* (*COL*, 124, emphasis added)

Before pointing out a last, significant difference from Kant, and in light of these mounting discrepancies and the fact that Hart seldom mentions Kant, we might wonder why we might wish to continue this comparison. Again, it is my impression that Hart maintains what is perhaps the central insight of the *Critique* (that objects are internalized within representation or judgment) but that his subject matter requires certain innovations that, consciously or not, take him away from Kant—for example, that experience and rules may split, that cases may in certain circumstances be constitutive of rules, and, now, that the judge must choose between rules with which to subsume the case. My concern has not been to map Hart strictly onto Kant but only to trace a Kantian inheritance effective in his theory of judgment. Thus I readily admit that choice is foreign to Kant's concept of judgment. For Kant, the work of judgment is never voluntaristic, nor could it be. It is not as if we choose which category to apply; instead, all the categories spontaneously apply themselves in experience, to make up experience.

For Hart, it is different. A rule will be *selected* to apply to the fact-situation in order to adjudicate it. This notion of choice is a function of Hart's theory of subsumption. Recall that a fact-situation is turned into a case when a rule is applied to it; a case becomes a case by virtue of a judgment or a subsumption. In such a scheme, the case is unable to modify the rule, for it is an artifact of that rule. Insofar as Hart conceives of the case as internal to the representation of the law, two features of adjudication are necessitated: (1) noncreativity and (2) choice.

1. Let us return to the passage quoted earlier (*COL*, 124). What does Hart mean by resemblance? He means that the judge applies a rule to a fact-situation and thereby encodes the rule in the image of the plain case that signifies the rule. The fact-situation is determined by the judge to resemble the rule, a resemblance that suppresses its singularity and transforms it into a case, the latest instantiation of a line of cases identical in view of the relevant respects. It is not that the rule is creative of the situation itself but only of its legal character, of its standing as a case. The rule does not and, on a Kantian interpretation, cannot modify itself according to the situation; rather, the judge considers whether the situation can be appropriately modeled on the rule and turned into a case included in that line. If a theory of adjudication adapts the judgment of the categories of the *Critique of Pure Reason*, then the case will be powerless to modify the

law insofar as it owes its very character as a case to the rule. As we have seen, a judge is charged to identify new circumstances as "instances of the general classifications which the law makes" (*COL*, 121).

2. It may happen in the course of adjudication that the rule does not fit and that another will have to be selected. The judge is positioned between a variety of prima facie valid rules and a new fact-situation. Faced with these many rules, there is always "something in the nature of a choice between open alternatives" available to the judge (*COL*, 125). If, as I have suggested, the rule cannot be modified by the case because it establishes it as a case in the first place, then choice is a necessary feature of Hart's theory of judgment. If the rule cannot be modified in its application and yet the judge must treat an unforeseen situation as an instance of a rule, then he or she must choose between rules that can best provide for the situation, that can transform it into a case, and thereby adjudicate it. Without choice, the rule would potentially have to accommodate new fact-situations to the limit of its own transformation. With the possibility of choice, however, adjudication is able to maintain the identity of its rules.

2

Reflective Judgment and the Law with Organs: Dworkin

In the *Critique of Judgment*, Kant proposes a unique and necessary presupposition of our faculty of judgment: Empirical nature, together with its diverse laws, must be judged as if it were a coherent unity. In a teleological judgment, we add that nature must be judged as if it were purposively designed for our faculty of judgment. In this chapter, I argue that Kant's concept of teleological judgment—the least commented on element of the critical philosophy—is rigorously adopted (but without direct attribution)[1] by Ronald Dworkin for his philosophy of law and adjudication. Central to my interpretation is that Dworkin's concept of integrity takes Kant's presupposition of the overall unity and systematicity of empirical laws as the necessary condition for adjudication.

The Principle of Principle

In the *Critique of Judgment* Kant draws a preliminary distinction between two types of judgment: reflective and determinative. For Kant, judgment in general is "the ability to think the particular as contained under the universal" (*CJ*, 18, §4). If the universal is given (as a rule or a law), judgment subsumes the particular under it. This operation is *determinative*. In determinative judgment, the law is marked out a priori and judgment need not devise a law, or reflectively presume a coherent system of laws, in order to subsume. If, on the other hand, only the particular is given and judgment is charged to find the universal under which to subsume it, the operation is *reflective* (*CJ*, 18–19, §4). In such a situation, only unrepresented "raw material," as Deleuze calls it, presents itself to the subject, having not yet been subsumed and expressed by a law or rule.² Reflective judgment must ascend from this lawless material to the universal (rule, concept, category, law); as such, it needs a principle to guide its discovery of laws for cases. This principle, we shall see, is the "finality of nature"—a presumption that empirical nature is coherently and systematically arranged for our power of judgment (*CJ*, 19, §4).

Let us turn directly to Dworkin and to the distinction he draws between plain-fact and realist adjudication, which, I argue, is based on a deeper but tacit distinction between determinative and reflective judgment. The first chapter of *Law's Empire* establishes an antinomy between plain-fact and realist views of adjudication. As in the *Critique of Pure Reason*, an antinomy occurs when two positions share an underlying presupposition that they develop in antagonistic directions. In these early pages of *Law's Empire*, the presupposition is that judges always judge *determinatively*—that for every case a rule at hand exists, and that judgment consists of nothing other than subsuming the case under this ready-made rule. On Dworkin's account, plain-fact and realist views are both committed to a determinative image of judgment.

For the plain-fact view of law, "popular among laymen and academic writers," legal disputes "can always be answered by looking in the books where the records of institutional decision are kept" because "the law is only a matter of what legal institutions . . . have decided in the past" (*LE*, 10, 7). From this perspective, judgment is simply a question of searching the archive and correctly applying the right rule to the case.

Alternatively, realists (and critical legal scholars, Dworkin adds) submit the plain-fact position to a "sophisticated" and skeptical consistency: Because every case is unique and can never exactly match the law applied to it, realists "conclude that there is never really law on any topic or issue, but only rhetoric judges use to dress up decisions actually dictated by ideological or class preference" (*LE*, 9). By this logic, realist judges consider themselves free from the strict constraints of law and proceed according to their own and their community's sense of justice.

Thus characterized, Dworkin elegantly establishes an antinomy between the plain-fact and realist camps. Because both positions commit to determinative judgment as the sole operation of judgment, two exclusive and antagonistic views of adjudication result. The plain-fact view says that adjudication must faithfully apply the written word of the law. The realist view claims that because no rule exactly fits a new case, the question of fidelity is misguided—the case provides nothing to which we can be faithful. At its limit, the "sophisticated" realists point out the inadequacy of a strictly determinative view of judgment but without calling into question the dubious image of determinative judgment that underwrites both positions.

By formulating the problem in this way, Dworkin sets the terms of the solution: The concept of reflective judgment provides a position to critique and thereby escapes from the antinomy. A consistent feature of Dworkin's philosophy, from *Taking Rights Seriously* all the way to his contemporary work, is the distinction between rules and principles.[3] For Dworkin, determinative judgment is allowed a limited place in adjudication in the application of rules. Rules always have an antecedent "if" clause that specifies the situational features of the application. Rules bear their own criteria of application (whether a speed limit or the constitutional rule that all members in the House of Representatives must be age 25 years or older), and once the facts of a case are settled they can be subsumed under the applicable rule. In our antinomy, both the plain-fact and the realist positions are inadequate because they conceive of adjudication as the simple application of rules to cases.

By contrast, principles (e.g., equal protection of the law without discrimination, or maxims such as "no one should profit from his own wrong") are not determinative and provide no stated criteria under which we can subsume the particular case. For Dworkin, law is significantly more than a collection of rules. Take, for example, the U.S. Constitution. Here we find few rules that specify their application; instead, the Constitution is replete with broad principles intended to orient and to guide judgment and legislation. Constitutional law is inherently unsuited to subsume cases through determinative judgment.

Without considering principles—that is, if we were confined to the simple subsumption of determinative judgment—we find that disagreement over law is puerile and insignificant. It is just a question of making sure the rule fits the facts (*LE*, 45–46). True legal disagreement speaks to conflict over principles and, more important, to conflict over their *interpretation* in relation to our legal institutions and history. For Dworkin, "interpretavism" is the attitude of judging according to principles. It has two central requirements: first, that law has value—that is, serve a purpose and express a principle; and second, that law remain sensitive to its principles (*LE*, 47). With the interpretive attitude, judges must "now try to impose *meaning* on the institution—to see it in its best light—and then to restructure it in the light of that meaning" (*LE*, 47).

We might say that at issue for Dworkin is the *principle of principle*—that is, the idea that the rules of law are principled and have value, not any specific principle. To suppose that the law embodies principles is, for Dworkin, to give adjudication a basis to investigate legal history and find the best law to judge the case at hand. When judges and lawyers disagree about law, it is a disagreement about which principles and constructions best express the purposes and principles law is assumed to honor. What is not disputed, according to Dworkin, is the notion of principle in general—that is, the assumption that principles inhabit our law. This assumption provides a shared basis for theoretical disagreement about and over law (*LE*, 42–43, 90).

Adjudication, in this sense, is a thoroughly Kantian endeavor of lifting and justifying the sensible (rules and cases) into the intelligible (practical purposes and principles). When Nietzsche exclaims that law "savors of morality," Dworkin could not be quicker to agree, for it is only thanks to a basis of principles that we are freed from the limitations of conceiving law as a collection of rules.[4] In determinative judgment, once the facts of a case are clarified, a rule comes to subsume it. The presupposition that our law is principled, by contrast, is quite different from rule application; it does not determinatively subsume anything. By assuming that our laws are *principled*—that, as Habermas puts it, an "embodied practical reason . . . extends through [legal] history" (*BFN*, 203)—we assume that we can investigate the specific principles said to inhabit law and adjudicate cases by means of those principles. The presupposition of principle acts as a focus or horizon for our power of judgment such that law appears as a purposive enterprise and as an expression of principle. This does not mean, however, that judgment is not subsumptive in Dworkin. It means only that, to bring a case under a rule, an anterior presupposition (that our rules embody principles) is necessary.

For Dworkin, decisions of law "contain not only the narrow explicit content of [past] decisions," which would qualify as rules, "but also, more broadly, the scheme of principles necessary to justify them" (*LE*, 227). It is the presupposition of principle in general that provides a reflective guide for judgment. This presupposition does not deliver a law to apply; instead, it enables an examination of our legal institutions as embodying principles with which to adjudicate cases. I characterize Dworkin's theory of judgment as reflective because of its presumption of purpose. Such a presumption is transcendental—it serves as the a priori condition that enables meaningful interpretation and judgment of particular purposes, laws, and cases.

Purposive Interpretation

Let us now turn to Dworkin's account of the interpretation of specific purposes and principles in law. Dworkin claims that "all genuine interpretation is purposive" and that interpretation is "by nature the *report of a purpose*" (*LE*, 51, emphasis added). It is possible to observe an apparent contradiction in the nature of this report. On the one hand, Dworkin proposes that we must see what is interpreted "*as if [it] were the product of a decision to pursue one set of themes* . . . rather than another" (*LE*, 59, emphasis added). Here, interpretation seems charged with the discovery of effective intentions present in the genesis of the phenomenon (e.g., the law) under examination. We presume that the law really was produced by the intentions we purport to find in it.

On the other hand, just pages earlier in *Law's Empire*, Dworkin claims that the concept of purpose that guides our investigations does not aim to report antecedent intentions that produced the law in question: "The purposes in play are not (fundamentally) those of some author but *of the interpreter*. Roughly, constructive *interpretation is a matter of imposing purpose on an object or practice* in order to make of it the best possible example of the form or genre to which it is taken to belong" (*LE*, 52, emphasis added). The contradiction is now registered: Guided by the reflective presupposition of purpose, we assume that the laws we investigate are the product of a decision to pursue certain actual purposes, and yet we realize that these purposes are imposed by the interpreter.

To reconcile these two statements, it is fruitful to call on the analogical dimension of Kant's *Critique of Judgment*: Reflective judgment proceeds *as if* the purposes we introduce into the laws we examine had been adopted in their very formulation. This *as if* is at the foundation of reflective judgment and reflective teleology.

> A teleological judgment compares two concepts of a natural product; it compares what the product is with what it is meant to be. Here our judging of the object's possibility is based on a concept (of a purpose) that precedes a priori that possibility. . . . If we think that a product of nature was meant to be something, and judge the product as to whether it actually is that, then we are already presupposing a principle that we cannot have derived from experience. (*CJ*, First Introduction, 429, §10, emphasis added)

In this description of teleological judgment we find the basis for Dworkin's philosophy of adjudication. In judging a thing teleologically, we presume that the possibility of this thing (product) depends on a concept (purpose) that precedes it and makes its existence possible. The only way that we are able to judge such a product is to assume a purpose that preceded it. For example, the only way to make sense of, and find a concept for, an organized body such as an eye is to presume a purpose that precedes its possibility; thus an eye (and each of its parts) is meant for seeing (*CJ*, First Introduction, 425, §9). This principle (of a purpose for products we judge teleologically) is a priori and is not drawn from experience of the product; the presumption of purposiveness is the formal condition by which we are able to make sense of and judge a natural product. Without a presumption of purpose we would perceive not a product but an inchoate thing.[5]

In making a teleological judgment, Kant consistently stresses that we are making a reflective and not a determinative judgment. Teleology says nothing about the object itself or its conditions of real causality; all that we can say is that for us to understand this thing before us, we must judge it *as if* it had been produced by purposes and preceded by a concept. *Teleology indicates only the conditions under which something is judged* (*CJ*, 34, §8). If we said that nature intentionally and purposively produced a thing by means of a concept, we would make a determinative (not to mention dialectical or illusory) judgment. Teleological reflective judgments indicate nothing about the object or real purposiveness in nature; they signify only the limitation of our judgment (that it is finite and bound to certain conditions: discursive and nonintuitive) that necessitates the use of this reflective principle of judgment (*CJ*, 291–292, §77).

In my reading of Dworkin I find Kant's insights on reflective teleological judgment scrupulously applied toward a theory of adjudication.[6] First, judgments at law are based on principles, or, more exactly, such judgments depend on the presumption of principle and purpose in our laws. Second, Dworkin preserves the strictly reflective sense of teleological judgment. Earlier we saw an apparent contradiction: At once we judge our laws as if they were the product of specific purposes adopted in their formulation, and, at the same time, we acknowledge that the purposes we impose are none other than our own (*LE*, 59, 228). The *as if* expresses the operation of teleological reflective judgment. In Dworkin's reflective teleology we make no claim as to the actual intentions of lawgivers. Instead, a merely subjective principle—the crucial reflective *as if,* which Dworkin carefully indicates—guides our investigations by reflectively imputing to laws a purposiveness and principle by which we can judge (or impose on) them with our own purposes. Given that Dworkin's interpretive theory of adjudication is grounded in the conviction that law is principled and purposive, various discernible purposes must be found in the history of the law and must be able to connect with the principles of the present (*LE*, 87). According to the requirements of reflective judgment, law must be purposive in general and inhere various purposes to be interpreted purposively; without reflectively presupposing purpose and principle in their history and formation, laws would be unsuitable for principled interpretation. To make the law the best it can be (a watchword of Dworkin's), we impute purposes and intentions throughout our legal history but make no claims that these intentions were present in the actual genesis of law.[7]

I have made two claims about Dworkin's philosophy of law. First, to avoid reducing adjudication to rule application, Dworkin proposes reflective judgment as a basis for adjudication that presumes purpose in our laws. Second, Dworkin maintains the strictly reflective sense of teleological judgment in his description of judging specific purposes in law. Purposes are interpreted as if they were present in the formation of law, and this is the condition by which we impose our own purposes. In the next section of this chapter, I deepen this teleological interpretation by concentrating on Dworkin's teleological concept par excellence: integrity.

Elegantia Juris: Integrity and the Lawfulness of the Contingent

In the Transcendental Deduction of the first edition of the *Critique of Pure Reason*, Kant assumes that the "order and regularity" in what we "call nature" is entirely provided for by the pure concepts of the understanding (A125). There, the pure concepts of the understanding guarantee a "necessary, i.e., *a priori* certain unity of the connection of appearances" (A125). The *Critique of Pure Reason*, however, deals with transcendental laws and objects of *possible* experience (*CJ*, First Introduction, 393n, §2). The *Critique of Judgment*, by contrast, poses the problem of judging the *content* of phenomena and of the problem of *a* nature in its real particular laws and organization. Contrary to the general laws of the understanding, these laws of nature are empirical and therefore contingent (as far as we know). For this reason, the *Critique of Judgment* faces a potential crisis of the unity of experience and cognition: Empirical nature (contrary to transcendental "nature as a whole") may not be unified, coherent, and systematic but may be a "crude chaotic aggregate without the slightest trace of a system" (*CJ*, First Introduction, 397, §4).

The organizing problem of the *Critique of Judgment* is to theorize how experience "*must* constitute a *system* of possible empirical cognitions, and do so in terms of both universal [transcendental] *and* particular [empirical] laws" (*CJ*, First Introduction, 397, §4, emphasis added). For Kant, this means that judgment must have a transcendental capacity of its own to match the understanding; only in this way can both transcendental and empirical laws constitute nature as a unified system. "If there is to be a concept or rule that arises originally from the power of judgment, it would have to be a concept of things of nature insofar as nature conforms to our power of judgment" (*CJ*, First Introduction, 392, §2). Insofar as we maintain the concept of a unified empirical nature (which we must, to match the unity of transcendental laws and experience), the power of judgment must assume for itself a purposive unity of nature in order to judge. We must assume that in principle we can judge nature systematically and that its laws cohere in a unity for our capacity to judge it. As usual, this is a merely reflective (and not determinative) power of judgment. The unity we presume claims nothing of nature itself. It merely says that if we are to judge nature coherently and consistently, we must do so as if it were a system. When Kant moves to treat teleology proper, the role of reflective judgment endowing empirical laws with maximum unity is kept. Added is the presupposition that this unity is (reflectively) conferred on phenomena by an understanding other than our own, that is, by a purposive causality: "We are absolutely unable to form a concept of how such a world is possible except by thinking of it as brought about by a supreme cause that *acts intentionally*" (*CJ*, 281, §75).

At this point I return to Dworkin to see how this presumption of unity and intention are necessary for adjudication. Among all the principles that Dworkin treats, one has special, "sovereign" importance: integrity (*LE*, 218). There are two variants of integrity. The first, which concerns us less, is integrity as the foundational principle of *political* community. The second is that of integrity as the significant principle of *adjudication*.

I begin with the first. Integrity is a distinct political ideal because we as a community "want to treat ourselves as an association of principle, as a community governed by a *single and coherent vision* of justice and fairness and procedural due process in the right relation" (*LE*, 404, emphasis added). Integrity demands that our principles be common and compatible and the best they can be (*LE*, 263). It is a bedrock of our moral and political culture that our principles neither adopt inconsistent applications nor contradict one another. "Integrity is flouted . . . whenever a community enacts and enforces different laws each of which is coherent in itself, but which cannot be defended together as expressing a coherent ranking" (*LE*, 184). Integrity shares an ambition with reflective judgment in that it assumes and insists that our principles are systematically ordered. Integrity thus has two functions. First, it orders our various principles into a coherent and responsible scheme, that of the community; and second, it ensures that members of the community may view and identify themselves as part of a collective undertaking of ordered principles in their best possible relation.

In order for our community to govern itself according to a single vision of principles (i.e., according to integrity), Dworkin claims that it is necessary to view the state as if it were a moral agent that adopts and upholds a system. It is not to be viewed as a mere aggregate of principles. Through its officials—judges, for example—the state is expected to "speak with *one* voice . . . toward all its citizens" (*LE*, 165). And according to Dworkin, "Integrity becomes a political ideal when we make the same demand of the state or community taken to be a moral agent, when we insist that the state act on a single, coherent set of principles even when its citizens are divided" (*LE*, 166). This is not a specious metaphysical hypostatization of the community; instead, the concept of a single community of principle is a necessary reflective assumption if its members are to uphold the principle of integrity. "We must not say that integrity is a special virtue of politics because the state or community is a distinct entity, but that the community *should be seen* as a distinct moral agent because the social and intellectual practices that treat community in this way should be protected" (*LE*, 187–188, emphasis added). This is a strong application of Kant's teleological judgment: Integrity can be upheld as a political value *only if* we reflectively presuppose that our state is a unified community intentionally practicing integrity. The state is neither a real nor an actually intentional moral entity; it is a reflective artifice that we must presume in order to maintain integrity in our laws, judgments, and moral orientation. Integrity is conceivable only if we reflectively posit an intentional state or community as its unified author. In this way, Dworkin's state is Kant's "understanding other than our own" by which we can formulate and experience our sovereign principle: integrity as a systematic arrangement of principles.

This leads us to the second, adjudicative variation of integrity. In adjudicating, the judge begins from the position of political integrity; in other words, he or she is "require[d] . . . to treat our present system of public standards as expressing and respecting a coherent set of principles" (*LE*, 217). But not only do judges presuppose the coherence of principles and community, they are also bound to abide and strengthen it. Therefore, a judge must "test his interpretation of any part of the great network of political structures and decisions of his community by asking whether [the interpretation] could form part of a coherent theory justifying the network as a whole" (*LE*, 245). Before, I argued that *the* reflective presupposition of judgment for Dworkin is that our laws are principled. I may now add a crucial corollary rule: Judges reflectively presuppose that our laws are principled *and* that these principles can be coherently organized and expressed in our law. The latter requirement is nothing other than integrity in adjudication.

Judges who honor integrity (and all conscientious judges do for Dworkin) must view themselves as guardians of the set of principles their community is taken to embody. The principles by which they adjudicate are not discretionary. Judges, in truth, understand that they are themselves mouthpieces for the reflectively presupposed state that speaks with a single voice (*LE*, 218). Not only should judges reaffirm the integrity and continuity of principles they find in the history of law and legal practice, but they must also make plain in their opinions the path "later judges guided by integrity will follow" by giving clear and definite expression to "convictions about morality that are widespread through their community" (*LE*, 248).

Judges must assume that the principles of their community are coherent. They are not, however, blind or naive. They know that the law is not perfectly consistent in its principles. Some statutes receive a force inconsistent with others; some precedents in force are atavistic, and so on. But, Dworkin adds, the judge "*assumes* that these contradictions are not so pervasive and intractable within departments of law that his task is impossible.... He *assumes* that some set of reasonably plausible principles can be found, for each general department of law he must enforce, that fit well enough to count as an eligible interpretation of it" (*LE*, 268, emphasis added). Or, again, law as integrity asks judges to "*assume that the law is structured by a coherent set of principles about justice and fairness and procedural due process*, and it asks them to enforce these in the fresh cases that come before them, so that each person's situation is fair and just according to the same standards" (*LE*, 243, emphasis added).

These decisive citations reveal a striking application of teleological reflective judgment to adjudication. Borrowing a phrase from Oliver Wendell Holmes, we can call Dworkin's theory an *elegantia juris*, the "cohesion of part with part" (*CL*, 36). As in Kant, Dworkin realizes the real danger and possibility that our laws (now juridical, not physico-empirical as in Kant) may not cohere, that there may contradictions, or, at best, an aggregate of unsystematized laws.[8] And, as in Kant, Dworkin summons a principle of judgment that is not determinative, that does not subsume anything, but that provides the necessary presupposition for judgment: coherent, purposive, and principled laws. Consider again these lines from Kant: "Experience too ... (*ideally*), *must* constitute a system of possible empirical cognitions" (*CJ*, First Introduction, 397, §4). Kant's and Dworkin's claims are strictly reflective; they claim nothing of the real unity of laws but only that we *must*, *ideally*, presuppose this unity in order to judge. Reflective judgment is presumptive in this fashion, and we can see its operation in Dworkin's repeated phrase, "we must assume that . . ." This assumption is the transcendental power of reflective judgment. It provides the hope that judgment may endow its territory of laws and their principles with maximal integrity.

Natural Purposes: The Law with Organs

For Kant, reflective judgments of purpose (i.e., teleology) are indispensable when judging an organized body (*CJ*, §65). Organized bodies are judged as natural purposes, for this is the only way we can make sense of them (i.e., to judge them). Such a judgment has three requirements: (1) The possibility of each part of the body depends on its relation to the whole (the purpose); (2) the purpose covers the entire thing, and each part must make reference to it; and (3) the purpose expresses internal finality. This means that the product is not a work of art with an exterior cause (an artist, God, etc.), for in that case we would make a determinative judgment as to its purposive causality. Rather, with internal finality the reciprocal actions of the parts on one another (e.g., "organs" or retina and lens) combine into a whole (i.e., the "organism" or an eye that sees), and it is the reflective concept of the whole (the eye that sees) that allows us to judge the parts *as if* they were purposively determined to combine and interact according to the design of the whole. In such a judgment the concept of a purpose does not actually produce the whole (as it would in art) but is merely the reflective basis by which someone judges the systematic unity and combination of the manifold parts as a whole. It is the whole purposively judged that gives meaning to the parts. In Kant's words, in order to judge a thing as a natural purpose, "what is needed is that all its parts, through their own causality, produce one another as regards both their form and combination, and that in this way they produce a *whole* whose concept . . . could, *conversely*, be the cause of this body according to a principle" (*CJ*, 252, §65). In brief, a connection of efficient causes could be judged in terms of purposive causation (final causes).

With these considerations, let us return to *Law's Empire*. Dworkin uses a suggestive metaphor for integrity in law: the chain novel (*LE*, 228–238). As we have seen in adjudication, the concept of intention does not aim to rediscover actual purposes of particular historical persons; rather, the interpreter strives to "impose purpose over the text . . . being interpreted" (*LE*, 228). A similar process occurs, says Dworkin, when writing a chain novel. With a chain novel, one author writes a chapter of a narrative and passes it on to a second author, who then writes a second chapter and passes it on, and so on. If the authors take the charge of continuity seriously, each will endeavor to write a chapter that makes a unified story the best it can be (*LE*, 229). Crucially, this involves an "overall judgment" on the part of each contributing author, "or a series of overall judgments as he writes and rewrites," as to what the intention of the story is, what its salient themes and features are, and how best to extend and contribute to the story. The interpretation the author adopts "must have general explanatory power, and it is flawed if it leaves unexplained some major structural aspect of the text" (*LE*, 330). The interpretation by which each author trusses together the text and weaves its strands into a coherent whole makes it appear as if a single author had written the text with an intentional consistent design in mind: "He must try to make this the best novel that can be construed as the *work of a single author* rather than, as is the fact, the product of many different hands" (*LE*, 229).

Step by step, Dworkin develops a reflective judgment of natural purposes. In judging the chain novel, the author imagines that each of its chapters (organs) are purposive parts in a coherent work (an organism). The whole text (organism) is not given beforehand and furnished to the author; instead, the author must construct a novel-in-process from the unformed text. He must first assume that a coherent interpretation is possible in principle (the founding presupposition of reflective judgment), and then he must design an overarching interpretation that can account for as many themes from the story as possible, implicating each part in a whole as if it were designed to play such a part.

This causality is not external or artistic. The parts bear an internal purposiveness within a whole that has been reflectively presupposed. The chain novel is reflectively judged as if it were written by a single author in order to obtain an evaluation of its purpose. In truth, however, the author does not write the whole story but only the last chapter of an ongoing narrative; the author merely adds another organ. Yet, for this organ to have been created, an overall purpose must be introduced into each of the parts; only in this way can the last chapter be written. The reflective judgment that presumes a whole (an organism with working parts) reorients each of the parts, including the last, and sets them all down within this whole such that each part purposively and reciprocally acts on each other within a whole scheme of significance. The parts make sense only as purposive units within a presupposed unity, and in this way the parts produce the unity (the whole interpretation) presupposed in order to judge them.

Mutatis mutandis, this characterization applies to Dworkin's theory of adjudication. Judges too must "interpret contemporary legal practice [as] an unfolding political narrative" (*LE*, 225). In constructing a judgment, a judge who abides by integrity endeavors to support and pursue a principle as consistently as possible through the history of the legal tradition. In this narrative, Dworkin's reflective teleology achieves its full power and extension: The history of law is assumed to be interpretable in terms of integrity—that is, its overall story can add up in a coherent account of our laws and practices—and is presumed to have been intentionally "created by a single author—the community personified" (*LE*, 224). In adjudicating, a judge's decision must provide an interpretation of what has gone on before in legal practice, and his judgment is the last chapter of an ongoing construction. The judge constructs the best and most coherent line of interpretation of his legal practice and history, and proceeds to compose his own chapter in which each precedent and organ of legal history upon which he draws—and indeed, the one he composes—is interpreted (reflectively judged) to inhere the purposive design of the whole organism effectively produced.[9]

By comparing this argument to Kant's reflective judgment of natural purpose, I call Dworkin's theory a *law with organs*. In order to adjudicate a case according to integrity, the judge must presuppose that the law is like a gigantic organism and that each principle is one of its organs. In this way, the best principle (i.e., the one that best shows off the coherence of principle and community) is selected to adjudicate the case at hand.[10] Just as in Kant, where the concept of the organism is both the reflective principle by which we judge the purposive relations of the organs and also the effective result of these relations, with Dworkin integrity is both the reflective concept that we bring to judge the history and principles of law and also "*the actual present law* [that] provides the best justification available for the doctrines and devices as a whole" (*LE*, 400). Using Deleuze's words with respect to Kant, we claim that the regulative aspiration of

Dworkin's adjudicative principle is for "a maximum of unity in the greatest possible variety, without the limit of this unity being clear."[11] To find a judgment so comprehensive that it approaches "a full interpretation of all [the judge's] community of law" is nothing but the dream for an organism of law in which each "part of that great network of political structures and decisions of community" finds itself accounted as purposive organs in this story (*LE*, 245). Such is the dream of reflective judgment.

We might say, in fact, that Dworkin's dream realizes Deleuze's depiction of an infinite economy of judgment, wherein "nothing is left but judgment, and every judgment bears on another judgment" (*CC*, 129). To add up these judgments: Dworkin reflectively presupposes that (1) laws are principled; (2) taken together, these principled laws are coherent; and (3) principles express the intention of the community personified. But these are only the three preliminary judgments. With natural purposes, the empire of judgment expands: (4) In a natural purpose not only do we judge a body or thing purposively but we also presuppose internal finality so that each part of the body is marked by purposive judgment alongside other parts, which are also marked according to this scheme. In such an organism all we see are judgments (purposive organs) that interact with other judgments. Finally, (5) each judge in the ongoing political narrative rejudges and reinterprets an organism (the law and its principles in toto) and its organs (specific laws and purposes), which are, in fact, nothing else than the product of a formally identical judgment undertaken by a preceding judge, and before him, his predecessor, and so on.

3

Communication, Judgment, Retrospection: Habermas

In this chapter I attend to Habermas's theory of adjudication from his major work on law, *Between Facts and Norms: Contributions to a Discourse Theory of Law and Democracy*. I argue that Habermas's theory of adjudication is subsumptive and expressly precludes creativity. This has to do with how he envisages the encounter between case and law. Although a case is judged within the institution of adjudication, for Habermas this judgment is reached by anticipating what participants in democratic discourses *would have thought* of the case had they considered it. I claim that adjudication in Habermas involves a sophisticated and *retrospective* temporality that secures continuity, and therefore legitimacy, between the application of rules in adjudication discourses and the creation of rules in democratic justification discourses. This relationship between application and justification discourses allows us to conceive of judgment as communicatively achieved.

Habermas: Communicative Kantian

Habermas extensively develops Kantian concepts toward his own philosophy of law and right. Indeed, one commentator characterizes Habermas, especially as a legal theorist, as a "communicative Kantian."[1] And not only is Habermas a strongly identified Kantian, but, as critics have pointed out, the discourse of human rights is dominated by a massive "return to Kant."[2]

As Deleuze and Guattari claim, "If one can remain Platonist, Cartesian, or Kantian today, it is because one is justified in thinking that their concepts can be reactivated in our problems and inspire those concepts that need to be created" (*WP*, 28). What is the nature of the Kantian reactivation? Theorists of discourse ethics transpose Kant's practical philosophy into a dialogical conception of practical reason.[3] This communicative turn reactivates Kant's practical and political thought within postmetaphysical thinking.

The primary insight of Kant's Doctrine of Right (*Rechtslehre*) is that law is both rationally acceptable and valid, and, contrary to the moral law, enforceable and factual.[4] In Kant's political theory, the legitimacy of law is rational but counterfactual; the legislator must frame laws in such a way that they *could* have been willed by each affected subject. Habermas takes this strong internal relationship between validity and facticity to formulate his concept of the discourse principle: "Just those action norms are valid to which all possibly affected persons could agree as participants in rational discourses" (*BFN*, 107). For Habermas, laws are action norms; indeed, they are the principal kind of action norms for modern societies.[5] An action norm or a law, therefore, is both rationally acceptable and enforceable.

Although the discourse principle might appear counterfactual ("possibly affected persons *could* agree"), for Habermas this is not the case. An action norm or law is legitimate (valid) and effective (factual) once it has been *dialogically* agreed on by all those affected. In other words, an enforceable law is always at the same time valid and rational by means of communicative agreement. This gives Kant's practical and political philosophy a democratic turn. Instead of being rational and acceptable in principle, laws are created through actual communication that participants find rational and acceptable. We, the authors of law, are really and simultaneously the addressees of law. Action norms are therefore relations that have their basis in dialogically achieved recognition and accord; they presuppose the first-person plural, communicatively achieved (*BFN*, 88).

It is crucial for Habermas that the discourse principle not remain merely counterfactual: "It is only politically autonomous legislation [*Rechtsetzung*] that makes it possible for the addressees to have a correct understanding of the legal order as a whole" (*BFN*, 121, translation modified). What the discourse principle needs, therefore, is a democracy principle to ensure the communicative creation of action norms and laws. According to the democracy principle, all citizens (and their elected representatives) are authors and addressees of their laws. What the democracy principle requires is a legal procedure for legitimate lawmaking that can ensure symmetrical rights to participation and deliberation in legislative processes. It finds this in an institutionalized discourse principle.

The discourse principle is intended to assume the shape of a principle of democracy only by way of legal [*rechtsförmigen*] institutionalization. The principle of democracy is what then confers legitimating force on the legislative process. The key idea is that the principle of democracy derives from the interpenetration of the discourse principle and the legal form. I understand this interpenetration as a *logical genesis of rights*. . . . Hence the principle of democracy can only appear as the heart of a *system* of rights. The logical genesis of these rights comprises a circular process in which the legal code and the mechanism for producing legitimate law—hence the democratic principle—are *co-originally* constituted. (*BFN*, 121–122, translation modified)

Developing this text, I distinguish two levels of rights: basic rights and derivative rights.

    1. *Basic Rights*. Most fundamentally, we have basic rights (*Grundrechte*) that guarantee citizens equal participation in determining the action norms that affect them. The institutionalization of the discourse principle establishes procedures necessary to legitimately legislate action norms: "The *substance* of human rights . . . resides in the *formal* conditions for the legal institutionalization of those discursive processes of opinion- and will-formation in which the sovereignty of the people assumes a binding character" (*BFN*, 104, emphasis added). Here, what is shared and recognized is not any particular action norm or right but the very form of democratic participation and communication. This is why Habermas calls the substance of human rights formal—at stake is the right to equal participation in the determination of all future norms. In brief, "*human rights* institutionalize the communicative conditions for a reasonable political will-formation."[6]

    The institutionalization of the discourse principle is nothing other than the idealized genesis of the democratic legal medium. In other words, to grant reciprocal rights of participation in democratic discourse *is* the founding act of the state as legal-administrative power (*BFN*, 89).[7]

The universal consent required for valid and enforceable action norms is no longer counterfactually assumed as it was in Kant; rather, the state form is established to enable and protect—to proceduralize—the communicative activity that generates action norms. "The sought-for relation between popular sovereignty and human rights consists in the fact that the system of rights states precisely the conditions under which the forms of communication necessary for a politically autonomous legislation [*für eine politisch autonome Rechtsetzung*] can be legally institutionalized" (*BFN*, 104, translation modified). By virtue of this internal relation between sovereignty and human rights, Habermas argues that human rights are always already positive and juridical by nature; rights do not preexist the procedural democratic association of the state but are co-original with this formation.[8] As Seyla Benhabib writes, "*les droits de l'homme et de citoyen* do not contradict one another; quite to the contrary, they are coimplicated."[9] For Habermas, all constitutional democracies are iterations of the basic grounding of participative rights. "We can understand the catalogs of human civil rights [*Grundrechtsabschnitte*] found in our historic constitutions as context-dependent readings of the *same* system of rights" (*BFN*, 128). There may be apparent differences to various constitutional democracies, but, at root, rights to will formation underlie all historic instantiations.[10]

2. *Derivative Rights*. With fundamental rights to participation anchored by the legal medium, citizens enter into deliberations to generate specific laws and rights (e.g., statutes, constitutional amendments). With the basic procedures of participation in place, justification discourses are enabled. "At the posttraditional level of justification, *the only law [Recht] that counts as legitimate is one that could be rationally accepted by all citizens [Rechtsgenossen] in a discursive opinion- and will-formation*" (*BFN*, 135, emphasis added, translation modified). Habermas envisages a law's legitimacy on the basis of universal accord—it is accepted for good reasons by *all* citizens. Justification requires a basis of universal rational consent. "We" mutually convince one another that a law is valid by means of criticizable argument. Habermas calls this moral argumentation after the cognitivist turn of Kant's practical reason (i.e., practical judgments that are not prudential but rational).[11] Moral arguments are not grounded in a shared substantial understanding of the good (ethical level), nor is a consensus achieved through a bargaining process, as in

a balance of diverse interests (pragmatic level) (*BFN*, 108–109). A law is valid "if and *only* if equal consideration is given to the interests of all those who are possibly involved"—that is, only if it can be impartially justified (*BFN*, 108). In ethical argumentation a norm is valid for those who share a way of life, and in pragmatic argumentation outcomes are acceptable for various interested reasons; neither is impartial. These levels of justification lack universal and ever-expanding consensus. Impartial justification demands universally shared reasons.

We have seen that the democracy principle presupposes the possibility of valid moral judgments. In fact, democracy is co-original with the institutionalization of (communicative) moral judgment. With these procedures in place (basic rights), legitimate laws and rights can be created (derivative rights): "the democratic principle states that only those *statutes* [*juridischen Gesetze*] may claim legitimacy that can meet with the assent [*Zustimmung*] of *all citizens* in a discursive process of legislation that in turn has been legally constituted" (*BFN*, 110, emphasis added). Action norms or laws are legitimately produced in and by a communicative legal medium. Because they are moral, norms are not bound to a determinate group or interest; they are human in the strongly Kantian sense of respecting the humanity—the communicative reason—of all those they affect.

A Deleuzian Reply

At this point, and in preliminary fashion, I raise two of Deleuze's objections to philosophies of communication. My objective is not yet to present his famous distaste for communication but to introduce criticisms that will help to develop Habermas. Of our three dogmatic theorists Habermas is the only one with whom it can be said Deleuze engaged (more or less) explicitly, and so, my justification for bringing Deleuze in at this stage is to guide the elaboration of Habermas's theory of adjudication and to prepare the critical discussion in Part 2.

I begin by stating that if philosophy's task is, as Deleuze consistently maintained, to create concepts, a philosophy of communication must be indicted on two counts. First, its philosophical ambition is to establish the conditions for opinion (*doxa*) to be shared and sanctified (*DR*, 131). And second, it is content to create consensus and exchange ideas that resolve into empty generalities (*WP*, 28–29). Because of these characteristics, the philosophy of communication "has not produced the least concept" (*WP*, 6, translation modified). We can coordinate Deleuze's two critiques with the two levels of rights I have outlined from *Between Facts and Norms*.

1. *Critique of Basic Rights*. Habermas's co-originality thesis establishes a legal medium in which communication backed by rights is at the core of democracy and political philosophy. In Deleuze's terms, Habermas's theory does not advance any particular *doxa* or substantive truth, "not a particular this or that," but, rather, thematizes "*the form of representation or recognition in general*" (*DR*, 131, emphasis added). If for Habermas human rights protect and provide for intersubjective deliberation and consensus, then for Deleuze they guarantee and entrench the form of recognition and representation.

2. *Critique of Derivative Rights*. With the communicative legal medium in place, citizens enter into deliberations to produce action norms. The formation of statutes and laws takes place within an economy of criticizable opinions and ideas pitched at a necessarily high or indeterminate level (*BFN*, 217). From Deleuze's perspective, moral discourses—the plane on which Habermas insists that derivative rights are legitimately secured by all those affected—produce abstract and senseless propositions. All participants may indeed agree on a proposition—against arbitrary detention, for example—but what they agree on is abstract, for it is without reference to a determinate situation or problem. For Deleuze, such agreement would be like a proposition arbitrarily detached from its context and devoid of sense (*DR*, 154). Shared moral discourses are propositions so abstract as to be empty. Not only, then, are communicative discourses unable to create philosophical concepts; they also are equally incapable of creating effective, determinate rights.

Reply: Application Discourses

Let me take these two criticisms as an opportunity for Habermas (and his close ally, Klaus Günther)[12] to reply, especially to the second criticism, and to introduce a central concept: application discourses as distinct from justification discourses. Justification discourses are those discourses that seek to generate norms that are intersubjectively shared and affirmed for good reasons (e.g., the plane of legislation, where a law is accepted by all those affected). Application discourses are those discourses in which a norm is applied to a case in order to treat it (e.g., the plane of adjudication, where a judge decides which norm applies to the case at hand).

It is not exactly accurate to say that moral discourses and the norms they produce have no content because the consensus needed to secure them was too abstract to begin with. Every norm has a situational index by virtue of its semantic content and always already incorporates reference to situations.[13] In this respect, and as a thought experiment, Günther imagines a *perfect norm*, one that a priori and publicly includes all its possible cases of application. Citizens in justification discourses could readily adopt a particular norm of this kind because it would immediately notify them of all its future applications.

Such a "perfect" norm could regulate its own application because each of those situations where an interest might be violated would have been taken into consideration beforehand. The participants of a discourse would be certain that there will be no situation where observance of a norm will violate a universalizable interest.[14]

In this situation all is given in the structure of anticipation. In a way, the perfect norm replies to the Deleuzian critique: The norm is not abstract but brims with content. As Günther observes, all citizens would know in advance on what they agree; none of their expectations could be violated by unexpected events and encounters. The discourse principle for such a norm would read, "A norm is valid and in every case appropriate if the consequences and side effects arising for the interests of each individual as a result of this norm's general observance *in every particular situation can be anticipated by everyone.*"[15]

Of course, as Günther quickly points out, perfect norms are a regulative ideal—our willed historical norms are inextricably finite and cannot anticipate all possible applications. Finite norms willed under conditions of limited knowledge and time can, however, foresee a range of cases in which their application would be appropriate. "In this way [the discourse principle] is equipped with an index that ties its application *to the level of knowledge at the current point in time.*"[16] Correspondingly, the exigencies of the discourse principle become weaker, diminished to the *expected* possible cases of application at the time of our justification discourses: "Only those interests *expected* to be affected by the consequences and side effects of applying a norm *can be considered*."[17]

Adoption of a strong discourse principle of norm justification is not only impossible (because it presupposes the availability of perfect norms), but also ethically suspect. A strong justification discourse would spuriously reduce new experiences and situations to those anticipated in justification. It would lead, in other words, to insensitive and inappropriate applications.[18] In light of our finitude, Günther and Habermas recommend a weak version of the discourse principle: Participants "examine contested norms in view of *foreseeably typical* cases . . . [that] can be applied *directly* only to the standard situations that have already [*von vornherein*] been considered in their antecedent clause" (*BFN*, 162). With this weaker principle, justification discourses leave open the potential for new and unanticipated situations for which we will need a different kind of operation, application discourses (*BFN*, 162).

Günther's innovation is to separate two moments that Habermas's previous work collapsed: justification and application. Let us examine Habermas's treatment of adjudication to illustrate these two moments. In adjudication we must carefully examine the individual situation to see precisely which norm applies to, and is able to consistently treat and subsume, the situation:

Except for those norms whose "if" clauses specify application conditions in such detail that they apply only to a few highly typified and well-circumscribed standard-situations . . . *all* norms are *inherently* indeterminate. . . . [Norms]—and not just constitutional rights and principles that justify the legal system as a whole—*remain indeterminate in their references to situations and have need of additional specifications in the individual case* [emphasis added]. Because such norms are only *prima facie* applicable, one must first enter a discourse of application to test whether they apply to a given situation (whose details could not have been anticipated in the justification process) or whether, their validity notwithstanding, they must give way to another norm, namely, the "appropriate" one. Only if a valid norm proves to be the single appropriate one in the case at hand does that norm ground a singular judgment that can claim to be right. That a norm is *prima facie* valid means merely that it has been impartially *justified*; only its impartial *application* leads to a valid decision about a case. (*BFN*, 217)

Adjudication faithfully applies the norms that are deliberatively generated because these norms deserve legal obedience and respect; they are embodiments of universal communicative agreements (*BFN*, 198). But, as Habermas observes, norms generated in justification discourses are indeterminate and make reference only to a few general application scenarios (*BFN*, 162). Given this indeterminacy, several norms will be prima facie applicable. The role of application discourses is to consider whether a particular norm is appropriate to the (fully described) situation, and, if not, to select another. With both moments of justification and application in mind, we say that "an action [is] right because it is the result of the *right* (appropriate) application of the *right* (valid) norm."[19]

But what is the nature of this application? Does application to the case leave the norm unchanged, if only more determinate? Or does the application modify the norm in a creative application? In sum, the first represents Habermas's solution, the second Deleuze's.

Consider the line just cited: "[Norms] . . . remain indeterminate in their references to situations and have need of additional specifications in the individual case." What sort of specification is this? We find a model in Kant's *Critique of Judgment*: A universal or generic concept is divided and specified by the species and subspecies it subsumes. Such a specification makes "the universal concept specific by indicating the diverse that falls under it" (*CJ*, First Introduction, 402–403, §5). For example, we do not encounter a mammal in itself, but this indeterminate concept is specified by various species that are explained through, but do not modify, the generic concept. Considered this way, an indeterminate norm preserves its identity while being applied to different cases; the cases are only specifications of that norm.

In specifications of this sort, impartial norm applications simply close the gap that remained open in justification. They adjudicate the case by full descriptions of situations as instances of this or that norm. The norm remains unaffected. The application discourse recontextualizes the norm that was cut off from its context in validity. In so doing, the ideal of the perfect norm is reached reconstructively. "The concepts of validity and appropriateness mean the same if and only if we could justify the consequences of the general following of the norm for each of all possible cases of application beforehand. So we have to apply a valid norm *as if* we could have foreseen this situation in a discourse under the conditions of unlimited knowledge and time."[20] This *retrospective temporality* is essential to what follows: A norm application is appropriate only if it could have been foreseen in justification discourses. To meet the standard of appropriateness, we must say—but this can only be done retrospectively—that the application had already been anticipated in the justification discourses that established the norm.

Although the perfect norm is merely a regulative ideal, it is nevertheless imperative for discourse ethics to ensure its retrospective possibility. Without retrospective possibility, application threatens to annul the validity of the justification discourses that brought the norm into being. Application must not modify the norm in any substantial way. Were it to do so, renewed justification discourses would be necessary to guarantee universal assent to the norm's new sense. Application discourses must therefore always operate in the future perfect to honor the moral agreement that generated the norm in the first place: Future cases *will have been* considered in the genesis of the norm at the level of justification. The decisive separation in discourse ethics between justification and application is necessitated by our finitude. The theory of appropriateness in norm application is an attempt to overcome our finitude and achieve perfect norms by other means—a specification of norms in application through cases that are retrospectively included in discourses of justification. This is precisely the Kantian specification: The norm is determined but not modified by the differences it contains within itself.

To repeat, the danger for discourse ethics in application discourses is that the specification of the indeterminate norm may alter the sense of that norm and thereby compromise the consensus to which it owes its validity. It is apparent that William Rehg, translator of *Between Facts and Norms*, is aware of this risk. Himself a scholar of discourse ethics and the philosophy of law, Rehg adds a telling interpolation into Habermas's text, one that attests to the anxiety around the problem of application and norm alteration. The text in question concerns precisely this issue of the modification of a norm in application. Habermas starts: "*The relations among valid norms change depending on the relevant constellation of features of the case to be decided*. . . . The latter enter into a specific order of relations with one another only when it becomes clear how the currently appropriate norm refers to the situation" (*BFN*, 219, emphasis added). At this point, Habermas's text continues by citing Günther:

If every norm must be coherently complemented by all other norms applicable in a situation, then the meaning of the norm (*subtly*) changes in every situation

[*Wenn jede gültige Norm auf eine kohärente Ergänzung durch alle anderen in einer Situation anwendbaren Normen angewiesen ist, ändert sich ihre Bedeutung in jeder Situation*]. In this way we depend on *history*, since it alone provides us with the unforeseeable situations that compel us at each point a different interpretation of the set of all valid norms. (*BFN*, 219, emphasis added)[21]

No mention of the subtlety of the modification of the norm is indicated in the German text; the addition of the word *subtly* is Rehg's intervention. But it is interpolated for good reasons. If "both guarantees, certainty and legitimacy, must be simultaneously redeemed at the level of judicial decision making," then modification in the meaning of the norm must be subtle indeed to assure the certainty of the application, the legitimacy of the justification, and the continuity between the two (*BFN*, 198).

It is important to note how and why the norm changes—subtly or not—in application discourses. It has nothing to do with the case or circumstance directly modifying the norm. Instead, the inclusion and exclusion of appropriate cases within each norm varies the relationships between the norms, and, by consequence, (subtly) alters their meaning.[22]

In justification discourses, norms are pitched at too indeterminate a level to conflict; however, norm collisions do occur in concrete situations.[23] As Günther explains, hard cases are always cases of collision; they have nothing to do with validity, only appropriateness.[24] We need application discourses to settle which particular norm is appropriate to treat the case at hand. With an appropriate application we *retrospectively* project back into the justification discourse foreknowledge of the "new" case at hand, *as if* it were already included within the norm. In this way, the norm had always *reconstructively* included this particular instantiation and can be affirmed by all those affected by it. But this retrospective inclusion does not modify the substance of the norm itself—it couldn't, for this would upset the consensus of justification—but instead alters relationships *between* the norms themselves.

With respect to application, Habermas quotes Günther (approvingly) as follows: "Every valid norm must be coherently complemented by all other norms applicable in a situation" (*BFN*, 219).[25] This puts the judge in a curious position. He must simultaneously describe the case at hand and also anticipate what citizens in justification discourses would have thought of the case if they had considered it. In adjudication, a situation is fully described, and it is this description that determines which norm is said to have included the situation all along, that is, according to the retrospective temporality of application discourses. An appropriate judgment requires that the judge undertake a sensitive evaluation of the new situation while at the same time acting as if his judgment was always already contained in, or subsumed by, the norm that he applies.

The jurisprudence of discourse ethics is animated by the pursuit of perfect norms. We have seen that an appropriate application does not alter the norm; rather, this norm is seen to include the case at hand as if it has already been accounted for at the time of justification. In this view, to say that the norm changes, even subtly, is uncertain. As Günther states, appropriate applications attempt to anticipate "the end of history with the ideal of a coherent system of all valid norms which allows only one appropriate answer to each situation."[26] Not only do the norms not change in application, but with the idea of the end of history the relations between the norms do not change either. Each and every judgment will fill in only what we retrospectively knew at the time of justification—that this norm appropriately treated this case. Adjudication is rendered noncreative. Judgments neither add to the norm nor modify the relations between the norms. As witnessed by Rehg's interpolation, this noncreativity is fundamentally required for discourse ethics. Only in this way can we be certain that jurisprudence does not forfeit the communicative structure of our laws and of the legal medium itself.[27]

To conclude, let's sum up the reply on the part of discourse ethics to the Deleuzian critique before recapitulating the image of law at play in our three theorists. Deleuze's initial complaint was that the norms agreed on in justification discourses are too indeterminate and abstract to make any real sense. Communicatively envisaged rights were said to be null because they are formal, bearing only impossibly vague reference to problems they can neither appreciate nor improve. Habermas's and Günther's reply separated application from justification discourses. It laid out the ideal of the perfect norm, in which all future content is disclosed a priori. It continued by advancing a theory of adjudication that acknowledges the finitude of both justification and application discourses, but in so doing, endeavors through the concept of appropriateness to attain the perfect norm indirectly. It does so through a peculiar retrospective temporality: A norm application is appropriate only if it *will have been possible* for participants in justification discourses to have acted as if they anticipated this case. The judge projects back into the norm the very application he has performed.

In Part 1, I have argued that Hart, Dworkin, and Habermas tacitly follow Kant in seeing judgment as subsumptive. It is important to recognize, however, that all three theorists start off by criticizing a simpleminded conception of subsumption: (1) Hart rejects a separation of case and rule in favor of a transcendental judgment wherein cases appear only from within the representations of rules; (2) Dworkin criticizes determinative judgments of rule application and proposes a concept of reflective judgment; and (3) Habermas warns that judgments are inappropriate unless rule applications preserve justification discourses through a retrospective operation. But although each theorist submits subsumptive judgment to a thorough reworking, I have tried to demonstrate that subsumption itself is still upheld. Specifically, it is upheld in an implicit or tacit form—as an assumption, or better, as an image of what judgment is and does. In rich and divergent ways, all three theorists establish the conditions under which subsumption can be properly understood and executed. What Hart, Dworkin, and Habermas all say—and use Kant to say it—is that we do not yet have an adequate account of how subsumption works. Each of them endeavors to supply the conditions for such an account—whether transcendental, teleological, or communicative. Common to all three is a shared assumption or image that judgment and adjudication are, by nature, subsumptive.

PART TWO

THE IMAGE OF LAW: BERGSON AND TIME

> Herein, perhaps, lies the secret: to bring into existence and not to judge.
>
> DELEUZE, *Essays Critical and Clinical*

In the afterword to the English edition of *Bergsonism*, Deleuze tells us what a "return to Bergson" might mean.

> A "return to Bergson" does not only mean a renewed admiration for a great philosopher but a renewal or an extension of his project today, in relation to the transformations of life and society, in parallel with the transformations of science. Bergson considered that he had made metaphysics a rigorous discipline, one capable of being continued along new paths which constantly appear in the world. (*B*, 115)

This injunction sets two specific and concerted tasks for us. The first is obvious: to extend Bergson's philosophy to the juristic sciences. My major ambition is to use Bergson toward a theory of adjudication, one that creates a concept of judgment sufficient to explain how adjudication works, how it is creative, and how (playing with Deleuze's words) law is necessarily transformative. Jurisprudence is a new path along which to renew Bergsonian metaphysics.

The second task is to renew Deleuze's comments on law and judgment through Bergson. Although the order of this renewal might seem backwards—for is Deleuze not, as Badiou puts it, a magical reader of Bergson, is he not Bergson's great renewer?—I systematically extend and renew Deleuze's remarks on law, judgment, and jurisprudence by relating them to Bergson. I claim that it is by reading Deleuze's remarks on law alongside Bergson that they gain their life and force. My second task, therefore, is tightly coordinated with the first: to extend Deleuze's theory of jurisprudence through Bergson. Such an extension of Deleuze is entirely permissible, for not only does Deleuze claim that the injunction holds for the reading of any philosopher, foremost for any reading of himself, but, moreover, that it is itself inspired by Bergson's insistence that thought develops only in the creation of new problems.

Part 2 is organized as follows. In Chapter 4, I relate Deleuze's observations on law, judgment, and jurisprudence. This involves, on the one hand, a preliminary presentation of the positive concepts of our jurisprudence (encounter, problem), and on the other hand, an examination of what Deleuze diagnoses as the dogmatism of law. In Chapter 5, I introduce Bergsonian jurisprudence through a reading of Oliver Wendell Holmes. Reading Holmes with Bergson allows us, on the one hand, to radicalize certain pragmatic themes in Holmes and, on the other hand, to make Bergson's concepts immediately relevant to law. In this chapter, I argue that law is inventive by virtue of its temporality and I criticize dogmatic theorists of law for systematically repressing the force and inventiveness of time. The next two chapters—the heart of the book—are to be taken together. I start with distinguishing pure perception and the pure past from Bergson's *Matter and Memory* and investigate their relevance for adjudication. Next, I develop two concepts of judgment that spring from the same source, the actualization of the past. Insofar as both are necessary to adjudication, neither kind of judgment is preferred to the other, but each has different effects. The first, inattentive judgment, will be shown to account for the regular and automatic application of law to cases; the second, attentive judgment, will be shown to account for the creativity and inventiveness intrinsic to adjudication.

4

Deleuze and the Critique of Law

This chapter bridges the critical and positive parts of this book. Because of this role, it is the only chapter devoted entirely to Deleuze. Although Deleuze has without doubt inspired this book, his presence is more or less subterranean. Here, I make explicit certain themes of his in order to frame the critique of the dogmatic image of law *and* to introduce concepts that we will pursue with Bergson and Spinoza. I start with Deleuze's few comments on jurisprudence. I use them to introduce two concepts: the encounter and the problem. Next, I carry out Deleuze's critique of dogmatism, specifically the dogmatism of law and judgment. To this end, I relate his broad critique of law and judgment and then connect it to the criticism of philosophies of communication and human rights that I sketched in Chapter 3. Here, and also in the coming chapters, I show how dogmatic theories of law foreclose an appreciation of those positive concepts in a Deleuzian jurisprudence that enable us to understand how and why adjudication is creative.

Jurisprudence vs. Law

An excellent way to introduce Deleuze's observations on law is to track their astonishing consistency over the course of his career. In his first and very early book, written on Hume in 1953, Deleuze establishes an opposition between law and institution of which he never lets go. In his reading of Hume, Deleuze develops a concept of the social as "profoundly creative, inventive, and positive."[1] Given this germinal conception of society, Deleuze concludes that *institutions* are necessary to concretely coordinate and resolve specific, ever-emerging problems. If, however, society is understood to form in order to guarantee certain preexisting rights, then *laws* are necessary to limit the harm subjects may do to each other.[2] Law and institution, therefore, correspond to, or map onto, two different appreciations of the social. It is not as though Deleuze says that there are no laws in Hume, or for that matter that there are no institutions in Locke (Hume's interlocutor). Rather, institution and law correspond to different ways to understand the need for and function of the institution of law; the terms designate perspectives, not entities.

Although I will not pursue this reading of Hume, we can already see an opposition forming: If society is understood as creative and dynamic, then institutions are needed to resolve existing problems and, perhaps, to invent new, more helpful ones; but if society is understood to guarantee rights, then laws are needed not to invent but rather to safeguard rights.

If we fast-forward thirty-five years to the *Abécédaire* interview (1988), we find the same opposition in a different vocabulary:

[This] respect for human rights, it's really . . . one wants to become . . . to take odious positions, it's . . . It belongs so much to soft thought [*pensée molle*] . . . from the impoverished period we spoke about. It's . . . it's pure abstraction. Human rights [*droits de l'homme*], what is that? It's pure abstraction, it's, it's empty. It's exactly what we were talking about just then about desires, what I was trying to say about desires. Desires don't consist in setting up an object, in saying I desire *this*. We don't desire liberty, for example . . . that's stupid. We desire . . . we find ourselves in situations. . . . All these are cases for *jurisprudence*. To act for liberty, to become revolutionary, yes, is to operate in jurisprudence. When we address ourselves to justice . . . justice, it doesn't exist, human rights, they don't exist. What counts is jurisprudence. That's the invention of rights. So, those who are satisfied to recall human rights and the respect for human rights . . . well . . . well . . . they're imbeciles. (*ABC*, G)[3]

Reading *jurisprudence* for *institution*, and *rights* for *law*, the antithesis remains unaltered from the book on Hume. According to Deleuze, rights theorists envisage a subject bearing a set of a priori and inviolable rights—rights to liberty, for example. In this view, human rights encode natural rights and endeavor to preserve a universal subject from harm. On the one hand, this proposal is negative in that it sees law as a contrivance designed to limit harm and preserve a closed set of rights. On the other hand, this proposal is abstract because it refers to rights independently of concrete situations; that is, it "say[s] nothing about the immanent modes of existence of people provided with rights" (*WP*, 107). Or, as Deleuze claims in another interview, "These days it's human rights [*droits de l'homme*] that provide our eternal values. It's the constitutional state and other notions everyone recognizes as very abstract. And it's in the name of all this that thinking's fettered, that any analysis in terms of movement is blocked" (*N*, 122, translation modified). I will come back to this critique.

Jurisprudence, by contrast, is neither abstract nor limiting. Although for the moment the term remains undefined, we see that jurisprudence operates only within situations. In other words, it is not abstract. And as the invention of rights, jurisprudence is positive and creative. Unlike theories of human rights discourse, jurisprudence is not content to identify a universal subject and enumerate a priori rights. As with Hume's institution, jurisprudence operates within a social field to resolve specific problems and create rights.

We could draw up the following list: Law and rights are negative, abstract, obfuscating, useless; institutions and jurisprudence are positive, concrete, creative, effective. Maybe because it was an intensely held conviction, or maybe because he never directly worked on it, the opposition between law/rights and institution/jurisprudence remained in play for more than forty years in Deleuze's work. The concepts of institution and jurisprudence consistently appear as concrete and positive alternatives to the negative and abstract strictures of law and rights.

In this chapter I reconstruct these occasional remarks on jurisprudence, law, and rights as topical and consistent expressions of a philosophy. I start with jurisprudence. Whenever Deleuze uses the term *jurisprudence* (and he does so almost exclusively in interviews),[4] he performs an innovative combination of the various meanings of that word, a combination of which he may have been unaware. In English,[5] jurisprudence means many and apparently opposite things: "The study of the first principles of the law of nature, the civil law, and the law of nations"; "the study of the general or fundamental elements of a particular legal system, as opposed to its practical and concrete details"; "judicial precedents considered collectively"; "caselaw."[6] Jurisprudence, then, appears to combine the highest and the lowest, the most general principles of law together with the concrete elements of precedents and case law. We will see that this apparent contradiction is, in fact, the seed of a Deleuzian jurisprudence.

Although Deleuze never defines quite what he means by jurisprudence, he appears to have in mind a system of case law, one that creates law out of its concrete encounters and the controversies of its litigants; something more akin—but this remains conjecture on my part—to an Anglo-American (common law) approach and not a Continental (civil law) approach.[7] In this view, a philosophy of law—or jurisprudence, properly understood—appreciates the *case*, that is, the legal singularity, as the fundamental element and first principle of law. "Codes and pronouncements are not what creates rights [*ce qui est créateur de droit*] but jurisprudence does. Jurisprudence is the philosophy of right [*du droit*], and proceeds by singularity, by prolonging singularities [*procède par singularité, prolongement de singularités*]" (*N*, 153, translation modified). Or again: "[François] Ewald has shown that you need more than just a legally constituted subject [*sujet de droit*] to have human rights, that you have to confront juridical problems that are in themselves very interesting" (*N*, 152). I take these remarks on jurisprudence to point to a creation of rights and law from cases as these represent and evolve into juridical problems. Deleuze, then, appears to have in mind a definition of jurisprudence that combines rights and principles with cases and singularities, and he then qualifies this as a creative relationship.

In *What Is Philosophy*, Deleuze and Guattari give us another hint as to what jurisprudence might mean. They write that *political philosophy* "designates that conjunction of philosophy, or of the concept, with the present milieu" (*WP*, 100). Two possible, noncompeting interpretations of this line can help to specify the jurisprudence Deleuze has in mind.[8] The first is that the concepts of a political philosophy must be *created* alongside, as a response to, the exigencies of specific situations. As such, the situation is formative of the very concepts that make sense of and intervene in it. A second interpretation is that rather than be created *tout court*, a concept may predate the situation in question but take on a particular effectivity in relation to it, perhaps undergoing modification as a result. Either way—whether a concept is created or merely determined—a jurisprudence that satisfies Deleuze's criteria for political philosophy must be characterized by engagement with, or susceptibility to, the situation (the *case*), coordinating its concepts and rules according to the shifting exigencies of the present milieu.

It is useful to turn to an actual case—especially given Deleuze's advice that "it is always worthwhile in analyzing concepts to begin with very simple, very concrete situations, rather than with philosophical antecedents or even with the problems as such . . . stick to the concrete, and always return to it"[9]—to illustrate what he might understand by jurisprudence.

I'll take an example I like a lot, because it's the only way to explain what jurisprudence is. . . . I remember the time when it was forbidden to smoke in taxis. Well, I used to smoke in taxis. There came a time when we no longer had the right to smoke in taxis. It was a big deal when the first taxi drivers forbade smoking because there were lots of smokers. They made a fuss. There was one, a lawyer . . . I've always been passionate for jurisprudence, for law . . . if I hadn't done philosophy, I would have done law but precisely not human rights [*droits de l'homme*], I would have done jurisprudence. Because, that's life. That is to say that there are no human rights, there is life, and there are rights of life [*il y a des droits de la vie*]. Yes but, life, it's case by case [*Seulement, la vie, c'est cas par cas*]. And well, the taxis. There was some guy who didn't want to be stopped from smoking in taxis and he took the taxi [company] to court. I remember very well, because I paid attention to the grounds for the decision. The taxi was found guilty. Today, no question, had there been the same trial the taxi wouldn't have been found guilty, it would be [the smoker] who would be found guilty. But, at first, the taxi was guilty. On what grounds? Because once someone hired a taxi he was a tenant. So the user of a taxi was likened to a tenant. The tenant has a right to smoke at home, that's his right. . . . It's as if one were renting a place, it's as if my landlord said to me, no, you can't smoke at home. Oh yes, if I'm a tenant I can smoke at home. So, the taxi was likened to an apartment on wheels, of which the user was a tenant. Ten years later . . . and now it's universal, there are no more, or practically no more, places where one can smoke. A taxi is no longer likened to the tenancy of an apartment, it's likened to a public service. With a public service, one has a right to forbid smoking. (*ABC*, G)

Here we have a situation, a problem. This taxi example is "not a question of a right to this or to that"; instead, it signifies two different juridical problems, two different juridical constructions (*ABC*, G). At first, the cab is assimilated to the status of an apartment with attendant user benefits of privacy (i.e., noninterference with one's actions). Later, the same taxi space is identified as a public service. What we see is a differential distribution or evolution of rights according to the construction of a juridical problem—is it an apartment or a public service? Modest though it may be, this example is what Deleuze means by jurisprudence: the conjunction of a right (here, the right to smoke) with a present milieu (the taxi as it *was* an apartment, as it *is* a public service). The question of "a right (to smoke)" does not make sense outside the situation in which it is adjudicated; jurisprudence creates and determines rights in coordination with concrete situations. From this we can draw a positive and a negative proposition: Rights exist and are effective only through juridical, case-based problems; and without relating rights to their originating situation, they remain abstract, ineffective, and incomprehensible. Before taking leave of this example, let us make clear that Deleuze is not recommending flux and destabilization in law. Instead, quite concretely, Deleuze is attempting to understand how a judgment about an apparently identical issue—smoking in a cab in Paris—could have been reversed over a relatively short period of time. By virtue of appreciating the connection or coordination between right and milieu, Deleuze opens up a perspective to see and explain innovation in law. Taking the necessary precautions, we might say that Deleuze is committed to renewing analytical jurisprudence, not to advocate but to understand how a case can affect a rule and to appreciate that the rule requires precisely that for its effectiveness. Taking words from another context, "how it works is the sole question."[10]

To Deleuze's concept of jurisprudence we can now add a further specification. If rights emerge simultaneously with, and only through, concrete situations, then we can say that the case is at once *accidental* and *necessary*. The accidental character of cases is obvious. Courts do not determine which cases come to them.[11] But although it is true that the case is accidental, we also appreciate it as necessary to the operation of law and to the genesis of rights. A Deleuzian philosophy of law must affirm both the case as it is accidental and as it is necessary to the formation of law and rights.

This double nature of the case as accidental and necessary takes us to a fundamental concept of Deleuze's philosophy: the *encounter*. A great theme of Deleuze's is that thinking occurs only under the constraint of an encounter and of an outside. The concept of the encounter is one that Deleuze takes from Proust and is rich in potential for legal analysis.[12] In his final novel, *Time Regained*, Proust describes the accidental yet necessary quality of the encounters that provoke reminiscences: "Their first character was that I was not free to choose them, that they were given to me as they were.... Precisely the *fortuitous, inevitable* way in which the sensation had been *encountered* governed the truth of the past that it resuscitated" (cited in *PS*, 96). In order for thought to think, it must be visited by an outside, an encounter, which is neither of its own making nor anticipated. "It is the *accident* of the encounter that guarantees the *necessity* of what is thought" (*PS*, 16, emphasis added). The encounter, therefore, is the name for a relation wherein thought engages with an outside irreducible to itself.

With this preliminary account of the encounter, it isn't hard to see why Deleuze privileges case law and puts it at the heart of jurisprudence. Cases simultaneously introduce exteriority into the law and serve as the germ from which law begins.[13] Law is placed in a constitutive relationship with its outside—*with cases*—which forces it into action and invention. A jurisprudence envisaged on the basis of case law meets Deleuze's requirements for political philosophy. The law encounters cases that are both necessary and accidental to its operation, that arrive from the outside, and that connect law to its present milieu.

Critique of Dogmatism in Law and Judgment

The concepts of jurisprudence and the encounter will be developed throughout Part 2. I now turn to the critique of dogmatism, especially to the critique of dogmatism in law and judgment. This will prepare Deleuze's criticisms of human rights and also develop the concept of the encounter.

Why might an exposition and critique of dogmatism afford an understanding of the encounter? Because it is the suppression of encounters that makes thought dogmatic. According to Deleuze, the essence of dogmatism is the assumption, implicit or explicit, that everything encountered can be recognized. Bergson is helpful to characterize a dogmatic approach.

In what drawer, ready to open, shall we put [the thing]? In what garment, already cut out, shall we clothe it? Is it this, or that, or the other thing? And "this," and "that," and "the other thing" are always something already conceived, already known. The idea that for a new object we might have to create a new concept, perhaps a new method of thinking, is deeply repugnant to us. (*CE*, 48)

An approach that seeks only to *recognize* is dogmatic because it a priori assigns a representational form to the outside; it presumes that the encountered thing is only another identifiable instance of an existing concept.[14] As Bergson tells us, the possibility that something might be genuinely new, that is, that we may *encounter* something unprecedented and experience a shock to thought, is an anathema to thought premised on recognition. As a consequence, both the genuine exteriority of the outside and the chance for encounters is forfeited—these are both interiorized, as it were, into our representations before the fact of an encounter. A genuine encounter is missed; it simply becomes an opportunity for the instantiation of prepossessed concepts. "We miss our finest encounters, we avoid the imperatives that emanate from them: to the exploration [*l'approfondissement*] of encounters we have preferred the facility of recognitions" (*PS*, 27). For dogmatic thought, encounters promise only their eventual recognition, and thought is kept from its creative capacities in favor of acts of identification.

But thought-as-recognition is dogmatic not only by virtue of suppressing encounters but also by virtue of its role and status as an *opinion*—or, as Deleuze puts it, as an *image*—as to what it means to think. According to Deleuze, if philosophy has a point and a right to exist, it is to fight opinion. In this respect, Deleuze is profoundly Platonic: Philosophy's vocation is none other than to break with *doxa*.[15] This brings us to the dogmatic image of thought. Schematically stated, Deleuze distinguishes between two levels of opinion: explicit and implicit. Without a doubt, philosophy has always denied every particular and explicit opinion with which it has been presented (*DR*, 134). Maybe the most famous example is the total rejection of opinion Descartes announces in the *Discourse on Method*.[16] But in addition to these explicit and easily dismissible kinds of opinion, Deleuze discerns a more pernicious and implicit variety in effect. As we will confirm through a series of examples, a consistent and long-standing set of unexamined opinions has haunted and compromised thought since its beginning. These opinions are of the nature of unquestioned assumptions as to what it means to think and include the goodwill of thinker, the upright nature of truth, and perhaps most important, *a model of recognition* on which thought bases itself (*DR*, 130–138).

For Deleuze what is at once so trivial and so dangerous about these opinions is that they are drawn from the realm of psychological consciousness. The dogmatic image of thought "has based its supposed principle upon extrapolation from certain facts, particularly insignificant facts such as Recognition, everyday banality in person" (*DR*, 135). Everyday recognitions such as "this is a piece of wax" (Descartes's *Meditations*), or "cinnabar is heavy and red" (Kant's *Critique*), or "hello!" as said to a friend (Plato's *Theaetetus*) are assumed to be what is at stake in thought, and recognition is taken as the exercise of thought. The concept of the dogmatic image of thought, therefore, designates this illegitimate adoption of commonplace facts and activities of life as both ground and destination of thought. Obviously, this concept is critical, for if opinion has surreptitiously smuggled itself into the very basis of thought and if as a consequence there results a total confusion of the empirical with the transcendental—a confusion that mistakes its most trivial and empirical exercise as its principle and potential—then philosophy is bereft of the means to realize its critical vocation of breaking with *doxa*. For his part, Deleuze does maintain that there are transcendental conditions of thought and experience, and although we have to investigate what this might mean, we can straightaway see that they cannot be assimilated into acts of recognition drawn from empirical psychological consciousness, for this consciousness is by definition not transcendental. To confuse the two would be illusory and illegitimate—dialectical, as Kant would say.

Equipped with this concept of a dogmatic image of thought, Deleuze proposes a sweeping revaluation of the history of philosophy as premised on a shared impotence and illusion. According to this account, (nearly every[17]) philosophy assumes and reinstates recognition at an implicit level, as an image of thought. Of course, in terms of their explicit propositions and concepts, different philosophies are irreducibly different; but according to the concept of a dogmatic *image* of thought, Deleuze can postulate in *Difference and Repetition* that a "*single* Image in general," held "in the realm of the implicit" as a presupposition or opinion, traverses all philosophy and compromises it equally (*DR*, 132, emphasis added).[18] In short, and with few exceptions, the history of philosophy has been hampered by a dogmatic set of opinions, recognition foremost among these, as to what it means to think. This association of thought with recognition—that thought takes and mistakes itself as recognition, that philosophy tries to secure the conditions for recognition—is doubly dogmatic. On the one hand, it prevents a genuine engagement with an outside of thought and with encounters; and on the other hand, it saddles thought with an ineradicable basis in opinion and everyday consciousness that frustrates any critical aspirations it might set for itself.

It is significant that three of the extended examples of dogmatism Deleuze gives in *Difference and Repetition* directly concern law and judgment. Although he never states so directly, it is as though law and judgment are avatars of dogmatism, as though they always imply and install dogmatism and recognition and thereby preclude appreciation of encounters, difference, and the true conditions of thought and experience. To situate these examples within a long dogmatic history, we can loosely call them *ancient*, *modern*, and *critical* moments. Investigation into these moments is rewarding to flesh out the concept of the dogmatic image, to detail the precise reasons for Deleuze's hostility to law and judgment, and, finally, to identify the dangers and illusions against which nondogmatic jurisprudence must guard itself.

Ancient (Aristotle): Judgment and Difference

In *Difference and Repetition*, Deleuze undertakes a dense critique of Aristotle (*DR*, 30–35). I will not attempt to reproduce the entire argument, only his critique of judgment insofar as it concerns subsumption, recognition, and dogmatism.

In the first chapter of *Difference and Repetition*, Deleuze begins to formulate a concept of difference defined neither in terms of identity and representation nor in terms of chaos and total indetermination. Deleuze's goal is to create a concept of difference in itself (difference as such) as distinct from a tradition that sees it only in terms of *conceptual difference*, that is, as something that concepts isolate and identify. Foremost, this means confronting a conception of difference as obtaining only *between* things (*DR*, 28). If difference is understood along the lines of "difference between," two consequences follow. First, difference becomes negative insofar as a thing is defined by what it is not; and second, difference becomes conceptual insofar as it is assigned and upheld by a concept that represents distinct things.

Aristotle stands at the front of a tradition that sees difference as negative and conceptual. Let us turn to Book VII of the *Metaphysics*, where Aristotle proposes how definitions are reached by a method of division. In this method, one starts with the broadest genus (e.g., "animal") containing the species to be defined and proceeds to divide it into subgenera by means of a criterion (e.g., "with feet," "without feet"). One then draws subsequent distinctions within the subgenera (e.g., "with feet") according to finer criteria (e.g., "cloven-footed," "noncloven footed") until eventually a definition of the species is arrived at. A species is defined when one comes to the end of the line with respect to further division and reaches a "species that contains no differences." At this point, the *specific difference*, which Aristotle also calls the last (or complete, *teleutaia*) difference, is obtained, capturing the specific essence of the thing, the "substance of the thing and its definition."[19]

In his critique, Deleuze focuses on *contrariety*, which he claims exemplifies Aristotle's attempt to reconcile the requirements of representation with difference. Every step in Aristotle's division effects a difference between two terms according to criteria that set them in opposition. Nevertheless, although these two terms ("footed," "nonfooted") are contrary with respect to a criterion ("footed or not?"), they remain contained or expressed by a broader genus that remains the same ("animal"). "Contrariety alone expresses the capacity of a subject to bear opposites while remaining substantially the same (in matter or in genus)" (*DR*, 30). Difference manifests itself in contrariety, all the while preserving identity for the concept that contains the opposition.

Where, we might ask, does contrariety best show itself? In *specific difference*. Specific difference (difference between species) represents the full achievement of the Aristotelian arrangement. Two special qualifications make it the ideal sort of difference: It is neither too big nor too small. On the one hand, differences between genera are "too large" and tend "to become simple otherness and almost escape the identity of the concept," for what concept can cover (and stay self-identical while covering) the broadest divisions of being (*DR*, 30)? On the other hand, concrete existents are too small; they have all sorts of accidental differences (e.g., black and white, tall and short for humans) that fail to represent the essence of the thing (*DR*, 30). Specific differences, by contrast, oppose each other while being contained within the genus *and* they provide the essence or definition of a concrete existent. They can, in other words, preserve the identity of the genus *and* give the concrete existent its identity (its difference with respect to other species, its identity with respect to itself and to other existents of its species). Specific difference, therefore, secures identity and reconciles difference with the concept on two levels: generic and concrete. Although it may fail to capture both universal (differences in being) and singular (differences in existents) difference, specific difference nevertheless represents a "propitious moment" in the history of philosophy insofar as it accommodates difference into the philosophy of the concept, identity, and representation (*DR* 32). At the root of Deleuze's criticism is that Aristotle thinks he provides a concept of difference, whereas in truth he only shows the inscription of difference within the identity of the concept (*DR*, 32).

In this scheme of conceptual difference, judgment plays an enormous role, for with generic and specific difference comes a *distributive concept of judgment*.

> Judgment has precisely two essential functions, and only two: distribution, which it ensures by the *partition* of concepts; and hierarchization, which it ensures by the *measuring* of subjects. To the former corresponds the faculty of judgment known as common sense; to the latter the faculty known as good sense (or first sense). Both constitute just measure or "justice" as a value of judgment. In this sense, every philosophy of categories takes judgment for its model—as we see in the case of Kant. (*DR*, 33; see also *CC*, 128–129)

Later in *Difference and Repetition*, Deleuze ascribes precise meanings to common sense and good sense. Common sense "*is the norm of identity*" with respect to an unspecified object, whereas good sense "*is the norm of distribution*" with respect to empirical objects "qualified as this or that kind of thing" (*DR*, 134, emphasis added). In this passage, judgment performs two functions that map onto common sense and good sense. First, it partitions being into its genera and upholds identity for each genus through its subdivision into species. In this sense, judgment is not merely complicit with but fundamentally underpins the kind of conceptual difference Deleuze opposes; it establishes differences between things as negative (contradiction and contrariety, what the thing is not) and as conceptual (the counted differences are those identified by the concept). Second, judgment distributes empirical existents into a covering concept that gives to them their (conceptual) difference (i.e., their specific identity). This is the empirical exercise of *judgment as subsumption*; subjects are measured and distributed into their appropriate category. The value, or justice, of a judgment is evaluated according to its capacity to maintain the identity of a concept through the exercise of empirical distribution of existents.

"Philosophy of the category" is Deleuze's term for this generic scheme that accommodates difference to the requirements of identity and representation. Judgment has an absolutely crucial job in philosophies of the category. Not only is it responsible for the adequate distribution of existents, but it also sustains the identity of each individual concept. Judgment, therefore, entrenches recognition at two different levels: at the level of the form of identity of each concept and at the level of the empirical subsumption of existents into concepts. Accordingly, the only kind of difference that judgment is able to acknowledge is difference *between* things: either between different concepts or between different things under different concepts. In a word, judgment appreciates only *discrete* and *conceptual* differences.

I note four things in closing. First, although recognition is not an express purpose of philosophies of the category, it is presupposed in the subsumption and classification of existents by covering concepts. Second, the encounter is eliminated insofar as only discrete and conceptual differences can be acknowledged. Third, if contemporary theories of adjudication envisage judgment as subsumptive, then they participate, however unaware, in a philosophy of the category that admits only conceptual difference. Here too the encounter with the case is null insofar as judgment apprehends and subsumes only "that which conforms to the general" (*DR*, 38). Fourth, if judgment concerns itself only with the form of identity and distribution under that identity, it becomes unable to pose or respect the problem of novelty. Hence we come back to Deleuze's maxim: "to bring into existence and not to judge" (*CC*, 135).

Modern: Law and Repetition

It is well known that the scientific revolution of the seventeenth century replaced the genus-species relationship with laws of nature as the principle by which science proceeds. Explanation ceases to be a question of distributing existents under categories that represent their essence and perfection and instead becomes a search for laws that cut through what were previously considered qualitatively different domains. But what does Deleuze make of this shift? The first five thematic pages of *Difference and Repetition* are devoted to a critique of repetition in scientific and moral law.[20] Note, however, that Deleuze is not criticizing the methodology of the natural sciences *tout court*; or if he is, and if he accepts the rough distinction between the "language of poetry in which every term is irreplaceable" and the "language of science [as] dominated by the symbol of equality," he has in mind "the eighteenth-century model" of fixed laws that govern and order all things (*DR*, 2).

In the introduction to *Difference and Repetition*, Deleuze begins to develop his concept of *repetition*. As a preliminary summary, repetition has nothing to do with an identically repeating series; instead, repetition is differential, which means that difference is always introduced by repetition, and that in repeating, a thing becomes different from itself. Repetition, to offer a definition we will revisit, is Deleuze's concept for a creative conception of time or of becoming. Turning now to the opening pages of *Difference and Repetition*, Deleuze straightaway identifies law (both scientific and moral, as we will see) as an obstacle to his concept. Why? Because, on the one hand, law establishes resemblances and equivalences between the subjects it designates, and, on the other hand, it postulates only bare and calculable repetition. Law, according to Deleuze, makes its subjects substitutable *and* it also makes time and the future predictable. He has specific terms for these twin functions: Law represents singular things as *particulars*, and law represents repetition as *change*. As he states in the opening lines of his critique, "Far from grounding repetition, law shows, rather, how repetition would remain impossible for pure subjects of law—*particulars*. It condemns them to *change*" (*DR*, 2, emphasis added). To elaborate this text, I raise two specific questions. First, why is a subject of law called a particular? And second, what could it mean to condemn a particular "to change"? That is, why does this preclude repetition? I take these questions in turn.

First, law for Deleuze represents a *general* perspective from which to view things. Take a childhood truism: No two snowflakes are alike; every snowflake is different. From the perspective of scientific laws, we lose sight of that fact. For example, atmospheric science is concerned with postulating laws that represent how snowflakes form in general, for example, how they form sixfold symmetries or how water crystallizes at given temperatures and under given conditions. From the perspective of these laws, the differences between snowflakes (and their unique processes of formation) disappear; far from being singular, they become *particular* expressions of a *general law*. The particular is what a singular thing looks like, or what a singular thing is converted into, when put under a law. Defined by the criteria a law designates, a particular stands in for an indefinite number of equivalent, substitutable subjects. In short, a subject is transformed into a particular exemplification of a general law and is put into relation with other particulars (which also exemplify laws). In terms of our concept of dogmatism, a major consequence of this scheme is that things under law are *recognized* as particular instantiations of that law; a particular, *as* particular, has no other existence or meaning besides the one given to it by a law. A particular, therefore, can never be encountered, for it is always already recognized by the law it incarnates; a particular can only ever be recognized.

Second, there is an important double meaning in Deleuze's claim that law "condemns its subjects to *change*." The first we have just seen: Law compels something singular to *change into a particular*, that is, to change into an expression of a general law. But there is in this phrase also the sense that law condemns the thing to a particular *kind* of change, a particular understanding of what change is. Law depicts repetition as calculable, predictable change (e.g., "under these conditions snowflakes will form," "this outcome results as a function of that law"). A thing is arraigned by a law that changes not only it but also the concept of change (of becoming and time) itself. When Deleuze writes that change is an "invariable form of variation," he claims that the future is apparently laid out by laws able, perhaps only in principle, to predict it (*DR*, 2). With law comes a conception of time as given, to which all particulars submit; it substitutes an effective and creative conception of time with a calculable one. In lieu of differential repetitions, the particular is confined to the predictable change allocated to it by law.[21] The consequences of understanding repetition or time under the form of change are obvious and striking. First, the future is recognized in advance inasmuch as it is in principle as predictable as an eclipse; and second, nothing in the future (or the future itself) can be encountered inasmuch as it is calculable in advance. Again, it is not that Deleuze dismisses the value of scientific laws or that he denies their usefulness; he only indicates the limitations of the conception of time they necessarily adopt.

Kantian moral law, another product of the eighteenth century, functions analogously to scientific law—it too converts singular actions and affects into particulars. "The application of the moral law can be conceived only by restoring . . . the model of the law of nature" (*DR*, 4). Moral law is enacted through a test of repetition, a test of the types of habits and behaviors that can in principle be repeated without contradiction: "What is Kant's 'highest test' if not a criterion which should decide what *can* in principle be reproduced—in other words, what can be repeated without contradiction in the form of moral law? The man of duty invented a 'test' of repetition; he decided what in principle could be repeated. He thought he had thereby defeated both the demonic and the wearisome" (*DR*, 4). At the expense of singular actions, practices, and dispositions, moral law grounds us in the arrangement between the general and the particular; actions are converted—tested—into repeatable particularities of a general moral law. Affective, practical becomings are replaced by a moral law that in advance gives a principle by which to recognize actions that conform to it. Such an operation recovers the concept of law with its calculable temporality on the plane of practical reason.

For these reasons, true repetition denounces the relationship of the law to its particular in favor of the differential and creative repetition of the singular. Repetition is extralegality itself and everywhere puts law into question: "[*Repetition*] *is against the law*: against the similar form and the equivalent content of law. If repetition can be found, even in nature, it is in the name of a power which affirms itself against the law, which works underneath laws, perhaps superior to laws" (*DR*, 2, emphasis added). Moreover, as Deleuze will later argue in *Difference and Repetition*, it is positive and differential repetition that gives rise to the legal order, which then turns around and obfuscates its own genesis by representing everything as legal particulars, as dependent on the form of the law. But my point is not yet to relate authentic repetition; it is simply to note its adamantly antilaw formulation.

Critical: Transcendental Judgment and Experience

For Deleuze, Kant represents a special moment in the history of dogmatic thought. On first impression, "he seemed armed to overturn the Image of thought" (*DR*, 136). With his discovery of the transcendental, with his substitution of rich illusions of thought for mere errors of recognition, with his devastating challenge to rational theology and rational psychology, and with his late disordered conception of the faculties, Kant appears ideally poised to inaugurate thought free from dogmatic, empirico-psychological consciousness. But no, on the contrary, "in spite of everything, and at the risk of compromising the conceptual apparatus of the three Critiques," Deleuze concludes that Kant "did not want to renounce the implicit presuppositions of [dogmatic thought]" (*DR*, 136).

Deleuze often asks how, despite all his promise, Kant reinstalls (indeed, reinvigorates) the dogmatic image of thought. For example, even as he reverses the relationship between the Good and the Law, Kant secures a model of recognition and dead repetition through practical maxims that test actions as to their pure practical worth (*CC*, 31–33; *DR*, 4). Or, despite his concept of a temporalized and fractured ego, Kant reinstates the unity of the subject in unity of apperception (*CC*, 29–30; *DR*, 136). A third example, the one I pursue here, is that despite demolishing a precritical concept of judgment that separates objects from representations, Kant creates a concept of transcendental judgment that forcefully entrenches a dogmatic image of thought. The criticism that Deleuze levels at transcendental judgment is that it is *abstract* and, consequently, that it suppresses the chance for encounters (the true transcendental basis for thought, as we will see).

In a famous trope from the first edition of the *Critique of Pure Reason*, Kant announces a "Deduction" to prove the existence of the pure concepts of the understanding and to show their necessary relation to possible experience (A84). Specifically, he wants to justify "how these concepts can be related to objects that they do not derive from any experience" (A85). A deduction is itself a legal term, and with it Kant speaks in the manner of a "jurist" who seeks to justify a claim to a contested possession by showing that the circumstances in which it has been acquired are rightful and are therefore entitled and acknowledged. In the case of the *Critique*, the possession in question is possible experience, and Kant sets out to prove that experience is possible only insofar as it fulfills the conditions stipulated by the a priori concepts of the understanding. This is a complex, involved argument, and I will only (briefly) touch on one (small) aspect of it: empirical and transcendental judgment.

According to Kant, to experience empirical objects, we require the concept of an *"object in general"* (A93/B126).²² If, from an empirical standpoint, we were to describe such an object, we would have to "abstract from all content of a judgment in general, and attend only to the mere form of the understanding in it" (A70/B95). But, of course, the concept of the object in general is not empirical but transcendental; it provides for the conditions of experience while not being of experience. To make empirical judgments about this or that object (or, in the terms of the deduction, to ground a claim to necessary, objective empirical judgments), a *transcendental power of judgment* is required to deliver the form of the object in general. This means that judgment has a transcendental capacity able to provide the form of the object in general; or, in more technical terms, synthetic a priori judgments coordinate the pure concepts of the understanding to provide the concept of the object in general, which structures experience and yields real, empirical objects.

Deleuze's criticism is the following.

> The elementary concepts of representation are the categories defined as the conditions of *possible experience*. These, however, are too general, too large for the real. The net is so loose that the biggest fish pass through. . . . Everything changes once we determine the conditions of *real experience*, which are not larger than the conditioned and which differ in kind from the categories. . . . It is in this direction that we must look for the conditions, not of possible experience, but of real experience. (*DR*, 68–69, emphasis added)²³

When I said that Deleuze was a Platonist in terms of critique, it was only half the story, for, as this passage shows, he is also uniquely neo-Kantian. If Deleuze and Kant are both *critical* philosophers, it is by virtue of their shared insistence that philosophy must endeavor to address the conditions of experience. But, unlike Kant, philosophy for Deleuze must not seek the conditions for *all possible* experience; it must instead endeavor to reach the conditions of *real* experience. In this sense, Deleuze can direct a Kantian criticism at Kant himself.²⁴

If transcendental judgment reinstates all the rights of the dogmatic image of thought, it is because it represents philosophy's most radical form of recognition and, to that extent, prevents any encounter (*WP*, 46).²⁵ In the *Critique of Pure Reason*, reality appears to us only within the transcendental horizon, and judgment structures the field of experience according to the requirements of representation: Possible experience is generated out of a set of a priori categories along with the synthetic activity of the subject. In such a scheme and at this depth (i.e., at the level of the object in general), encounters (as the outside of thought, as the unrecognized) are impossible insofar as experience is always already given in the form of the object in general, an object that the unified subject recognizes. Kant's concept of the transcendental delimits the frame for every possible experience and event before it occurs and defines if not what does occur, then at least what *can*—or *cannot*—occur. As such, Kant secures three constitutive features of the dogmatic image: recognition of all experience, subjective unity, and elimination of encounters.

Inasmuch as thought and experience presuppose encounters as their real (as opposed to possible) condition (*DR*, 139), Kant's transcendental judgment is indicted as abstract on two counts. First, without considering encounters in their specificity—encounters not already organized and assigned into the form of a recognizable general object, a form that simultaneously confirms the apperceptive unity of the subject—we lack an explanatory mechanism for experience. Transcendental judgment might be able to account for everyday acts of recognition that require no more than a general concept of an object together with psychological memory, but it finds itself unable to account for (or even to acknowledge) experiences or encounters that challenge the form of representation itself. Deleuze's first criticism, therefore, is methodological: Transcendental judgment cannot provide an analysis of sensible and singular experience and thought because it installs an abstract account of a transcendental object and subject. The conditions of an experience must be no broader than the experience itself; if not, we are left with indifferent, abstract conditions that lack both explanatory force and real potential.

Deleuze's second criticism turns on the issue that transcendental judgment concerns itself only with *possible*, that is, *nonnecessary*, experiences (*DR*, 139). Genuine encounters, to anticipate the discussion of the next section, *force* themselves on us and compel us under their pressure to think and experience. In this sense transcendental judgment is abstract, for within its confines nothing forces itself on us. Instead all experience is equally and indifferently structured according to the general form of the object (except, of course, in exceptional "sublime" experiences that manage to break down, however temporarily, this form of the transcendental object = x [*CJ*, §26]). Thus, to revisit our three dogmatic moments, if

Aristotelian judgment substitutes a concept of difference with conceptual difference and if modern law substitutes differential repetition with calculable change, then Kantian judgment substitutes the real conditions of experience with the conditions of all possible experience. In all three cases, the facility of recognition replaces the exploration of encounters.

The Transcendental Encounter (Transcendental Empiricism)

As we have seen, in Kant's transcendental philosophy, a priori representations, together with the subject's synthetic activity, structure all possible experience according to a recognized, contentless object. But although Deleuze may criticize Kant's transcendentalism as doubly abstract (as general, as nonnecessary), we cannot conclude that Deleuze does not preserve a transcendental basis for his own philosophy. The *encounter* is presupposed in, and necessary for, experience. As such, it is *critical* and *transcendental*. The encounter alone accounts for the conditions of real thought and experience. By virtue of the concept of the encounter, Deleuze calls his philosophy a *transcendental empiricism*. According to Deleuze, only an unanticipated and violent encounter can stimulate thought past the purview of recognition and force it to think. In this section I give a preliminary account of the encounter. The concept of the encounter will be fundamental to our investigation, and it will be adapted toward the following formula: the encounter with the case is the transcendental condition of law.

Deleuze's preliminary definition of the encounter is negative. The encounter is the unrecognized or, more exactly, that which challenges the form of recognition. For Deleuze, what is at stake in an encounter has nothing to do with rewriting, multiplying, or making more supple the concepts and categories used to recognize objects (*DR*, 303). If that were the case, thinking would still be premised on recognition, and although the exact category in which the thing ought to be put may not be known, faith in its eventual discovery would be kept intact. Deleuze's claim is more radical: We think when we do not recognize. Deleuze does not deny recognition its necessity. What he does deny is the identification of recognition *as* thought, for that identification eliminates the potential for encounters which provoke thinking. It is true that we recognize all the time and that we are ceaselessly involved in this practical activity; we must not, however, think that recognition is what is primarily at stake in thought.

The unrecognized—or the encounter—is a metaphysical violence. An encounter occurs whenever clichés, habits, categories, and propositional certitudes are no longer sufficient to account for, think, and react within a situation. This is a claim that Deleuze never abandons, from the encounter in *Difference and Repetition* to the time image in *Cinema 2*. It is with force and necessity that encounters cause us to break from dogmatic thought and the recognizable form that dogmatism assigns to the outside.

> Concepts only ever designate possibilities. They lack the claws of absolute necessity—in other words, of an original violence done to thought; the claws of a strangeness or an enmity which alone would awaken thought from its natural stupor or eternal possibility: there is only involuntary thought, aroused but constrained within thought, and all the more absolutely necessary for being born, illegitimately, of fortuitousness in the world. . . . Do not count on thought to ensure the relative necessity of what it thinks. Rather, count upon the contingency of an encounter with that which forces thought to raise up and educate the absolute necessity of an act of thought or a passion to think. The conditions of a true critique and a true creation are the same: the destruction of an image of thought which presupposes itself and the genesis of the act of thinking in thought itself. (*DR*, 139)

It should not be surprising that this passage is directly evocative of Kant's preface to the *Prolegomena*. Here too we find ourselves in a "dogmatic slumber" or a natural stupor.[26] Only, with Deleuze, what rouses is not the skeptical challenge and transcendental reply; on the contrary, the identification of recognition as the vocation of thought is soporific. Recall that Kant is criticized on three bases: The conditions of possible experience do not address the conditions of real experience; possible experience never attains necessity; and possible experience annuls encounters insofar as it is always already recognized. In this passage, we find the positive expression of these same three criticisms: The encounter is singular, necessary, and violent (unrecognized). Contrary to Kant, the fundamental and transcendental problem for Deleuze is not to determine the conditions of possible experience; rather, it is to determine the conditions for a specific, necessary thought. For thought to address its own possibility, it must find a way to affirm and engage the outside without reducing or assigning to it its own form. The encounter is the concept that Deleuze creates to indicate a transcendental genesis of thought that is necessary and specific and attains a constitutive relationship to an irreducible outside.

To attain this relation to the outside, we require a disposition that is receptive, however minimally, to encounters. Deleuze is fond of citing Heidegger's claim that we are not yet thinking, that thought remains a potential and not a necessary capacity (*DR*, 144, 275; *C2*, 156; *WP*, 55).[27] Given its emphatic definition as distinct from recognition and everyday consciousness, it is clear that thought cannot always be operative and that it is engendered only in specific, occasional situations. "We search for truth only when we are determined to do so in terms of a concrete situation, when we undergo a kind of violence that impels us to such a search" (*PS*, 15). The danger for Deleuze is that we remain insensate to encounters by virtue of a prejudiced dogmatism—prejudiced in the exact sense of judging everything in advance according to the form of representation, if not to actual, given representations.

At this point, we can specify two dimensions to an encounter, roughly speaking: external and internal. The distinction is perhaps not quite exact, for no encounter fails to simultaneously join the two, but it is clarifying. Moreover, it will be of service in our discussion of adjudication as encountering cases from the outside and as constructing problems from these.

In an external encounter something truly does, in the plain understanding of the phrase, come from the outside. Borrowing from Bergson, Deleuze twice uses the example of swimming. When we learn to swim, we do not simply mimic the motions taught to us on land. Instead, "a body combines some of its own distinctive points with those of a wave, it espouses the principle of a repetition which is no longer that of the Same, but involves the Other—involves difference, from one wave and one gesture to another, and carries that difference through the repetitive space thereby constituted" (*DR*, 23, 165, 192; see *CE*, 192). Swimming is this entanglement or encounter between the points of my body and the points of a wave to constitute a space and an action. This encounter and the response it creates—swimming—is forced (if not, we drown) and it is singular (these points of the wave with my body).

Another, more properly philosophical, example of an encounter with the outside is Kant's concept of the sublime in the *Critique of Judgment*. A sublime experience is one that defies our powers of representation and recognition par excellence. On the one hand, a mathematically sublime experience confronts us with a phenomenon (an ocean, an abyss, etc.) whose boundless magnitude defies our intuitive power to synthesize it (*CJ*, §25). On the other hand, a dynamically sublime experience frightens us with the might of the infinite (*CJ*, §28). In both cases we are forced into thinking. In the former the boundlessness of nature compels us to think of the concept of the infinite; in the latter terror turns our thoughts toward reason. With the concept of the sublime—and perhaps this is why so many contemporary commentators are drawn to its investigation[28]—we witness in Kant a unique respect for the encounter: A singular aesthetic experience overwhelms our representational capacities, forces us to think, and requires a disposition sensitive to it.

The second kind of encounter I call, perhaps infelicitously, internal. By this, I mean that an encounter indicates not only that which comes from the outside but also the *problems that thought creates*. On this theme of the problem, Deleuze again takes his inspiration from Bergson. "What is required in philosophy and even elsewhere, is to find the problem and consequently to pose it, even more than to solve it. . . . But stating the problem is not simply uncovering [*découvrir*], *it is inventing*. . . . The effort of invention consists most often in raising the problem, in creating the term in which it will be posed" (*CM*, 51, emphasis added, translation modified). The direct identification of the encounter with the problem is my own, but, given the criteria for what counts as an encounter, it is illuminating and not unwarranted. For Deleuze as well as for Bergson, thought occurs only in the invention of problems. When one philosopher criticizes another, it is never on the basis of shortcomings that could be recognized from within the latter's terms (e.g., errors or contradictions in a vulgar sense); rather, criticism always forms new problems in light of which the outdated philosophy shows itself to be inadequate. Using the resources of an old text, new problems are created that are initially unrecognizable from the perspective of that text (if not, they would have already been stated). The problem, then, is like an encounter proper to thought insofar as from criticism comes genuine creation.

Pushing this interpretation, the concept of the problem satisfies four transcendental conditions established by the concept of the encounter. First, the problem is the *presupposed condition* for philosophical thinking.

Second, the problems of philosophy are deemed *necessary* and not merely possible. Third, a problem is *singular* to the philosophy that develops it. And finally, problems are *not recognized*; they are created, not uncovered. This last point is worth stressing. Insofar as they are created, problems are irreducible to recognition. They are, in a sense, outside recognition and come from outside representational thinking. It is difficult to explain this point, but for Deleuze the process of creating problems—especially at first, before the specific problem is settled and before its concepts are fully determined—is subrepresentative and nondiscursive but *not* in the intuitive or private sense that a contemporary philosophy of language promptly criticizes. Problem creation is something of a capacity or aptitude of perception, or of sensibility, that can upset and unsettle a text without yet having, but on the way to having, the terms with which to do so.[29] There is, in other words, a process that happens *between* two philosophies that Deleuze calls the "posing of problems," and this is a process of searching for new terms with which to simultaneously criticize a predecessor and create a philosophy. As Deleuze puts it, critique *is* creation. This formula introduces us to a new critical transcendentalism adequate to think about the necessity, singularity, and unrecognizability of philosophical thoughts as they are related to their animating problems. In short, for Deleuze the problem is like an encounter proper to thought, the instance and condition in which thought is set in motion. Problems give us a reason to think and a singularity to these thoughts and thus satisfy the requirements of the encounter.

Again, we can go back to Kant. The *Critique of Pure Reason* is an inquiry into the appropriate way to set and to treat the intractable problems posed by reason. A wonderful turn of phrase from the fourth section of the Antinomy of Pure Reason shows us just how aware Kant was of the transcendental nature of problems in the history of philosophy: "Where do you get the ideas the solution to which involves you in such difficulties?" (A482/B510). There are two layers to this complex little phrase. First, Kant acknowledges that rational dogmatism and skepticism alike are animated by ideas or problems that prompt the invention of solutions. This shows the *genetic* quality of problems. But second, and more important, the fact that Kant can criticize dogmatism and skepticism for their wild problems and unaccountable solutions (of the beginning of the world, of freedom, of God) is purely a consequence of the way he himself has posed the problem *of* dogmatism and skepticism. This is the creative move of the antinomies. Instead of a simple opposition, Kant sees that rationalism and skepticism share a deep, implicit basis (that experience concerns objects in themselves), which they develop in opposite ways. Framing the problem in this way (*as* an antinomy, not as an opposition), Kant simultaneously reinvents the sense of dogmatism and skepticism, criticizes both of them, and, in so doing, creates his own concepts (specifically, transcendental *idealism* emerges as set against the two leading positions of transcendental *realism*). This shows the *creative* quality of problems—creative of criticized text, creative of the new text. And Kant himself is perfectly well aware of the power of problems and states as much both in the *Critique* and in a letter that explains how his philosophy came to him only once he had posed the problem of the antinomies.[30] This problem-posing aspect of Kant's philosophy is one that Deleuze deeply admires, and in *Difference and Repetition* he opens the chapter on Ideas with Kant's transcendental account of problems: "For every solution presupposes a problem, that is to say the constitution of a systematic, unitary field that orients and subsumes the researches or investigations in such a manner that the answers, in turn, form precisely cases of solution" (*DR*, 168, translation modified). Thus both Deleuze and Kant establish an equivalence between ideas and problems that serves as the transcendental feature that stimulates the singularity of, and the necessity for, any philosophy.

I conclude by repeating that the division of encounters into external and internal/problematic is not absolute. It is, as scholastics might say, a mere distinction of reason, for what philosophical problem is not animated by an outside? Equally, what outside encounter does not formulate a problem? Of course, all encounters simultaneously concern both the outside and problems; all I have done is prepare an analytical separation of these two constitutive features for later investigation.

Critique of Communication

In the last two sections of this chapter, I turn to Deleuze's only sustained criticism of institutional law: human rights. Deleuze consistently links human rights with a critique of philosophies of communication. By exploring this connection, we can at once elaborate this critique and connect it to the concepts of dogmatism and encounter and, in addition, put Deleuze into direct dialogue with Habermas, one of the dogmatic theorists of law.

It is well known that Deleuze is both personally and philosophically repelled by discussion. To the phrase "let's discuss this point a little," the true philosopher will get up and run away as fast and as far as possible (*WP*, 28, and elsewhere). Why? Because the kind of communication we find in discussions and conversations is anathema to the creation of problems, that is, to philosophy. For the creation of problems, communication substitutes the exchange of opinion (*doxa*).[31]

As I said, in his critique of *doxa*, Deleuze is both a Platonist and a political philosopher. Philosophy must fight opinion, for "it is in this very struggle against the power of opinion that Deleuze's ontological and political critique of representation finds its justification."[32] What Deleuze will later oppose to philosophies of communication is forcefully in evidence in his early critique of dogmatism.

> Philosophy is left without means to realize its project of breaking with *doxa*. No doubt philosophy refuses every particular *doxa*; no doubt it upholds no particular propositions of good sense or common sense. *No doubt it recognizes nothing in particular. Nevertheless, it retains the essential aspect of* doxa—*namely, the form.* . . . *The image of thought is only the figure in which* doxa *is universalized by being elevated to the rational level*. However, so long as one only abstracts from the empirical content of *doxa*, while maintaining the operation of the faculties which correspond to it and implicitly retains the essential aspect of the content, one remains imprisoned by it. . . . The form of recognition has never sanctioned anything but the recognizable and the recognized; form will never inspire anything but conformities. (*DR*, 134, emphasis added)

Deleuze is quite clear that philosophy rarely if ever upholds particular opinions of common sense; instead, it preserves *doxa* in a more covert and also more profound way. Philosophers never presuppose an *empirical* opinion—"a particular this or that"—but rather install a more fundamental *doxa*—"*the form of representation or recognition in general*"—as the basis of their philosophy (*DR*, 131, emphasis added). As Deleuze says, one can deny every possible kind of opinion and yet still be mired in it if its image or form is not also acknowledged and denied. And this is precisely what happens. With recognition as its image of thought, dogmatic philosophy can simultaneously criticize every particular opinion while developing concepts that raise its form to rational, discursive standing.

This entire endeavor, however, rests on a confusion of the empirical with the transcendental in that *empirical* acts of recognition are assumed as the basis or image of thought (*DR*, 131–138).[33] This is of extreme significance. If thought is based on recognition, it remains locked in a conformity of which it is unaware. Moreover, we will see that recognition precludes appreciation of the real transcendental basis of thought: the encounter and the problem. In short, with recognition as its image of thought, philosophy is without the means to challenge *doxa* and realize its raison d'être.

If we take Habermas as exemplary of a dogmatic image of thought, it is with a few caveats. Doubtlessly, few thinkers have been as careful to steer clear of confusing empirical opinion with rational discourse. Returning to *Between Facts and Norms*, Habermas distinguishes between moral and ethical justification discourses. Ethical discourses occur within determinate groups and address shared substantial understanding of the good. In ethical argumentation an empirical and substantial norm is valid for those who share a form of life (*BFN*, 94–97). Moral discourses, by contrast, are postmetaphysical and require "a perspective freed of all egocentrism or ethnocentrism," freed, that is, from all empirical *doxas* that pass in ethical life (*BFN*, 97).

But despite barring empirical opinions, and just as Deleuze anticipates in *Difference and Repetition*, moral discourses instantiate a profound form of *doxa*. In moral discourses, participants advance criticizable arguments to reach a universal understanding with one another about something. This something must be "impartially justified" through a discourse principle that "reflects those symmetrical relations of recognition built into communicatively structured forms of life in general" (*BFN*, 109). Almost as if taken word for word out of *Difference and Repetition*, Habermas establishes a communicative practical reason by raising the *form* of *doxa*—recognition, intersubjective goodwill, and so on—to an explicit rational level. What Deleuze calls *doxa* is preserved within the form of communication itself.[34]

To sharpen the contrast between Habermas and Deleuze, we can ask how participants of moral discourses resolve *problems*. Moral discourse is itself a solution to a problem (that of legitimate discussion and agreement in a posttraditional age) and is used as an intersubjective, communicative medium to resolve problems. For Habermas, "thoughts are propositionally structured" and to each proposition a speaking subject can take a yes or no position (*BFN*, 11–12). In moral discourses, participants come together to discuss a shared problem and reach consensus by means of propositions to which subjects say yes or no.

> One has the possibility of taking a yes or no position to a criticizable validity claim only if the other is willing to justify the claim raised by her speech act, should this be necessary. Communicatively acting subjects commit themselves to coordinating their action plans on the basis of a consensus that depends in turn on their reciprocally taking positions on, and intersubjectively recognizing, validity claims. From this it follows that only those reasons count that all participating parties *together* find acceptable. It is in each case the *same* kinds of reasons that have a rationally motivating force for those involved in communicative action. (*BFN*, 119)

A problem for Habermas is cashed out by propositions to which participants take a yes/no position, working toward a consensus affirmed by all and for good reasons. The questions are formed according to yes or no responses interlocutors may give. This communicative account of the problem and problem solving strongly recalls what Deleuze calls interrogation in *Difference and Repetition*. In interrogation, the questions put to subjects are "always traced [*calquée*] from givable, probable or possible responses" (*DR*, 156). Questions are propositions traced from their possible responses; or, changing the phrase, the genesis of questions—and by consequence, the genesis of the represented problem—is empirical. As Deleuze puts it, interrogation "dismembers problems and questions, and reconstitutes them in accordance with the propositions of the common empirical consciousness—in other words, according to the probable truths of a simple *doxa*" (*DR*, 157; also *ABC*, Q; *WP*, 80). According to this concept of interrogation, which I claim reflects Habermas's position, a problem has the following characteristics: It is propositional; it is formed by the possible responses to questions put to participants; and it works toward a consensus of recognizable propositions. Conceived in this way, this sort of problem is a strong instantiation of *doxa*: A problem is dismembered into recognizable propositions traced from the probable empirical responses given to them. *Doxa* insists itself both at a transcendental level (the form of recognition in exchangeable propositions) and at an empirical level (formation of questions through probable responses).[35]

The Deleuze-Habermas opposition is expressed by the following. For Habermas, problems are propositional, whereas for Deleuze "the problem is extra-propositional, [it] differs in kind from every proposition" (*DR*, 157).

The problem is extrapropositional because it is transcendental; it delimits a field of real experience and defines the meaning of the questions one can pose and prefigures the cases of solution. Simply put, questions and answers depend on problems as their condition, not the other way around. We can identify four differences in kind between Deleuze's concept of the problem and Habermas's conception of the problem as propositional: (1) Problems are *singular*; propositions are *general* and circulated through a universal community. (2) Problems are *transcendental*; propositions are *empirical*, modeled as they are on possible responses of a rational community. (3) Problems *force* themselves to be thought; propositions are *voluntary* and based on communicative goodwill. (4) Problems are *created* and unrecognized; propositions, inasmuch as they embody the form of *recognition*, are *doxa*. To hold, as Habermas does, that thinking is propositional obliterates, according to Deleuze, any appreciation for the true basis of thought: problems. With communicative propositions, we instate an intransigent form of *doxa* at the heart of philosophy; moreover, we deny the extrapropositional problem as a transcendental basis of philosophical thought and experience.

To establish the proposition as the stake of philosophy is, in the strong sense, nonsense for Deleuze. "Philosophy finds no final refuge in communication, which only works under the sway of opinion in order to create 'consensus' and not concepts. The idea of a Western democratic conversation between friends has not produced the least concept" (*WP*, 6, translation modified). Communication and conversation have no philosophical standing for Deleuze. Communication is, instead, the modern incarnation of a dogmatism that obfuscates an appreciation of the nature, conditions, and intrinsic creativity of philosophy. It is not as if Deleuze proposes a rival philosophy to communication; rather, he constructs a concept of philosophy that excludes communication and makes its claim to philosophical standing nonsensical.[36]

But to say that a communicative philosophy is nonsensical does not mean that it is not harmful. Dogmatic philosophies of communication threaten to separate philosophy from what it can do: create problems and concepts. Hence Deleuze's claim that philosophies of communication are inspired by *ressentiment* is not mere polemic; *ressentiment* and slave morality separate a thing from its powers, which is precisely what communication does (*WP*, 29).[37] Thus the least harm conversation can do is to introduce imprecision into the discussion of problems (either by dismembering and distorting a problem into criticizable propositions or by attempting to establish conversations within the history of philosophy).[38] But it is much worse: In the putative name of democracy and universalism, philosophies of communication install *doxas* of recognition and of participative goodwill and foreclose appreciation of and sensitivity toward problems and encounters. And, again, this is for Deleuze pure *ressentiment*. Communicative dogmatism separates us from the productive powers of problems and encounters.

Critique of Human Rights

In this last section I present Deleuze's provocative dismissal of human rights or, more specifically, of human rights *discourses*. We will see that this dismissal closely parallels and builds from his critique of communication. I proceed by citing from interviews given by Habermas and Deleuze, both late in their respective careers, on the subject of human rights.

Habermas's interview, titled "America and the World," offers him an opportunity to reflect on the current status of international law and human rights. The interviewer, Eduardo Mendieta, calls Habermas "a defender of the Kantian project second to none," and Habermas promptly honors the designation by drawing a Kantian distinction.[39] Pessimistic about the chances for effective reform in the United Nations—based as it is on a federation of interested sovereign nations (Kant's *foedus Amphictyonum*)— Habermas remarks that the "properly Utopian element of the status of world citizenship" lies in continental governments such as the European Union, where citizens, and not merely states, would be subjects of international law (Kant's *ius cosmopoliticum*).[40] Envisaging nothing less than a "parliament of world citizens," Habermas is aware that his claim could "give rise to humbug." But, he persists, although a positive association of a category as disparate as world citizens may be difficult to envisage, we might imagine such an institutional body bound together *negatively*.

In view of the limited functions of the United Nations, one must keep in mind that representatives in this parliament would be representing populations which of necessity would not be bound together, like the citizens of a political entity, by thick traditions. In place of the positive solidarity of a national citizenry, *a nega-*

tive consensus would suffice, to wit: a common outrage at the aggressive warmongering and human rights violations of criminal gangs and regimes, or a common horror over acts of ethnic cleansing and of genocide.[41]

Such a proposal would institutionalize a world public, perhaps unable to share a substantial ethical life but nonetheless capable of identifying egregious infractions of human rights and expressing properly universal—and universally shared—outrage. Although the universal outrage appears almost as aesthetic as it does discursive (we *feel*, almost through a shared aesthetic sense, a common horror), we again see processes of recognition, goodwill, and consensus. What we *feel* in common will doubtlessly be propositionally expressed in common.

Now, I cite Deleuze's criticism of human rights from the *Abécédaire*. These texts of Habermas and Deleuze are ideal to compare, for it seems that, although given a dozen years earlier, Deleuze anticipated a word-for-word rejoinder to Habermas.

I'll take the recent example of Armenia . . . it's very recent, that one. What's the situation? . . . There is this enclave within a Soviet republic. There is this Armenian enclave. There is an Armenian republic, there is an enclave, ok, that's a situation. That's the first thing. There is this massacre [by] some Turks, those pretend, those pseudo-Turks [*des semblants de, des espèces de Turcs*] . . . well I guess the Armenians are massacred one more time. OK. In the Enclave. OK. The Armenians flee to their republic—I think, you correct all my errors—and, on top of all that, an earthquake. Well, we'd think we're in the Marquis de Sade. Those poor people went through the worst, the worst possible ordeals, and the moment they get shelter nature butts in. We say human rights [*les droits de l'homme*]. But finally, these are discourses for intellectuals, and for odious intellectuals at that, for intellectuals without ideas. First, I remark that these declarations of human rights are never made in conjunction with those concerned, with Armenians societies, with Armenian communities, etc. But it's funny, the problem, it's not about human rights. What is it? It's . . . "what are we going to do?" Here's an assemblage [*Voilà un agencement*]. . . . [What can we do] to make this enclave livable? . . . It's not a question, I would say, it's not a question of human rights, it's not a question of justice. It's a question of *jurisprudence*. All the abominations people suffer are cases. These aren't elements with abstract rights, they're abominable cases. We might say that these cases resemble each other, but these are situations of jurisprudence. The Armenian problem is exactly what we could call an extraordinarily complex jurisprudential problem. What to do to save the Armenians and how can they save themselves from this crazy situation they're in? . . . All of this is jurisprudence. It's not a question of a right to this or to that. It is a question of situations and situations that evolve, and to fight for liberty is in fact to do jurisprudence. So, the Armenian case seems typical. Human Rights . . . you invoke human rights . . . what does that mean? It means, "Ah, Turks have no right to massacre Armenians." OK. The Turks have no right to massacre the Armenians, then what? And then we're supposed to have advanced with that? They're really idiotic. Or, I think they're truly hypocrites, all those who think human rights [*qui pensent les droits de l'homme*]. It's philosophically null, just null. And the creation of law [*du droit*], it's not . . . it's not declarations of human rights. Creation in law, it's jurisprudence. Only that exists. So, to fight for jurisprudence, indeed. (*ABC*, G)

Before moving to these difficult, prickly remarks, it is helpful to briefly situate them within the evolution of Deleuze's thinking about the political. As Paul Patton observes, between the earlier writings with Guattari (1972, 1980) and *What Is Philosophy* (1991) we find in Deleuze a growing and insistent awareness of normative political issues.[42] Whereas *Anti-Oedipus* and *A Thousand Plateaus* were mostly concerned with establishing a political ontology that conceptualizes creativity and movement (hence the almost unreasonable repetition of the twin concepts of territorialization and deterritorialization in one Plateau after another), the later interviews, and most especially *What Is Philosophy*, reflect on normative political categories, such as dignity, shame, distributive justice and material inequality, rights, and democracy. Of special pertinence to his Armenian example from the *Abécédaire*, Deleuze claims that philosophy provides a way of responding to the intolerable (*WP*, 108), which, as Patton comments, "implies that this resistance may assist the emergence of new forms of individual and collective life that, in specific ways, are *better than* existing forms."[43]

The Armenian example is obviously an instance of the intolerable. It is, as Deleuze puts it, an abominable case, a complex multiplicity or assemblage that must be taken up as a problem in and for jurisprudence. It has unique features (geopolitical, natural, etc.) and poses a singular problem to law: how to make this situation livable? To the questions "How do we create rights?" "Which rights would these be?" "With what coordination?" we see a double construction. On the one hand, rights would have to be tailored to this problematic situation, and on the other hand, the situation would be constructed, and hopefully ameliorated, through jurisprudential intervention. Or, in Deleuzian terms, the situation is an encounter that forces the law into the invention of a problem, which creates rights to modify and to improve that situation. This Armenian case is similar to the earlier taxi example: A situation is encountered; law and situation form an assemblage, a juridical problem, or a case (for now these terms are equivalent); rights are created and implemented.

Now what kind of response could philosophy or jurisprudence make to such an intolerable, abominable case? We have already seen Deleuze insist in *What Is Philosophy* that a basic criteria for (the success of) political philosophy is that its concepts connect to the present milieu, with the effect that both are modified or recreated from within the context of their mutual encounter. This is perhaps why in the *Abécédaire* (and also in *Negotiations*, 169–170) Deleuze states his frustration that declarations of rights are seldom made in conjunction with those whom they concern; these declarations, in other words, fail to connect to a milieu and hence fail to be determined by the situations they are designed to improve. The fundamental problem raised by Deleuze's *Abécédaire* example is, roughly, how are these people to live, in this enclave, as Armenian people? The conjunction or encounter between concept and milieu arises in the relationship between this concept and the details of the Armenian situation (call this geophilosophy). More generally, if philosophy is meant to be untimely, that is, critical of its milieu, then in order for that criticism to be effective, it must not abstractly negate or decry that milieu but draw on "processes and tendencies that are immanent to [it] and that embody a potential for change."[44] That is why declarations of rights are no help and why Deleuze is so aggressive toward them. In the Armenian example a connection to the situation—which might, perhaps, generate new and appropriate determinations of the rights to amnesty, to property, even, as Deleuze seems to suggest, to liberty—is severed in favor of preexisting categories whose implementation could barely help to clarify or affect the catastrophe at hand.

Obviously, Deleuze is not against rights per se (whatever that would mean), but he opposes how they are articulated by human rights *discourses*. As Patton comments on these *Abécédaire* remarks, "Nothing in what [Deleuze] has to say implies rejection of human rights, the rule of law or democratic government as such. His criticisms have to do with the manner in which these are represented: as 'eternal values,' 'new forms of transcendence,' 'new universals.'"[45] Human rights discourses are the juridical arm of philosophies of communication, and, as such, they are subject to the same criticisms. First, human rights have no politico-philosophical standing; and second, they are inspired by *ressentiment* (they separate a thing from its powers). We must take Deleuze's claim that human rights are for intellectuals without ideas of their own strictly and not pejoratively; human rights have no claim to be a concept because they are established by (dogmatically) suppressing encounters, problems, and the creativity intrinsic to jurisprudence.

Habermas's recommendation founds a global community on the vulnerability of the human subject. If we can't agree on anything positive, we must be able to recognize breaches of preexisting rights wherever they may occur. Rights exist by virtue of a universal communicative agreement that certain human faculties are inviolable (an agreement that is, hopefully, coordinated with forces to police and preserve these rights). The basis for these rights is universally recognized propositions secured before the fact of violation. Or, reverting to Kantian terms, human rights a priori (i.e., before the event of their violation) postulate the conditions for *all possible* breaches of right, such that when a breach occurs, it is recognizable.

By Deleuze's definition, this is dogmatic and misses the genesis of rights from concrete situations. Habermas's theory of rights substitutes the case or encounter as the basis for rights with communicatively circulated propositions. Understood as communication or as discourses, human rights fail to indicate a meaningful conjunction of a right with a present milieu—the requirement for political philosophy and jurisprudence. As such, they are subject to both a Kantian critique, in order to raise awareness of encounters as their transcendental basis, *and* a Platonic critique, in order to urge a break with *doxa* and with the propositional form in favor of effective, singular problems. In short, human rights discourses fail to satisfy the requirements of political philosophy in that they substitute the genetic encounter and the juridical problem with the general and recognized proposition; and they also effect *ressentiment* by separating rights from their creative capacity and from what they can do. As Deleuze says in an interview with Raymond Bellour and François Ewald, if the human rights movement "means reconstituting transcendence or universals, restoring a reflective subject as the bearer of rights, or setting up a communicative intersubjectivity, then it's not much of a philosophical advance [*invention philosophique*]" (*N*, 152, translation modified).

We could object that Habermas's proposal is designed to alert a global community to rights violations where local courts and governments either ignore or have insufficient powers to redress the problem. And, in this light, Deleuze's call to a creative jurisprudence would be an irresponsible fantasy leading either to a blind eye to intransigent global violence or, maybe worse, to hideously creative jurisprudences (disenfranchisements, show trials, etc.). But, and here I speculate, Deleuze would not be against international interventions into abominable situations—only, he would not call them interventions to protect inviolable rights but interventions into problematic situations to create rights. These are cases to be judged, not instances to be subsumed by existing laws or rights. The difference is not semantic; it directly addresses how we conceive of rights and their genesis and creativity.

I have tried to strongly distinguish between a communicative and a Deleuzian approach to rights. I have suggested that a Deleuzian jurisprudence invokes the necessity of transcendental singular encounters in contrast to a communicative philosophy of law based on universal, recognizable propositions. Although my concern is not to elaborate the institutions and protections of a global Deleuzian jurisprudence, I insist that the difference between conceiving rights along the lines of human rights violations and problematic situations is substantial and, as we will see in the coming chapters, a matter of the nature of judgment and adjudication itself.

5

The Time of Law I:
Evolution in Holmes and Bergson

In my treatment of the dogmatic image of law in Part 1, I said that dogmatism consists in taking subsumption as its model of judgment. I also said that subsumption is an image because it is assumed to be what is at stake in adjudication: to recognize cases as instances of rules. It is not by virtue of their image of law that dogmatist theorists differ but by virtue of how they work it up, whether by schematism (Hart), by reflective teleology (Dworkin), or by application discourses (Habermas). Judgment as subsumption does not come into question, only the method by which subsumption is accomplished.

At this point, I add an important complexity to Deleuze's concept of the image of thought: It changes over the course of his writings. In his earlier work, as represented by *Proust and Signs* and *Difference and Repetition*, the image is identified with dogmatism and, as such, is rejected as a spurious, nonphilosophical foundation for thought. "A single Image [of thought] in general" spans from Plato to phenomenology and saddles philosophy with presuppositions (common sense, goodwill, and recognition) that separate it from its critical vocation of breaking with *doxa* (*DR*, 132). And so, Deleuze calls for "a thought *without image*," one able to find its difference and beginning for being "without any kind of presuppositions" (*DR*, 132, emphasis added). But two decades later, in the preface to the English edition of *Difference and Repetition* (1994), Deleuze proposes the possibility of a "*new image* of thought—or rather, a liberation of thought from those images which imprison it" (*DR*, xvi–xvii, emphasis added).

What could be the characteristics of such a new image? Given that it remains an image, what place does it preserve for prephilosophical, albeit nondogmatic, departures? I propose two answers, one here and one in the next chapter, both of which turn to Bergson. The first answer consists of finding in Bergson *an image of thought irreducible to dogmatism*.

If we were to identify a single proposition of Bergson's to summarize his philosophy, it would be the following: "Time is invention or it is nothing at all" (*CE*, 341). If the future is given alongside the present (either as a calculable function of it or as a plan to realize out of it), then time means nothing; in other words, a meaningful conception of time must allow for unpredictability or inventiveness. As we will see, Bergson relentlessly pursued the implications of this proposition and gave it a concept: duration. Nevertheless, there is a sense in which this proposition is perhaps not primarily a concept but rather an image, a hunch, or an intuition that multiplied into so many examinations of the relationship between time and creativity in psychic life (*Time and Free Will*), ontology (*Matter and Memory*), cosmology and evolution (*Creative Evolution*), physics (*Duration and Simultaneity*), and the sociopolitical (*Two Sources of Morality and Religion*). As Bergson comments in the opening pages of *Creative Mind*, even as a youth reading Spencer, long before he had formalized any concept of duration, he had a strong impression of dissatisfaction in that "real time" was eliminated from philosophical systems (*CM*, 11–12). As he says, "I perceived one fine day that, in [Spencer], time served no purpose, did nothing. . . . Nevertheless, I said to myself, time is something" (*CM*, 93, translation modified). And, speaking just as autobiographically in that same text, Bergson claims that any great philosopher has, in all honesty, only one or two ideas that serve as simple and concrete starting points to elaborate over the course of his or her life. These are insights so "extraordinarily simple that the philosopher has never succeeded in saying it. And this is why he went on talking all his life" (*CM*, 108–109). For Bergson, his so-called simple insight was that the task of philosophy is not to think the eternal but to think the new as it makes itself in time, for it is nothing other than time itself. I suggest, therefore, that when Bergson claims that time is invention or it is nothing at all, this insight is as much an image as it is a concept. In other words, a rigorous and formalized concept of duration is inspired by a simple and inchoate image, by Bergson's stubborn insistence to look for real and inventive time right from his youth and on to his most sophisticated discursive constructions.

Stretching them slightly, Deleuze's commentaries on Bergson seem to corroborate the suggestion that Bergson's philosophy is based on a nondogmatic *image* of thought (time as inventive). In *Cinema 1*, Deleuze remarks that if time is no longer set in the image of eternity but is instead committed to thinking "the production of the new, that is, of the remarkable and the singular," then what we witness is "a complete *conversion* of philosophy" (*C1*, 7, emphasis added). Deleuze's term *conversion* is suggestive of a theological interpretation in the sense of a faith in this new image of time. If, as Deleuze claims, an image of thought is necessarily nonconceptual (as the prephilosophical foundation that inspires and orients conceptual inquiry), then it operates as an indemonstrable point of departure or inspiration that launches thought and not as a discursively defended concept. In this sense, when dealing with an image we cannot but *convert*, we cannot but change our *beliefs* from a dogmatic image of thought that longs for the eternal to a new image of thought for which time is invention.

The phrase "a new image of thought" simultaneously indicates the newness *and* the imagistic nature of this thought. The image continues to designate a "prephilosophical" foundation for thought (*WP*, 40). Only now this image is new insofar as it is committed to the thought of creativity and novelty, of time as invention. In this sense, a new image of thought becomes inassimilable to opinion, with the consequence that thought can be based on an image and simultaneously execute a critique of *doxa*. As inventive or untimely, a new image of thought shakes off and finds a unique perspective from which to criticize the dogmatic image (whose opinion-ridden postulates (goodwill, recognition, etc.) profoundly inhibit the ability to think the new). And so, I suggest that the discovery of a nondogmatic image of thought in Bergson may be one of the reasons that, late in his work, Deleuze comes to affirm the potential for (and the powers of) a new image of thought.

This chapter begins the search for a new image of law that can appreciate the inventiveness of time and adjudication or, more exactly, the inventiveness of adjudication insofar as it is *in time*. To start, I introduce two concepts of Bergson—internal difference and differentiation—that start from and develop the notion that time is inventive. Next, I turn to Oliver Wendell Holmes's *Common Law* and claim that its image of thought is not dogmatic but, like Bergson, starts from the presupposition that time is inventive. The orienting image of this great work of American jurisprudence is that adjudication is based on the desire of a society insofar as desire changes in time. This means that creativity is an inescapable feature of adjudication. Finally, by way of contrast, I return to Dworkin and Habermas to claim that their respective conceptions of adjudication strive above all to eliminate the inventive power of time.

Bergson: Time as Invention
(Internal Difference and Differentiation)

I have spoken of creativity, but what does it mean? What are, according to Bergson, the requirements for creativity? Foremost, the future must not be calculable from given elements of the present. If the future could be anticipated or prophesied from the basis of the present, all would be given and time would be deprived of its efficacy. Time would be a mere chronological withholding of that which cannot be given at once and in which nothing new, that is, nothing unpredictable according to the elements of the present, could happen. It is helpful to look at two positions—mechanism and finalism—usually considered in opposition, that Bergson identifies as committed to the calculability of the future.

The essence of mechanism is to foresee change as the displacement and rearrangement of parts that do not change. "To foresee consists of projecting into the future what has been perceived in the past, or of representing for a later time in a new grouping, in a new order, elements already perceived" (*CE*, 6, translation modified). We can draw three consequences of a mechanistic conception of time. First, we deal with *unchangeable* parts, unalterable by time. Change occurs only in the displacement and combination of parts, never in the parts themselves (if the parts change, we merely isolate smaller parts, from organisms, to organs, to corpuscles, to atoms, etc.). Second, change is *reversible* in that if basic parts remain unmodified, then, in theory if not in fact, there is nothing to prevent their return to an initial position. And third, by way of conclusion, *nothing is created*—what the set will be is always already present in what the set is.[1]

In *Creative Evolution*, Bergson radically rejects the received opposition between mechanism (with its inexorable yet fortuitous laws) and finalism (with its intelligible designs and purposive ends). In fact, he establishes an antinomy: Mechanism and finalism develop a shared illusion in opposite directions. The shared illusion is that the concepts of the intellect are intended for speculation when, in fact, they are meant for action. As Bergson puts it, in a formula that condenses pragmatism to a point, "originally, we think only to act" (*CE*, 44, translation modified). It is with action in mind that mechanism identifies closed systems and discrete parts to enable calculation. Such an approach is perfectly legitimate for purposes of action, but when mechanism believes it can offer true knowledge of the singularity and becoming of things, it falls into an illusory and illegitimate extension of its action-oriented concepts. Finalism too is perfectly legitimate, as a doctrine of action. "In order to act, we begin by proposing an end; we make a plan, then we go on to the detail of mechanism to realize it" (*CE*, 44, translation modified). For Bergson, human beings are fundamentally artisans and builders, *homo fabers*, who act according to designs. A doctrine of ends strays into illusion when it takes this uncontestable pragmatic doctrine of human ends and action and claims that the universe is likewise oriented. When finalism dialectically extends itself and claims that the universe also operates with ends in mind, it falls into the same illusion as mechanism: All is given, only this time in accordance with the realization of a plan. Time becomes nothing but the realization of a program (*CE*, 39, 44–45).

In *Creative Evolution*, Bergson rejects mechanism and finalism because their mutual image of time—"all is given" (*CE*, 345)—suppresses the most striking feature of life: creativity and the invention of differences. Creativity, therefore, cannot consist in a conception of time wherein all is either given in the present or in the future; it always consists of the production of the new. In what follows, rather than comprehensively relate Bergson's *Creative Evolution*, I outline two central concepts from this text as they anticipate the discussion of creativity and time in the law and in Holmes. These two concepts, both committed to explicating Bergson's image of thought that time is invention or it is nothing at all, are *internal difference* and *differentiation*.

I begin with internal difference. Internal difference is that which differs from itself; it is the unity of a subject and its becoming. At the outset of *Creative Evolution*, Bergson proposes the following psychological example, which soon develops into an ontological thesis. Every day I apparently pass through many moods and states. "I am warm or cold, I am merry or sad, I work or I do nothing, I look at which is around me or I think of something else" (*CE*, 1). For the sake of convenience, these states are spoken of as if separate blocks: *Earlier* I was bored; *now* I'm merry; *later* I'll be sad, and so on. Doubtless, this is an expedient mode of expression, but it leads to a number of absurdities. First, moods are said to be self-same entities that endure over a period of time. If a mood were seen to vary, it would be broken down according to the principles of mechanism toward an infinitesimal limit, into shorter and shorter moods in order to guarantee a self-identity to each mood unit. Second, the process of change from one mood to the next remains incomprehensible. If each mood is self-same, it is utterly mysterious as to how I can *pass* from one state to the next. Third, in order to reunite these moods, we must posit an artificial bond: that of an underlying and indifferent ego that threads together these psychic states to ensure their continuity within a same subject.

Bergson instead proposes that we grasp psychical life as ceaseless variation over time. There is "no feeling, no idea, no volition which is not undergoing change every moment" (*CE*, 1). On the one hand, each state is in constant variation and so forfeits any designation as a self-same unit; on the other hand, if our psychic life is constant variation, the "passing from one state to another resembles, more than we imagine, a single state being prolonged; the *transition is continuous*" (*CE*, 2, emphasis added). With this, Bergson resolves each of the absurdities: Moods are no longer divided into self-same units but constantly vary; the passing of moods becomes explicable as the uninterrupted alteration and blending of states (strictly, we can no longer speak of states); and the notion of an indifferent, underlying ego is replaced in favor of a subject with a singular becoming in time.

This is Bergson's concept of internal difference: the unity of a subject and its becoming. And there is no reason to limit this concept of internal difference to psychic life; more fundamentally, it is ontological. Here, it is rewarding to draw on Deleuze's powerful and systematic reading of Bergson. Deleuze observes that with internal difference Bergson proposes a fundamental and novel concept of difference no longer confined to distinguishing *between subjects* as in specific or generic difference.[2] Despite what the exigencies of action and common sense say, difference is not primarily the delineation of two things determined as different, identified or subsumed by different concepts. As Deleuze puts it, Bergson's insight is that "*difference is not exterior or superior to the thing.*" Difference *is* the thing itself; it is the very being of the subject.[3] A being is neither an indifferent and stable subject, nor is it modified through multiple states; instead, a being is nothing other than its *continuous modification* in time. In brief, Bergson's concept of internal difference is a concept of ontological difference: Beings are, and express nothing other than, difference (duration). This is the meaning of Bergson's most famous concept, duration: time *as* internal difference, *as* becoming.

Evolution exemplifies internal difference. What is evolution in fact? It is *life in time*. This expression must be strictly construed as internal difference. As Bergson puts it, "Wherever anything lives, there is, open somewhere, a register in which time is being inscribed" (*CE*, 19). In other words, and this is not a banality, *life occurs in time*—it can be understood only by a concept of internal difference, that is, continuous change in time. In relation to life as internal difference (evolution), Bergson repeatedly insists that organisms are expressive not of states but of *tendencies* (*CE*, 12–15, 128, and elsewhere). In *Creative Evolution*, Bergson is primarily interested "not [in] the thing produced or evolved but the activity of evolution itself," which is why organisms are expressive not of states or definitions but of movement and directions.[4] Organisms are representative of directions—or *tendencies*—of life over time and the continuous alteration of life that accretes over time. "[Organisms] are therefore relatively stable, and counterfeit immobility so well that we treat each of them as a *thing* rather than as a *progress*, forgetting that the very permanence of their form is only the outline of a movement" (*CE*, 128). Indeed, without considering internal difference, change in evolution could only be accidental and would occur only as a result of an extrinsic determination (see *B*, 99). With the concept of internal difference, however, Bergson is able to provoke a reading of evolution as both modification *between* organisms over time and also the *internal variation* of an organism.

At this point, I turn to the other main concept from *Creative Evolution*, differentiation. What characterizes evolution for Bergson is the increasing complexity and differentiation of life over time. Contrary to mechanism and to finalism, which both hold that life operates by association and reorganization of parts, life always proceeds by processes of "dissociation and division" (*CE*, 89). This is, of course, consistent with time as the invention of the new, as a productive and positive power.

> We said of life that, from its origin, it is the continuation of one and the same *élan*, divided into divergent lines of evolution. Something has grown, something has developed by a series of additions which have been so many creations. This very development has brought about a dissociation of tendencies which were unable to grow beyond a certain point without becoming mutually incompatible. (*CE*, 53, translation modified)

If there is a doctrine of finalism in Bergson, it is found in the notion of the simplicity of an origin that over time divides itself into all kinds of life forms, themselves representative of lines or tendencies of development (*CE*, 51). In Bergson's evolutionary scheme we see a major initial differentiation between plant and animal; subsequently, in the animal line we see a differentiation between those animals with centralized nervous systems (vertebrates) and those with decentralized nervous systems (arthropods). And, as evolution continues, or, as time goes on, we witness more and more differentiations and creations.

But why does life divide itself? Why is evolutionary creation manifested through this process of dissociation and differentiation? To answer this question, I must introduce what is perhaps the fundamental biological category for Bergson: the problem. Let us take an example of a single problem—the use of instruments and tools to survive—that receives two divergent evolutionary solutions. It is through this problem that the sense of two great lines of evolution can be comprehended: instinct and intelligence. On the one hand, instinct is the faculty of using inborn organized instruments toward determinate and invariable ends; on the other hand, intelligence is the faculty for making and using unorganized instruments toward a variety of indeterminate ends (*CE*, 140). Faced with a problem (the use of instruments for survival), life proposes two solutions that represent different evolutionary lines (instinct culminating in insects; intelligence culminating in humans). In a beautiful phrase, instinct and intelligence "represent two divergent but equally elegant solutions to one and the same problem" (*CE*, 143, translation modified).

As Deleuze states in a lecture course on *Creative Evolution*, "The living [*le vivant*] is essentially a being with problems that it resolves at every moment."[5] Each line of life is, therefore, related to a problematic situation (an environment or an ethology) in relation to which a body and form must be invented. This is why for Bergson, the living being "appears primarily as the stating of a problem, and the capacity to solve problems: the construction of an eye, for example, is primarily the solution to a problem posed in terms of light" (*B*, 103; also *CE*, 58, 87–90). And if life proceeds according to the posing of singular problems with correspondingly singular solutions, it is easy to see why evolution is divergent. Every problem (e.g., how to use instruments, how to adapt light) is an original situation with its own temporal index and "imparts something of its own originality"; as such, life proceeds by an increasing dissociation according to the demands of problems and their corresponding solutions (*CE*, 28). Life is composed of tendencies in time differentiated according to problems encountered.

To conclude, it has not been my intention to exhaustively relate Bergson's philosophy of life in *Creative Evolution* or to examine it in light of contemporary science.[6] Rather, I have introduced an image and two concepts to guide our examination of Holmes. I began with Bergson's opening image that time is invention or it is nothing at all, which I contrasted with the ineffective temporality of mechanism and finalism. Next, I introduced the concepts of internal difference and differentiation. The first of these concepts shows the identity between subject and alteration; a subject is a continuous multiplicity, and the true subject of Bergson's text is not a state or a product but a movement or a tendency. The second concept showed that tendencies are differentiated into new and inventive lines according to problems encountered and the corresponding solutions engendered. To sum up, we say that evolution is life in time: tendencies creatively differentiated according to problems.

Holmes: Evolution and the Time of Law

Immediately, I say what I will *not* treat in this examination of Holmes and evolution: eugenics. I state this upfront, as the literature on Holmes and evolution obsessively turns on this point.[7] It is fact that the private, public, and professional writings of this famous turn-of-the-century jurist consistently recommend eugenics and the engineering of a race. One polemical commentator goes so far as to identify eugenics as the only positive political project Holmes ever advanced.[8] In this vein I can cite his speeches: "Perhaps in the future we shall care less for quantity and more for quality and try to breed a race"[9]; and "I think it probable that civilization somehow will last as long as I care to look ahead—perhaps with smaller numbers, but perhaps also bred to greatness and splendor by science."[10] With greater notoriety, I can cite Holmes's majority judgment in *Buck v. Bell* defending forced sterilization of the "mentally defective": "It is better for all the world, if instead of waiting to execute degenerate offspring for crime, or to let them starve for their imbecility, society can prevent those who are manifestly unfit from continuing their kind."[11]

Although criticism of Holmes's statements on eugenics and the intersection between law and biology is necessary, I have a different aim: the question of time in Holmes as he articulates duration and creativity in law, or *law in time*. As with my reading of Bergson, I propose an image and two concepts. I claim that the image that launches Holmes's thought is that adjudication is based on the desires and interests of a society *as these change in time*. Holmes never bothered to explicitly articulate (or, perhaps because of the obviousness, could he articulate) his so commonplace and so taken-for-granted image that, in the most basic sense, the desires of a society change over time. The claim, to use an inapt term, that desires change over time is not a premise or a concept (both of which would be stated and actual) but rather an unarticulated starting point that, we will see, launches a theory of adjudication that acknowledges the creativity inherent in judgment. Reading Holmes through this underlying image allows us to create two concepts that, although not identified by name, are rigorously grounded in his text: *duration in law* and *differentiation of law*. My intent in establishing a strict symmetry with Bergson is not to suggest that Holmes was in any way a disciple of Bergson's or that he adhered to his philosophy of time or that he applied it to law. Such claims would be untenable, for if Holmes's attachments to American pragmatism are doubtful, his relation to Bergson is more distant.[12] Instead, Bergson is useful not for any direct filiation but because his philosophy of time and creativity formalizes certain strands of argument within Holmes.

Let's jump right into the famous first page of Holmes's major work, *The Common Law*, in order to see against whom his philosophy of law is directed.

The object of this book is to present a general view of the Common Law. To accomplish the task, other tools are needed besides logic. It is something to show that the consistency of a system requires a particular result; but it is not all. The life of the law has not been logic: it has been experience. The felt necessity of the time, the prevalent moral and political theories, intuitions of public policy, avowed or unconscious, even the prejudices which judges share with their fellow-men, have had a good deal more to do than the syllogism in determining the rules by which men should be governed. The law embodies the story of a nation's development through many centuries, and it cannot be dealt with as if it contained only the axioms and corollaries of a book of mathematics. (*CL*, 1)

To start, observe how the opponent is styled along the lines of Bergson's mechanist. The contemporary reference is to Christopher Langdell, dean of law at Harvard, who looked on law and adjudication as an exercise in logical consistency, extracting general principles from particular cases and applying these without reference to "anything outside of [logic]."[13] What does Langdell's view repress according to this account? Desire and interest in time. Let us look closely at the passage. Logic, as in Bergson and as in pragmatism generally, is assimilated to the status of a tool. It is a tool used, as Holmes says, to secure consistency. It is used within a system that has been isolated by eliminating reference to the outside, that is, to elements not included in its mathematics. Given that it is axiomatic, logic is in the service of calculation and prediction; propositions will be deduced from one another to ensure the consistency of the system. Just as in mechanism, all is given; logic is rigorously atemporal in that it isolates a system of given principles and, by virtue of axiomatic reasoning, secures for itself consistency and calculability. In brief, by eliminating or ignoring those variable elements with a temporal index—such as desires, prejudices, forces, experiences, and so on—logic forecloses the creativity and efficacy of time. This is how I interpret the remarkable line that "the life of the law has not been logic"; logic, in the sense that Holmes depicts it, annuls the creativity of time, or rather, the very livingness of life.

Obviously, the identification of mechanism in the first paragraph of *Common Law* is not identical to Bergson's account in *Creative Evolution*. In their particulars both texts are motivated by different problems. But, to adopt a broader perspective, an affinity can be claimed in that both writers are fundamentally concerned with animating time as a productive power. To see this point clearly, we can look at how *finalism*—the other position in *Creative Evolution* for which "all is given"—is criticized by Holmes. Although not entirely consistent on this basis, Holmes repeatedly insists on the need for a theory of law freed from historicism.[14] In other words, to think the becoming of law outside teleology and the realization of a plan,

> we are not bound to assume with Sohm that his Frankish ancestors had a theory in their heads which, even if a trifle inarticulate, was the majestic peer of all that was done at Rome. The result of that assumption is to lead to the further one, tacitly made, but felt to be there, that there must have been some theory of contract from the beginning, if only you can find what it was. It seems to me well to remember that men begin with no theory at all, and with no such generalization as contract. They begin with particular cases, and even when they have generalized they are often a long way from the final generalizations of a later time.[15]

In this essay, Holmes reproaches the use of teleological explanations to account for the growth and genesis of law. To repeat Bergson's characterization, in teleological accounts the underlying conception of time is that all is given, and here we see that a mature theory of contract is postulated in the inception of a legal system. If granted, the realization of this contract theory would consist of cleaning up that which was at first, naturally, a "trifle inarticulate"; in other words, the genesis of law would be the fine-tuning of an existing, possible plan. As Holmes warns in the first pages of *Common Law*, we must not suppose "because an idea seems very familiar and natural to us, that it has always been so. Many things which we take for granted have had to be laboriously fought out or thought out in past times" (*CL*, 2). Accordingly, legal scholarship must maintain an appreciation for the growth and becoming of law—which proceeds from particular situations and cases unfamiliar with later ordering principles and generalizations—without subjecting these to a scheme of ends or final causes. An awareness of the becoming of law makes us sensitive to the new in law.

This puts even the most sensitive historical scholarship in a tricky predicament. Both Bergson and Holmes are acutely aware that the study of history is necessarily oriented toward the present; as such, the past can be explicated only from the perspective of the present, its categories, and its interests. Although we may know that the present does not bear a prepared and planned future waiting only to be realized, our historical accounts will scarcely be able to avoid such finalism, for our explanations always illuminate and identify those aspects of the past relevant to, and responsible for, our present condition *from the perspective of that condition*.[16] It is within the context of this aporia—an ineradicable finalism from which historicism must extricate itself—that I read Holmes's claim that "history has to be rewritten because history is the selection of those threads of causes or antecedents that we are interested in—and the interest changes in fifty years."[17] Thus, on the one hand, Holmes constantly renews a struggle against the illusion of a finalism that would order the history of law according to given plans and principles; and yet on the other hand, he concedes that all historical scholarship, even his own, writes from the interests of the present and is at least minimally historicist. In this bind, Holmes can only but recommend revisable history (not because of any facile relativism as certain interpreters would have it),[18] because history is always touched by a finalism that compromises sincere efforts to relate the becoming and creativity of law as it develops over time. As Holmes says in a fine line, "a development is hard to describe."[19]

In this tension between the history of law (finalism) and the time of law (the becoming of law), we can begin to formulate Holmes's image of time and the creativity proper to law. I have said that the interests of the present provoke the fall into finalistic history. But, at the same time, the interests of the present are the ground for legislation and for adjudication. Recall that according to the first paragraph of *Common Law*, the "life of the law" is animated by "prevalent moral and political theories, intuitions of public policy, avowed or unconscious, even the prejudices which judges share with their fellow-men."

I must make explicit a latent insight of Holmes's theory. Perhaps it is too obvious an observation and perhaps this is why Holmes does not expressly raise it, but the interests and needs of a society are in constant and continued flux. Although Holmes never conceptually develops this thought—and this is precisely why it is an *image*, as an unthought or preconceptual departure—it informs his philosophy of law and provides the reason that law is *necessarily creative*.

We get at this image only indirectly, by reconstructing its secret, animating power: What the courts declare to have always been the law *is in fact new*. It is legislative in its grounds. The very considerations which judges most rarely mention, and always with an apology, *are the secret root from which the law draws all the juices of life*. I mean, of course, considerations of what is expedient for the community concerned. (*CL*, 35, emphasis added)

Why is the law new? Why is it not merely sometimes, but rather always, new? It would be disastrous to think that Holmes indicates a kind of decisionism wherein the judge can break with tradition at his or her discretion and legislate for contemporary interests and power. To think this way is to ruin both the sense of the new and of the legislative in this passage. According to this reading, the new would be the realized occasion of a power play and the legislative would be an illegitimate suspension of the separation of powers such that the judge would be, temporarily and irresponsibly, a lawgiver.

This passage has a different, more radical sense. If the desires (or interests and needs, if one prefers) of a society are the ground for adjudication and if these interests are continuously changing, then adjudication is *necessarily creative*, for the ground that serves as its secret root changes in time. Furthermore, if judgment is inevitably creative by virtue of having a temporally mobile root (a rhizome, we might say), then judgment is necessarily legislative because the new judgment will suit the needs of the present and thus be discrepant, however slightly, with the past. If, according to this passage, strict adherence to tradition is impossible, it follows that every judgment will be legislative in that it bears, however minimally, novelty. Another way of stating the same point is that if the root of law is a mobile ground of desires, then the rule cannot strictly repeat, for it must be adapted to the requirements of a new ground, and judgment—which adapts tradition to desire—is consequently unavoidably novel and legislative. Law, perhaps contrary to our preliminary expectations, exemplifies *differential repetition* (a repetition that changes, that *is* change). Judgments are necessarily novel because they reflect changes at the level of desire of a community. For Holmes, desire—insofar as it is properly comprehended in time—is a perfectly productive power that accounts for what is at once the most striking and the most necessary characteristic of law and of adjudication: creativity. Holmes must not be understood as recommending creativity or advocating invention in adjudication; rather, his texts are committed to understanding why—to properly formulate the problem as to how and why—creativity is inevitable in law.

Judgments actualize a temporally mobile basis of interest and desire in conjunction with tradition. Let us look at a profound text from *Common Law* that explicates this *creative* relationship between the past of the law (traditions, precedents, etc.) and the interests of the present.

A very common phenomenon, and one very familiar to the student of history, is this. The customs, beliefs, or needs of a primitive time establish a rule or formula. In the course of centuries the custom, belief, or necessity disappears, but the rule remains. The reason which gave rise to the rule has been forgotten, and ingenious minds set themselves to inquire how it is to be accounted for. Some ground of policy is thought of, which seems to explain it and to reconcile it with the present state of things; and *then the rule adapts itself to the new reasons which have been found for it, and enters on a new career.* The old form receives a new content, and *in time* even the form modifies itself to fit the meaning which it has received. (*CL*, 5, emphasis added)

If Richard Posner takes the liberty to claim in this and other similar passages a genealogical method *avant la lettre* and goes so far as to call Holmes the American Nietzsche, I hesitate only slightly to propose this text as an account of *duration in law*.[20] This is my first concept.

Holmes begins with a provocative thought: rules without sense, or rules whose sense has been forgotten over time. In this passage, a judge is always confronted with a rule that has lost its reason and its sense, both of which must be newly provided. The expression must be strictly constructed: The rule is *senseless*. It is not the case that the judge disregards a past rule or overturns reasons previously given; according to Holmes, the rule arrives without reason or explanation and is without sense until furnished by the adjudicative process. What judges do, therefore, is provide a sense for the rule, which is to say that a judgment creates a rule insofar as it connects together the old form (tradition, the rule) and a new content (the reasons provided for the rule). The new career of the rule is nothing other than the differentially repeated rule, or the newly created rule. We must not think that the identity between a rule and its reason is found only in a real or imagined past—as if the first and only time a rule is one with its reason. Rather, this state of identity between rule and reason occurs each and every time a judgment is rendered, because only judgment can establish this identity by creating the rule, once again. The law is nothing other than this creative activity of judgment.

As Holmes says, and I underline, the rule is "*in time*," which means that it is set within a field of desires or interests in flux and change, such that when the rule is received, its reasons have been forgotten; it can no longer be understood because contemporary reasons and interests have changed. I stress this point: It is not that the reasons for the rule have been lost by the empirical destruction of documents or by the real absence of reasons (as if the library had burned down, or that the Twelve Tables or the Ten Commandments had come without supporting documentation). This would be to reduce Holmes's theory to its most empirical and trivial aspect. Rather, it is that the reasons that have held in the past are no longer tenable and satisfactory. They are no longer fit to give acceptable sense to the rule. What arrives before a judge is a forgotten or a senseless reason in that it is no longer for us—it has ceased to make sense as a legitimate explanation for the rule. The judge is charged with coordinating this senseless rule with contemporary interests and with providing acceptable, sensible reasons to uphold the rule according to current interests. Only in this way can the rule take on a sense, and only in this way can reasons be given for a judgment.

In a famous essay, Holmes writes, "We do not realize how large a part of our law is open to reconsideration upon a slight change in the habit of the public mind. *No concrete proposition is self evident.*"[21] This statement, and other similar statements found throughout Holmes's work, situates interests and reason giving in time and claims that it is precisely these interests and reasons that give sense to rules. A rule, by virtue of being *in time*, has had its reasons forgotten and its sense lost; and now, no matter how self-evident it may seem, this rule must be created anew according to interests and reasons able to account for it. *Adjudication can follow tradition only by creating rules.* A simple formula can be given: Rules are in time. Or, rules are available (actionable, justiciable, appreciable) only from within the context of temporalized interests and reason giving.

At this point, I should say that adjudication for Holmes has nothing to do with subsumption. In subsumption, a rule is applied and determines a case. This implies, first, that the rule's sense is apparent and ready to be applied; second, that the rule preserves its sense before and after its application; and third, that the case is unable to affect a rule beyond instantiating it within a present state of affairs. But everything is different with Holmes. On account of being in time, the rule cannot be said to make sense before its application. And, as it is only within the process of adjudication that the rule takes on its sense, we must conclude, first, that judgment modifies the rule, and, second, that the case participates in the construction of the rule. In short, this adjudication is not subsumptive; a judge never subsumes but instead always brings a rule into existence.

In *Common Law*, Holmes provides a charming, almost quaint, example of this temporality of law, this forgetting and inventing of sense that brings rules into existence: the "deodand." According to Holmes, a common feature of ancient and superstitious societies (whether Hebraic, Roman, English, or German) was to punish and destroy objects that caused harm. It was as if the thing itself had volition and was culpable and punishable—in other words, liability attached to the object doing the damage (*CL*, 11). For example, if an ox were to gore someone, it would be stoned; if a tree were to fall and injure someone, it would be chopped up (*CL*, 7, 24). Such a thing was a deodand: an "accursed thing" (*CL*, 7). What is surprising about the law and ceremony surrounding the deodand, however, is how long it lasted in a special branch of law, admiralty. As Holmes writes, "A ship is the most living of inanimate things," and thus "the old books say that, if a man falls from a ship and is drowned, the motion of the ship must be taken to be the cause of death, and the ship forfeited" (*CL*, 26). The ship was treated as if endowed with personality. Almost incredibly, the treatment of ships as a willful and responsible agent endured all the way to 1844 when Justice Story of the U.S. Supreme Court approvingly cites Chief Justice Marshall: "This is not a proceeding against the owner; it is a proceeding against the vessel for an offence committed by the vessel" (*CL*, 29). Obviously, the Court no longer thinks that an inanimate thing is capable of committing an offense. And yet, we see a renewal of the deodand rule under a different scheme of interests and reasons. First, the ship is considered as the limit of liability so that its forfeiture is the maximum penalty; and second, if a ship causes damages, it is expedient to "arrest" the ship in that location and oblige the owner to claim it there, rather than to pursue the matter in a foreign court (*CL*, 30–34). Using this example, we can say that the reasons for the rule of the deodand were truly forgotten by the nineteenth century, yet the rule was revived and effectively invented according to new interests and reasons. The deodand is a single example of a process common to all law for Holmes: evolution.

So far, I have shown that time is an inventive and creative power insofar as changing desires are the basis for law and for adjudication. We can say, therefore, that the law is in continuous difference from itself and that *the life of the law is nothing but its internal difference.*

Although the term *internal difference* is foreign to Holmes, evolutionary expressions are among his favorites to characterize law as it differs from itself through time, that is, as it *evolves*: "One is made to feel the complex antecedents . . . out of which the plant has grown, and one is made to see the growth. . . . The difficulty in remembering the details is the difficulty of marking the steps of an organic process. One sees that the *embryo* has taken form, gained size and coherence, more readily than one marks the moments of the change." And, "The history of law is the *embryology* of a most important set of ideas." And, "For the last thirty years we have been preoccupied with the *embryology* of legal ideas; and explanations, . . . [which means] tracing origin and growth."[22] The recurrent use of the embryology analogy is significant for our Bergsonian reading of Holmes, given that Bergson notes "the development of the embryo is a perpetual change of form. Any one who attempts to note all its successive aspects becomes lost in an infinity, as is inevitable in dealing with a continuum" (*CE*, 18). The embryo stands in Holmes as a figure of internal difference, as continuous change of form. This sense is striking when Holmes writes that he is "interested to trace the transformation [of law] throughout its whole extent" and that this study "afford[s] an instructive example of the mode in which the law has grown, *without a break*, from barbarism to civilization" (*CL*, 5, emphasis added). Like an embryo, law never ceases to change continuously, and so it is artificial to lay any claim to breaks in law, in between which law could be said to maintain a relative identity and stability with itself. Instead, Holmes is explicit in characterizing the law through internal difference; the law grows and changes without interruption, and this growth and alteration is nothing but the being (or becoming) of the law. This is certainly why Holmes, like Bergson, stresses that any analysis of law is much less concerned with states and breaks than with "a study of *tendencies*" (*CL*, 2, emphasis added). If I have concentrated intensely on the opening few pages of *Common Law*, it is because there Holmes provides a perspective on what can only be called an ontology of law: the being of the law as tendency, that is, as difference in time.

From the internal difference of law and its substratum of temporal desires, we can deduce the second concept of our analysis: differentiation in law. Over and over Holmes uses evolutionary and vitalistic tropes to characterize the development, or growth, of law. Recall that in Bergson, life differentiates itself according to problems that are encountered (various species are understood as so many equally elegant solutions to the problems of life). In Holmes too we witness the same process of differentiation, for in the history of law "we watch the metamorphosis of the simple into the complex."[23] A legal system begins with only a few categories but, over time, becomes an increasingly sophisticated and differentiated system with many and ever increasing branches and rules.

What is the mechanism by which the law differentiates itself? It should not be surprising to propose that Holmes, like Bergson, understands the differentiation of life according to problems encountered. Judgments for Holmes, like species and organisms for Bergson, are kinds of solution to problems; judgments express the constellation of desires and rules from within a problematic situation. I conclude with the following statement of Holmes's from a speech.

My keenest interest is excited, not by what are called great questions and great cases, but by little decisions which the common run of selectors would pass by because they did not deal with the Constitution or a telephone company, yet which have in them the germ of some wider theory, and therefore of some profound interstitial change in the very tissue of law.[24]

The image of "interstitial change" and of the "interstitial legislator" was a favorite of Holmes to describe the process of adjudication, and it recurs in his judgments.[25] I suggest that *all* legal judgments—some minimally and others profoundly—introduce alteration or interstitial change into the law. This is a consequence of how the problem is effective in the differentiation of law.

Because the concept of differentiation in law is implied in what I have already said, I only briefly treat it. According to Holmes, a case before the court poses a problem with two distinct aspects. First, the case is more or less a novel fact-situation and introduces unforeseen distinctions and differentiations in the law. To take a famous example, what happens if someone murders his benefactor to gain his own inheritance?[26] This case introduces a new distinction into civil law to punish and prevent this kind of conduct; a new rule is born as a solution to this problem.

I have already introduced in this discussion of the sense of the new rule the second aspect of the problem. If interests and desires are the ground on which rules are adapted, and because this ground is in time, then every adjudicative situation represents a problem of adapting rules to desires. We need only recall the deodand: Each judgment that evokes this rule and keeps it from desuetude must reinvent it along the lines of the needs and desires appropriate to contemporary society. The rule is differentiated and made actual in each case it is called on to adjudicate. Just as in Bergson, the evolution of law develops like an explosion—new cases and desires differentiate the law, and what began as a simple system evolves into tendencies that fork in divergent directions.

Following Bergson, we can say that the judicial decision is a solution to the problems of law. Each decision is therefore, at least minimally, a differentiation of law in that it performs a double and simultaneous adaptation of any rule according to both new situations and new desires. Given that law is in time, that it encounters new factual situations and is based on mobile desires, judgments are interstitial modifications of a tissue of law that becomes ever differentiated, indeed *ever invented*, over time.

All Is Given: The Possible in Dworkin and Habermas

In reading Holmes with Bergson, I claimed that adjudication is creative by virtue of being in time. But what happens when we turn back to Dworkin and Habermas and examine their respective conceptions of adjudication with special attention to the problem of time? We will see that they both implicitly hold an image of time wherein all is given in advance, an image that denies to adjudication an inherent, creative power. In so doing, I hope to show that a key means to distinguishing between dogmatic and nondogmatic jurisprudence is the way in which the relationship between time and law is imagined.

I start with a case. In *Law's Empire*, Dworkin calls on Justice Hercules (the persona for the ideal judge of his theory) to adjudicate *McLoughlin v. O'Brian* (*LE*, 23–29).[27] In *McLoughlin*, the plaintiff's family was seriously injured in a car crash at which the plaintiff was not present, but when she rushed to the hospital and learned that her daughter was dead and her husband and other children seriously injured, she suffered nervous shock and sued the defendant to compensate her injuries. How does Hercules proceed? He starts by laying out the six possible principles to adjudicate the case.[28] The details need not concern us, only, as Dworkin might say, the underlying temporal principle. Hercules, with his infinite time, patience and vision, will pursue each possible principle and each possible ruling within the context of integrity. Recall that integrity is the teleological reflective principle that acts as if law were structured according to a coherent and closed set of principles. In such a context, Hercules must select one principle from the six that best represents this reflectively presupposed totality. Hercules is a little like Leibniz's God, for he contemplates possible principles as if they were possible (and hence incompossible) worlds to realize. In brief, Hercules has six possible choices of which only one will be realized. According to Dworkin, therefore, all is given in advance and the job of the judge is to narrow the field to the most appropriate principle. This is an image of time defined by prospective possibility.

With Habermas, we need only repeat our characterization from Chapter 3. What happens in application discourses? Recall that to the problem of the perfect norm Habermas invokes a temporal solution. A perfect norm generated through justification discourses must include all possible situations to which its application would be appropriate. Of course, this is impossible in advance, given that situations are unforeseeable. Instead, Habermas proposes that perfect norms are *retrospectively achieved*. In choosing a norm to adjudicate a case, the judge acts *as if* justification discourses had already considered and approved of application in this particular case. Retrospectively, the norm bears all its possible applications and thus achieves a retrospective perfection. Thanks to this operation, *the norm contains all its possible cases*, and when one of these comes up in an application scenario, the norm is *instantiated* and *realized*. For the norm, then, all is given and this is an image of time defined by retrospective possibility.

For both Dworkin and Habermas adjudication realizes a possibility. For Dworkin it is selecting the principle that best shows a community of principle; for Habermas it is applying a norm to a case retrospectively contained within it. Either way, time is rendered ineffective in that all possibilities are given in advance before their realization.

I have imposed the terms *possibility* and *realization* to bring us directly to Bergson. Neither Dworkin nor Habermas uses these words—nor, I should add, do they directly treat the problem of time and law—yet these terms are apt to characterize the underlying temporality of their theories of adjudication. For Bergson, the categories of the possible and the real designate a false approach to time wherein the possible preexists and is less than the real. I cite an illuminating anecdotal text from Bergson's 1920 lecture, "The Possible and the Real."

During the Great War certain newspapers and periodicals sometimes turned aside from the terrible worries of the day to think of what would happen later once peace was restored. The future of literature particularly preoccupied them. Someone came one day to ask my opinion. A little embarrassed, I declared I had none. "Do you not at least perceive," I was asked, "certain possible directions? Granted, one cannot foresee details; but as a philosopher you have at least an idea of the whole. How do you conceive, for example, the great dramatic work of tomorrow?" I shall always remember my interlocutor's surprise when I answered, "If I knew what was to be the great dramatic work of the future, I should be writing it." *I clearly saw that he conceived the future work as being already stored up in some cupboard of possibles.* . . . "But," I said, "the work of which you speak is not yet possible."—"But it must be, since it will be realized."—"No, it is not. I grant you, at most, that it *will have been possible.*" "What do you mean by that?"—"It's quite simple. Let a man of talent or genius come forth, let him create a work: *it will then be real, and by that very fact it becomes retrospectively or retroactively possible.* It would not be possible, it would not have been so, if this man had not come upon the scene. That is why I tell you that it will have been possible today, but that it is not yet so. . . . As reality is created as something unforeseeable and new, its image is reflected behind it into the indefinite past; thus it finds that it has from all time been possible, but it is at this precise moment that it begins to have been always possible, and that is why I said that its possibility, which does not precede its reality, will have preceded it once the reality has appeared." (*CM*, 100–101, emphasis added, translation modified).

This passage is excellent in light of our analysis, for it depicts both our main characters: The journalist plays Dworkin, and the Bergson of the passage plays Habermas. We start with the first character. For the journalist, seeing that the next great work is bound to happen, its possibility must be anterior to it; for Dworkin, seeing that a judgment is bound to happen, its possible principles must also be anterior to it. Because the possible is the reflection of the present in the past and because the future succeeds the present, we make the unwarranted conclusion that the possibility of the future lies ready-made in the present, or in its past. As Bergson says for metaphysics and as we say for jurisprudence, "The consequences of this illusion are innumerable" (*CM*, 22). With respect to Dworkin and the adjudication of *McLoughlin*, I identify three consequences.

1. *The concept of the possible eliminates creativity in law.* As Deleuze writes, "The idea of the possible appears when, instead of grasping each existent in its novelty, the whole of existence is related to a preformed element, from which everything is supposed to emerge by simple 'realization'" (*B*, 20). Rather than see either the case or the principle as novel (as in Holmes), Dworkin's judge Hercules lays out preexisting principles and selects one to subsume and illustrate the adjudicative truth of the case. Everything is, in Deleuze's words, preformed: The principles are given before their application, and the case represents the realization of one of the principles.[29] Because there is no conceptual difference between the possible and the real, the process of realization cannot be creative, nor can it provide an understanding of creativity.

2. *The case becomes inexplicable and trivial.* According to our journalist and to Hercules, a possibility is *less than* the real but is conceptually identical to it: Possibilities are almost perfect and complete; they lack only reality. For Deleuze, the possible "simply has existence or reality added to it, which is translated by saying that, from the point of view of the concept, there is no difference between the possible and the real" (*B*, 97)—a writer need only grab an idea out of the air and put it to paper, and a judge need only select the right principle. Turning to adjudication, we ask, What can a case do for a principle? It can give it a body, a reality, a concrete existence. A case provides a concrete but indifferent opportunity for principles to leap into existence—concrete because cases are vehicles to realize principles, and indifferent because cases do not modify, but only instantiate, principles. For example, the concrete multiplicity that is *McLoughlin* does not modify the six possible principles; it only gives them existence. In this schema of possibility, the only difference between a possible principle and a real principle is realization, nothing more. On Dworkin's account, the difference of the case—its being unique, the being of its uniqueness—becomes inexplicable and trivial. It is inexplicable because the only differences admitted are between principles; it is trivial because all the case is good for is to realize a principle. As Deleuze puts it, when a possibility is realized, "it is difficult to understand what existence adds to the concept when all it does is double like with like" (*DR*, 212). The case offers the top-up of existence; beyond this, it is inexplicable and indifferent.

3. *The possible introduces a false concept of choice into adjudication.* On first impression, the judicial freedom of Hercules appears to be one

of indetermination, an open competition between possibles. So, Hercules would evaluate one principle and then consider the next and so on. But this facile kind of freedom is rejected by Dworkin, for if all principles were in fact truly and equally possible, this freedom would lead either to an arbitrary exercise of judicial discretion or to an inability to decide. One principle is best and necessary; the others are considered only out of conscientiousness.[30] We witness a process of limitation whereby one by one Hercules knocks down the competing possible principles to reach the eventual winner (principle 5—compensation for reasonably foreseeable injuries), and, finally, we are left wondering in what sense these ostensible competitors really have been said to be possible except as a puerile and retrospective exercise.

It is true that for Habermas this false problem of choice does not arise. Just as Bergson counters the journalist, for Habermas the possible works only in the future perfect: The case *will have been* included within the norm only in the moment of its application. How does this work? The judge applies a norm to treat a case, but the norm application is appropriate only if it *will have been possible* for the participants in justification discourses to have acted as if they anticipated this case. Thanks to a retrospective process, the norm is said to bear all its possible applications in advance, and when one of these situations comes up, it is applied. As Klaus Günther, whose major influence on Habermas's theory of adjudication (application) was discussed in Chapter 3, writes, "We have to apply a valid norm *as if* we could have foreseen this situation in a discourse under the conditions of unlimited knowledge and time."[31]

To illustrate this theory of adjudication and its peculiar temporality, we can look at *Riggs v. Palmer* (1889), which raises the question of whether an heir who murders his benefactor, but serves punishment for it, is entitled to inherit. According to Habermas, the judge that forbids the murdering grandson his inheritance will act as if the participants in justification discourses who established the testamentary rule had already considered the possibility of murdering heirs and decided that it ought to be forbidden. It is no accident that Habermas makes use of such a peculiar temporality within adjudication. Only through this retrospective activity can the judge guarantee continuity with justification discourses and therefore guarantee the appropriateness of the application. Without such (retrospective) continuity there is always the danger that judges could override the communicative processes that legitimately establish norms. The operation of the possible in Habermas is therefore precisely parallel to Bergson's reply to the journalist. For Dworkin, there is a prospective possibility in that many possible principles could be selected and applied. For Habermas, the category of the possible does not involve choice among competing possibilities. His problems are of a different nature: How can a norm be appropriately applied within the limits of discourse theory? How can a justified norm anticipate its possible cases? To answer these questions, Habermas proposes a retrospective temporality of the possible.

If Habermas apparently follows Bergson, then what objections do we raise? Our trouble with Habermas is that nowhere in the passage from *Creative Mind* does Bergson claim that retrospection or the concept of the possible actually assists in the creation or constitution of anything; instead, Bergson explains to the journalist only how we can give an account of the concept of the possible, how it makes sense only retrospectively, and how it leads us into metaphysical absurdities when used prospectively. At no point is an explanation of the possible confused with the effective genesis of phenomena. For Habermas, by contrast, the possible is effective in the genesis of appropriate applications. The judge proceeds as if participants in justification discourses had anticipated the case and, thanks to its retrospective inclusion within the norm, can make an appropriate application. Again, this is the only way—a retrospective *via indirecta*—to achieve the ideal of a perfect norm, one that has anticipated all its application situations. So, although Habermas may be correct in his assessment that the concept of the possible has only a retrospective sense, he is dogmatic insofar as it is put to positive use to secure continuity between justification discourses and application situations. We identify the positive and productive use of the possible and its retrospective temporality as dogmatic for the same two reasons we reproached Dworkin: Creativity is eliminated and the case is trivialized.

With respect to the first objection that Habermas's theory vitiates an understanding of creativity within adjudication, another text from *Creative Mind* is relevant.

Things and events happen at certain moments; the judgment that notes [*constate*] the occurrence of the thing or the event can only come after; it therefore has its date. But this date at once fades away, in virtue of the principle anchored in our intellect, that all truth is eternal. *If the judgment is true now, it seems to us it must always have been so. It matters not that it had never yet been formulated: it states itself by right before being stated in fact [il se posait lui-même en droit, avant d'être posé en fait].* To every true affirmation we attribute thus a retroactive effect; or rather, we impart to it a retrograde movement. As though a judgment could have pre-existed the terms which make it up! (*CM*, 22, emphasis added, translation modified)

Habermas's theory of adjudication commits precisely this retrospective fallacy of judgment. Rather than appreciate their work as novel, as initiating an inventive and unique genesis of law, judges for Habermas must throw back their norm application onto the plane of justification as if it had already been considered and approved. Exactly as Bergson says, the judgment postures as if eternal, as if judgment was nothing else than the rediscovery and recuperation of its origin within justification discourses. By retrospective inclusion of the case in the norm, it is as if the judgment has always existed in right, if not in fact. And because this retrospective judgment is committed to an image of thought wherein time is as if eternity, it cannot grant to the case any genetic value or give to the norm any novelty. This is our second criticism: By virtue of a retrospective temporality, the case forfeits any interest beyond a correct description of it, as required for an appropriate application. The novel case or new juridical problem becomes, in this view, latently contained within the norm that will be applied to it. Precisely because the norm anticipates and always already includes its applicable cases, the relationship between a norm and a case can be neither new nor inventive. In the perfect norm reconstructively achieved, all is given in advance, that is, all the cases to which it could appropriately be applied.

To conclude, Dworkin and Habermas operate with a conception of time that shields adjudication from the inventive power of time. Or, we can say that with a dogmatic image that takes judgment as subsumptive comes an image of thought or time that longs for the eternal. Reading Holmes with Bergson, I have tried to propose an alternative theory that admits an inventive power to time and that, as a consequence, appreciates the ineluctable creativity of adjudication. In the next two chapters I continue this task by turning directly to Bergson.

6

The Time of Law II: Bergson, Perception, and Memory

To use Bergson toward a pragmatist theory of law and adjudication is unusual for at least two reasons. On the one hand, if Bergson is mentioned at all in connection to law, it is usually as its radical critic; on the other hand, Bergson's pragmatist theses sit uneasily with those of mainstream legal pragmatism. Thus, on both legal and pragmatic grounds, Bergson seems an unpromising candidate on which to base a pragmatic theory of law. By way of introduction, let us take each of these objections in turn.

1. *Bergson and Law.* With respect to law, Bergson is seen as either silent or hostile. If it is only seldom that Bergson directly treats political questions, it is even less so that he addresses questions of law.[1] Even when compared to Deleuze, there is little in the nature of direct observation to draw on. And if, on equally rare occasions, the relationship between law and Bergson's wider philosophy is raised by commentary, the conclusions are overwhelmingly negative or, worse, discouraging. For example, Gadamer observes that Bergson represents a "criticism [of] legal thinking," and Gillian Rose criticizes Bergson's apparent attack on law and juridicism.[2] Moreover, Deleuze's concept of repetition—extensively (and I would insist primarily) informed by Bergson—is set "against the law: against the similar form and the equivalent content of law" (*DR*, 2). Finally and explicitly, Michael Hardt warns those who would attempt to turn Bergson, especially through Deleuze's commentaries, toward the subject of law: "Deleuze's investigation of Bergson is focused primarily on ontological issues, and, although it flirts with the question of ethics, it gives no solid grounds for a discussion of law."[3]

Taking up Hardt's remark, it is indisputable that Bergson had little to say about the institution of law and that his problems primarily address ontology. But it is precisely these ontological insights that I press into service for jurisprudence. As Eric Alliez remarks, "What is funny is that whenever the question of political philosophy is dealt with institutionally, everything happens as if there were no link with any kind of ontological investigation."[4] Already in our work on Bergson and Holmes we have tried to uncover an ontological insight: that the being of law is internal difference, based as it is on desires set in time. In this chapter I develop major ontological themes—matter, movement, and perception, and most important, time—from Bergson's *Matter and Memory* to appreciate Deleuze's comments on jurisprudence and, more important, to formulate a nondogmatic jurisprudence. Specifically, I start from Bergson's account of matter and perception and demonstrate its application to law with a famous case of Cardozo's. From there, I relate Bergson's theory of time and memory by drawing on Deleuze's systematic formalization in *Difference and Repetition*. In brief, this chapter isolates and develops the two major ontological themes from *Matter and Memory* (matter, movement, and perception on the one hand, and time on the other). All this prepares the discussion in the next chapter, which shows that the substance of adjudication consists in the relationship between perception and time. (Or, to anticipate our terms, adjudication consists in actualizing the virtual past of the law in coordination with a present perception of the case.) In this way, I show that Bergson, together with Deleuze, can contribute a fundamental and profound understanding of law and adjudication.

2. *Bergson and Pragmatism*. Although it is true that both William James and John Dewey valued Bergson's work not merely as a complement to but also as an integral part of the pragmatist project, contemporary American pragmatism has all but dropped it from consideration.[5] What's more, legal pragmatism has never given Bergson serious notice. Maybe this has to do with the teleological theory of judgment and the temporality that underpins it. American legal pragmatism espouses an openly teleological conception of adjudication. According to this theory, judges can judge only from within specific circumstances to advance certain determinate ends. Cardozo's exemplary formulation—which Posner calls "pragmatism in a nutshell"[6]—in *Ostrowe v. Lee* condenses this teleological orientation to a line: "The soundness of a conclusion may not

infrequently be tested by its consequences."[7] And in *The Nature of the Judicial Process* Cardozo elaborates that "the teleological conception of his function must be ever in the judge's mind. This means, of course, that the juristic philosophy of the common law is at bottom the philosophy of pragmatism. Its truth is relative, not absolute" (*NJP*, 149). With Holmes, we have seen teleology effective from the first lines of *Common Law*, where "felt necessities" and not "logic" are determinative of "the rules by which men should be governed" (*CL*, 1). And this teleological orientation extends to the present day. Posner, for example, claims that pragmatism "means looking at problems concretely . . . and above all the insistence that social thought and action be evaluated as instruments to value human goals rather than as ends in themselves."[8] Thomas Grey identifies the two mainstays of pragmatic jurisprudence: First, "juristic thinking is contextual"; and second, "it is instrumental, aiming to make [adjudication] serve human purposes."[9]

It is granted that, on the surface, Bergson could not be allied with this kind of teleological pragmatism. This is for two reasons, which I develop in due course: First, its conception of time is finalistic; and second, it risks judicial voluntarism. But this is not to say that Bergson fails to develop themes that share concerns with, or define a family resemblance to, legal pragmatism, even if they cannot be directly assimilated into it. Using Bergson, I intend to develop a theory of *ontological pragmatism*. What I mean by this is a theory in which time *does* something effective and creative, and in which need and action are radicalized as the condition and criteria for perception and recollection.[10] This places Bergson at once very near and very far to legal pragmatism: near, in that need and desire remain the basis for adjudication, but far, by ridding itself of all voluntarism and by proposing an effective, inventive temporality. But beyond these affinities and differences there is something more important at stake. In developing a pragmatic theory of law with Bergson, we will be able to preserve a central and constitutive insight of legal pragmatism—that adjudication creates law, that it is a creative activity—while simultaneously making it immune to criticisms that say it *recommends* change and promotes activism. Precisely by radicalizing the concepts of need into a theory of memory and perception and by developing a creative ontology of time, we will see that invention is a necessary and constitutive aspect of adjudication, one beyond the question of whether or not it is desirable. In this sense, far from being incompatible with the problems of legal pragmatism, a Bergsonian analysis can appropriately reframe and invigorate these problems through an ontological *and* pragmatic undertaking.

Pure Perception: Image and the Case as Image

In the last chapter, I started to account for why the preface to the English edition of *Difference and Repetition* calls for "a new image of thought" in the context of an argument that denounces the image as inherently dogmatic. There I proposed that Bergson's image of thought ("time is invention or it is nothing at all") meets the qualifications for a nondogmatic image, and I speculated that, perhaps, this opened up the concept of a new image of thought.

But let us now take Paola Marrati's lead and propose that Deleuze's interim work between *Difference and Repetition* (1968) and its English translation (1994), namely, the *Cinema* books (1983, 1985) and *What Is Philosophy* (1991), led him to revisit Bergson's theory of the image and its ontological status.[11] This revaluation of the image, I speculate, provides the second reason as to why and how Deleuze can suggest the possibility for a new image. But before going any further, I must warn that the term *image* is now being used in two very different senses. On the one hand, the image designates the set of presuppositions that orient thought. On the other hand, the concept of the image drawn from Bergson's first chapter of *Matter and Memory* (and worked up by Deleuze's commentaries) *designates the identity of matter and movement*. An explanation of this second sense follows immediately, and, unless explicitly noted, the term *image* is now taken in this second sense. But for the moment I suggest that it may be a combination of these two senses of the image that can account for Deleuze's shift in heralding a new image of thought.

I begin with the concept of the image from *Matter and Memory*. The first chapter of *Matter and Memory* establishes a theory of matter, movement, and perception. Bergson's text opens with a depiction of a universe of pure matter without perception, a world of *present* images and not *represented* images.

All of these [present] images act and react upon one another in all their elementary parts according to constant laws which I call laws of nature, and as a perfect science of these laws would doubtlessly allow us to calculate and to foresee what will happen in each of these images, the future of the images must be contained in their present and will add to them nothing new. (*MM*, 17, translation modified)

With the term *image* Bergson establishes an identity of movement and matter, which is why more conventional terms such as *matter* or *object* won't do. In this universe of images, no body is distinct from, or has added to it, movement; images exist in a state of universal variation and reciprocal action that makes the term *matter*, with its connotations of staticity and inert divisibility, inappropriate. An image, Bergson continues, "act[s] through every one of its points upon all other points of all other images, to transmit the whole of what it receives, to oppose to every action as equal and contrary reaction, to be, in short, merely a road by which pass, in every direction, the modifications propagated throughout the immensity of the universe" (*MM*, 36). In this depiction of a universe of images it is inappropriate to speak of images as discrete objects that could be identified and isolated. Instead, the universe of images is rather like, as Deleuze puts it, "a gaseous state," a field of continuous movement and interaction, each image being a road or passage to transmit the continuous movement of the universe (*C1*, 4). Or, in the fine formulation of *What Is Philosophy*, Bergson's universe of images depicts "the infinite movement of a substance that continually propagates itself" (*WP*, 49).

It is important to notice what Bergson expressly excludes at this early stage of his theory: temporality and subjectivity. In the given citations Bergson uses actively spatial language (points and parts) to depict a pure image—that is, a complete identity of movement and matter in a state of universal variation—as fully present and actual both to itself and, reciprocally, to all other images. So far, the image is unalloyed with perception or time. As I will explain, nothing in this universe is withheld by perception; nor is anything added by duration or by memory. In this whole all is given and time is suppressed in favor of a universal variation that operates according to constant laws.

It is equally significant that Bergson eliminates any concept of subjectivity as either transcendent to or closed off from images, movement, and variation. The subject, its brain and its nervous system, is an image among others.[12] The brain and its so-called representations are not of a different nature than other images, and neither is the universe of images immanent to a transcendent subject (*MM*, 24). At this stage, the subject deserves no special mention because, just like any other image, all it does is receive and execute movement; the subject is simply part of the continuum or road of universal variation. Deleuze doubly appreciates this feature of *Matter and Memory*. First, in *What Is Philosophy* Bergson is honored as the first author since Spinoza to have rigorously, and without compromise to transcendence, constructed a universe (a plane of immanence) not in any way immanent *to* consciousness but the other way around (*WP*, 48–49).[13] Second, given that images exist only within a plane of variation, it is impossible for any particular image—that is, for a subject or consciousness—to close itself off from that variation. "The plane [*plan*] of immanence is the movement (the face of movement) which is established between the parts of each system and between one system and another, which crosses them all, stirs them all up together and subjects them all to the condition which prevents them from being absolutely closed" (*C1*, 59, translation modified). For Deleuze, therefore, this universe of images avoids the dangers of both transcendence (a forteriori, of subjective transcendence) and the isolation of closed sets (a forteriori, of consciousness as a closed set).[14]

If more than one interpreter of Bergson calls this universe of images a "transcendental field without subject," how then do we account for the fact of subjects peopling it, immanent to or within it?[15] For Bergson, within the image universe are "centers of real action," that is, bodies and brains that live, act, and perceive (*MM*, 31). But although inanimate images act and react immediately on one another, living images display a unique capacity for discrimination and hesitation. "My body is, then, in the aggregate of the material world, an image which acts like other images, receiving and giving back movement, *with, perhaps this difference only, that my body appears to choose*, within certain limits, the manner in which it shall restore what it receives" (*MM*, 19, emphasis added). Contrary to images that instantaneously act and react according to invariable laws, living images, especially those with a central nervous system, have a special capacity to delay and to choose their actions and reactions. How does a living image choose its actions? *Pragmatically*, according to "greater or lesser advantage" derived from that action, that is, what we need to survive in a situation (*MM*, 20). And so, thanks to the unique function of a certain image (my body and the nervous system) that permits hesitation, deliberation, and pragmatic action, Bergson can reintroduce the subject without recourse to transcendent or transcendental subjectivity, or to a difference of nature between living and other nonliving images. No longer bound to the subject as it is from Kant on, now the universe of images is the presupposed milieu for the activity and experience of any particular image. "A transcendental field without subject" does not preclude the appearance of living images that organize a world according to the requirements of action; it states only that far from appearing through a subjective transcendental horizon, an acentered universe of images is the presupposed condition for any living image, for their actions and their representations. Consciousness is a property of the world, not the other way around.

It now becomes clearer how Bergson's concept of the image furnishes the conditions for a new image of thought. An image in the earlier sense indicates the presuppositions that are the condition of thought. These can be dogmatic and opinion ridden; or as in Bergson, they can be devoted to an untimely thought of novelty impossible to recuperate into *doxa*. Now, the second sense of the image operates much like the first; it too is the condition for all thought. But this time, the image is Bergson's concept for a moving universe that, here and there, gives rise to centers of action with a unique capacity for delayed action. Consciousness is nothing more than that. As such, the image and the universe of images is irreducible to consciousness; in fact, it is consciousness that requires the universe as its condition of existence and exercise (and not just for the trite reason that consciousness needs a world of images in which to live and think, but because consciousness *is* itself an image). Just as philosophy requires the prephilosophical (image in the first sense) as its condition, so does consciousness require an unconscious universe (image in the second sense) as its condition. Or, just as philosophy is itself *also* the nonphilosophical, so is consciousness itself *also* the unconscious.

No doubt, the two senses of the image are vastly different, to the point that it may seem like a coincidence that they both share the same term. Moreover, Deleuze gives no direct indication that this second sense of the image has anything to do with his own concept of the image of thought. Nevertheless, the two function in parallel insofar as both emphasize that thought or consciousness gets its start from an unthought or unconsciousness that remains irreducible to it. They coincide, in other words, in the insight that there is always an outside to thought, *which is its very condition*. An image of thought, we recall, is dogmatic if and when it suppresses the outside. Certainly, it too has a constitutive outside (a prephilosophical image); but unfortunately its outside is opinion, which perversely works to undermine the outside as if it were a mere function of thought; that is, it works to reduce the outside to something that appears only for thought and that thought recognizes. Bergson, by contrast, could provide Deleuze with a model for a new image of thought insofar as he simultaneously affirms an image of thought committed to the upsurge of novelty in time *and* holds that consciousness not only arises from a universe of images but is itself an image.

Returning to *Matter and Memory*, I said that the thesis of a transcendental field without subject is a reversal of Kant: Images appear not by virtue of a transcendental consciousness but instead consciousness appears only by virtue of a transcendental field. But this thesis is only the first reversal of Kant in the first chapter of *Matter and Memory*. The second, on the question of perception, brings us directly to law and the case. Bergson's theory of perception is radically pragmatist—we perceive only what we need according to the exigencies of action.

> Images must display in some way, on the aspect they present to my body, the profit which my body can gain from them [*sur la face qu'elles tournent vers mon corps, le parti que mon corps pourrait tirer d'elles*]. . . . [Images] send back, then, to my body, as would a mirror, its eventual influence. . . . *The objects which surround my body reflect its possible action upon them.* (MM, 20, 21)

In Bergson's initial presentation, images are totally and fully present; they do not reserve themselves and, in fact, every part and point of every image interacts with every other image in the universe. Whether rhetorical or not, Bergson says that the perception of an atom is "infinitely greater and more complex than ours" given that this "point gathers and transmits the influences of all the points of the material universe" (*MM*, 38). To perceive something completely would be to "descend to the condition of a material object," an impossible demand (*MM*, 49). In comparison, our own perception—that is, perception by any living image—is thin and poor. It reflects and isolates only those aspects of an image that interest potential action. But an image reflected by a (living) image is exactly what Bergson calls a perception. *What makes up perception is nothing other than our potential action as it is prefigured and reflected in those images we can use.* Because our nervous system is only an instrument of analysis with respect to movements received and an instrument of selection with respect to movements executed, we can only perceive potential movements; or, changing the phrase, we do not perceive for any speculative reason but rather to receive and execute movements, to act and to survive. In operating according to these exigencies, pragmatic human perception isolates interests, and, in this act, images are perceived.[16] The perceived image indicates "that part of external matter which has been carved out as an object for the purpose of our action."[17]

This is to say that perception is *subtractive*. For Bergson a perceived image is always *less than*, and never *other than* or *more than* the image in itself. If the represented image were other than (of a different nature) the image in itself, we would encounter intractable and empty problems of schematism and mind-world correspondence; equally, if a represented image had more to it than the image in itself, we would be forced to return to the "mysterious" thesis that, instead of screening movements, the mind produces representations said to correspond to and exceed things (*MM*, 35). Bergson rejects both options and holds that between images in themselves and our representations of them is "merely a difference of degree, and not of kind" (*MM*, 37). In perceiving, we take away from the image everything in which we are uninterested; images "abandon something of themselves" in being perceived (*MM*, 37; also *B*, 52).

According to Deleuze, Bergson establishes a double system of reference for images. "There is firstly a system in which each image varies for itself, and all the images act and react as a function of each other, on all their facets and in all their parts. But to this is added another system where all vary principally for a single one, which receives the action of other images on one of its facets and reacts to them on another facet" (*C1*, 62; see *MM*, 22, 76). Thus the image and the perception of the image are one and the same thing, and if there is dualism here, it is merely one of detail and degree. On the one hand, images in themselves act and react according to their parts and capacities. With this thesis, Bergson discovers a whole reality of images that exceeds the conditions of natural perception (*C1*, 2). And on the other hand, a living image perceives by eliminating whatever does not interest it. With this thesis, Bergson rejects the Kantian difference in kind between represented and unrepresented images and restores faith in the common sense that the images we perceive are of a kind with those images themselves (*MM*, 10, 17).

Turning to law, we see that the case is an image in the Bergsonian sense in that it underlies and exceeds its representations. What is the most basic activity of any judge or lawyer? Is it not to select a few relevant points of a case and coordinate these into arguments and judgments? Any case has an infinity of points and sides that go neglected, facts irrelevant to the interest at hand that exceed its eventual legal construction. Here, we can draw a distinction between a case as it is not yet represented, as it is a pure event or image in the world, and a legal case as it is pragmatically perceived, as it is reflected according to interests. Any case, therefore, has an infinity of sides and points available for selection; this selection will yield a legal case with a set of finite features. The perception of a case—that is, its representation as a legal case—is limiting and subtractive; *only certain crucial points* are advanced and construed into legal argument, but underlying these points is the case in itself, unperceived, or giving to perception that part that interests the perceiving parties. Any good judge or lawyer knows this. "There is a constant need to separate the accidental and the non-essential from the essential and inherent" (*NJP*, 116–117). Or, as Llewellyn put it:

> What is the relation of this statement of "the facts" to the *brute raw events* which happened long before? What is left in men's minds as to those raw events has been canvassed, more or less thoroughly, more or less skillfully, by two lawyers. *But canvassed through the screen of what they consider legally relevant*, and of what each considered legally relevant to win his case. It has then been screened again in the trial court through the rules about what evidence can be admitted. The jury has then reached its conclusion, which—for purposes of the dispute—determines contested matters for one side. The two lawyers have again [at the appellate level] sifted—this time solely from the record of the trial—what seemed to bear on point upon appeal. Finally, with a decision already made, the judge has sifted through these "facts" again, and picked a few which he puts forward as essential—and whose legal bearing he then proceeds to expound. It should be obvious that we may be miles away from the case.[18]

Llewellyn's point may be that the further along the legal process we go, the more distance we put between the origin of the case in its raw state and the case considered at law. But Llewellyn also marvelously demonstrates the pragmatic process of perception as it applies to law. Something happens in the world, a case as raw event, and this event—this image—is subsequently apprehended and represented according to interest, that is, according to what is legally important and relevant. This makes it a case at law, a legal case. The legal case is constituted through a process that drops and subtracts everything except for a few salient aspects. And this process is repeated over and over. Each different judicial level sifts different points from that event according to interests that change (e.g., what is considered legally relevant by the lawyers at the trial level might be different at the appellate stage). The universe of case images is a transcendental field without subject, for courts and lawyers and judges presuppose these events and are themselves established only from within them as living images that mirror back an impoverished but usable reflection. And, extending this point, the case in itself always exceeds natural or pragmatic perception. Its facets and features surpass representation but nevertheless remain revisitable for subsequent (appellate or retrial) perceptions.

A famous case of Cardozo's—"perhaps the most famous case in the history of tort law"[19]—exemplifies this conversion of the pure image case into a perceived legal case. Strictly speaking, any case would do, but *Palsgraf v. Long Island Railroad Co.* (1928) is especially illuminating because Richard Posner took it up in his study on Cardozo and provided a supplementary account of the facts, facts that Cardozo is said to have underplayed or simply ignored. Here is Cardozo's summary:

Plaintiff [Helen Palsgraf] was standing on a platform of defendant's [Long Island Railroad Company] railroad after buying a ticket to go to Rockaway Beach. A train stopped at the station, bound for another place. Two men ran forward to catch it. One of the men reached the platform of the car without mishap, though the train was already moving. The other man, carrying a package, jumped aboard the car, but seemed unsteady as if about to fall. A guard on the car, who held the door open, reached forward to help him in, and another guard on the platform pushed him from behind. In this act, the package was dislodged, and fell upon the rails. It was a package of small size, about fifteen inches long, and was covered by a newspaper. In fact it contained fireworks, but there was nothing in its appearance to give notice of its contents. The fireworks when they fell exploded. The shock of the explosion threw down some scales at the other end of the platform, many feet away. The scales struck the plaintiff, causing injuries for which she sues.[20]

This case, like any case, embodies a set of features. In this description we have a perceived case: Cardozo isolates and identifies certain points and parts of an event within a represented image, *Palsgraf*. In other words,

Cardozo's perception of the case is limited to these features and no more. But why these features? What principle guides Cardozo's judgment? What principle determines precisely which points and parts of the case are perceived, reflected, and represented?

The novel principle advanced in *Palsgraf*—one that substantially influenced negligence and tort law—is liability based on external standards of foreseeability. A wrong is actionable if a reasonable person could have foreseen it. Helen Palsgraf lost her case because the railroad company could not be reasonably expected to have foreseen that the package was dangerous; hence the conduct of its employees was not negligent. "If the harm was not willful, [the plaintiff] must show that the act as to him had possibilities of danger so many and apparent as to entitle him to be protected against the doing of it though the harm was unintended."[21] So, the only set of facts relevant to Cardozo—the only facts that can be relevantly perceived according to this principle—is how the package looked to the guards helping the person onto the train. Because this package in no way looked dangerous—it was small, only fifteen inches, anonymously wrapped—nothing else in the facts of the case need be considered. Where Mrs. Palsgraf was standing in relation to the accident or the magnitude of the blast matters as little as, for example, the weather or time of day.

It is instructive to compare Cardozo's principle with the one it overturned, as represented by the original trial and also by Justice Andrews's dissenting judgment. At the time of *Palsgraf*, the standard principle in such cases was to "ask first whether the defendant had been negligent and second whether, if so, that negligence had been the *'proximate cause'* of the plaintiff's injury."[22] The principle of proximate cause is a kind of rough justice, where liability is upheld if the plaintiff is directly affected by the defendant's actions.[23] Mrs. Palsgraf had won $6,000 in her initial trial on that basis. Her injuries were said to have been within proximity of the accident. If proximate cause is the principle by which the case is to be adjudicated, many facts that Cardozo does not relate spring into consideration, such as the force of the blast and Mrs. Palsgraf's location. Moreover, there are many facts to which Cardozo seems oblivious and yet are reported in the briefs.[24] For instance, it is not certain whether it was the blast or the panicked crowd that caused the scales to topple onto the plaintiff. Moreover, contrary to what Cardozo reports, Mrs. Palsgraf is not suing because of the impact of the scales but because the shock of the event led her to develop a serious stammer and eventually to go mute. Obviously, these facts are of enormous importance if the proximate cause principle is used, and they will not go unperceived and unreported. The case in itself has all these other features (plus an indefinite number more), which, if the principle guiding the investigation is different, get noticed and become perceptible and relevant. The fact is that for Cardozo all this is irrelevant; all that matters is how the package looked and whether the guards could have been expected to know it was dangerous.

What is the advantage of appreciating the case as an image and the legal case as a represented image? It is that prima facie judges and lawyers can no longer be suspected of misreporting or neglecting the facts of the case. In short, we protect pragmatism from both its critics and its devotees. Posner, for example, is full of admiration for Cardozo's rhetorical technique, praise that he admits "cannot be taken as wholly complimentary in evaluating a judicial opinion, for one element of the technique is the selection of facts with a freedom bordering on that of a novelist or a short-story writer, and another is outright fictionalizing."[25] But if we admit Bergson's pragmatic theory of images, action, and perception, we cannot level Posner's compliment at Cardozo or any other judge or lawyer. Cardozo's actions are not rhetorically clever, only pragmatically necessary at the level of perception, for what is criticizable is only the merit of the principle. To the extent that this principle performs a selection of relevant features of the case, it is neither good nor bad but unavoidable. The judge, just like any living image, exists in a universe of images and can only represent these by eliminating and subtracting the extraneous according to a criterion of interest.

The Pure Past and the Four Paradoxes of Time

In the last section, I isolated Bergson's theory of pure perception and introduced its relevance for law. But this theory remains incomplete: ontologically, psychologically, and juridically. First, this theory of pure perception does not yet address the ontology of time; second, it does not treat the question of memory in psychological experience, and third, it does not confront the problem of the use of rules in adjudication. To remedy these shortcomings and, most important, to prepare my theory of jurisprudence, I now turn to the problem of time in Bergson and Deleuze.

In *Matter and Memory*, Bergson admits that his theory of pure perception is principally heuristic and "exists in theory rather than in fact," for it describes a being immersed in the present at the exclusion of "every form of memory" (*MM*, 34). In truth, any perception involves two operations of memory. On the one hand, no living image can obtain an instantaneous perception, for perception *contracts* a multiplicity of moments "so as to grasp them in one relatively simple intuition" (*MM*, 69). In the perception of matter, for example, a living image contracts together "an enormous multiplicity of [molecular] vibrations which appear to us all at once, although they are successive" (*MM*, 70, also 34, 82; *CE*, 301). On the other hand, perception always calls forth a recollection suitable to treat and know what to do with it. Here too perception involves an act of memory. In short, perception involves "memory [*mémoire*] in these two forms, covering as it does with a cloak of recollections [*souvenirs*] a core of immediate perception, and also contracting a multiplicity of moments" (*MM*, 34, translation modified).

The awareness that perception simultaneously involves a relationship to memory and time leads us into the most complex sections of both Bergson and Deleuze. As testimony to both the difficulty and richness of the third chapter of *Matter and Memory*, Deleuze multiplied his own commentaries over the course of twenty years.[26] In what follows I draw chiefly on Deleuze's highly economical account of Bergson's four paradoxes of time in *Difference and Repetition*:[27] (1) contemporaneity of the past and the present, (2) coexistence of all the past with the present, (3) preexistence of the past, and (4) repetition in the past. Together, these paradoxes work to create a concept that Bergson calls the pure past, or what Deleuze calls the virtual past.

This concept of the pure or virtual past—created, among other reasons, to account for both the passing of time and for the use of the past in recollection and perception—will prove fundamental to my theory of judgment. In a nutshell, I claim, first, that judgments are composites of perception and memory; second, that in order to explain how a case is joined to rules, we need recourse to the concept of the virtual or pure past of law; and third, that the two ways to connect a case to rules (or, as we will see, to connect a perceived case to the pure past of law) explain why judgments sometimes seem as though they are subsumptive and why judgments are sometimes creative. To arrive at these conclusions, we need a sustained analysis of the four paradoxes of time; and, given their complexity, my immediate account will not make reference to law. In the conclusion to this chapter I do, however, begin to consider the pure past in relation to a Bergsonian pragmatic theory of adjudication.

Paradox 1: Contemporaneity of the Past and the Present

The negative point on which all these paradoxes insist is the inadequacy of a chronological interpretation of time. Or rather, they state that if time appears to be chronological, it is due to a different and more profound temporal operation. My presentation of the first paradox stresses this negative point.

I have said that for Bergson the present is constituted by a contraction of external moments, or as he puts it, of vibrations. On several occasions, Bergson emphasizes that perception never defines or takes place within a purely present instantaneity—that is, a moment of time that is strictly and only present. Instead, perception contracts together an infinity of infinitesimally distinct moments to constitute a present perception (e.g., a color). As Bergson says, "What you are considering is the concrete present such as it is actually lived by consciousness, we may say that this present consists, in large measure, in the immediate past" (*MM*, 150). By virtue of contraction, therefore, the past exists alongside the present. Were it not for this contractive quality, our present would not be experienced as continuous (as *durée*) but would instead be a series of disconnected instants.

But immediately we encounter a problem and a paradox. The problem is, How is it that the present flows? How is one present replaced by another? Or, how does the present pass? What is implied in saying that the present passes? The solution is a paradox: For the present to pass—for there to be a continuity of time rather than a series of juxtaposed and infinitely decomposable present instants—Deleuze argues that the present must be "past 'at the same time' as it has been present" (*DR*, 81, translation modified). To account for the passing present, in other words, we must posit a contemporaneity of the present and the past; the past and present must occur at the same time.

What is so puzzling about the passing present is that it reveals a temporal constitution of time—"to constitute time while passing in the time constituted" (*DR*, 79). The fact that the present passes—that it is never entirely present but is always also past—requires for its possibility and explanation "*another time* in which it can occur" (*DR*, 79). We will see that this other time is the *past*; it is the past that makes "the present pass," and therefore it is the past "which must be considered the ground [*fondement*] of time" (*DR*, 79). The past is that time in which, or by virtue of which, the present can take place and pass. But we must take care to recognize that the past can no longer designate a series or sequence of former presents; it does not indicate something chronologically "after" the present. This interpretation is disqualified because the past is simultaneous with the present; it is not past in a chronological sense. No, as Deleuze explains in *Bergsonism*:

> *The past and the present do not designate two successive moments but two elements which coexist*, one of which is the present, which does not cease to pass, the other of which is the past, which does not cease to be but through which all presents pass. It is in this sense that there is a *pure past*, a sort of "past in general": the past does not follow the present, but on the contrary is presupposed by it as the pure condition without which it would not pass. (*B*, 59, emphasis added, translation modified)

As contemporaneous, the present is at once past, and, vice versa, the past does not wait to pass but is immediately and now past. In the next paradox I explain why the past and present differ as two elements. For now, I stick to the negative point: The problem of the passing present forces us to reject a chronological conception of time. Certainly, there is no denying a chronological succession between the present and former presents that have passed; Deleuze's point, however, is that only the contemporaneity of present and past can account for the manifest chronology of passing presents. In response, therefore, to the problem of the passing present, Bergson and Deleuze create the concept of the pure or virtual past that functions as a ground of time, that is, as the grounding of the present by the past. As we will see, the pure past is a time "in which" the present can take place and pass.

Paradox 2: Coexistence of All the Past with the Present

Why does Deleuze say that the past and present differ in kind as two elements? Because if we suppose that past and present differ merely by degree, then we face intractable problems of ontology and psychology. This point is made apparent in the associationist psychology that Bergson attacks in *Matter and Memory*. For associationism, as for everyday psychological consciousness, the past is constituted *after* the present and appears to consciousness as a less vivid impression of a present perception. Thus a *chronological* difference of degree between past and present (the past as "earlier" than the present) introduces a difference of degree between perception and recollection (recollections are weakened perceptions). For Bergson this is suspect on two counts. First, as we have seen, chronological difference cannot account for the passing of the present; and second, if memories are merely faded impressions, it is impossible to see how or why a present perception should attract them (*MM*, 67, 164). Therefore to suppose a mere difference of degree between past and present vitiates an account of both temporality and memory.

Instead of a difference of degree, Bergson and Deleuze conclude that present and past are two coexisting elements that differ in kind. In fact, between the two lies an *ontological difference*: The present *becomes*, whereas the past *is*. The criteria used to establish this difference is pragmatist and not chronological: The present is that which is useful and active; the past is that which is useless and inactive. And, as they coexist, one no longer comes after the other.

What is the fundamental characteristic of the present? It is always passing and in a constant state of becoming. Why? Because in the present, all images are *actual*, *active*, and *useful to* one another. This is clearly shown in the universe of images from the first chapter of *Matter and Memory*. First, a present image is fully actual in that all its points are made available to, and interact with, all other points of the universe. Images are actual insofar as they cannot help but affect other images, and likewise, they cannot hide from being affected by other images. Second, a present image is active in that it acts on and reacts to all other images. By virtue of this activity, a single present image is in a constant state of individual variation; and, taken altogether, the images constitute a plane of immanence that is itself a state of universal variation. Third, a present image is useful in that it is available for perception and can be acted on by other living images. Given these characteristics of the present image—actual, active, useful—we are led to conclude that the present is never able to subsist and is always outside itself; it is, as Deleuze puts it, a "pure becoming" (*B*, 55). This reverses, Bergson argues, our ontological expectations or predications. "You define the present in an arbitrary manner as *that which is*, whereas the present is simply *that which is being made*" (*MM*, 150). Pragmatically defined by its actuality, activity, and usefulness, the present indicates a becoming or flux always in the process of being made.

The *past*, by contrast, is not "present." It is neither actual, useful, nor variable. This is not to say, however, that the past has ceased to *be*.

> Useless and inactive, impassive, it IS, in the full sense of the word: it is identical [*il se confond*] with being in itself. It should not be said that it "was," since it is the in-itself of being, and the form under which being is preserved in itself (in opposition to the present, the form under which being is consummated and places itself outside of itself). At the limit, the ordinary determinations are reversed: of the present, we must say at every instant that it "was," and of the past, that it "is," that it is eternally, for all time. This is the difference in kind between the past and the present. (*B*, 55)[28]

Again, on pragmatic grounds Bergson and Deleuze reverse the ontological determinations usually associated with the past and the present. By virtue of being useful and actual, the present is always in the process of passing and becoming; and by virtue of being useless and inactive, the past remains what it is.[29] The past is real and it exists; unlike the present, however, it is not actual. Once the temporal difference is no longer characterized by chronological degree, past and present become distinct elements both equally present (chronologically speaking) but ontologically distinct on the basis of use and uselessness. In other words, the inactive and impassive (pure) past *coexists with* the active and actual present.

This paradox follows the first and shifts the emphasis. Whereas the negative point of the contemporaneity paradox was to show that the difference between past and present is not chronological, the paradox of coexistence asserts a positive ontological difference between a past and a present that coexist. We need no longer take refuge in psychological explanations that identify the past as a weakened or past present, for the past has a being all its own, one that remains outside a present redefined as actual, useful, and active. And because the past has its own proper register of being—impassive and subsisting—we appreciate it as simultaneously coexisting with a present from which it differs in kind. In speaking of the past, we cannot say "it was," only it "no longer exists," or rather it is no longer actual from the perspective of the action-oriented present and its actual images (*DR*, 82). Or, as Bergson says, from the vantage of psychological consciousness the pure past is "unconscious," that is, not present as an actual and usable image in the service of action; but this is not to say that because the past has ceased to be conscious, it has, as associationism would have it, ceased to be or degraded its being (*MM*, 141). For Deleuze's part, he never tires of citing Proust's exemplary formulation of the pure past as "real without being present, ideal without being abstract" (*PS*, 58; *B*, 96; *DR*, 208; *TP*, 94)[30]—which is to say that the past has its own proper ontological reality that fully coexists with, without being actualized in, the present.

What, according to Bergson, is the payoff of this complex ontology of the past and passing present? It is to provide us with a theory of recollection and memory that avoids the intractable problems of associationism. Ignoring the pure or virtual dimension of the past and its difference in kind from the present, associationism situates itself entirely in the actual present and "attempts to discover in a realized and present state the mark of its past origin," which can only be a distance of degree or magnitude between the vivid present perception and a distant similar memory (*MM*, 135).[31] Stuck in a chronological imagination of time and a psychological imagination of memory, associationism can neither explain what the relationship between past and present consists in beyond a misguided chronological succession, nor can it help us to understand why a particular memory is sought and what use it could be to the present if it is merely a faded doubling of the present.

With what does Bergson propose to replace the discredited associationist theory of memory? First of all, he establishes a difference of kind between (present, actual) perception and (pure, virtual) memory such that we are prevented from reducing both to a single genre of stronger or fainter representations. But this is certainly not to say that the two do not positively and continuously interact. Perception always calls up (or actualizes) useful recollections from the past to aid action; as such, perception is always alloyed with recollection. Although recollections can be either of a motor-habit nature (e.g., orienting oneself in a room, singing a familiar song) or of an intellectual nature (e.g., remembering specific instructions for a task), what is common to both is that they are searched for, and brought forth from, the past. Again, this past is not a former present but a coexisting reality in which recollections have a pure or virtual existence. As Deleuze puts it, "It is with respect to the pure element of the past, understood as the past in general, as an *a priori* past, that a given former present is reproducible and the actual present [*l'actuel présent*] is able to reflect itself. Far from being derived from the present or from representation, the past is presupposed by every representation" (*DR*, 81, translation modified).[32] Only from within the pure past can a chronologically former present be reproduced within the actual present. The pure past is the element in which we focus on a particular former present; it is the element from which we extricate and actualize a specific recollection within the present. We can call this the "actualization of the virtual": Present perception seeks out a recollection in the pure or virtual past, and, in so doing, the recollection is made actual within the current problems of action it was called on to help solve. At no time does the recollection alter its chronological temporality, for past and present are contemporaneous (paradox 1) and coexist (paradox 2); what has changed is the mode of being, from virtual to actual existence (*MM*, 140).

Paradox 3: The Preexistence of the Pure Past

I can now clarify the positive sense of what could only be put negatively in the first paradox: the passing of the present and the past as the ground of time. According to the second paradox, it is the whole virtual past—*all* of the past—that coexists with the actual present. As Bergson says in *Creative Evolution*, the past in its entirety "follows us at every instant," but, because it is virtual, we remain unaware of it except for "the two or three recollections that in some way complete our actual situation [*situation actuelle*]" (*CE*, 5, 167, translation modified). But regardless of our conscious awareness of the past, the present situation always actualizes some particular element (or recollection, in terms of psychic life) sought from a coexistent virtual dimension. It is precisely this process of actualizing and inserting the past into the present that produces a chronological continuity between former presents and the present present. As Deleuze says, "It is right to define duration as a succession, but wrong to insist on it; it is, in effect, *a real succession only because it is virtual coexistence.*"[33] The present solicits its coexistent pure past in order to actualize a former present and to establish a chronological continuity. In this capacity, the virtual past is the *ground of time* in which, or by virtue of which, the present chronologically passes.

According to Deleuze, in its role as the ground of time, the pure past is nothing other than the "transcendental" condition of the present and of its passing (*DR*, 81). This is a bold identification that we must inspect, especially given that since Kant transcendental argumentation had to be preserved and kept separate from ontology.[34]

What, broadly speaking, is the main qualification for a transcendental argument? To provide the conditions of experience while not being of experience. The pure past satisfies this requirement to the letter. On the one hand, the pure past is the condition of the present and its passing. The pure past is, I have argued, the ground and condition for the actual present. And, given that the actual present is the only time in which all images exist, it is safe to say that the pure past is the condition of experience. On the other hand, Deleuze defines the pure past as a priori, that is, as separate from experience (*DR*, 81). And later, Deleuze calls the virtual past "a past which was never present" (*DR*, 83). These last two identifications—as a priori and as never present—bring us to the paradox of preexistence. The paradox is, How could the past, which we think has already happened, ever be a priori? How could the past, which we think of as having passed, have remained outside experience?

Yet these identifications are perfectly consistent with the concept of the pure past; insofar as it is virtual, the past is never actualized within the present. We never experience the virtual past per se (at best, maybe, we glimpse a "morsel of time in the pure state" [*PS*, 61; *C2*, 82]) but only its actualized recollection; as such, its designation as a priori, as distinct from actual experience, is appropriate. In its role as the ground of time, "the past does not make one present pass without calling forth another, *but itself neither passes nor comes forth*"—it remains purely virtual, outside experience, and therefore a priori (*DR*, 82, emphasis added, translation modified). Indeed, the pure past can serve as the transcendental condition for the actual present only insofar as it preserves itself, in a full and impassive ontological purity, alongside the actual. The virtual past is therefore a past that preexists—again, not in a chronological sense—as outside, yet is coexistent with, the actualized present. The pure past "posed as already-there, presupposed by the passing present and making it pass . . . there is thus a substantial temporal element (the Past which was never present) playing the role of ground [*fondement*]" (*DR*, 82, translation modified). The virtual past that was never present is therefore the transcendental or preexistent ground for perception, experience, and the passing of time.

The first three paradoxes, to round up the discussion, are three modes or expressions of the relationship between the actual and the virtual. One reason that Deleuze's account is so complex and provocative is that he uses temporal language (e.g., *pass, past, present*) to criticize and demonstrate the inadequacy of a chronological understanding of temporality. Thus *contemporaneity* stresses the simultaneity of past and present in contrast to chronological succession to explain the passing of time; *coexistence* replaces a chronological difference in degree with an ontological difference between a virtual past and an actual present to account for memory and recollection; and *preexistence* postulates that the past is not anterior and a posteriori but is instead the a priori and transcendental condition for a present that actualizes its continuity with the past.

Paradox 4: Repetition in the Pure Past

The last paradox departs slightly from the deep coherence of the previous three, and, in fact, Deleuze introduces it parenthetically near the end of his discussion of the paradoxes of time (*DR*, 83). But because it is central to my discussion of law, it is best to introduce it in and of itself.

As we have seen, living images actualize recollections to aid perceptions. The pure past has nothing to do with a mysterious dual or parallel world; instead, living images actualize and insert recollections drawn from the past into their actions and problems. Now, different situations call for different types of recollections with varying degrees of specificity. Bergson provides us with the following example:

A word from a foreign language, uttered in my hearing, may make me think of that language in general or of a voice which once pronounced it a certain way. These two associations by similarity are not due to the accidental arrival of two different representations. . . . They answer to two different mental *dispositions*, to two distinct degrees of tension of the memory; in the latter case they are nearer to the pure image, in the former, they are more disposed toward immediate response, that is to say, to action. (*MM*, 169)

What Bergson intimates here, and I will have greater occasion to discuss this, is that the whole of the past that coexists with the present also coexists with itself in different degrees of generality (contraction) and

136   *The Image of Law*

specificity (relaxation). This is the sense of Bergson's famous cone of time (Figure 1). Given the second paradox of time, it is *all* of the past, as a *total virtual past*, that coexists with the actual present. But because different situations can call for a different specificity of recollection—for example, must I only remember the language, or must I remember a specific occasion of having heard it?—Bergson postulates that the virtual past is repeated in its entirety at different degrees of tension.

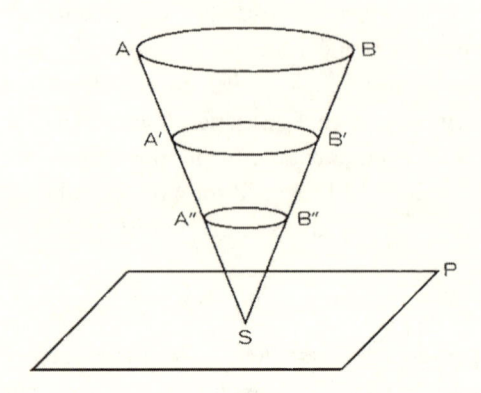

FIGURE 1. The cone of time

With reference to Figure 1, the inverted cone represents the virtual past, point S represents the present perception, and box P represents the plane of images available for perception. This figure shows, first, that the pure past coexists alongside the present and, second, that an actualized recollection is inserted into point S. But especially relevant with respect to the fourth paradox are the sections crossing the cone: AB, AB', AB", and so on. These sections do not represent a partial slice or portion of the past; rather, they indicate a particular state of tension at which the *entire* virtual past is contracted. Each section, therefore, differentially contracts *all of the pure past*. According to the variable exigencies of our needs at point S, we seek out a particular section or tension. Corresponding to the situation at hand, we choose the level (and the recollection therein) appropriate to our need and to our disposition: "Everything happens, then, as though our recollections were repeated an indefinite number of times in these many possible reductions of our past life. They take a more common [*banale*] form when memory tightens up, more personal when it dilates" (*MM*, 169, translation modified). This final paradox Deleuze calls ontological repetition: The pure past is repeated in an infinity of varying tensions such that a living image actualizes a recollection from a particular level based on the degree of specificity it requires (*DR*, 293). Summarizing all the paradoxes, Deleuze writes that the pure past "is constituted by the relations of virtual coexistence between the levels of a pure past, each present being no more than the actualization or representation of one of these levels" (*DR*, 83). Each present actualizes a level of the virtual whole characterized by a specific tension, and by virtue of this activity the present continually passes and virtual memories are made usable by present actuality.

Two Weak Points of Legal Pragmatism

In the introduction to this chapter, I proposed to use Bergson toward a theory of law, that, despite its distance from the mainstream tradition, calls itself pragmatist. Given this identification, I should ask for the pragmatic or cash value of the pure past for law. To this end, I examine two counts on which American legal pragmatism is on shaky ground: *gaps in law* and *time in law*. In so doing, I hope to use Bergson's theory of time to rescue central insights of legal pragmatism, securing these from their critics and devotees alike.

Gaps in Law

A favorite phrase of Holmes's describes the judge as an interstitial legislator: "I recognize without hesitation that judges must and do legislate, but they do so only interstitially; they are confined from molar to molecular motions."[35] Here molecular motions do not imply Deleuze's deterritorialization or continuous multiplicity; instead, as Cardozo comments, it means that judgment moves "untrammeled" in the gaps of the history of law, in areas where no prior judgment has yet been given (*NJP*, 134). Acknowledging that "the limits for the judge are narrower" than those for the legislator, Cardozo nevertheless insists that the judge "fills the open space in the law . . . [and] within the confines of these open spaces and those of precedent and tradition, choice moves with a freedom which stamps its action as creative. The law which is the resulting product is not found, but made" (*NJP*, 154–155). Today, too, legal pragmatism upholds the rights of privileges of the gap, with Posner arguing that

American judges are compelled to exert a gap-filling role given that the legislative machinery is slow and decentralized.[36] And what criterion, we might ask, guides the filling in of these gaps? "Social Welfare," a teleological standard sensitive to social needs and desires, adjudicates the hitherto ruleless case (*NJP*, 135).

On account of this theory of gaps, pragmatism has come under severe and, to my mind, justified criticism by conservatives. Scalia says:

> The common law grew in a peculiar fashion—rather like a Scrabble board. No rule of decision previously announced could be *erased*, but qualifications could be *added* to it. The first case lays on the board: "No liability for breach of contractual duty without privity"; the next player adds "unless injured party is member of household." And the game continues. This system of making law by judicial opinion, and making law by distinguishing earlier cases, is what every American law student, every newborn American lawyer, first sees when he opens his eyes. And this impression remains for life. His image of the great judge—the Holmes, the Cardozo—is the man (or woman) who has the intelligence to discern the best rule of law for the case at hand and then the skill to perform the broken-field running through earlier cases that leaves him free to impose that rule: distinguishing one prior case on the left, straight-arming another one on the right, high-stepping away from another precedent about to tackle him from the rear, until (bravo!) he reaches the goal—good law.[37]

Scalia's point is that a theory of gaps—endemic, he finds, to common as opposed to statutory law and exaggerated into a virtue by legal pragmatism and realism—is dangerously discretionary and decisionistic. Every case is unique and can always be distinguished from prior rules. If the judge is so disposed, a gap may always be opened and an interstice may always be made in order to adopt an illegitimate role, that of a lawgiver. If in an interview Justice Breyer can joke that searching for a precedent is like a cocktail party, in that "you look for your friends," cannot the same be said for a judicial mind-set that seeks some solitude, a bit of space to decide without guidance?[38] To allow for gaps in the common law is to admit a judicial "mind-set that asks, 'What is the most desirable resolution of this case and how can any impediments to the achievement of that result be evaded?'"[39] Pragmatic adjudication and its gaps, therefore, have the potential to enable judicial creativity in the pejorative and activist sense of the term; a judge can throw his or her hands in the air, say that there is no rule to cover this case, and invent one on the basis of what is deemed socially desirable.

Time in Law

Pragmatism is also compromised by its lack of a theory of time with respect to law and adjudication. To my knowledge, there is no pragmatist work directly on time with respect to adjudication. Indeed, there is little on the subject of time in legal theory generally. Rebecca French has recently made a survey of the concept of time in various disciplinary bodies of literature and considered their application to law.[40] Although French does not call herself a pragmatist, there are clues in her work to warrant such identification. Her article adopts a scattershot approach and surveys five different modes of time—eternal, cyclical, industrial, social, and saturated—and suggests that each mode finds a place and use in contemporary law.[41] Where French turns pragmatist is in her argument that these forms of time occasionally compete with one another and deserve explicit consideration to determine which one best represents the contemporary situation. For example, she identifies originalism (e.g., by Justices Bork and Burger and, in this respect, Scalia) as an attempt to "harken back to and compare a previous time when law was done correctly." Efforts like this, she argues, are out of step with our speeded-up and saturated times, such that we ought to demand for law and adjudication a "shift from conceptualizing time as a stable constant to the current cultural perception of time as a rapidly evolving, erratic, engine of constant change."[42] And so, she concludes her article on a pragmatic note, recommending one kind of temporality over another. "It is imperative that we, as academics and practitioners, critically reflect on our approach to legal time. This might involve consciously *promoting new ideas over traditional ones* and moving away from dualistic reasoning patterns, particularly the bipolar model currently employed by social and legal theorists."[43] French explicitly links the creation of new juridical ideas with an underlying temporality favorable to their emergence.

This conclusion is in its way perfectly pragmatist. One kind of time (dynamic) is preferred and recommended over another kind of time (traditional) as more indicative of our situation and hence desirable. Accordingly, we should be able to select the kind of time that should underlie adjudication—whether, say, it should promote original or living interpretations of the Constitution. But the trouble with this is that it lacks necessity; in other words, French's version of pragmatism is vulnerable because her concept of time is empirical, hence revocable. For French, time is empirically determined; it is something of a "social construction" open to debate, change, and contestation.[44] If time is indeed a product of social formation, then nothing in principle prevents a call for an eternal, static temporality to underlie adjudication, however unlikely its empirical realization and however distant its correspondence to our contemporary state of affairs. Because French does not establish a temporality necessary to law as either transcendental or ontological, and instead grounds her conception of time squarely within the empirical as socially constructed, her recommendation for a particular temporality in law is contestable precisely on her own grounds: preference and desirability. As such, this theory remains stuck in stalemate with conservatives who advance alternative determinations of time through different criteria of desirability, all the while sharing an appreciation of time as empirically determined by preference.[45]

*

These, then, are two weak spots of American legal pragmatism: gaps in which judges legislate and an empirical conception of time. What rescue, then, can Bergson provide? Although the full implications of Bergson's theory of memory are apparent only in the next chapter, I can make two preliminary suggestions that introduce its usefulness for law.

First, against American pragmatism and its critics, the issue of gaps becomes a nonproblem. The theory of gaps is itself caught in an externalist (or pre-Critical *and* pre-Bergsonian) conception of subsumptive judgment: On the one hand, we have a unique case; and on the other, we have a set of rules, none of which apply. Although subsumption fails (no rule fits), there can be no question that a notion of gaps demands, through its failure, an image of judgment as subsumptive. For Bergson, such a problem is unthinkable because *perception always implicates memory* such that for a case to appear at all, for it to be perceived or for it to be docketed, it must already be combined with recollected rules. As one commentator puts it, "It is when a theoretically pure perception is alloyed with memory that subjective consciousness emerges."[46] Perception always associates and actualizes a virtual recollection—this recollection is required to make sense of a perception, to help perception in its situation and problem (*MM*, 34). As I said, pure recollections are contemporaneous with present perceptions (paradox 1); they virtually coexist and are actualized by perceptions (paradox 2); and they are, in fact, the preexistent condition for perception and of the passing of the present (paradox 3). There are no gaps to be opened and no interstices to be occupied, for the unique case is perceived only according to the recollections it embodies. Moreover, we can mobilize the fourth and final paradox to deny gaps in the law. On first impression, the fourth paradox could seem to lend a hand to a theory of gaps. If the past is infinitely repeated in itself at different levels of tension (i.e., at different degrees of specificity and generality), could it not be said that a judge need only select a sufficiently dilated tension—the judge as dreamer[47]—such that all the recollections therein would be too specific to associate with the case at hand? But this too succumbs to the illusion of an externality between perception and recollection, as though a judge could be before a case and decide or choose which level of the pure past is appropriate to it. Perception for Bergson straightaway calls on the recollection appropriate to its need and situation. There can be no perception of a case before which we deliberate which level to call on. For the case to appear as a case, it has always already selected an appropriate level to manifest itself as a perception.

Second, the issue of pragmatism's theory of time is a good way to distinguish between American legal pragmatism and Bergson's ontological pragmatism. An *empirical* theory of time is not an accidental determination of American legal pragmatism but its consistent product. Given that this pragmatism bases itself on determinative teleology, for which the value of a conclusion is estimated by its consequences, it is only natural that its conception of time should also be measured by the desirability of its consequences and therefore should be open to modification and contestation. Bergson's theory of time, which I call ontological pragmatism, is foreign to this approach. Instead of an empirical or a psychological conception of time, Bergson proposes a simultaneously transcendental *and* ontological account of the actualization of the virtual to explain the passing of the present and the actualization of recollections within perceptions. Far from there being multiple and contestable times—times that we could say are internal to us, to our desires, and to our disputes as to their merits—"it is we," as Deleuze puts it, "who are internal to time, not the other way round.... Time is not interior in us, but just the opposite, the interiority in which we are, in which we move, live and change" (*C2*, 82).

My task in the next chapter is to develop the implications of the following proposition: *Adjudication and law are in time.* For now, I can say that a significant benefit of this proposition is to sidestep so many lame debates about whether a dynamic or static conception of time in adjudication is preferable. In fact, rather than an either/or proposition, by asserting that there is only a single time to law—the actualization of the virtual—it is possible to account for *both* the conservative and the creative capacities of judgment, for these capacities represent two different ways of actualizing the past and are both equally necessary to adjudication. In so doing, I claim that Bergson's theory of the pure past can revitalize valuable insights into legal pragmatism—notably, that law is inventive, based as it is on need.

7

The Time of Law III:
Judgment *sub specie durationis*

My account of Bergson's *Matter and Memory* isolated pure perception and the virtual past in order to lay the foundation for a theory of adjudication. I now propose a concept of judgment based on the actualization of the virtual past—that is, one that puts perception and the virtual past back into relation. This might be surprising given Deleuze's repeated criticisms of judgment and his professed ambition "to try and find the means to have done with the system of judgment, and to put something else in its place" (*ABC*, K). Nevertheless, I argue that Deleuze and Bergson furnish the means to reevaluate adjudication as premised on the actualization of the virtual. I intend, in other words, to use this concept of the actualization of the virtual to renew what Deleuze once described as a fundamentally Kantian undertaking, that is, to pose the problem of judgment "at the level of its technicality, or of its originality."[1] Far from being intractably dogmatic and committed to subsumption, I argue that adjudication (properly understood) is of a kind with the jurisprudence Deleuze favors: It depends on the encounter with the case, *and* it is inherently (not accidentally, not willfully) creative.

This chapter picks up where I left off, with the deceptively simple statement that adjudication takes place *in time*. From there, I explore how the virtual past of the law is actualized in connection with the actual perception of the case, and I introduce two different processes of judgment: inattentive and attentive. Inattentive judgment accounts for the great majority of judgments: the application of rules to recognized cases.

Attentive judgment, by contrast, accounts for the minority of judgments: the creation of rules for unrecognizable cases. It has been said (and then resaid in the context of law)[2] that if the exception cannot be explained, then neither can the general. In this sense, the advantage of a Deleuzian theory of adjudication is that it can explain both the ordinary (rule-applying) and the extraordinary (rule-creating) functions of adjudication as two different processes of the actualization of the past of law. It contributes not only an account of the everyday of adjudication but also one that includes within it the exceptional as part of its normal operation.

The Pure Past of the Law and the Law without Organs

We left the last chapter with the claim that law and adjudication take place *in time*. I articulated four paradoxes, each of which restates the thesis that the past virtually coexists with a present that actualizes it in order to draw recollections and to pass. To reintroduce the relevance of the pure past to law, we might draw on the distinction that Kant makes between private and public life in his article "What Is Enlightenment?" There, he argues that we all lead double lives. On the one hand, we lead "public" lives wherein we speak our minds with the fullest possible exercise of reason; on the other hand, we lead "private" (what we would call professional) lives wherein we serve institutional positions and adopt their personae (e.g., the tax collector, the cleric). Turning to Bergson, let's take the example of a judge. As a human (public) being, a judge obviously moves in a being-memory, a virtual pure past that enables the actualization of the lived present. But in his private or professional capacity as a judge, he also occupies an *institutional* being-memory, the being-past of the law. Although Bergson did not develop this specific insight, it is possible to claim that not only do living beings presuppose pure memory for present action, *but so do institutions and institutional personae* (e.g., judges). Insofar as judgment occurs in time, an ontology of the pure past is necessary to understand how adjudication works.

My claim is that *the judge, as judge*, exists *within* a pure institutional past, which I call the *pure past of the law*. This past of the law is virtual; it is the past in general (the pure past) in which all the rules for judgment are found.

This means that rules of law have a double existence. On the one hand, they fill and are found in the books (they are *actual*); on the other hand, they exist in or as a pure past (they are *virtual*). We must, therefore, take care to distinguish the pure past of the law (i.e., its virtual archive), from the published archive of law (i.e., the books, the corpus of legal rules we find in LexisNexis). On first impression, this distinction is bound to seem mysterious and unnecessary. We might ask, for instance, what's wrong with accounting for the past of the law solely through the archive of its published history? Why the need to evoke another (ontological) register for these rules? I have two replies. First, without the pure past of law, the case could never be perceived; it could never be considered at law. Second, without the pure past there would be no way to explain why a present case leads to one rule rather than to another. I expand the first reply in this section, and the second in the next section. My procedure broadly adopts the form of a Kantian deduction: to show that the appearance of a case in adjudication presupposes the pure past of law as its condition of possibility.

Consider the following: How does a state of affairs—a pure image, in Bergson's terms—become a case at law? *On its own*, can a state of affairs suggest a published legal term, rule, or principle? No, of course not. In order for a state of affairs to lead to a rule, or, in order for a rule to be embodied within a state of affairs so as to make it a case, something else must occur: an act of memory. Someone—whether a litigant, a lawyer, a judge, or someone else—must connect that raw event to law; only that can initiate the use of the actual, written texts. In Bergsonian terms, a pure recollection of law must be actualized so that a state of affairs can be perceived as a case. Or, we can restate the point by asking, What is a legal case? It is a composite of law and world, of rule and state of affairs, and something needs to happen—what we call an act of memory—in order to integrate the one with the other so as to form a case. This is so simple that it becomes difficult to say. Let's return to *Palsgraf v. Long Island Railroad Co.* (see Chapter 6). Helen Palsgraf's injuries are a raw event, an as yet (legally) unrepresented state of affairs: At such a time and at such a place an explosion caused scales to topple over and harm someone. How do we get from here to law? To do *that*, the event must be connected with the terms (words, concepts, rules) of (tort) law, such that in the recounting of that event, terms such as *obligation, injury, cause,* and *responsibility* take hold of it, make it relevant and a case for law, and direct the subsequent search for rules. The facts or datum of that event are apprehended and organized by the recollected rule—the event becomes literally perceived along the lines of the rule and converted into a case. This is the first point: For the event to be perceived as a case, it must be joined to or informed by law, and only memory can do that.

In theorizing adjudication, we must remember that perception is never independent of memory; this is analytically implied in the word *case* insofar as it combines rules of law (the past) with a present situation (perception). We must also remember that there are two distinct, interrelated senses of memory: on the one hand, *actual*, psychological recollections inserted into perception according to pragmatic criteria; on the other hand, *virtual* or pure memory from which recollections are drawn and actualized. As Bergson taught us in his critique of associationism, psychological recollections presuppose pure memory as their condition of possibility (see Chapter 6, paradox 2). The same holds within the context of law: Actual recollections (rules) are inserted into a perception (state of affairs) in order to form a composite (case), and presuppose the existence of a pure institutional past. This is my second point: The use of an actual, documented rule of law always presupposes the virtual existence of that rule in order for it to be actualized and embodied within a case.

This point is bound to seem bizarre, for what does it mean for an actual rule to have a simultaneous virtual existence? It does not mean that "actual" and "virtual" represent different contents of law, as though the actual was the more literal and the virtual the fuzzier version of the same rule. Instead, recourse to the virtual indicates a necessary condition implied in the use of a rule that exclusive attention to the actual misses and cannot explain. What the actual fails to explain is how, if there is an event on one side and a printed rule on the other side, the two could ever meet. For a case to exist, something must join the two. Here, the actualization of a rule within a perception depends as its condition on the pure past, that is, on rules that are not actual but virtual and hence actualizable within the event to make a case. In order to *use* a rule to perceive and to adjudicate a case, a judge (or lawyer, etc.) must formulate that event in terms of the rule and incarnate the rule in terms of the event. This is the very definition of a case (event + law). In order for the actual books of law to gain their effect, the rule must be actualized within an event, and, as such, the pure past and its actualization stand as the condition for a rule to come into play within the context of an event. It is not as though the judge has actual rules sitting in front of him, whether on the books or in his head, which he considers one by one before finally declaring "That one! That one best fits the case at hand." In order for there to be a case at hand, an event has always already been joined to, synthesized, or composed with a rule—a process that is the condition for the appearance of the case, and one that actualizes a rule from a virtual (or psychologically speaking, an unconscious) past that does not have the form of an actual rule catalogue for the judge to choose from but instead insists and actualizes itself within the (legally relevant) perception of the thing at hand. And so, even if Cardozo himself tells us that "the first thing [the judge] does is to compare the case before him with the precedents, whether stored in his mind or hidden in the books," we see that that's not quite right, that he gets ahead of himself: for the first thing a judge must do is place himself *in a pure institutional time* (*NJP*, 112). In order to consult the books, an (ontologically) anterior act of memory—one that joins perception (case) with recollection (rule)—always takes place. And for this to occur, the rule must not be actual but virtual and actualizable, which, again, requires the pure past of law as its condition.

What are the characteristics of the pure past of law? Here I quickly sketch two features, to which I will return later: first, its virtuality; second, its repetition. It cannot be sufficiently stressed that the pure past is not actual. The pure past of law designates the virtual whole of the past of law that coexists alongside the present that actualizes it. As in the paradoxes, the pure past of law is contemporaneous, coexistent, and preexistent to the present case (paradoxes 1, 2, and 3): It is simultaneous with, exists virtually alongside, and is the condition for the case at hand. It is within this pure legal past that a judge searches for appropriate rules to make the case perceptible and to adjudicate it (but we will see that these are not distinct moments). In addition to its virtuality, the pure past of law has another important characteristic for which the fourth paradox of time is of the greatest relevance: (ontological or virtual) *repetition* of the entirety of the pure past at different levels of tension. Bergson's claim is that the entirety of the pure past coexists with the actual present but on virtual planes of different degrees of specificity. As the cone of time (Figure 1, in Chapter 6) illustrates, recollections most removed from the present point of action preserve their singularity and distinctness, whereas those closer to the active present are general or generic enough to be of immediate use for most needs. For example, depending on the situation in which a foreign word is spoken, I solicit one level or another of the past in which that word is found contracted at a suitably specific tension. Carrying the example to law, depending on the situation (on the *case*), a judge will place herself on the level of the past in which the rule she is looking for is contracted at an appropriate tension. The sought-after rule could be, for example, *Riggs v. Palmer*. At one level, this rule could be recalled as a general maxim that "no one may profit from his or her wrongs"; at another level, it could be recalled as a specific case about a murderous heir. The example is perfectly arbitrary, but it shows how a rule exists at different tensions in the pure past and moreover that the demands of the present situation dictate the tension at which the rule will be sought and actualized.

That law takes place *in time* means two things: first, that the past of the law *virtually* exists in its entirety as a pure archive repeated on variously contracted levels; and second, that law *actually* exists as an alloy of recollections actualized in a present case. Leaving the second point aside for the moment, we can get a better sense of the pure past of the law by contrasting it with Dworkin's *reflective totality* of the history of law. Specifically, I argue that if the past of the law is assumed to be purely actual and reducible to its published letter (as I take Dworkin's scheme), then creativity is placed outside the proper exercise of judgment.

To summarize our findings from Chapter 2, Dworkin's concept of integrity adapts Kant's reflective judgment of teleology and its presupposition that nature and its laws must be judged as if they were a coherent and purposive unity. In order for a judge to honor the integrity of law, he must presume that the rules of law and the principles that inform them are a systematic and purposive whole. We went further in our characterization of Dworkin, calling his theory a law with organs. By this we intended a strict analogy with the internal purposiveness necessary to judge organisms in Kant's *Critique of Judgment*. In this vein, Dworkin tells us that each part of the history of law (each of its organs) must be judged within the presupposed context of a whole (an organism) that gives to each part its place and purpose. At its regulative limit, reflective teleological judgment identifies and assigns to every part of the past of law a purpose and place within the scope of the whole. Thanks to the presupposed whole, every part of the past of the law is fully present, identifiable, and *actual*: Each judgment that upholds integrity in law imposes an overall interpretation of every element of the past of the law.[3] In that interpretation every element of the past of law represents its purpose as assigned by a reflectively presupposed totality; or, in other words, each organ of law has its purpose laid out and identified within the presupposed whole.

It has been suggested that Deleuze could be seen to support Kant's concept of reflective judgment.[4] This support may well extend to reflective judgments of the beautiful and the sublime,[5] but not, however, to reflective judgments of teleology or finality. I argue that Deleuze creates a specific concept to oppose this kind of reflective judgment: the Body without Organs (BwO).[6] So far, the fact that the BwO attacks reflective judgment has been underappreciated, despite being a precise (indeed, terminologically exact) critique of it.[7]

Take one of Deleuze's stridently antijudgment texts, appropriately titled "To Have Done with Judgment." In this short piece, Deleuze raises five coordinated criticisms of judgment, one of which concerns us directly: his opposition to judgment "at the level of the body" (*CC*, 130). On Deleuze's account, "judgment implies a veritable organization of the bodies through which it acts." But what does it mean for judgment to act through the organization of bodies? How does judgment perform this organizing function? By transforming bodies into "*organisms*" (*CC*, 131). This transformation replaces a vital body with a concept that assigns a function to both the organism and its organs, coordinating both into a purposive whole. Without directly naming it—although strongly hinting at it when he states, "Kant did not invent a true critique of judgment; on the contrary, what the book of this title established was a fantastic subjective tribunal" (*CC*, 126)—Deleuze identifies reflective judgments of teleology as precisely those judgments that convert bodies into purposive entities called organisms. As Deleuze puts it, "Where we once had a vital living body, God has made us into an organism. . . . God has stolen [this body] from us in order to palm off an organized body without which his judgment could not be exercised" (*CC*, 131). By "God" I understand Deleuze to mean exactly what Kant took God to signify in relation to (legitimate and regulative, not constitutive) teleological judgment: a presupposed principle that assigns purpose and harmony to bodies and thereby enables adequate, scientific judgments.

Returning to the critique, reflective judgment transforms a vital body into an organism that each of its organs is made and meant to express. As such, judgment prevents "the emergence of any new mode of existence" inasmuch as it subsumes vital properties with a function, converting them into organs within a presupposed purposive totality (*CC*, 135). Deleuze's complaint is not so much with organs as it is with the organism, or rather with its "hidden" and "secret" reflective principle of totality and purposiveness (*TP*, 265–266).[8] "The enemy is the organism. The BwO is opposed not to the organs but to that organization of the organs called the organism" (*TP*, 158). But, if I may add an interpretation, the enemy is not really the organism either; it is, rather, reflective judgment that takes the organism as a purposive whole and assigns to its parts functions within that organization. It is judgment, specifically reflective judgment, that the BwO opposes (organs and organisms are merely fruits of this kind of judgment). "The judgment of God, the system of judgment of God, the theological system, is precisely the operation of He who makes an organism" (*TP*, 158). A Body *without* Organs is what results when we dispense with the principle of reflective judgment, for we no longer limit organs to an assigned purpose. So when Deleuze exhorts us to make ourselves into a BwO, it is to "escape judgment" or, more precisely, to escape the purposiveness and totality of reflective judgment (*CC*, 131).

If we are to construct a jurisprudence from Deleuze, it must be a *Law without Organs* (LwO), that is, law and judgment freed from teleology.[9] When Deleuze instructs us to "combat against judgment . . . and its personae," this must first and foremost be a struggle against Dworkin's Justice Hercules and the organized totality that reflective judgment presupposes (*CC*, 132). I have said that in this totality everything is actual: Every part or element of the history of law is assigned a place within an overall purposive interpretation. In this system, new cases are subsumed by existing rules and principles so as to complement the overall integrity. When, for example, Hercules adjudicates, he "deploy[s] arguments why the parties actually had the 'novel' legal rights and duties they enforce at the time the parties acted" (*LE*, 244). Because everything is actual within this presumed totality, judges never create but propose "improved reports of what the law, properly understood, *already is*" (*LE*, 6). Or, as in Dworkin's gloss on *Brown v. Board of Education*, "if someone says the judges discovered the illegality of school segregation, he believes segregation was in fact illegal before the decision that said it was, even though no court had said it before" (*LE*, 6). In brief, each new judgment is understood as if it were already contained in a past rule or principle, such that the judge need only select a rule or principle to subsume the present case. Guided by the ideal of integrity, Justice Hercules actualizes all rules and principles within a total, purposive interpretation of the law. With all rules and principles given, judges are charged to select and apply the appropriate one. The total actuality of the law from within a teleological horizon necessitates a concept of judgment as subsumptive: Either an existing rule is applied or, if a new rule is made, it is said to have tacitly existed all along.

The past, therefore, is fully actual, and one of its rules—the one that best satisfies integrity—is selected to subsume the present case. Accordingly (and what else can be expected from an image of time where all is given?), the future is already played out. The future is merely a matter of the capacity to realize one's principled vision. As Dworkin puts it, "philosophers of law" are "chain novelists with epics in mind, imagining the work unfolding through volumes it may take generations to write. In that sense each of their dreams is already latent in the present law; each dream might be law's future" (*LE*, 409).

Deleuze is no philosopher of law in this sense. On the question of the value of teleological judgments in law, he is nearest to Nietzsche's observation that "'purpose in law' is the last thing we should apply to the history of the emergence of law. No matter how perfectly you have understood the usefulness of any *physiological organ* (or *legal institution*...) you have not yet thereby grasped how it emerged."[10] As I said, Deleuze dedicates the BwO to combat the dogmatism of teleological reflective judgment. From a Deleuzian perspective, Dworkin is dogmatic on two counts. First, a judgment of natural purposes determines each organ according to the ordering of the judgment. This means that with such a judgment, at least in the regulative limit of Justice Hercules, every bit of the law is fitted within an overall interpretation. Second, a judgment of natural purposes projects principles into the past of the law in order to be discovered, recognized, and applied. Dworkin's approach vitiates an understanding of creativity in adjudication, which is reduced to something merely willful or accidental (see, for example, Dworkin's reading of pragmatism). This second critique sums up both: A teleological reflective judgment assigns to each part of law a definitive and exhaustive place (all the law is actual), which we then apply to the present case (judgment is subsumptive).

Leading back to our positive task of creating a Deleuzian jurisprudence, we may be surprised to learn that we do not dispense with the *totality* but with the *total actuality* of teleological reflective judgment. With respect to the concept of the pure past, we see that in no way is the idea of totality abandoned, only the fact of its actuality and its closure. Indeed, in Bergson and Deleuze it is the whole of the pure past that coexists with the present; moreover, it is the whole of the pure past that is contracted into various virtual tensions; and finally, as time goes on, this whole is added to and swells, making it into an *open whole* (on this last point, see Chapter 8). In fact, Deleuze pushes much further than Dworkin in this direction: The whole of the past is not merely presupposed as in reflective judgment but is postulated as absolutely real—it (ontologically) IS. The LwO reproaches reflective judgment for the *actuality*, and consequently the closure, of that totality. If all rules are entirely actual without appreciation of their virtuality, and if they are all given and enumerated from within a reflective transcendental horizon, then they are a closed set that calcifies the history of the law within an overall interpretation and reduces the present case to a mere function of it. A complete actuality of law, then, comes with dangerous consequences: The whole of the past of law is set within an interpretation, all rules are given for identification, and judgment subsumes the case under a rule. Teleology not only vitiates consideration of inventiveness in law but, as we will see in the next section, misrepresents the genesis of judgment.

Actualizing the Pure Past of Law

Consider, at the most basic level, a judgment of law. Is not its fundamental characteristic to combine past rules with a present situation? Is not a judgment, or a competent one at least, a perfect composite between past and present, such that, "there comes a moment when the recollection . . . is capable of blending so well with the present perception that we cannot say where perception ends or where memory begins" (*MM*, 106)? The great advantage of *Matter and Memory* for an investigation of adjudication is that it is devoted to analyzing just this alloy of past and present. How does

Bergson methodologically proceed? By division. He starts with a composite—pragmatic everyday experience—and divides it into its constitutive elements that differ in kind: pure perception and the pure past. With this done, Bergson can give us "the sufficient reason of the thing, the sufficient reason of the composite"; he can, in other words, reconstruct the genesis of composite pragmatic experience through the relationship of the pure past and perception. (*B*, 28). Our investigation has dutifully followed this method, separating out pure perception and pure past in the law. Now, finally, we are in a position to appreciate their combination: It results in nothing other than judgment.

As with his great contemporaries (we need name Freud and Nietzsche in this respect), memory is a function of the future for Bergson. Recollections are in service of action; they are called up and actualized to help us act—in this consists Bergson's pragmatism. But how does it happen? It starts with a leap into the past.

What does it mean to recover a recollection, to evoke a period of our history? We become conscious of an act *sui generis* by which we detach ourselves from the present in order to replace ourselves, first, in *the past in general, then in a certain region of the past*—a work of adjustment [*de tâtonnement*], analogous to the focusing of a camera. *But our recollection still remains in a virtual state*; we simply prepare ourselves to receive it by adopting the appropriate attitude. Little by little it comes into view like a condensing cloud; from the *virtual it passes into the actual state*; and its outlines become more distinct and its surface takes on color, it tends to imitate perception. (*MM*, 133–134, emphasis added, translation modified)

We leap into the pure past in order to recollect. But, as Bergson carefully specifies, we leap into a virtual or pure, not a chronological or psychological, past. This much follows from the paradoxes of time: We make an ontological and not a chronological move; we "leap into ontology," into the being of the past, "leaving psychology altogether" (*B*, 57). The leap may be hemmed in on both sides by psychological processes—a need starts us on a search of the past from which we emerge with a recollection—but in between it is the pure past that we inhabit.[11]

In searching for a recollection, Bergson tells us that we place ourselves within a certain *region*, or *level*, of the past. Although the recollections at each level remain in a virtual state, they are contracted at a specific tension (paradox 4: ontological repetition). In language suggestive for adjudication, Deleuze writes, "*Depending on the case [suivant le cas]*, I do not leap into the same region of the past; I do not place myself on the same level; I do not solicit the same essential characteristics" (*B*, 62, emphasis added, translation modified). Although it is true that we place ourselves in the past in general, Bergson adds that our leap is always directed at a particular level, as dictated by our need. Once placed in or on that level, the recollection we receive is no longer pure. It sheds its virtuality by joining with the perception that solicited it. At this point, the recollection inserts itself into the plane of action, indicates to our body reactions appropriate to the situation, and is as fully actual as any other image. According to Bergson, this whole process, which takes so much adjustment and so much psychological finesse, happens every time we endeavor to localize a recollection to help us in a situation; which is to say that it happens all the time, with every perception. It also, I claim, happens with each and every judgment.

That the pure past differentially repeats on multiple planes is one of Bergson's toughest and most suggestive ideas. It is also one of the most rewarding for our analysis. In Bergson's initial account the contracted base of the cone of time contains the past in its most general form, as motor habits, whereas the higher expanded levels bear the infinitesimal detail of our past (*MM*, 166–167, and elsewhere). What distinguishes planes, therefore, is increasing specificity, such that when we need a detailed recollection (e.g., "who said that word and when?" and not merely, "what does this word mean?"), we leap into higher and higher planes of the past (see Figure 1 in Chapter 6). But this account is overlaid by the following terrifically difficult text:

If, here again, we suppose a multitude [*une foule*] of possible repetitions of the totality of our recollections [*souvenirs*], *each of these copies of our past life will be cut up* [*se découpera*], *in its own way, into definite slices* [*en tranches déterminées*], and the mode of division will not be the same if we pass from one copy to another, *for each of them is characterized by the particular kind of dominant recollections* [*souvenirs*] *on which the other recollections* [*souvenirs*] *lean as on supports.* . . . It is sufficient to remark that these systems are not formed of recollections [*souvenirs*] juxtaposed like so many atoms. *There are always some dominant recollections* [*souvenirs*], *veritable shining points around which the others form a vague nebulosity.* These shining points are multiplied in the degree to which our memory expands. (*MM*, 170–171, emphasis added, translation modified)

This text poses (at least) two specific problems for interpretation. First, before this passage the principle organizing each plane was sought in tension; now, Bergson brings in a different, thematic criteria of "shining points" and "dominant recollections." Second, it is a central thesis of Bergson's that each level contains the past in a whole and *undivided* state, for division is always a characteristic of the actual (and of space and number). Bergson always holds that if the virtual divides, it changes in nature; that is, it becomes actual.[12] It is surprising, then, to see that in its virtual state the past can be said to be cut up and organized by shining points. Perhaps by addressing the second problem of how an undivided plane can be cut up and dotted with points, we can also answer the first.

To restate the problem, the pure past exists undivided at each level and yet contains dominant recollections and shining points. Is this not a contradiction? How can the undivided be cut up by points and recollections? I propose that the points and recollections are indicative not of a pure virtual consistency but of a plane and its recollection *in the process of actualization*. This is one of the rare times I go against Deleuze, who insists that the points and dominant themes in the pure past are "completely real but only virtual" (*DR*, 327–328n23).[13] It is not my claim that the points and themes depict fully actual, detached recollections; I do, however, argue that the plane organizes itself in this way only under the pressure of a search of memory. The future tense of Bergson's passage—"each of these copies of our past life *will be cut up* [*chacun de ces exemplaires de notre vie écoulée* se découpera]"—suggests that the organization of the plane of memory into shining points is indicative of something that will happen under pressure of a search, of a process to be accomplished, rather than its virtual sempiternal state.

How, then, does the search of pure memory initiate an organization of the undivided plane of memory into shining points and dominant recollections? Further, how can a recollection be isolated and actualized—that is, how can it be fully divided and extracted from the pure past and inserted into perception? In short, how does the plane divide and yield the recollections with which to address the problems of the present? For Bergson, the selection of recollections is accomplished through *translation* and *rotation*.

Memory, laden with the whole of the past, responds to the appeal of the present state by two simultaneous movements, one of *translation*, by which it *moves in its entirety to meet experience, thus contracting more or less, though without dividing*, with a view to action; and the other of *rotation* upon itself, *by which it turns toward the situation of the moment, presenting to it its most useful side*. (*MM*, 121, emphasis added, translation modified)

Here we see a complex process of actualization that resolves the apparent contradiction between an undivided plane of memory contracted at a specific tension and its simultaneous fracture into shining points. According to Bergson, the specific recollections that fracture a plane of memory are the function of *rotation*, where a plane presents its most useful side, a side divided and spatialized, ready to be plucked out and actualized. These rotations are called up by the needs of the present for a *specific* recollection, and yet the leap is said to select an *undivided* plane of useful tension. The leap chooses a level of undivided tension and not a specific, isolated recollection. Thus the search initiated by the present need organizes virtual memory into the specific undivided tension required for the situation. This is the work of *translation*: the degree of virtual tension that contracts or expands a plane of undivided recollections into useful tension. Translation (undivided tension) and rotation (divided actualizations) are strictly simultaneous. At once Bergson presents us with an undivided plane (which provides recollections at an appropriate tension, with an appropriate specificity or generality) and with a fractured plane (in which the present need looks for and finds the discrete, particular recollections embodying the tension of the whole). This complex simultaneity is such that we pick out useful recollections (rotation) that *divide* the virtual tension, yet it is this *undivided* tension (translation) that offers a suitably contracted recollection.[14]

The processes of rotation and translation help resolve the two problems I set earlier. First, before fully fracturing and actualizing the plane into a specific recollection, rotation starts by organizing and cutting up the plane into dominant recollections and shining points according to its need. Given that actualization is a process, one characterized by constant adjustment, we cannot say that it happens all at once—as though the pure past were suddenly shattered like a plate—but instead that it actualizes itself by degrees: from a purely undivided plane to one organized by shining points and, finally, as divided into useful recollections. In the middle of this process, therefore, the plane is whole and divided, or, in other words, virtual but being actualized and divided. Second, the work of translation organizes the past by specific tensions, and we select the one suitable to our needs. But if translation is always accompanied by rotation and if in the process of rotation the plane becomes cut up on its way to actualization, then there is no problem in saying that the plane is organized simultaneously by a specific tension and by thematic shining points and dominant recollections. What this means, and what my interpretation of Bergson's passage amounts to, is that translation and rotation are always corollary to our leap into the past and, by consequence, that we leap never into the absolutely pure past but always into some degree of its actualization. This is not, of course, a return to a psychological reading of Bergson (as if our past were always psychically present to us); it is only to say that the leap into the pure past always initiates a process of actualization and organization of memory.

I have refrained from giving examples from law because the process that Bergson describes—leap, translation and rotation, actualization—characterizes all judgments. A problem comes before a judge, the case as image. Before consulting any text, the judge has already leapt into the pure past of law to try to find a rule suitable for this case. This, I have said, is the only way for the case (as pure image) to appear before the judge as a *legal case* (a composite image of perception and recollection, a case joined to rules). Given that the virtual past of the law is by definition nonactual and thus also subrepresentative, we cannot describe it or give an account of its layers. But in keeping with Bergson's theory, I claim that the judge jumps into a specifically contracted level of the pure legal past and proceeds, by a work of adjustment, to actualize a rule in the present and in coordination with the case.

Let's revisit our warhorse, *Palsgraf*. Before being perceived, a case bears infinite aspects, only some of which are deemed legally relevant. What is relevant in *Palsgraf* shrinks down to how the package full of fireworks appeared to the station guard, whether it looked dangerous. How does Cardozo manage to subtract everything else? Thanks to a recollected rule. Although the clear enunciation into case law of an external standard of liability is Cardozo's doing, this rule had already been proposed at great length and detail in Holmes's *Common Law* and suggested in prior rulings.[15] What we can say, therefore, is that Cardozo leaps into the pure past and actualizes this rule. Accordingly, the only relevant fact in the case is the one Cardozo describes: the look of the package with respect to foreseeability.

What I mean to say, in the simplest way possible, is that the combination of a recollected rule(s) with the perception of the case *is* the judgment; that is, the composite, or the process of combining perception with recollection, is the judgment. A state of affairs is presented to a judge (an explosion at a train station harms a plaintiff); a rule must be selected to make a legally relevant determination of the facts (Holmes's external liability standard); the rule joins together with the state of affairs to select its salient characteristics, and judgment is rendered (only the appearance of the package is relevant; the package looked safe; Helen Palsgraf's suit is dismissed). Thus the very composition of the rule with the case results in a judgment.

But why, we might persist in asking, do we need Bergson's complex theory to reach this conclusion? For four reasons, two of which I will treat later.[16] The first reason I have already touched on: A case is always a composite of perception and memory, such that in the presentation of a case it must already be joined to rules. With an incisive phrase Holmes says, "Continuity with the past is not a duty, it is only a necessity."[17] In Bergsonian terms, a judge never hears (in the figurative *and* literal sense) a case as a pure image but only as a composite *legal* case. Therefore we cannot conclude that the actual archive of law (i.e., its texts) exhausts or is even primary in relation to the past of law, for an anterior and immediate connection of the case with the past is presupposed in every reference to it. A search of the books implies a search of memory. Indeed, without the concepts of the pure past and the leap, the connection of the case with the past of the law remains mysterious, for how can a state of affairs dictate which rule corresponds to it on its own? Neither the pure image nor the text can suggest the one to the other, for that is the function of judgment: to actualize a (past) rule within the context of a (present) case. As I argued in the previous section, the coexistence and actualization of the pure past in law reveals itself as the condition for the most basic feature of judgment: its coordination of past rules with a present case.

The second advantage that speaks in favor of Bergson's theory is that with the repetition of the pure past on different planes of specificity and association, we have a mechanism to explain how and why a present case leads to and actualizes one rule rather than another, at one generality rather than another, without recourse to an implausible notion of the decision or "choice" of the judge. Now, given that the pure planes of memory are subrepresentative, we can show their existence only by implying their necessity (i.e., we once again follow the method of the Kantian deduction). Returning to *Palsgraf*, Cardozo cites a general formulation of the external liability standard: "It was not necessary that the defendant should have had notice of the particular method in which an accident would occur, if the possibility of an accident was clear to the ordinarily prudent eye."[18] This rule is attributed to a number of cases, all of which are singular, but still encapsulated by its generality.[19] Without Bergson's concept of the repetition of levels of the past, how, we ask, could these cases ever be associated by Cardozo? Without being brought down to a sufficient generality, these cases are inassociably different. We cannot say that the judge generalizes only from the written record of one case and then another, for according to my last point, a search of the books of law always presupposes an act of memory. The text of one case cannot refer to the text of another unless by virtue of an association of memory. For example, *Munsey v. Webb* does not on its own lead to other cases, but rather Cardozo *recalls* that *Munsey* articulates a rule similar to both *Condran v. Park & Tilford* and *Robert v. U.S.E.F. Corp.* In short, the association established between these cases cannot be explained merely by virtue of an actual printed archive of law, no matter how well cross-referenced. Instead, we require an operation of memory that can establish a correspondence between them. The association of cases from *Palsgraf*, therefore, serves as a *ratio cognoscendi* for what we must presuppose in order for the case at hand to be possible at all: a differentially repeated pure past that enables recollections to (pre)exist at a tension suitable for their insertion into the present case. *Palsgraf* (and I have taken this case almost at random) demonstrates the Bergsonian thesis that rules of law exist at various virtual tensions and, moreover, that the need of the present determines at which tension they will be sought. Cardozo needs cases to back up his rule and recalls three as being similar from this standpoint; in other words, he locates these three rules together on a pure plane of memory and actualizes them all at once as alike. Irreducible to the actual archive of law, the theory of the differentially repeated pure past, together with a pragmatic theory of perception and recollection, can at once account for the associations between past cases and for their inclusion within the present judgment.

On this question of the actualization of rules, it is worthwhile to distinguish between H. L. A. Hart's theory and my own. The two may seem miles apart, but there exist, despite appearances, substantial affinities. Of the so-called dogmatic theorists, it is Hart to whom I am by far the closest, for we share an understanding that case and law are not external instances. In reconstructing Hart's criticism of John Austin, I argued that for Hart rules do not subsume a conduct external to them but instead simultaneously constitute and judge conduct. This, I said, adapted Kant's fundamental insight from the *Critique of Pure Reason*—that judgment occurs only within representation itself—toward an adjudicative theory that states that for a legal case to appear, it must always already be informed by concepts of law. In this respect, I find Hart's theory exemplary. My criticism of Hart is twofold. First, he fails to consistently maintain his theory of subsumption, abandoning it in his conception of judicial choice: A judge sits before a case and selects one of the many prima facie applicable rules (see Chapter 1). Hart thereby introduces a distance and externality between the case and the law (the judge sits before a case and deliberates *which* rule to pick) and thus reintroduces the very subsumption he had criticized: A rule is chosen to cover a case. Second, the rule that subsumes the case is all too similar to an a priori category of the understanding given that in its application it is unmodified, only exemplified. Rule application, therefore, can instantiate a rule but is incapable of creating one.

I address the concept of judicial choice, reserving the question of creativity. What is interesting about choice is that on the face of it Bergson's theory of perception precludes any such concept, for although perception always actualizes a recollection, which recollection is actualized is not a matter of choice. Choice would not make sense; we spontaneously call up recollections according to the exigencies of life, such that a situation summons a recollection to deal with it. But Bergson persistently and affirmatively uses this word *choice* in *Matter and Memory*. Why?

He introduces it with respect to perception: "My body appears to *choose*, within certain limits, the manner in which it shall restore what it receives." "Our consciousness only attains to certain parts and to certain aspects of those parts. *Consciousness*—in regard to external perception—*consists precisely in this choice.*" "The sole question is, then, to know how and why this image *is chosen* to form part of my perception, while an infinite number of other images remain excluded from it," and so on.[20] I could easily multiply mentions of choice, but these are sufficient to show that Bergson is attempting to create a rigorously pragmatic and nonvoluntaristic concept. By radicalizing the notions of want and desire typically associated with choice—or at least a facile conception of it[21]—Bergson overturns the commonplace understanding of it. Choice has nothing to do with a selection made between options, for this betrays a superficial understanding of need, want, and desire. Needs, wants, and desires are, in fact, much more basic, for Bergson's thesis in the first chapter of *Matter and Memory* states that we perceive what we need: Our need chooses our perception; it chooses what we perceive, such that everything we do not need is subtracted away or not chosen from the image.[22]

This use of *choice* isn't limited by Bergson to perception but is also extended to memory and our search of it: "The representation which is analogous to the actual perception has to be *chosen* from among all possible representations" (*MM*, 95); "the *choice* of one resemblance among many . . . is, therefore, not made at random: it depends on the ever-varying degree of the tension of memory" (*MM*, 243). Just as in perception, a need chooses which recollection is actualized and at what tension. Here too, a radical concept of need is used to develop a nonvoluntaristic concept of choice. But Bergson is quite clear that the choices made in perception and recollection are not independent; in fact, they are two sides of a single process. The selection of potential movements that defines a perception also determines in which region of the past the recollection shall be sought (*MM*, 95, 179). A major innovation of Bergson's theory of memory, therefore, is to reconcile *involuntary memory* with *choice*: Our needs *spontaneously choose* which level of the past we leap into and what recollection we actualize.

What does this imply for adjudication? *A theory of judgment without decision*. This phrase indicates that, unlike Hart, there can be no separation between case and rule, for such a separation introduces decision and subsumption, which our theory calls undesirable and impossible: undesirable because decision leads to sterile debates of judicial choice and because subsumption, for all the reasons we have discussed, is dogmatic; and impossible because Bergson's concept of choice prevents any separation between case and rule, and with it decision and subsumption. According to Bergson, choice in adjudication indicates a spontaneous activity that at once eliminates all that is legally irrelevant from the pure image of the case and also leaps into memory to actualize the right rule at the appropriate tension. Deleuze says it perfectly: "*Depending on the case* [*suivant le cas*],

I do not leap into the same region of the past" (*B*, 62). But we must not be hasty at this point and conclude that Bergson posits a judicial automaton who, the minute a case appears, has already perceived, drawn a rule for, and adjudicated it. In the next section I show two irreducible operations of memory and reintroduce the concept of the encounter, which frustrates any notion of mechanical recognition or application of law.

Inattentive Judgment

I have argued that the pure past is the transcendental condition of possible experience and that all perception is impure, that is, alloyed with memory (see Chapter 6). But following Bergson's and Deleuze's injunction for precision in philosophy, we must delve into the conditions of real, and not merely possible, experience (see Chapter 4). If the *real* conditions are to be addressed, the Bergsonian question cannot be "why something rather than nothing, but: why *this* rather than something else? . . . Why will a perception evoke a given memory, or pick up certain frequencies rather than others?"[23] Or, as Bergson states in *Matter and Memory*, "The real question is to understand how a selection is made [*est de savoir comment s'opère la sélection*] among an infinity of recollections that all resemble in some way the present perception, and why only one of them—this one rather than that one—emerges into the light of consciousness" (*MM*, 165, translation modified). If real experience always implicates memory, we must investigate why a particular experience calls up a specific recollection.

Bergson's distinction between two kinds of memory is a major step in this direction. This distinction is introduced in *Matter and Memory*, modified within that text, and then reworked in Deleuze's commentaries. For now, I can list the distinction with its permutations: habit memory and recollection memory (*Matter and Memory*, ch. 2); inattentive perception and attentive perception (*Matter and Memory*, ch. 2); inattentive recognition and attentive recognition (*Cinema 2*, ch. 3); and action-image and time-image (*Cinema* books, passim). None of these pairs maps directly onto another, but they share a motivating problem, which could roughly be stated as, Why do certain situations call up not merely different recollections but precipitate us into different processes of memory altogether?

Why do we have ready responses for some situations, whereas for others we are unprepared? And, when caught unprepared, what happens? What kind of search of memory happens then?

To my mind, the distinction between not simply two sorts of memories (i.e., habits and recollections) but between two irreducible processes of perception and memory (i.e., inattentive and attentive) represents Bergson's full importance for jurisprudence. Not only does this distinction furnish a theory of adjudication with a profound taxonomy and not only does it account for the real conditions of judgment, but it also explains why judgment looks as though it were subsumptive and how judgment can be creative. Corresponding to this last distinction between subsumption and creativity, I formulate two concepts proper to a nondogmatic jurisprudence: inattentive judgment and attentive judgment.

To begin my examination of the two kinds of memory, it is helpful to restate Bergson's pragmatist rule of thumb: We perceive and remember only as much as we need to, as much as the situation demands. We don't look for, nor do we let in, more detailed recollections than are necessary. "Consciousness, attentive to life, only admits, legally [*ne laisse passer, légalement*], those [recollections] that can offer their assistance to the present action."[24] Given this principle, Bergson establishes a division between two types of memory: recollection memory and habit memory. Remember that for Bergson the pure past is preserved in its entirety on more or less contracted levels, each of which contains all of the past (paradox 4). As shown by the cone of time (Figure 1 in Chapter 6), the levels closer to the expanded base preserve recollections in all their unique specificity, neglecting no detail (*MM*, 81). These are recollection memories. The sections of memory closer to the plane of action, by contrast, are narrower and "enclose the same recollections grown smaller [*diminués*], more and more removed from their personal and original form" (*MM*, 106). These are habit memories. To show how the same memory can be contracted on different levels—now as a recollection and now as a habit—Bergson uses the example of a poem we learn by heart. On the lowest, most contracted level we only remember the poem and can recite it; whereas on the highest, most expanded level we have a recollection of each occasion we have tried to learn it (*MM*, 79–80).

Although between the levels of the cone there is only a difference of degree, it is nevertheless significant for Bergson to distinguish between recollection memory and habit memory (*MM*, 79–90). By pragmatic criteria, there is big difference between the two: One is useless, the other useful. "Essentially fugitive" recollection memories are "materialized only by chance," when an exactly similar situation prompts us to leap into an expanded level of the cone to seek out a detailed recollection (*MM*, 106). A recollection memory has no occasion to actualize its fully detailed self, for that detail is unnecessary and useless to the present. "Essentially incapable of being repeated," consciousness sets aside all recollections that cannot be coordinated with the present perception (*MM*, 83). A habit recollection, by contrast, can incarnate itself at any time precisely because it is sufficiently general to "throw light upon and complete in a useful way the present situation" (*MM*, 85). Regardless of whether this kind of memory is motor (e.g., navigating a room) or intellectual (e.g., recognizing a word),[25] it ceaselessly integrates itself into perception and creates a composite with it. Experience, therefore, overwhelmingly solicits the lowest planes of memory to guide action within the present situation. "Of these two memories that we have distinguished, the second, which is active, or motor, will, then, constantly inhibit the first" (*MM*, 85). Because habit memory is so much more useful, it is constantly being inserted into perception and thereby makes unnecessary or inhibits the actualization of a more detailed recollection.

This distinction between habit memory and recollection memory is obviously salient for law. In a line that might as well be from Bergson, Holmes tells us that "it is to make the [rules] easier to be *remembered* and to be understood that the teachings of the decisions of the past are put into *general propositions* and gathered into text-books, or that statutes are passed in a general form."[26] As in *Matter and Memory*, a general rule is more likely to be remembered—that is, used and actualized in a present situation. In another essay, Holmes tells us that the reason we generalize is "because of the ease of mind and comfort which it brings."[27] Ease of mind is just what habit memory is after, promising the know-how to act within a situation. Moreover, the principal drive behind Holmes's work on the history of law is to reduce the apparent multiplicity of historical rules down to its underlying principles—for example, "to show that there really is a Law of Torts, not merely a number of rules of law about various kinds of torts."[28] It is as though we see the cone contracting before our very eyes: from the history of law as a bewildering profusion of singular rules, down to that same history as a manageable handful of principles.

With respect to adjudication, I need only cite Cardozo's surprisingly Bergsonian formulation that a past rule "is the source from which new principles or norms may spring to shape sentences thereafter. If we seek the psychological basis of this tendency, we shall find it, I suppose, *in habit*" (*NJP*, 113, emphasis added). Again, we can conveniently look to *Palsgraf.* Here, Cardozo makes three distinct precedents equivalent by citing them together without distinction in service of the same rule. These precedents were the source from which he shaped his own judgment, and they were actualized within the present as though they were a habit. Chosen not at the level of their uniqueness and singularity as recollection memories, these cases, grouped under the articulation of a single general rule, have been selected from a plane of habit memory that gives to them their generality at the expense of their difference. Adjudication has an obvious penchant for general rules that are easily actualizable within a present case as opposed to highly circumstantial and seldom-used recollections.

From recollection memories and habit memories, I proceed to Bergson's second division between inattentive and attentive processes of memory and perception. This new distinction does not exactly correspond to, but neither does it overwrite, the previous one. The organizing principle of this new distinction is *how we react to encounters*. Bergson observes, together with Deleuze, that most of the time the actualization of the past happens smoothly and, as it were, imperceptibly: We recognize a familiar situation and select appropriate habits or recollections in order to act within it. At other times, however, there occur encounters we do not recognize, ones for which we have no ready-made habit or recollection and that frustrate the ordinary process of the actualization of the past. The first kind of situation I call the *unproblematic encounter*, and the second I call the *problematic encounter*; respectively, these provoke either inattentive or attentive processes of perception and memory. I devote the rest of this section to the unproblematic encounter and inattentive perception; the problematic encounter and attentive perception will be discussed next.

I start by asking how this new distinction (reactions to encounters) reworks the previous distinction (between habit memory and recollection memory). Doubtless, from a certain practical point of view there is a huge difference between habit memory and recollection memory (see *MM*, 80–81). From this practical perspective Bergson explains what determines the association of memories: usefulness for action. But in truth, between habit memory and recollection memory there can be only difference of degree. The rote memory of a poem and the memory of a time that I struggled and stammered to learn it are undeniably different from the point of view of usefulness; but the fact remains that they are the same memory, only contracted at different tensions. In either case, if a situation arose in which that particular recollection was needed, it would be actualized; the only difference is that habit memory is far more likely to be of service. Both types of memory can be actualized as responses to possible situations; they can both be used in the service of recognition and action. Therefore, from the new perspective of how we react to a situation, habits and recollections become one of a kind, alike insofar as both have the capacity to come forward to respond to the demands of a situation.

In a situation, therefore, memory images (which include both habits and recollections—from now on I will designate both of these as recollections for short) rush to the support of a perception and create a composite with it. But in *Matter and Memory*, Bergson describes a crucial reversal of this relation between perception and memory, or rather of the relative importance of its terms. On first impression, it looks as though perception is primary, for it initiates the search for recollections that come to its aid; in this view, memory would be a kind of supplement to experience. But this neglects the extent to which experience is pragmatically oriented, for our perceptive apparatus, in fact, is not so much devoted to *perceiving* as it is to *actualizing* useful recollections.

It is indisputable that the basis of real, and so to speak instantaneous, intuition, on which our perception of the external world is developed, is a small matter compared with all that memory adds to it. Just because the recollection of earlier analogous intuitions is more useful than the intuition itself, being bound up in memory with the whole series of subsequent events and capable thereby of throwing a better light on our decision, *it supplants the real intuition of which the office is then merely . . . to call up the recollection, to give it a body, to render it active and thereby actual. . . . We must take into account that perception ends by merely an occasion for remembering* [une occasion de se souvenir], that we measure in practice the degree of reality by the degree of utility, and, finally, that it is our interest *to regard as mere signs of the real those immediate intuitions* which are, in fact, part and parcel of reality. (*MM*, 66, emphasis added)

For the most part, the primary function of perception is to motivate the manifestation of memory. No longer can we say, as might be expected, that memory is useful to perception, but instead that perception is useful to memory insofar as it serves as a vessel in which useful memories can be embodied.

I call this particular arrangement between perception and memory *inattentive judgment*. Admittedly, the term is foreign to both Bergson and Deleuze, who opt for inattentive perception and inattentive recognition, respectively. By using *judgment* rather than *perception*, I do not mean to introduce a new sense to Bergson's analysis; I claim only that insofar as every perception actualizes a recollection, every perception is a judgment in the sense that it makes an assertion of a subject. What I wish to say is that an inattentive perception *is* an inattentive judgment insofar as a recognizable situation calls up recollections in order to act. These recollections recognize, evaluate, and use perceptions toward an eventual action; in this capacity, they are judgments. And later, I will say that an attentive perception *is* an attentive judgment insofar as an unrecognizable encounter initiates a creative relationship between perception and memory. I intend, in other words, to show not only that there is a rich theory of judgment to be explored with Bergson but that *Matter and Memory* has already proposed its two modes: inattentive and attentive.

I begin with the first mode: inattentive judgment. What is unique about this kind of judgment is that instead of lingering over an encounter (a thing, a situation, etc.) as though it deserved a prolonged and singular analysis, the encounter is used merely as representative, as a sign of, the recollection it is meant to solicit. "In most cases, *these memories supplant our actual perceptions*, of which we then retain only a few hints, thus using them merely as 'signs' that recall to us former images" (*MM*, 33, emphasis added). Inattentive judgment, therefore, designates the process whereby perception straightaway actualizes recollections in order to deal with an encounter.

Habit memories are especially important to inattentive judgment. To prepare his discussion of habits in *Matter and Memory*, Bergson returns to his early depiction of a perceiving subject amid a universe of images. These images are interrogative, inquiring as to the potential action that will eventually define them. "So many points of space are there able to solicit my will and to pose, so to speak, an elementary question to my motor activity. Every such question is what is termed a perception" (*MM*, 45). The whole point of habits, Bergson says, is to equip us with a stock of ready responses in order to quiet these questions, not to have to answer them at every instance. And with an extraordinary analogy, Bergson likens habitual responses to neurological damage. "Perception is diminished by one of its elements each time one of the [neural] threads termed sensory is cut because some part of the external object then becomes unable [*impuissante*] to solicit my activity, and also whenever a stable habit has been formed, *because this time the readymade response renders the question unnecessary [inutile]*" (*MM*, 45, emphasis added, translation modified).

Thanks to inattentive perception and habits, the questions and problems posed by each encountered image can be circumvented by prepared reactions. An inattentive perception has the unique function of seeing unique images as just another occasion of something recollected. In this sense, the question or problem posed by the image is suppressed in favor of the recognition and activity supplied by a recollection. Or, to return to the terms of our discussion, for each encountered image, we have a snap judgment prepared, one that can immediately identify what the image is and what we are to do with it. This kind of judgment blocks out the questions and problems it may pose; it turns a uniquely encountered image into a familiar occasion. With inattentive judgment we gain decisive and immediate recognition and action at the expense of genuine or singular engagement.

I must be clear that neither Bergson nor Deleuze criticizes inattentive perception (or, I conjecture, inattentive judgment) as such. Both of them are aware that it would be an overwhelming and impossible demand to let each image address its unique question to our possible action. But Bergson and Deleuze do criticize habits and inattentive perception when they are taken beyond their proper and legitimate sphere of necessity and pragmatic action. As a guiding thread to the reading of *Matter and Memory*, Bergson warns that "the habits formed in action find their way up to the sphere of speculation, where they create fictitious problems, and that metaphysics must begin by dispersing this artificial obscurity" (*MM*, 16).[29] For his part, Deleuze never derides the principle and formation of habits; in fact, he devotes some of his favorite pages in *Difference and Repetition* to their exploration.[30] But habits become dogmatic when the ends of pragmatic experience—namely, identification and recognition—confuse themselves with the ends of thought.

Leading back to law, I show that inattentive perception is vital to the operation and success of adjudication. But where I turn critical is by identifying inattentive judgment as the source of our illusion about judgment, namely, that it is subsumptive. Let me explain this. If we take judgment in the sense of predicating claims of a subject, we can claim that for Bergson all judgments are composites of perception and memory: The perception of an object actualizes a recollection in order to act. Judgment for Bergson has nothing to do with subsuming under rules; it has everything to do with actualizing recollections in the present, with connecting a virtual past to an actual present. A judgment is a connection or a composition of perception and memory; it is not a subsumption of perception by memory.

How, then, is the illusion of subsumption formed? It arises by virtue of the peculiar role of memory in inattentive judgment. Here, the office of perception is to suggest memories to orient action. Perception downplays or minimizes itself as much as possible, and recollections, usually drawn from habit memory, are given full reign. The consequence is that the composite nature of judgment is disguised by the heavy emphasis on applying general recollections to thin perceptions. Bergson repeatedly describes this process. "These [recollection] images *constantly mingle* [*se mêleront*] with our perception of the present *and may even take its place*. For if they have survived it is with a view to utility; at every moment they complete our present experience . . . [and] must end by *covering up and submerging* [perception]" (*MM*, 66, emphasis added, translation modified). Bergson's diagnosis is acute; initially memory and perception are composite (they mingle), but memory will come to achieve dominance as though it were subsumptive (it covers and submerges).

Later in *Matter and Memory*, habit memory, in service of inattentive perception, again appears to forfeit composition with perception in favor of subsumption.

[As recollections are] more and more removed from their personal and original form, [they become] more and more capable, from their lack of distinguishing features [*dans leur banalité*], of being *applied* to the present perception and of determining it *after the manner of a species which defines and absorbs the individual* [*de la déterminer à la manière d'une espèce englobant l'individu*]. (*MM*, 106, emphasis added)

Here Bergson likens judgment—or as he calls it, the determination of a perception—to subsumption par excellence: categorical judgment. Just like the relationship between a species and an individual, recollections are applied to an individual perception that they define and absorb. This should come as no surprise, given that one dwells on an object as little as possible, alighting only long enough to actualize a recollection that does all the determining work. Although in truth—and perhaps this is why Bergson says that memory determines merely "after the manner" of subsumption, as in not quite fully subsumptive despite its dearest wishes—a judgment always implies a reciprocal determination of the image by perception and memory, here that reciprocity is so faint and memory so strong that it looks as though memory alone effects the determination. Working in concert, an inattentive perception ignores the appeals and questions posed to it by the image and thereby prepares the image as just another specimen to be gathered under a recollection, which, actualized from the lower plane of the pure past, appears precisely in the guise of a rule or species competent to subsume the perception. By diminishing as much as possible the composite nature of any judgment—insofar as recollections are only actualized within perception and work concertedly together to determine the object—inattentive judgment is able to give rise to a convincing illusion: that judgment is categorical and subsumptive. In its way, *Matter and Memory* gives us a dialectical analysis worthy of Kant. By its very nature inattentive judgment gives rise to pernicious and almost intractable illusions about judgment generally.

Let us look now to law. Considering that nearly all cases—not just appellate cases but also all minor matters that go to trial—are adjudicated according to inattentive judgment, it is no wonder that illusions about the nature of judgment are commonplace. For every open-and-shut case (or borrowing from Dworkin, for every "easy case") a process of inattentive judgment is active in that a certain set of facts leads a judge to unhesitatingly actualize a certain rule. The perception of a certain situation poses a problem to a judge who will straightaway actualize a rule by which to act and resolve it, that is, *to judge it* (judgment is the judge's kind of action). And this is absolutely necessary. If judges did not have at their disposal so many prepared answers for so many cases—if, in other words, judges heard the solicitations and questions posed by each and every case—then not only would the courts collapse under the weight of backlog, but, more important, the predictive and regular application of justice would be at risk.[31]

Inattentive judgment performs a crucial regularizing function in adjudication. It is of chief importance to litigants that the judge, as far as possible, respond to the present case just as it has been responded to in the past. In this sense, stare decisis and habit memory are coincident: "to stand by things decided," that is, to uphold the doctrine of precedent whereby a court will follow earlier judicial decisions when the same points recur in litigation. But of course the same points *never* exactly recur in litigation—as an image, every case is different—and this is precisely why inattentive judgment is invaluable. To actualize a leading rule or precedent, judges must ascertain that the same conditions apply—that is, that, legally speaking, the present case and the precedent are identical—which is precisely what the evaluation made by inattentive judgment is suited to do. A thin perception of the present case enables a link to the leading case, which is then actualized in the present. Inattentive judgment is requisite for stare decisis and with it the predictability and regularity of the courts. To evoke a specific recollection—for a judge to evoke the leading case—the present perception must be such that it can spontaneously choose that recollection. Or, negatively put, a perception sensitive to all the questions and problems posed by an image would be unable to evoke a generalized recollection. This kind of recollection could never do the image justice; it just wouldn't fit and so would never be called on and actualized in the first place. If a judge were to see every angle and every possible question raised for action by a case, it would be with great difficulty that the general leading rule could be identified and actualized. But thankfully, inattentive judgment always aims at action, at muting the problems posed by an image in favor of a prepared recollection. This kind of perception captures the outline of the case just enough to suggest a general recollection; as such, it is the precondition for the successful application of a leading precedent and stare decisis.

But understood improperly, inattentive judgment raises two dangers for adjudication: first, to confuse judgment with subsumption; and second, potentially, to be insensitive to the new. In a subsumptive judgment, a rule is applied to a case such that the case is determined and the rule is instantiated but unmodified. By their nature, judgments of inattentive judgment can easily be mistaken for subsumption. Why? Because these sorts of judgments adjudicate a case by actualizing a rule that does not undergo modification. As I said, the aim of inattentive perception is to prompt the instantiation of a recollection in order to act; to this end, inattentive percepts are offered up to determination by memory. These inattentive percepts are by nature nonspecific, abstract. Likewise, a judge will perceive a case in such a manner as to immediately call to mind a rule to recognize and treat it, that is, by which to judge it. For most cases there can be no question of concertedly probing perception and memory in a sensitive adaptation of the one to the other that will modify both. The demands of regularity, time, and money—in short, of action—forbid it. Instead, a perception of the case is sought to incite a mechanical repetition of the past rule to determine it. The goal, therefore, of inattentive judgment is to disguise itself as, or at least reap the rewards of, subsumptive judgment: one in which the rule is applied to and determines the case. It is a form of judgment that operates just like a categorical judgment, wherein a species covers an individual such that the nature of the individual is expressed through the determination of the species concept. This type of judgment offers enormous practical advantages for the courts, for only in this way can unique situations be judged as just another manifestation of a rule. But for all that, and despite appearances, judgment does not relinquish its connective nature; it only underplays it to extract the obvious benefits for action that subsumption offers. A Bergsonian analysis, therefore, provides an etiology of the illusion of subsumption and an appreciation of its desired effects without relinquishing an understanding of its underlying condition in the connective actualization of the pure past within a present perception.

The second danger follows from the first. If the exigencies of adjudication cause it to adopt a subsumptive orientation, then this comes with the danger of insensitivity toward the new. This is not necessary, for although inattentive judgment is essential to adjudication, it is not exhaustive of it. But if we forget that subsumption is only a disguise, and by consequence forget the connective origins of judgment, then we run the risk that a new situation will be approached only by asking what rule suffices to cover it. Cardozo complains that "some judges seldom get beyond that process in any case. Their notion of their duty is to match the colors of the case at hand against the colors of many sample cases spread upon their desk. The same nearest in shade supplies the applicable rule. . . . The man who had the best card index would also be the wisest judge" (*NJP*, 113). What is to be feared, therefore, is application of rules to situations for which they are no longer adequate. In Deleuze's idiom, this danger can be called the sterile repetition of rules. As Holmes says,

> Every living sentence which shows a mind at work for itself is to be welcomed. It is not the first use but the *tiresome repetition* of inadequate catchwords which I am observing—phrases which originally were contributions, but which, by their very felicity, delay further analysis for fifty years. That comes from the same source as the dislike of novelty—intellectual indolence or weakness—*a slackening in the eternal pursuit of the more exact.*[32]

Between the necessary repetitions of rules in inattentive judgment and this tiresome repetition that Holmes describes lies a fine balance. How, then, are we to steer between necessary recognitions and subsumptions, and their potentially violent and outmoded extension? How can adjudication be, as Holmes urges, exact without being either dangerously repetitive or dangerously ingenious?

Attentive Judgment

It may seem surprising to have affirmed, within limits, inattentive judgment in light of our critique of the dogmatic image of law. First, does this theory not reinstate the kind of subsumption we saw in Kant and Hart? Is inattentive judgment not designed to circumvent encounters by securing recognition in the appearance of a perception as overcoded by memory? Is this not transcendental judgment by another name in that objects of appearance (perceptions) appear only from within the horizon of the concepts of the understanding (recollections)? What's more, we also upheld the necessity of a kind of judgment that pretends to subsumption. This too smacks of dogmatism in that cases would gain their difference and being by sheer conceptual determination of a rule, itself unmodified in application. Does this kind of subsumption not vitiate an authentic concept of repetition (in the sterile repetition of rule application to new cases) *and* an authentic concept of difference (in the conceptual determination of the singular case)?

But, and to turn a Bergsonian phrase, inattentive judgment is only one half of judgment. This isn't to say that within or behind inattentive judgment lies its other half; no, it stands alone, sufficient for its purpose of action. Instead, there is another kind of judgment, one that I call attentive judgment.[33] The basis to distinguish between the two, and by which to move from one kind of judgment to the other, is the encounter—that is, what the encounter does to us, how it is engaged, and what it provokes.

A simple formula can summarize Bergson's inattentive perception: Situation → Action → Modified Situation. A situation presents itself as a problem for action; perception along with memory determines an action to solve it; the situation is modified accordingly. If judgment is the kind of action peculiar to judges, then we have the following: A case appears before the court; the judge perceives it in connection with recollected rules (this *is* judgment); the case is modified, that is, adjudicated. In this sort of judgment, recollections insert themselves between perception and action—or better, the insertion of a recollection into a perception *is* the action, it *is* the judgment. In its immediate presentation the case is judged, already determined by the rules with which it is associated. In this scheme, there is no genetic or problematic encounter: This case is recognized and judged as an example of that rule. This is why with inattentive perception or judgment there are never any true encounters, only this or that situation to which we react. As Cardozo tells us—and, given that he served as an appellate judge, the true ratio is surely higher—this fate awaits nearly all cases: "Nine-tenths, perhaps more, of the cases that come before a court are predetermined—predetermined in the sense that they are predestined—their fate established by inevitable laws that follow them from birth to death."[34]

But what happens in that tiny minority, in that less than ten percent? An unrecognized encounter, that is, a true encounter, one that does not come predetermined by an inevitable law. Here, the court is caught unprepared in the sense that it cannot cancel out the encounter with a ready-made rule up its sleeve. "It is when the colors do not match, when the references in the index fail, *when there is no decisive precedent, that the serious business of the judge begins*" (*NJP*, 113, emphasis added). In no uncertain terms, Cardozo tells us that the real work of the judge and of judgment starts with a failure of recognition.

This question of recognition and its failure offers a promising lead into Bergson and Deleuze. From the discussion in Chapter 4, we can enumerate the characteristics of the encounter: It is *unrecognized*; it is *singular*; it is *forceful*, it forces thought to think; and it is the *transcendental* condition for thought, that which breaks thought away from routine recognition. In sum, we might say that the encounter is an *interruption*. An encounter interrupts the links between perception and recollection in inattentive judgment; it interrupts that smooth process whereby a percept immediately calls to mind a recollection to recognize it.

In connection with this notion of interruption, Deleuze's discussion of the breakdown of recognition and the encounter in *Cinema 2* is exemplary. Although it may seem odd to draw on his *Cinema* books for a theory of law, these two texts represent some of Deleuze's best and most sustained thinking on Bergson, time, and movement. With respect to the concept of the encounter, it is helpful to look at Deleuze's distinction between pre- and postwar cinema, even if we are not concerned with the details. According to Deleuze, what separates pre- from postwar cinema is that postwar cinema evidences the "shattering of the sensory-motor schema" (*C1*, ix). The sensory-motor schema is defined by the action-oriented exchange between perception and memory characteristic of inattentive perception. Prewar cinema exhibits this sensory-motor schema because its movies are organized by characters who encounter an initial situation that provokes a series of reactions that modifies (and almost always resolves) the situation. Inattentive perception operates according to the sensory-motor schema: We perceive enough of a situation to actualize a recollection that will, in turn, respond to the situation at hand. Most of these reactions, we have seen, are induced by perceptions that actualize habits and general recollections suitable (by virtue of their generality) to act within any number of situations. For this reason, Deleuze gives the sensory-motor schema (and indirectly, inattentive perception) a severe characterization.

A cliché is a sensory-motor image of the thing. As Bergson says, we do not perceive the thing or the image in its entirety, we always perceive less of it, we perceive only what we are interested in perceiving, or rather what it is in our interest to perceive. . . . We therefore normally perceive only in cliché. (*C2*, 20)

Given what I said about Deleuze not abjuring habits or inattentive perception per se, this identification of sensory-motor images as cliché might seem harsh. In his defense, I could note that this particular passage raises the question of cliché in connection with type-set emotional schemata that tolerate systematic poverty and oppression (a "civilization of the image" [*C2*, 21]). But this historical index of cliché is not necessary for us: It is undeniable that cliché always lurks within inattentive perception insofar as recognizable formulas and characterization are of inestimable use. This, as I pointed out earlier, is both the advantage and the danger of inattentive perception: We perceive in order to recollect and act, not to perceive as such.

What happens in postwar cinema is the breakdown of cliché, or in Bergsonian parlance, an inhibition of the relays between perception and memory necessary for action. It is not exactly that the cliché comes under more intense criticism; rather, it is that perception is unable to call up clichés as it used to; cliché can no longer do what it once did. In the postwar period, according to Deleuze, the situations to which we no longer know how to react are multiplied, and "what tends to collapse, or at least to lose its position, is the sensory-motor schema which constituted the action-image of the old cinema" (C2, xi). In other words, what happens when sensory-motor linkages jam and break in the face of certain situations is the experience of an encounter, the unrecognized. Such an encounter provokes a shift away from acting toward perceiving.

> It is here that situations no longer extend [*prolongent*] into action or reaction in accordance with the requirements of the movement-image. These are pure optical and sound situations, in which the character does not know how to respond.... But he has gained in an ability *to see* [*en voyance*] what *he has lost in action or reaction*: he SEES so that the viewer's problem becomes "What is there to see in the image?" (and not now "What are we going to see in the next image?"). The situation no longer extends into action through the intermediary of affections. It is cut off from all its extensions, *it is now important only for itself*, having absorbed all its affective intensities, all its active extension. This is no longer a sensory-motor situation, but a purely optical and sound situation, where the seer [*voyant*] has replaced the agent [*actant*]: a "description." (C2, 272)

A genuine encounter interrupts recognition by suspending the spontaneous linkages between perceptions and recollections. This is the negative function of the encounter; it inhibits recognition and reaction. In the terms of the *Cinema* books, the sensory-motor linkage that aims at action is shattered. But there is also a positive function to the encounter: It teaches us to see, to properly perceive. The theme of striving "to see in order to see, and no longer to see in order to act" is taken from *Creative Evolution* (*CE*, 298). It is also implied in the concept of inattentive judgment. This kind of judgment has no intention of properly seeing or perceiving; its office is to act and recollect. But when an encounter is such that no suitable recollection can be spontaneously actualized to match it, we are forced, for once, to perceive and to see, that is, to acknowledge and exceed the limitations imposed on us by pragmatic perception. The less we recognize, the better we see, for instead of being cut short by a ready-made reaction, the encounter imposes itself. It is not as if we voluntarily choose to dwell on or properly see an encounter; instead, an encounter catches us unprepared. Without ready recollections to recognize and react to the situation, we are disarmed, left with no choice but to dwell on and really see it. We can at last describe something rather than have it provoke repetitive and predictable reactions. This kind of encounter, therefore, is not just a transcendental condition for (authentic and not dogmatic) thought (*DR*, 139); it is also the transcendental condition for perception, for a perception that has regained its rights and is no longer merely ancillary to recollection (*DR*, 144–145).

I can give two examples of this kind of breakdown in which perception becomes primary and attentive. First, and as so often happens with Deleuze, I find an illustrative philosophical antecedent in Kant. What, according to Kant, happens in an aesthetic judgment of the beautiful? We experience a sensible phenomenon without determining it by rules. "[It] keeps us in the state of having the presentation itself, and [keeps] the cognitive powers engaged in their occupation without any further aim. We *linger in our contemplation of the beautiful*, because this contemplation reinforces and reproduces itself" (*CJ*, 68, §12, emphasis added). The similarities among Kant and Deleuze and Bergson are numerous on this point. First, a singular encounter provokes an aesthetic judgment of beauty; it is *this* particular thing before me, and not things in general, that provokes an aesthetic experience of the beautiful.[35] Second, this encounter is not covered or treated by a concept. Indeed, the definition of a reflective judgment of beauty is that it eludes conceptuality; not only does an aesthetic judgment of beauty resist the determinations of an empirical concept ("What a beautiful *rose*!"), but it also eludes the pure concepts of the understanding ("This rose *is* . . .").[36] Third, Kant expressly says that we dwell and linger in contemplation; the experience and intuition of the object becomes an end in itself, its own aim, and not subservient to determinative or practical judgment. My intent is not to belabor this comparison, only to point out that in Kant there are depictions of encounters wherein representational determination is suspended in favor of a different mode of judgment.

The second example is from law, or a movie about law: *Twelve Angry Men* (1957, directed by Sidney Lumet). Now, in *Cinema 2* Deleuze gives this movie short shrift, identifying it as part of a "genre of literally judicial films" aimed at "pointing out the difficulty of reaching the true, taking into account the shortcomings of the investigation and of those who judge" (*C2*, 138). This seems hasty and, in fact, we ought to reconsider whether this movie merits its designation as judicial, that is, as a movie that reaffirms judgment and the search for truth despite all obstacles.

In *Twelve Angry Men* a young man is tried for murder and the evidence doesn't look good. Eleven of the twelve jurors initially find the defendant guilty; one holds out, saying he's not sure (Juror 8). This one juror raises doubts as to all points of evidence and eventually convinces the others to acquit the accused one by one over the course of the film. The movie opens with the jurors chatting about how the case is "open-and-shut" and how it will be over with time to spare to "make the ball-game." But after the preliminary vote it becomes clear that they are not unanimous; one does not recognize what all the others do. It is telling that Juror 8 says that he votes "not guilty" *not* because he thinks the accused is innocent but because he simply doesn't know; he is in doubt. Juror 8 here is like Dostoevsky's idiot that Deleuze so admires, the one who denies what everyone else claims to know (*DR*, 130; *WP*, 62).

In the initial go-round, when the other jurors try to convince Juror 8 of the defendant's guilt, it is quite clear that they have inattentively made up their minds, as it were. For these jurors, a quickly garnered perception of the case was sufficient to call up recollections that led to an inevitable guilty verdict. And so, the accused is guilty because he's from the slums (Jurors 3, 4, and 10), because he had a motive in revenge (Jurors 6 and 4), because his alibi is flimsy (Jurors 3, 4, 7, and 10), because he's an ungrateful kid (Juror 3), and because of conclusive testimony (all jurors, except Juror 8). But this list should not lead us to conclude that some of these reasons are at the level of prejudice and that others are at the level of fact. What the film shows is that all these putative reasons have the same status as cliché in the specific sense that they are drawn from perceptions more concerned with actualizing decisive recollections than with carefully perceiving. This is why Juror 8 can oppose all of them with the same denial. In this respect, he jams up the sensory-motor linkages and insists that the case be encountered and not evaded.

And so, the rest of the movie *dwells* on the circumstances of the case, carefully probing a detailed perception and joining it to the recollections of the jurors (drawn both from the case and from their own lives) until, finally, an acquittal is delivered. Far from being a juridical movie where the truth-seeking value of judgment is affirmed against all odds, *Twelve Angry Men* is a vivid demonstration of the breakdown of a certain type of (inattentive) judgment in the realm where it was ostensibly most secure, the law. The acquittal the jurors return does not affirmatively pronounce the accused innocent; instead, this verdict is testament to the thick layer of doubt that has disabled the basic resource and mainstay of adjudication: inattentive judgment. The movie does not resolve in a judgment of recognition (guilt or innocence) but in the indetermination of reasonable doubt.

A final quality of the film that deserves attention, one directly tied to the experience of dwelling on a single perception, is how long the film feels to the viewer despite running only an hour and a half. To my mind, what gives this impression is the often hysterical objections raised by the jurors to Juror 8's denials of what they all recognize. These objections are all of a nature: "Is he going to keep us here *forever*!?" "We could talk *all night* and not get anywhere!" "He's wasting our *time*!" and the like. But what these jurors violently object to is not, it seems to me, the delay or wasting of chronological time but something much more profound: the challenge to expeditious perception and quick judgments. Dwelling on the case for these jurors is insufferable not for the ostensible reason of lost time (that would be silly, given that the movie takes place in real time) but because dwelling on a perception assails a mode of judgment that sees the case only as an opportunity for fast and ready action. In other words, the movie seems so long because it opens the viewer up to a qualitatively different kind of temporality, one that eschews the pragmatic exigencies of ready responses and the spontaneous actualization of the past in favor of a sustained exploration of the pure past in conjunction with an attentive perception.

The delightful candor of *Twelve Angry Men* cannot be matched in actual judgments, for what judge would openly say "I can't recognize this case" or "I'm in doubt"? Nevertheless, despite its clear demonstration of the breakdown of inattentive judgment, this film is limited in three ways for our analysis (which is not, of course, to criticize it). First, it remains confined to questions of fact and not of law, asking only whether or not the accused could have done it. Second, it gives the impression that a case attentively judged is only a case better described, with more details brought into relief. Third, it does not show a necessary connection between attentive judgment and creativity.

To take up the second point, the transition from inattentive to attentive judgment cannot rest on a more accurate or fuller description of empirical reality. It is, as Deleuze explains, more significantly based on the difference the encounter provokes in the relationship between memory and perception.

> The sensory-motor image effectively retains from the thing only what interests us, or what extends into the reaction of a character. Its richness is thus superficial and comes from the fact that it *associates with the thing many different things that resemble it on the same plane*, insofar as they provoke all the same movements: it is grass in general that interests the herbivore. It is in this sense that the sensory-motor schema is an agent of abstraction. Conversely, the pure optical image [i.e., the encounter] *may be only a description*, and concern a character who no longer knows how or is no longer able to react to the situation: the restraint of this image, the thinness of what it retains, line or simple point, "slight fragment without importance," bring the thing each time to an essential singularity, *and describe the inexhaustible, endlessly referring to other descriptions*. It is, then, the optical image which is really rich. (*C2*, 45, emphasis added)

At a superficial level the difference between a sensory-motor and an optical image—that is, between an image acted on and an image encountered—appears to be richness of detail: the sensory-motor image is abstract and drops what is superfluous for action; the optical image is rich and results from a prolonged description. But what is the nature of this description? Deleuze is clear that it is not the image itself that is richly described. Far from it: From this we retain a thin account, a line, or a point. The richness results from referring the image to other descriptions, that is, with repeated reference to memory. An empirically richer description of an image might be at stake for a perception utterly divorced from memory; but wed as it is to memory, this is not the nature of our perception. At issue, therefore, is not an image more or less empirically described, but rather the relationship between perception and memory in its inattentive and attentive modes: from one where perception consistently actualizes recollections from the same plane of memory to provoke the same movements, to the other where a few aspects of a perception are dwelled on so

Judgment sub specie durationis 181

as to elicit descriptions that, once actualized together in the perception, cohere as an essential singularity.

I call this act of attention, this new relationship between perception and memory, a *circuit*. Bergson is fond of this metaphor, proof of which is his first diagram in *Matter and Memory* (*MM*, 105). This diagram (Figure 2) is of central importance for us, for not only does it bring us to the other half of judgment (i.e., attentive judgment), but more significantly, it substantiates our guiding claim as to the creativity of judgment.

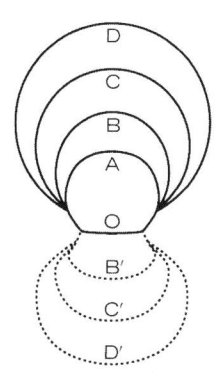

FIGURE 2. Circuit diagram

A circuit can be established only by virtue of an encounter that inhibits or arrests movement. This encounter is, in the plainest sense, something we do not know what to do with. Rather than evoke a ready response, it initiates a prolonged, experimental search.

Memory thus creates anew the present perception, or rather doubles this perception by reflecting either its proper image or some other recollection-image of the same kind. If the retained or remembered image will not cover all the details of the image that is being perceived, *an appeal is made to the deeper, more distant regions of memory, until other details that are already known come to project themselves upon those details that remain unperceived* [*ceux qu'on ignore*]. And the operation may continue indefinitely—memory strengthening and enriching perception, which in turn becoming wider, draws into itself a growing number of complementary recollections. . . . Metaphor for metaphor [*Image pour image*], we prefer to compare the elementary work of attention to that of the telegraph clerk who, on receipt of an important dispatch, sends it back again, word for word, in order to check its accuracy. (*MM*, 101–102, emphasis added, translation modified)

This passage is crucial toward developing a concept of attentive judgment. Again, I admit that Bergson did not develop an explicit theory of judgment. Nevertheless, by combining his concept of attentive perception together with the emphatic sense of the encounter in Deleuze, we can formulate a concept of judgment that is inherently creative. This is a kind of judgment that creates by the very nature of its activity. But before we leap to this conclusion, let me identify five characteristics of attentive judgment in coordination with Bergson's text.

We have already heard its first characteristic, but it bears repeating: It dwells. Inattentive judgment uses perceptions as opportunities to instantiate recollections and rules for action. But now we are caught up with an encounter, with the unrecognizable, such that sensory-motor extension is suspended. Because the encounter cannot be resolved into movement, judgment dwells in it, or judgment is a process that dwells with it.

This brings us to the second characteristic of attentive judgment: It reveals itself as in time. Of course, all judgment is in time in that it actualizes the pure past. But only the interruption of recognition fully reveals the virtual past as the condition and element of judgment (see *C2*, xii, 54). Given the spontaneity of inattentive judgment, we lose an awareness of the pure past, for we come into contact only with those actualized recollections that inhabit present perception. But in the prolonged search of memory implied by attentive judgment, we enter into sustained exploration of the (pure or virtual) past. When Bergson writes that we make appeals to the "deeper, more distant regions of memory," we cannot subject this phrase to a chronological interpretation. Given that the entire past coexists with itself (paradox 2), the claim can only be ontological: We leap into, inhabit, and dwell in a time that is distant and deep by virtue of its virtuality. Once engaged with the process of attentive judgment, the relationship to time is made visible and perceptible. Attentive judgment reveals the pure past—and no less important, the search of the pure past—presupposed in every judgment and perception (see *DR*, 211).

The third and fourth characteristics of attentive judgment go hand in hand: It is experimental and cumulative. Because no recollection can treat the encounter (this is what makes it an encounter), we choose one recollection image after another to launch "in the direction of a new perception" in the hope of illuminating it (*MM*, 102). In this sense, attentive judgment adopts an experimental attitude, trying one recollection out after another on the perception.

But what is fascinating about this experimentation is that it is a cumulative process. As Bergson's passage suggests, the encountered perception productively and positively resists recognition. On the one hand, no single recollection suffices to treat or to recognize it; it remains an encounter. On the other hand, each recollection we try out reveals what was at first unperceived. Bergson's phrase to describe this process is complex: "If the retained or remembered image will not cover all the details of the image that is being perceived . . . other details that are already known come to project themselves upon those details that remain unperceived [*ceux qu'on ignore*]." A preliminary interpretation would suggest that recollections bring to notice details in the perception that initially went unperceived. But there is more to it, for each newly discovered percept brings us to another area of memory, another recollection—we are ceaselessly made to revisit the deep and distant pure past. We must conclude, therefore, that perception and memory mutually explore one another: An encounter prompts one to experimentally try out recollections to help make sense of it; these recollections, while not recognizing the encounter per se, illuminate its previously unperceived and ignored aspects; and these new discoveries in turn incite more leaps and continued exploration of the pure past, bringing to light new memories, and so on. In this cumulative experimentation—in this shuttling to and fro from the plane of perception to the plane of memory—a rich composite of memory and perception grows. We retain a few features of an encounter and refer these, over and over, to the descriptions of memory; in so doing, an essential singularity is created.

At last, we reach the fifth, final, and most important feature of attentive judgment: It is creative. That judgment is creative seems unlikely. The very function (or, anticipating Spinoza, *conatus essendi*) of our sensory-motor schema is to recognize and act—by design, that's all judgment wants. Judgment has a one-track mind; it always takes on a pragmatic orientation of recognition in the service of action. Only the encounter frustrates this activity and interrupts its linkages. Yet, even within an encounter, judgment stubbornly pursues its course and calls up recollections in the hope that one might be successful. But precisely here lies Bergson's great reversal, transforming judgment into a creative capacity. In striving toward recognition, an experimental and cumulative process is initiated wherein perception and recollection shuttle back and forth and, in this activity, create a composite singularity. Try as it might, a recollection cannot be found to treat the encounter to satisfaction—this is what makes it an encounter—and so judgment tries one recollection on after another. From the perspective of inattention and recognition, this is a vain process, for none of them will fit; but from the perspective of attention and creativity, this is a productive process that will construct, rather than recognize, the encounter.

Thanks to the encounter, judgment will create or produce a unique product, an unprecedented composite of recollections and perceptions. When Bergson tells us that "memory thus *creates anew* the present perception," we must take the word *create* in the emphatic sense of novelty and invention, not as duplication or sterile doubling. Nor is it that the encounter is created out of thin air; it is instead built up and engendered by the process of attentive judgment. Through the process of attentive judgment, the encountered image becomes indissociably joined to memories that have described it, and equally, the recollections become inseparable from the encountered image in which they are actualized. *Attentive judgment, therefore, always creates a singularity.* Far from recognizing an image as it set out to do, judgment instead connects to an encountered image recollections that "discover in a perception that which could not be perceived in it at first" (*MM*, 102). And, as I said, the process does not stop there, for these newly discovered percepts lead back to a renewed search of memory, trawling for recollections to connect with this enriched perception. By virtue of this process, a composite image of perception and recollection is created.

With his concept of attentiveness, Bergson turns judgment on its head: It is precisely *because* judgment persists in trying to recognize an encounter that it creatively engenders the encounter instead. Initially, the encounter is purely negative; it is what defies recognition and the application of recollections. This defiance, however, provokes the positive, productive, and reciprocal explorations of memory and perception that cohere as a genuine creation. What starts with preliminary nonrecognition engenders a positive creation or "constructivism."[37] For Deleuze, the encounter is what forces thought to think and break from recognition; for us, the encounter is what forces judgment to judge and break away from inattentive judgment. Attentive judgment, therefore, constructs and creates the encounter as an essential singularity. Let's look to Bergson's decisive text on this matter in relation to Figure 2.

> An act of attention implies such a solidarity between the mind [*l'esprit*] and its object, it is a circuit so well closed that we cannot pass to states of higher concentration *without creating, whole and entire, so many new circuits which envelop the first and have nothing in common between them but the perceived object*. Of these different circles of memory, which we shall later study in detail, the smallest, A, is the nearest to immediate perception. It contains only the object O, with the following image that comes back and overlies it. Behind it, the larger and larger circles B, C, D correspond to growing efforts of intellectual expansion. It is the whole of memory, as we shall see, that enters into each of these circuits, since memory is always present; but that memory, capable by virtue of its elasticity, of expanding more and more, reflects upon the object a growing number of suggested images [*chose suggérées*]—sometimes the details of the object itself, sometimes concomitant details which may throw light upon it. Thus, after having rebuilt [*reconstitué*] the object perceived, as an independent whole, we reassemble [*reconstituons*], together with it, the more and more distant conditions with which it forms one system. Let us call B', C', D' these causes of growing depth, situated behind the object and virtually given with the object itself. *We see that the progress of attention results in creating anew not only the object perceived, but also the ever widening systems with which it may be bound up*; so that in the measure in which the circles B, C, D represent a higher expansion of memory, their reflection attains in B', C', D' deeper strata of reality. (*MM*, 104–105, emphasis added, translation modified)

I address three themes from this very rich text: the indiscernibility of the past and present, the creation of the object, and the creation of the past. I find the first theme, one already familiar to us, repeated in a sophisticated, concise fashion. A perceived object always coexists with the pure past repeated on different layers of contraction. From the perception of the object (O) we leap first into one layer (A) and then another (B, C, D). But if we leap into a layer, why does Bergson speak of circuits? It is because the circuit indicates the dynamic and productive *exchange* between the actual and the virtual. Thus, on the one hand, the circuit represents the actualization of a particular layer of the past within a perceived object; and on the other hand, the circuit represents the immersion of the perceived object in the virtual past. The circuit shows how the perceived object has one foot in the actual and the other in the virtual; it shows, in other words, that between the actual and the virtual there exists a "perpetual exchange" and indeed, "indiscernibility" (*C2*, 273).

Quickly sketched, we leap into the pure past to actualize a recollection from it, thereby creating a circuit. As Bergson says, each plane "reflects upon the object a growing number of suggested images" that throw light on the object, that can be actualized to help make sense of it. Now, with *in*attentive judgment we would quit here and execute a movement or action. But *attentive* judgment renews the leap, only this time into a different layer by virtue of the fact that our leaping point, the perceived image, is itself now different (for it is joined by the select recollections from the first leap; this is its cumulative nature—call this the irreversibility of time *within* a judgment). In attentive judgment, therefore, a perception travels back and forth from the virtual to the actual; it leaps into the virtual to return with an actualized recollection only to immerse itself again with a subsequent leap. Thus the indiscernibility between past and present indicates both the composite nature of any perception (that it coheres perception and recollection) and the restless exchange between actual and virtual modes of existence.

We pass now to the creation of the object. A repeated lament made by Bergson and Deleuze of metaphysics is that it lacks precision. We have seen this in two of Deleuze's critiques of dogmatism: The categories of the understanding fail to address the genesis of real experience in order to postulate the conditions of all possible experience, and generic concepts miss out on the singular in order to determine the particular (see Chapter 4). It is to overcome this generality that Bergson calls for an empiricism that dispenses with "ready-made conceptions" and "works only according to measure, sees itself obliged to make an *absolutely new effort for each new object it studies*" (*CM*, 175; also *B*, 28). I must be clear that the precision Bergson calls for—and that inspires *What Is Philosophy*—is not of the nature of a more exact and felicitous reference. Bergson refrains from taking this path. He is not looking for a concept that can designate or sign a state of affairs more exactly (this is, according to Bergson, for the natural sciences to do).

Straightaway, we see how Bergson's circuit scheme fulfills the demand for a new effort of analysis for every new object studied. The encounter is, by definition, a new object: It is one that does not fit ready-made conceptions, and it frustrates the endeavor to actualize a recollection and execute an action. But we are not left helpless. The encounter provokes many leaps into, with many actualizations of, the pure past. Around the perception of the object—around the encounter—recollections gather like clouds condensed on a particle.[38] In fact, the only thing these various recollections have in common is the perception that connects them. Gathering unto itself these recollections, the object or encounter is constituted as a rich artifact of the travel between perception and the planes of memory. The object is not so much perceived as it is created.

Attentive judgment is a constructivism. However unlikely, we find that a positive concept of judgment can affirm a Bergsonian metaphysics freed from inflexible concepts in favor of "mobile, almost fluid representations, always ready to mold themselves on the fleeting forms of intuition" (*CM*, 168) while simultaneously being amenable to a Deleuzian conceptual practice that stresses that "it's not enough simply to say concepts possess movement; you also have to construct intellectually mobile concepts" (*N*, 122). If it is true that the preferred tool of judgment is the ready-made rule or recollection, in an encounter, together with the attentiveness it excites, judgment is transformed into a power that performs the most subtle and singular combinations of recollections to objects. When forced to rise to the occasion, judgment can become, in other words, a faculty for the construction of intellectually mobile representations. (Call this an interpretation of necessity being the mother of invention.)

A famous example from Proust's *Swann's Way* might help us, Marcel and the madeleine. For years Marcel tasted madeleines without thinking twice, but the specific conjunction of one dipped in lime-blossom tea sets off an encounter.[39] He takes one sip, then another, each time exerting himself and leaping into a region of the past only to come up empty-handed, with only the feeling of some recollection "shift, try to rise."[40] What tries to rise is the "visual memory which is attached to this taste," and, as in attentive judgment, Marcel uses this sought-after visual memory to elucidate the taste, to ask of it "to translate for me the evidence of its contemporary, its inseparable companion, the taste, ask it to tell me what particular circumstance is involved, what period of the past."[41] Traveling from the plane of perception to memory and back, Marcel reciprocally interrogates taste with memory to discern the truth of the one in the other until finally, after many failed leaps, the recollection manifests itself (Sunday tea with Aunt Léonie). But it is clear that the object is perceived not as just another madeleine but as indissociably bound up with a whole psychic life; its very taste and perception is wedded to this past.[42] The encountered object—very different from the one recognized day in and out as a pastry—is created for Marcel in its connection to memory.

But it is not only the object or perception that is created, for as Proust makes plain, the recollection of Combray (the town of his childhood) is properly engendered, not merely found: "Seek? Not only that: *create*. It is face-to-face with something that does not yet exist and that only it can accomplish, then bring to light."[43]

This brings us to the third and last theme from the circuit diagram: the creation of the past. To stay with our example, we say with Deleuze that "Combray reappears, not as it was or as it could be, but in a splendor which was never lived" (*DR*, 85; *PS*, 59–61). There are two specific connected senses to this claim. On the one hand, what appears to Marcel is a Combray that never *was* in the sense that it is the virtual or the pure past; it never was because it coexists with the present and, in a way, it never is, if this is taken to mean actualized and representable. On the other hand, when Combray *is* recalled and represented, this is not in the sense of a duplication of how it appeared to him as a child but as a differential actualization within the context of the present perception. Bergson, Proust, and Deleuze are all of a mind on this point: The past is always modified by its actualization, which is to say that the repetition of the past is differential.

This differential (or creative) actualization of the past is made clear in Figure 2: "The progress of attention results in creating anew not only the object perceived, *but also the ever widening systems with which it may be bound up*" (*MM*, 105). Perception O establishes an initial circuit with A. Next, another leap is made and another circuit created (B); from there additional connections or links come to mind, and more circuits are made (D, C, etc.).

There are three distinct ways in which the past is differentially actualized in this process. First, a recollection is always actualized in a unique and unrepeatable situation; to this extent, even the most sterile habitual repetition always involves a (however minimal) modification to its instantiation (see Chapter 5).

Second, the encounter is an unrecognizable situation that precipitates a unique organization—rotation and translation—of the selected plane of memory. Bergson is clear that we actualize not just the one recollection but also the entire plane of memory specific to it, "the ever widening system." With the actualization of specific recollections comes an entire organization of the past. Thus, although the planes of memory fully preexist in the present (paradox 3), their actualization into circuits—what we have already interpreted as their gradual organization of a plane of memory into shining points and dominant recollections (see our earlier discussion)—occurs only under the pressure and constraint of the search of memory.

Third, and most important, the relationship between the circuits consists solely in the encounter that coheres them. In this sense, the recollections drawn from A, B, C are in an original configuration possible only in light of the encounter that searched for them. As Bergson says, we create "so many new circuits which envelop the first and have nothing in common between them but the perceived object." Attentive judgment constructs a unique constellation of recollections within the perception. This process is simultaneously creative of the perceived object and of the recollections, actualized as they are in an unforeseen and unprecedented coordination. The madeleine is a good example of this. Memories rush back not as they were, that is, as former presents, but instead as they inhabit the perception that solicited them. Actualized in the perception, they entertain new and unprecedented relations. For example, in the perception of the madeleine, Marcel actualizes a unique configuration of recollections that, while they all come from his childhood, could never have been gathered together in this way at that time (e.g., Swann and the young Marcel as counterparts: a connection made possible only much later than their time together at Combray). As we will see, this process is exemplified by the making of a legal decision. Any innovative judgment actualizes precedents and rules in a unique arrangement. To anticipate the next chapter, an attentive judgment actualizes a manifold of past rules toward the determination of its own unique and unprecedented juridical problem. But for now, the point is that through so many leaps into the pure past of law, a judgment combines rules into a unique collection or assemblage.

By way of conclusion, I can sum up the three themes of attentive judgment. (1) In attentive judgment we shuttle back and forth between the plane of perception (the actual) and the plane of memory (the virtual). In so doing, we simultaneously (2) create the perceived object or engender the encounter (the encounter coheres the many recollections actualized from the many leaps) and (3) create the past (the recollection is actualized in a new situation; the entire plane of memory is actualized by virtue of the circuit established with it; and finally the recollections drawn from multiple leaps entertain a new and unprecedented relationship within the perception). Now, in the conclusion to this chapter, I attempt the preliminary application of the concept of attentive judgment to adjudication.

Griswold and Attentive Judgment

Using Bergson and Deleuze, I have argued that a case can be judged in one of two ways: inattentively or attentively. In the first, which constitutes most decisions, a case is heard and straightaway recalls a rule. Operating always with a view to action, judicial perception will strip this case down to its bare essentials in order to cover it with a rule. This process has all the appearance of subsumption: A rule (a species) is applied to a case (an individual) in such a way that the rule appears unmodified (sterile and not differential repetition) and the case is determined entirely by the rule (its difference is the property of the rule). Inattentive judgment, I said, accounts for the regularity and expediency of adjudication. Where it can go wrong, however, is to take its subsumptive appearance as its reality and either forget or repress its origins in the actualization of the virtual past of the law.

Attentive judgment, by contrast, is illustrative of the actualization of the pure past. Always initiated by an encounter, judgment is stymied. At the outset, an encounter is a purely negative figure; it is the unrecognizable that interrupts the linkages of recollection and action. Nevertheless, judgment persists in selecting recollections to shed light on the encounter and, as a consequence, it becomes experimental. By experimental, I mean that judgment is forced to try out one recollection after another to illuminate and make sense of the encounter. As a result of this process, judgment changes its orientation, from recognition to creation. Rather than recognizing the encounter, judgment chooses one memory after another to build it up; in so doing, judgment creates so many circuits with the pure past, held together only by the encounter that provoked the search of memory, that a veritable creation of a new object occurs. And we said that this creativity is twofold and simultaneous: On the one hand, the encounter is positively engendered through the search of memory and the manifold circuits this creates; and on the other hand, the past is creatively actualized both because it is recollected in new circumstances and because the coordination between the various recollections within the encounter is unprecedented.

Unlike inattentive judgment, attentive judgment cannot be confused with subsumption. It reveals the two essential features of all judgments that we repress in the name of expediency: the encounter and the actualization of the past. *In*attentive judgment avoids encounters by securing minimal perceptions in order to call up recollections; moreover, it disguises the actualization of the past—which is always, however, infinitesimally creative by virtue of actualizing recollections in new situations, by internalizing their difference one in the other—as a subsumption. But I must be clear that a judge does not choose whether a case will be judged attentively or inattentively; the encounter determines that. The transition from inattentive judgment (recognition) to attentive judgment (creativity) is nonvoluntary. The encounter, as unrecognized, forces itself to be judged attentively.

Let me at last give an example of attentive judgment in law: *Griswold v. Connecticut* (1965). I choose this particular case mainly because it is famous. But assuming that any great case is a result of an encounter—or otherwise put, is not reducible to an automatic rule application—I might very well have chosen another. I am trying to achieve an account of two modes of judgment to explain regularity and creativity in adjudication, not to contribute a reading of a specific case.

In *Griswold*, the U.S. Supreme Court reviewed and struck down a Connecticut law proscribing the use of contraceptives. The appellants were the executive director and the medical director of the Planned Parenthood League of Connecticut, both of whom had been convicted as accessories for giving married individuals information on how to prevent conception and for prescribing a contraceptive device or material. The Court ruled that the Connecticut statute violated the right of marital privacy, which falls within the guarantees of the Bill of Rights. Now the reason that this is an example of *attentive* judgment is that the Constitution explicitly recognizes neither rights of association (marriage) nor rights of privacy (as in the state of being free from public attention and interference with one's decisions).

From Justice Douglas's majority opinion, let's take these questions in the order in which they arise: first, marriage as association, and then privacy. As Douglas admits, "The association of people is not mentioned in the Constitution nor in the Bill of Rights."[44] Nevertheless, Douglas observes that the Court has construed the First Amendment in terms wider than its letter.[45] Citing the Court's decision in *NAACP v. Alabama*, Douglas notes that "freedom of association was a peripheral First Amendment right."[46] With the term *peripheral rights*, Douglas indicates rights that deserve protection even though they are not explicitly stipulated, for without them "the specific rights would be less secure."[47] And so, given that the freedom of association is protected by the First Amendment and given that marriage is "an association for as noble a purpose as any involved in our prior decisions," marriage is argued to be protected by the Bill of Rights.[48]

The real innovation of *Griswold*, however, is in advancing constitutionally protected privacy rights for associations. Douglas approaches this issue on two fronts: the First and Fourth Amendments.[49] Again, Douglas starts off by noting that privacy is not explicitly mentioned by the Constitution. But as with the question of association, he invokes the concept of peripheral rights, citing two precedents to show that "the State may not, consistently with the spirit of the First Amendment, contract the spectrum of available knowledge," which, importantly, includes "the right to distribute, to receive, the right to read."[50] The right to receive information, that is, to receive information as to contraception, is guaranteed; or, in Douglas's famous words, "The First Amendment has a *penumbra* where privacy is protected from governmental intrusion. . . . The foregoing cases suggest that specific guarantees in the Bill of Rights have penumbras, formed by emanations from those guarantees that help give them life and substance. . . . Various guarantees create *zones of privacy*."[51] In his judgment, therefore, Douglas establishes two mutually reinforcing penumbras from the First Amendment: Marriage as an association protected by privacy rights. And with respect to the Fourth Amendment, which states the "right of the people to be secure in their persons, houses, papers, and effects, against unreasonable searches or seizures," Douglas finds that the Connecticut statute is impracticable and unconstitutional, for it involves the search and seizure of contraceptives within the marital home.[52]

At this point, we can evaluate this decision in light of our theory. I propose five points by which a Bergsonian analysis can elucidate how adjudication works.

1. *The encounter.* Before the Court in *Griswold* is an encounter: No specifically stated guarantee of the Bill of Rights can automatically apply to the statute under review. And, like all encounters, it comes from the outside (here, a doctor and a director arrested for disseminating information about contraception). The response to this encounter determines whether the mode of judgment is attentive or inattentive. For some judges, the lack of an explicitly stated rule is cause to support the statute, as evidenced by the dissenting opinion.[53] But for Justice Douglas, the case insists itself and must be dwelled on in connection with an exploration of the First Amendment. This precipitates a process of attentive judgment.

2. *Subtraction of the image.* This applies to both modes of judgment. The case is an image that presents an infinity of aspects, of sides and points to use Bergson's words. According to a criterion of need, only some of these points are joined with recollections and advanced as legally salient qualities. Bergson's pragmatic theory of perception accounts for why a judge notices only certain aspects of the case—for example, the domestic nature of marriage (to connect it with the Fourth Amendment) and its status as an association of two people (to connect it with the First Amendment). All other points of fact pass unremarked through the judge.

3. *Attentive judgment.* In *Griswold*, a statute comes before the Court that proscribes a certain conduct: the use and dissemination of contraception in Connecticut. A judge must ask whether this statute violates the Constitution. On the face of it, no, it doesn't. But this is just where Douglas's concept of the penumbra is effective, for it raises the following problem: Does the stated right tacitly, but necessarily, imply certain other rights, which this situation prompts us to consider? An encounter—this case—makes the judge stop to ask whether there is more implied in the First Amendment than meets the eye. In turn, this discovery rebounds onto the case and the perception: Not only is marriage sacred and basic, but it is also an association on par with any other and with attendant rights of privacy. Is this not attentive judgment par excellence? Douglas's opinion appears to exemplify the Bergsonian process whereby "an appeal is made to the deeper, more distant regions of memory, until other details that are already known come to project themselves upon those details that

remain unperceived." In an attentive judgment, case and law engage not in a subsumptive but in a mutually exploratory fashion, using one another to elaborate the details of the rule (the penumbra surrounding the First Amendment) and the details of the case (marriage as an association, as private, etc.).

4. *Judgment is a process.* Attentive judgment proceeds step by step, circuit by circuit. As Deleuze says, "In going from A to B and then B to A, we do not arrive back at the point of departure as in a bare repetition; rather, the repetition between A and B and B and A is the progressive tour or description of the whole problematic field" (*DR*, 210). In Part 3 I will try to fully develop this thought (especially the suggestion that adjudication might be the creation of problematic fields), but already Bergson's diagram shows us how a circuit reconstitutes its object such that subsequent leaps are taken from different departure points. This is the *cumulative* quality of attentive judgment.

Unfortunately, the text of a judgment is like a fetish commodity; we see only the finished result and not the production process that went into it. But it cannot be doubted that a judgment as complex as *Griswold* is not arrived at all at once but is secured through several successive leaps and actualizations. For example, a first leap connects the marital relationship with the First Amendment as an association; then, from this new departure point (marriage as association) there is another leap to actualize precedents dealing with privacy. Although my reconstruction is guesswork, it goes to show that judgment is a process that secures one point and moves to another until a finished result—which we call the judgment proper—is achieved. I leave off here with a magnificent line from Kafka: "The judgment isn't simply delivered at some point; the proceedings gradually merge into the judgment."[54]

5. *Judgment is creative.* Attentive judgment necessarily introduces innovation into law because it actualizes the past of law within unprecedented circumstances and different problems. It would be inadequate, verging on disingenuous, to simply say that *Griswold* finds the Connecticut statute unconstitutional and void, for it is not as though the First or Fourth Amendment or any particular precedent cited in *Griswold* is mechanically applied. Indeed, we can say that before the advent of *Griswold*, none of these rules existed in a shape adequate to adjudicate this case. Although it is true that peripheral rights (such as association and

privacy) predated *Griswold*, there was no specific rule that stated that the marital relationship is an association and, by consequence, is private. This was the specific innovation of *Griswold*.

Going back to Deleuze, the only way to provide a proper analysis of a judgment is to look at its real conditions of existence. The conditions of inattentive judgment are generic: A rule claims a perception as another instance of itself. But the conditions of attentive judgment are always singular. For example, in *Griswold*, we must at once acknowledge the novelty of the encounter that comes from the outside and, more important, we must see how this encounter is engendered through attentive judgment in order to be judged. Both aspects are singular: On the one hand, the negative function of the encounter shatters the sensory-motor schema of inattentive judgment, and, on the other hand, the positive function of the encounter initiates attentive judgment to construct the encounter as something justiciable. Let us return to the epigraph that began Part 2: "Herein, perhaps, lies the secret: to bring into existence and not to judge" (*CC*, 135). By combining Bergson's theory of memory and perception with Deleuze's concept of the encounter, I have tried to create a concept of attentive judgment that claims that in order to judge, one must create. Judgment brings into existence; far from being in opposition, judgment and creation are one and the same, albeit under certain (attentive) circumstances.

PART THREE

SPINOZA AND PRACTICE

> Ethics without metaphysics must be nonsense; we must first know what our potentialities are and what our situation is as parts of Nature; otherwise anything we say about human purposes and happiness must be relatively subjective; our statements will be no more than a projection of the desires and imaginations generated in us by our particular confined experience as finite modes in Nature.
>
> STUART HAMPSHIRE, *Spinoza and Spinozism*

I have tried to develop a concept of judgment from Deleuze. This effort has had nothing to do with reading Deleuze against the grain to claim that his denunciation of judgment is a passion matched only by its repression in his own text.[1] Instead, I have taken Deleuze at his word. On the one hand, I have created a concept of judgment commensurate with his insights on time, creativity, and encounters; on the other hand, I have shown how a widely held conception of judgment (the dogmatic image of law, subsumption) occludes those insights or realities. On the basis of these two points, I claimed that adjudication (judgment, in its legal institutional sense) has all along been practiced in accordance with the new concept of judgment (this is a transcendental and not a historical claim) and that confusions regarding adjudication, especially those surrounding its creativity, stem from a dogmatic concept of judgment unable to account for time, creativity, and encounters.

My procedure has been to take certain key Deleuzian concepts and develop them through another writer (most often Bergson, sometimes Kant), along with Deleuze's commentaries on that writer. In the final chapter, Chapter 8, because the complexity involved in an attempt to impose or integrate a full and independent analysis of Spinoza might risk the clarity of my foregoing concepts, I reverse the practice. Rather than treat Spinoza's political and legal theory in itself,[2] I take three themes from the *Ethics* to see how they are developed in Deleuze's commentaries and philosophy. Two motivations have guided the selection of the themes: first, to expand Deleuze's original interpretations of Spinoza and also to reveal the profound yet implicit presence of Spinoza in works that, on the surface, appear to have nothing to do with him; and second, to use each theme to extend and complete my theory of adjudication. Thus coupled with each section in Chapter 8 that examines Deleuze's reading of Spinoza is another section that integrates the argument into the context of law. The themes and their extension to law are as follows:

1. *Physics*. Upon arguing that Spinoza's physics provides the unacknowledged model for Deleuze and Guattari's philosophy of the concept in *What Is Philosophy*, I take this model to urge that judges create concepts just like philosophers do: by joining components together. This analysis provides another way to appreciate the creativity of adjudication and is a complement to the concept of attentive judgment.

2. *Affect and power*. In demonstrating how Deleuze's analysis of the concepts of affect and power in *Spinoza: Practical Philosophy* reveals an unlikely notion of duration in Spinoza, I use these concepts to evaluate a sad image of law and to show how law can become now more or now less adequate to its capacities. This analysis gives us a criterion to evaluate adjudication, that is, to show in what ways judgments are good or bad.

3. *Expression*. By tracking the term *expression* as it appears in *Expressionism in Philosophy: Spinoza* and in *Cinema 1*, we will see how Deleuze creates a concept of the plane of immanence that combines a philosophy of pure immanence (Spinoza) with a creative conception of time (Bergson), a concept that I use to orient the summation of this book. This last analysis articulates how law is itself a plane of immanence, with adjudication as its operator.

In Chapter 8, I use a contemporary case to illustrate the Spinozist theme under discussion: the Canadian Supreme Court's 1997 *Delgamuukw v. British Columbia* decision.[3] Now, the reader will be excused for thinking that every treatment of Deleuze and law must conclude with an analysis of an aboriginal land title case.[4] For my part, to the question of why this case and why this branch of law, I answer that the problem of aboriginal title represents an encounter insofar as Western jurisprudential analysis or common law concepts are not exactly suitable for it (aboriginal title is sui generis, as the judges say). In aboriginal title cases we get to see judges at work practicing attentive judgment. In this respect, *Delgamuukw* illustrates the explanative power of Deleuzian jurisprudence. Specifically, *Delgamuukw* shows the sensitive appreciation of a new situation for the law along with the Court's awareness that the only way to make it justiciable is by creating concepts alongside it.

8

Three Spinozist Themes in a Deleuzian Jurisprudence

Spinoza's Physics in Deleuze's Philosophy of the Concept

I want to claim not merely that Spinoza is an important source for Deleuze's philosophy of the concept, but that he provides its precise and technical model. To my knowledge this is an original claim, for although it is true that in *What Is Philosophy* Spinoza receives the highest honors for his uncompromised philosophy of immanence ("Spinoza is the Christ of philosophers, and the greatest philosophers are hardly more than apostles who distance themselves from or draw near to this mystery" [*WP*, 60]), it is also true that he is unmentioned in the first chapter of that text where Deleuze and Guattari spell out just what they mean by concept.[1]

To identify Spinoza as the unacknowledged model for Deleuze's philosophy of the concept, we must turn to the physics in Book II of Spinoza's *Ethics*. Schematically put, Spinoza holds that all individual bodies (and minds or ideas—we will come to this momentarily) are composed of a multiplicity of parts or bodies that share a relation of motion and rest.

When a number of bodies of the same or different magnitude form close contact with one another through the pressure of other bodies upon them, or if they are moving at the same or different rates of speed so as to preserve an unvarying relation of movement among themselves, *these bodies are said to be united with one another and all together to form one body or individual thing*, which is distinguished from other things through this union of bodies. (*E*, IIL3D, emphasis added)

202   Spinoza and Practice

Take a water molecule. A water molecule is composed of three parts or bodies (two hydrogen atoms and one oxygen atom) that share a relation of motion and rest. Insofar as these parts preserve this relation of motion and rest, they form an individual distinguished from other things. For Spinoza, an individual ceases to exist and becomes something else when its parts are determined to enter into relationships that no longer characterize it. For example, this water molecule will cease to exist when its oxygen atom is determined to enter into a new relationship with an iron atom to produce rust. Consider now a human body, composed as it is "of very many individual parts of different natures, each of which is extremely complex" (*E*, IIPos1). Just as the individual human body is made of parts, so too are those parts (e.g., organs) also made up of parts, ad infinitum (i.e., there are no simple bodies—see Spinoza's letter to Meyer [*L*, Letter 12]). All of these parts (and parts of parts) must be maintained in their delicate, characteristic relation.[2] Indeed, an individual body exists only so long as its parts retain and renew their characteristic relation of motion and rest; it ceases to exist, it dies or is destroyed in other words, when its parts are determined to enter into relations that no longer characterize it as a human body.

It is fundamental to Spinoza's physics that an individual may *take* the parts of another individual to persevere in existence. An individual may also *join* its parts to another individual and form a greater composite with it. For example, a human individual can forcefully annex the parts of another individual to preserve and enhance its powers (eating, for instance). Moreover, a human individual may combine its parts with those of another individual to form a greater and more powerful individual. Someone can join their powers to those of a tool and become a blacksmith; many people can join together in association to form a friendship, a business, a society, and so on. In short, whether an individual wishes it or not, its parts are constantly leaving one relation to temporarily enter into another. (Or, as Deleuze and Guattari would say, there is an ongoing process of deterritorialization and reterritorialization.)

From this simplified account of Spinoza's physics we can draw two points that will shortly become significant. First, an individual is *born* or *engendered* when formerly extrinsic parts are newly determined into a relation of compatible motion and rest. Second, an individual *dies* or *is destroyed* when its parts are taken from it, when they are determined to enter into a relation that no longer characterizes it. This last point signals Spinoza's notion of death as always external to the individual; death always comes from the outside in the form of a bad encounter that destroys the characteristic relation of the parts of that individual (*EPS*, 239; *SPP*, 100).

But what can all this have to do with Deleuze's philosophy of the concept, seeing as Spinoza's physics concerns an account of *bodies*? In this connection, and to readers familiar with Spinoza, I need only mention his theory of parallelism. For Spinoza, mind and body are the same modification of substance conceived now under the attribute of thought and now under the attribute of extension. Given that the human mind is an idea of the modifications that occur in the body, Spinoza can claim that the composite nature of the human body is mirrored or paralleled by the composite nature of the human mind. "The idea which constitutes the formal being of the human mind is the idea of the body, which is composed of a great number of very composite individual parts" (*E*, IIP15). A discussion of parallelism and the proofs leading to this proposition is beyond our present scope, but the conclusion Spinoza draws in this respect is certainly not: The ideas that the mind forms of the human body are composite; the idea itself is composed of many parts. Just like the body, the idea of the mind is born when extrinsic parts are determined into a characteristic relation (*E*, IIP23); and it dies—or at least terminates its existence in duration (this point becomes complex in light of the eternity of the mind in Book V)—when these parts are determined to enter a relation that no longer characterize it (*E*, IVP20S, VP21).

For Spinoza there are no simple (i.e., noncomposite) bodies; likewise, thanks to his doctrine of parallelism, there are no simple noncomposite minds or ideas. It is with an extraordinarily Spinozist gesture, therefore, that Deleuze and Guattari begin their chapter "What Is a Concept?" with the following: "*There are no simple concepts. Every concept has components and is defined by them*" (*WP*, 15, emphasis added). To see what this means, I can cite the example Paul Patton uses to illustrate this theory of the composite concept: Hobbes and the social contract.[3] To create his concept of the social contract, Hobbes relies on a number of component concepts (each of which has its own components—like Spinoza there are no simple components), such as the state of nature, the desire for power, the natural laws of human reason, and the sovereign that results from the contract.

When joined together in a particular way, these components create the concept of the social contract. In Spinozist terms, the idea (or concept) of the Hobbesian social contract comes into existence once its parts (or components) are determined into a characteristic relationship. What else would the idea be except for the characteristic relationship established between its parts? Or as Deleuze and Guattari say, "Every concept has an irregular contour *defined by the sum of its components* . . . each concept will therefore be considered as the point of coincidence, condensation, or accumulation of its own components" (*WP*, 15–16, 20, emphasis added). The concept is a kind of consistency or relation established between components, and it exists "in a state of survey [*survol*] in relation to its components, endlessly traversing them according to an order without distance" (*WP*, 20). Like a composite body, or the idea of that composite body, a concept consists in the relationship it establishes between its parts; and, as in Spinoza, a concept endures only insofar as its characteristic relation—the relation of motion and rest between its parts—is maintained. Perhaps this is why Deleuze and Guattari favor expressions of distance, movement, speed, and consistency to articulate their sense of a concept.[4]

For both Deleuze and Spinoza, bodies, ideas, and concepts are of the nature of *events* and *singularities*. In Spinoza a body is born and an idea engendered once external parts are determined to enter into the characteristic relation of that individual; in this sense, every individual is an event, a singular coordination or constellation of parts that temporarily cohere or travel together.[5] For Deleuze, too, the concept has the status of an event or a singularity insofar as every new concept represents an unprecedented assemblage of components.

In addition to being characterized as event or singularity, a concept can also be called "a multiplicity" (*WP*, 15).[6] Not only does this signify that the concept is composite, that it coheres many parts, but that the concept is an *open multiplicity* subject to change and destruction if its characteristic relation is disturbed. In Spinoza, composite bodies exist in duration. Although weak, impotent bodies are the most likely to be destroyed through bad encounters, no individual, however strong and durable, can forever resist all bad encounters (*E*, IVAx). It is inevitable that one individual will meet with another individual that fundamentally alters it, to the point of destruction (this is why everything that lives will die; no individual can altogether escape from the realm of encounters destructive to itself). Obviously, this is undesirable from the point of view of the dissolved mode or individual, but, in truth, all it means is that its parts will rejoin other individuals, other assemblages. On the one hand, death is always violent and external; on the other hand, it is merely an unavoidable and ongoing redistribution of parts.

On this point, it seems to me, Deleuze and Guattari follow Spinoza to the letter and to great effect. A concept is a multiplicity, yes, but an open multiplicity subject to destruction and death if its parts are redistributed. Patton's example is again illustrative. The concept of the social contract does not end with Hobbes but has a long and illustrious career in political philosophy. How does this happen? By changing one or more of the components, the initial concept will perish and another will be engendered. In other words, with the addition or subtraction of a part, the relationship that characterized the first concept will pass and another will be created. Thus Locke will replace Hobbes's power-hungry subjects with citizens who establish political society as a trust designed to protect what he calls property; Kant following on Rousseau will introduce a distinction between a pure or a pathological interest in the contract, which, later on, Habermas will take as dialogically grounded; and so on. As Patton puts it, "In each case, the outcome is a singular concept of a social contract where the nature of this singularity is determined by the components and the complex relation between them." For this reason, he calls Deleuze's concept of the concept an open multiplicity.[7]

A concept will endure only so long as its characteristic relation is maintained; if this relation is altered, if a philosophical encounter causes one or more components to migrate out of a concept and replaces them with other and different components, then the first concept will die and another singular concept will be created. It is no wonder, then, that the history of philosophy that Deleuze proposes evokes (yet without invoking) Spinozist physics.

When philosophers criticize each other it is on the basis of problems and on a plane [*plan*] that is different from theirs and that melts down the old concepts in the way a cannon can be melted down to make new weapons. It never takes place on the same plane [*plan*]. To criticize is only to establish that a concept vanishes [*s'évanouit*], that it loses some of its components or acquires others that transform it, when it is thrust into a new milieu. (*WP*, 28, translation modified)

And also:

The history of philosophy means that we evaluate not only the historical novelty of the concepts created by a philosopher but also the power [*puissance*] of their becoming when they pass into one another. (*WP*, 32)

Concepts die a Spinozist death: external, violent, and redistributive. As I have said, for Spinoza a thing never dies on its own but always as the result of a bad encounter, a poisoning (needless to say, an encounter is bad or a poison only from the point of view of the destroyed individual; it is not bad in general or bad for the mode that benefits from it). In these passages, Deleuze is clear that the criticism one philosopher makes of another is always external to that philosophy.[8] To criticize a philosophy is never to reveal a lack or inadequacy on its own terms (again, a thing does not die or self-destruct by virtue of its own relations), but only to show that when put into new circumstances (a new, unexpected philosophical encounter), its own relations can no longer stand unmodified; some of its parts will join the new philosophy, others will not, and yet others will be adapted by it, to the point where the original "criticized" philosophy will have been said to die, that is, to be superseded or transcended (but this, of course, only from the perspective of the superseding philosophy, which, in time, will suffer the same fate).

But if, from the vantage point of the criticized philosophy, criticism is a destruction or death, then from the perspective of the new philosophy and from the perspective of the history of philosophy, criticism is a power of creation: It is a renewal, different, to be sure, of the insights of that previous thought. From the point of view of the new philosophy there is a rebirth in that the components of a previous philosophy are combined with others to create new concepts. From the point of view of the history of philosophy there is a becoming of the parts of philosophy as they pass into one another, as they become actualized in ever new assemblages. In a word, and for quite specific Spinozist reasons, the conditions for a true critique and a true creation are identical. Philosophical criticism is by its nature concept creation. It is in this sense that we can understand Deleuze's claim that "a concept's power comes from the way it's repeated" (*N*, 147). A concept that can be repeated is powerful, for each repetition discloses or actualizes its potentials. It is indeed a sign of a concept's impotence or ineffectiveness that no one repeats it after its initial use. We could say that a concept only truly dies when it is left to itself, unmolested but neglected. By contrast, a concept only truly lives when it is disfigured and destroyed—that is, renewed—in a philosophical encounter. In this sense, there is no greater tribute to other thinkers than to criticize their concepts—that is, to take up and recreate their concepts in a new milieu.

Before turning our attention to law, I conclude this analysis with a summary of the two main points of comparison between Spinoza's physics and Deleuze's philosophy of the concept.

1. *Bodies and concepts are composite.* For Spinoza, all bodies are made of composite parts that maintain a characteristic relationship (and, by consequence of parallelism, the same holds for ideas). For Deleuze, all concepts are composite and are made up by the relationship between their various components. Both a body and a concept come into existence when their parts or components are determined to enter a certain characteristic relation.

2. *Bodies and concepts die (and their parts are renewed) by encounters.* For Spinoza, only an encounter can destroy the characteristic relationship of an individual by determining some or all of its parts to enter into a different relationship. For Deleuze, the history of philosophy proceeds entirely through encounters. A philosophy can create concepts only if it takes the parts of a previous philosophy into a new and different relationship. The history of philosophy, in this view, is nothing other than an ongoing decomposition and recomposition (deterritorialization and reterritorialization).

Delgamuukw I:
Creation of a Legal Concept (Aboriginal Title)

"The multiple *must be made*. . . . To attain the multiple, one must have a method that effectively constructs it (*TP*, 6, 22). This remark is precisely what is at stake in *What Is Philosophy*—Deleuze and Guattari create a concept of the concept *as* a created multiplicity and provide a method to investigate the history of philosophy accordingly. In what follows I claim that legal concepts, just like philosophical concepts, are both created and composite. To support this identification, I analyze the jurisprudence surrounding a particular legal concept: aboriginal title in the context of the Canadian Supreme Court's 1997 *Delgamuukw* decision.[9]

In *Delgamuukw*, the plaintiffs (and later, appellants), all hereditary chiefs of the Gitksan and Wet'suwet'en peoples, claimed 58,000 square kilometers in the province of British Columbia. Their initial claim at the British Columbia Supreme Court trial was for "ownership" of the territory and "jurisdiction" over it; later, at trial, and carried into the appeals, this was amended to a claim for aboriginal title over the land in question. Before this trial, the Province of British Columbia had refused to enter into treaty negotiations with the aboriginal peoples, a fact that made the courts the only means by which aboriginal peoples could make a land claim. *Delgamuukw* is a landmark case because, although the Supreme Court had in recent and successive cases given its opinion as to the source and existence of aboriginal rights, the question of the content of aboriginal title had so far been untested and undefined.

For the Gitksan and Wet'suwet'en peoples, the hope was to recognize rights to their land, to stop invasive trespass, and to fight the imposition of unconstitutional restrictions on their resource use. For the province, the hope was for the courts to ratify the extinction of aboriginal title.

To make a short story of this long and costly trial, the British Columbia Supreme Court (and, more or less, the British Columbia Appeals Court)[10] ruled that the plaintiffs did not have rights to their traditional territories; that if they did have rights, they were extinguished when the colony of British Columbia joined the Canadian Confederation in 1871; and that the province was under no obligation to enter into treaties with the First Nations.[11] The Supreme Court of Canada reversed this decision and ordered a retrial on the basis of a legal technicality (a defect in the pleadings). Although no verdict was issued concerning the land in question, the Supreme Court used *Delgamuukw* as an opportunity to define the content and limits of aboriginal title so as to benefit subsequent litigation. The Court held that aboriginal title is a right to land, protected both by common law and the Constitution; it further held that it is a right to exclusive use and occupation of the land for a variety of purposes not limited to traditions integral to distinctive aboriginal cultures, with the qualification that the land cannot be put to a use that is irreconcilable with the nature of that group's attachment to the land.

For our purposes the question of aboriginal title is fascinating because the term consistently used to characterize it is *sui generis*—literally, "of its own kind," unique, or peculiar. What could be more indicative of an encounter? In the context of Canadian common law jurisprudence, aboriginal title resists any satisfying recognition by common law concepts.[12] Indeed, in his majority decision, Supreme Court Chief Justice Lamer says that what defines aboriginal title is its very nomination as an exception. "The idea that aboriginal title is *sui generis* is *the unifying principle underlying the various dimensions of that title*" (*Delgamuukw*, ¶113, emphasis added). This is an extraordinary admission, for it clarifies the fact that each dimension or component of aboriginal title is unique. Furthermore, it states that the designation of aboriginal title as sui generis is only a consequence of the fact that its multiple dimensions go unrecognized in common law. We have direct evidence, therefore, that this concept provokes an encounter for the common law; and we have indirect or implied evidence that a legal concept is a composite that unifies its components. What are these dimensions? Lamer cites three.

First, as opposed to fee simple property interest, aboriginal title is *inalienable* to anyone other than the Crown.[13] Second, the *source* of aboriginal title is unique. Although it was initially held that the source for aboriginal title was the Royal Proclamation of 1763—and thus co-original with the declaration of colonial territoriality upon which it was to be a burden—*Calder v. British Columbia (Attorney General)* (1973) and *Guerin v. Canada* (1984) correct this view and acknowledge aboriginal title as "a legal right derived from the Indians' historic occupation and possession of their tribal lands."[14] Not only does this mean that title is derived from presovereign occupation of land, and not only does this mean that title is simultaneously grounded in aboriginal legal traditions outside the common law (as rightful possession), but it also means that the common law gives legal standing to these two dimensions and recognizes something outside itself. As Lamer explains, this places aboriginal title *between* traditions. "Its characteristics cannot be completely explained by reference either to the common law rules of real property or to the rules of property found in aboriginal legal systems. As with other aboriginal rights, it must be understood by reference to both common law and aboriginal perspectives" (*Delgamuukw*, ¶113).[15] Third, aboriginal title is held *communally*. Title cannot be held by individuals but must, by necessity, be held by all members of an aboriginal community.

But before I outline the specific content of aboriginal title, I should ask what problem it poses and how this problem is determined. The reason

I need to do so is specifically Deleuzian, for according to him, the concepts of a philosophy (or, I might add, of a jurisprudence) can be understood only with reference to the problems that inspire them. By examining the relationship between problems and concepts within the context of *Delgamuukw*, I hope to clarify the importance of this relationship for both politicolegal philosophy and the decision itself.

Turning now to the conclusion of the 1997 *Delgamuukw* opinion, Lamer pointedly states the fundamental problem set by aboriginal rights: how to achieve "the *reconciliation* of the pre-existence of aboriginal societies with the sovereignty of the Crown." And in what is at once the most preliminary and the most mature statement of the problem of aboriginal jurisprudence, he adds, "Let us face it, we are all here to stay" (*Delgamuukw*, ¶186). If we ignore for a moment the fact that this line comes at the end of the opinion and that the manner of the reconciliation has been set by the preceding judgment, could we not say that Lamer's concluding lines reveal the basic animating problem surrounding aboriginal title and that, in fact, the task of his judgment is to determine more fully the scope, content, and responsibilities of aboriginal title in light of the joint problem that reconciliation must be achieved and that we're all here stay? In this latter sense, the problem poses itself as a bare-bones imperative to which the judgment must give direction, sense, and precise determination. A concept of aboriginal title must be in service of—that is, give meaning and effect to—the problem of reconciliation.[16]

We have three distinct terms: encounter, problem, and concept. In a hard case they come together as follows: An encounter spurs the judge toward the formulation of a problem able to create concepts to adjudicate the encounter. We can unpack this formula with *Delgamuukw*. There is an encounter with an aboriginal land claim (as unrecognizable to the common law, sui generis); there is the problem of aboriginal title (how to achieve reconciliation and live together); and there is the concept of aboriginal title (which spells out its precise content).

We start with the encounter and the problem. An aboriginal land claim case is an encounter insofar as it cannot be treated by existing common law concepts and dealt with in the manner of inattentive judgment. Aboriginal title, insofar as the Court considers it a "species" of aboriginal rights, falls under a broad problem of how to achieve reconciliation between aboriginal and nonaboriginal peoples; it also falls under a more specific problem of how to reconcile the preexistence of aboriginal societies with Canadian sovereignty (*Delgamuukw*, ¶137). Given this encounter and this problem, the judge must honor the sui generis nature of this case while judging it within the context of the common law and its commitment to reconciliation. What will happen, therefore, is the creation of a concept of aboriginal title able to abide the encounter and to advance and further determine the problem.

In facing an encounter, the common law is not frozen but springs into action. In fact, it is by springing into action that it is able to specify the precise sense in which the case is an encounter. I have already hinted at this: Aboriginal title is indeed an encounter, but it is by virtue of its comparison with, and as we shall see, its adaptation of, inappropriate common law concepts that it receives its unique content and concept. The law does not remain dumb before an encounter but modifies its approach to construct and make sense of what is new for it. The encounter spurs adjudication to the formulation of a concept (aboriginal title) that makes sense within its terms of analysis *and* honors the singularity of the case before it.

Guiding this creation of a concept of aboriginal title through an encounter is the problem of reconciliation. Yet it is crucial to realize that, although the problem guides the formation of the concept of aboriginal title, it is the very formation of that concept that precisely determines the problem of reconciliation and affects the manner in which it is to take place. The adjudication of an encounter is animated by a problem that itself gains its sense and determinacy by the concept it motivates. A fully determined concept of aboriginal title, therefore, is a kind of solution to the problem of reconciliation. However, it is not a solution in the way of an answer to a ready-made problem; instead, this concept or solution gives a sense—that is, determination, direction, specificity, and meaning—to the problem that motivates it. It may be that the basic problem of reconciliation animates the jurisprudence on aboriginal title, but it is only with a formed concept of aboriginal title that the problem can appropriately express itself (through its solution). This is why, it seems to me, that Lamer's "let us face it" line comes twice in his judgment but with two different senses or degrees of determination: implicitly (or virtually) at first, as an undetermined imperative to guide jurisprudence on aboriginal rights and title; and then explicitly (or actually), as a more or less solved problem equipped with a concept that explains how, on the question of land claims, reconciliation ought to proceed.

Here we arrive at two of Bergson's most famous claims: Thinking occurs only in the formation of problems, and a determined problem is a solved problem.

The truth is that in philosophy and even elsewhere it is a question of *finding* the problem and consequently of *positing* it, even more than of solving it. For a speculative problem is solved as soon as it is properly stated. . . . *But stating the problem is not simply uncovering, it is inventing.* . . . The effort of invention consists most often in raising the problem, *in creating the terms* in which it will be stated. *The stating and solving of the problem are here very close to being equivalent*; the truly great problems are set forth only when they are solved. (*CM*, 51)

What does it mean to say, as Bergson does, that to state a problem is to solve it? And how does this relate to the task of inventing problems? To be expressed, a new problem must invent the means by which to do so. Or, in other words, a problem cannot exist apart from the expressions it creates for itself. Let us return to *Delgamuukw* to illustrate this point. I said that the problem of this judgment is reconciliation, that is, how to live together given this past we share and responsibilities to which we are committed. If this problem appeared at the beginning of the judgment, we would find it abstract, even wishy-washy. It would be more of a pseudoproblem, either an aspiration or a political move. But it is entirely different when we encounter this problem at the end of the judgment. By that time, at the end of a hundred pages of reasoning and equipped with the concept of aboriginal title (along with all its components), we are made aware that this concept has been invented not just to formulate and make determinate the problem of reconciliation; it has attempted to solve it. The concept of aboriginal title shows what is at stake in the problem of reconciliation (it makes the problem determinate and concrete), and, in so doing, it attempts to provide a solution to it. At the point where the problem (of reconciliation) is stated (by means of the concept of aboriginal title), it is solved.[17] This notion of the problem is paradoxical because it claims that a problem is not statable except by means of its solution—you cannot determinately say what the problem is without at once solving it. This is why Deleuze calls the problem transcendental: It makes thought possible while not itself experiencable; it is the condition for thought known only through its fruits of solution (*DR*, 159). In terms of our analysis, the concepts created in adjudication are responses to real problems that are invented, stated, and solved by means of these concepts. In this sense, problems are the transcendental condition for (attentive) judgments that are not straightforward applications of rules.[18]

Three grave consequences compromise our understanding of adjudication when we forget that it is problem creating. First, we account for disagreements with a puerile category of error (i.e., judges make mistakes of fact or application). Second, judgments appear as propositions divorced from their problems, like conclusions without premises.[19] Once the legal problem has been forgotten, we are left with an abstract (not to mention arbitrary) judgment without the means to support its generality.[20] Judgments may look like propositions (verdict: "he is innocent," "she was negligent," etc.), but that is only because they are in fact problems; propositions always have an underlying and inspiring problem. Third, creativity in judgment—to say nothing of judgment *as* creative—appears as either an accident or an abuse; in any case, it is a misapprehension of law.

But if, on the other hand, we appreciate that adjudication can be a problem-creating activity, then we see that disagreements in law occur through the transformation of problems: that the concepts of a judgment make sense when expressive of an animating problem and that adjudication is creative because, on occasion of an encounter, it must actualize—and thus invent by way of determining—problems in order to adjudicate the situation. What we appreciate, in words that anticipate the coming sections, is that the creation of problems is a fundamental power of law, and to deny this capacity is to misunderstand its situation and to forfeit its potentials.

I now turn to the question of the concept in adjudication. Drawing on the account of Spinoza, I investigate how legal concepts are created and composite. I can start with a few programmatic statements. Like *any* concept of law, aboriginal title is a composite made up of the relations between its components. There is nothing more to this concept than the relation between its components (it does not draw support from these components, it *is* the relationship of its components). The components of this concept, signed and dated parts of the history of law, are assembled into a novel configuration to create aboriginal title. This concept is created once its parts are determined to enter into a particular relationship. And, maybe one day, Lamer's concept of aboriginal title will be overturned and die when a new concept takes some of its components for itself in a new relationship critical of the old one.

To detail all the parts of aboriginal title in *Delgamuukw* exceeds our reach and need (it would, by definition, recreate the entire judgment). But I can draw attention to a few major components and their relations that, taken together, create the Court's concept of aboriginal title. I start with the constitutional part, section 35(1) of the Constitution Act, 1982: "The existing aboriginal and treaty rights of the aboriginal peoples of Canada are hereby affirmed and recognized." But section 35(1) is not enough; the rights protected by it do not stand alone in *Delgamuukw* but are put into relation with other parts or components of the law to achieve their relevant sense. This is how Lamer begins his judgment:

This appeal [*Delgamuukw*] is the latest in a series of cases in which it has fallen to this Court to interpret and apply the guarantee of existing aboriginal rights found in s.35(1) of the *Constitution Act, 1982*. Although that line of decisions, commencing with *R. v. Sparrow*, [1990] 1 S.C.R. 1075, proceeding through the *Van der Peet* trilogy (*R. v. Van der Peet*, [1996] 2 S.C.R. 507, *R. v. N.T.C. Smokehouse Ltd.*, [1996] 2 S.C.R. 672, and *R. v. Gladstone*, [1996] 2 S.C.R. 723), and ending in *R. v. Pamajewon*, [1996] 2 S.C.R. 821, *R. v. Adams*, [1996] 3 S.C.R. 101, and *R. v. Côté*, [1996] 3 S.C.R. 139, have laid down the jurisprudential framework for s.35(1), this appeal raises a set of interrelated and novel questions which revolve around a single issue—the nature and scope of the constitutional protection afforded by s.35(1) to common law aboriginal title. (*Delgamuukw*, ¶1)

As Lamer writes, the adjudication of *Delgamuukw* must proceed through an interpretation and application of the constitutional rights protected by section 35(1); but, he continues, the relevant sense and meaning (the framework) of section 35(1) has been established through a series of cases that now come into play. So, for example, Lamer draws from *Côté* to argue that the rights constitutionalized by section 35(1) are not limited to those recognized at common law (*Delgamuukw*, ¶136); he cites *Adams* to reject the idea that title is only a bundle of rights (¶137); and he upholds his own decision in *Van der Peet* that courts must be sensitive to the unique nature of aboriginal evidence (¶788); and so on. The list could go on, but from these examples we see that to create the concept of aboriginal title, Lamer combines section 35(1) with components from the jurisprudence surrounding it. A portion or dimension of *Delgamuukw's* concept of aboriginal title, therefore, results from holding *these* parts together in *this* characteristic relationship.

Of course, that's not all. Because this is a land claim case, Lamer must involve a series of common law property concepts, all the while realizing their insufficiency and adapting them accordingly. A major component of aboriginal title is the common law principle that occupation is proof of possession in law (*Delgamuukw*, ¶114).[21] Aboriginal occupation of the land results in a right to the land itself, and consequently title is more than a right to engage in certain protected practices on that land (*Delgamuukw*, ¶140). But, to name only two, this component is modified by other components in significant ways. First, unlike ordinary fee simple property, title land cannot be alienated to any party but the Crown (thus satisfying the Royal Proclamation); moreover, unlike fee simple property, the use of title land has an inherent limit in that it cannot be used in a manner irreconcilable with the nature of the claimants' attachment to it (*Delgamuukw*, ¶¶125–132). Second, given that the source of aboriginal title is sui generis, reference to aboriginal laws is relevant to establishing the occupation of lands (*Delgamuukw*, ¶148). In these two important ways—limits and sources—the component of common law property and occupation is modified to meet (or, more exactly, to *create*) the sui generis nature of aboriginal title.

And so here too is a cluster of components gathered around occupation, which will join up with the cluster around section 35(1), among others. From this sketch we see that this concept of aboriginal title exists only by virtue of a certain relation or tension between its components. We might, in fact, liken it to "a wall of loose stones, uncemented stones, where every element has a value in itself but also in relation to the others" (*CC*, 86). Like Spinoza's individuals and like Deleuze's concepts, a legal concept is created when its elements come together.

Before concluding, I make three remarks to tie this analysis into our overall project. The first concerns attentive judgment, the second law and time, and the third nonvoluntarism.

1. *Attentive judgment.* In attentive judgment, the judge performs multiple leaps into the pure past of law, actualizing this and that part of it into a perceived case. The current analysis of the legal concept as composite resonates closely with attentive judgment and, inasmuch as they share two crucial characteristic features, can be considered a repetition or

restatement. First, in both schemes a legal concept does not refer to a state of affairs, nor does a judge apply ready-made rules to a situation; instead, concepts must be created to adjudicate an encounter. Just as with attentive judgments, where rules neither designate nor refer to a case but are actualized within a perception, a (composite) legal concept is not applied to an independent state of affairs but is formed from within a situation whose facts are established by being taken up in the context of a jurisprudential problem. As we have seen, the concept of aboriginal title is created as a solution to, or an actualization of, the problem of reconciliation, a problem that itself provides parameters to establish the facts of the case (e.g., for Lamer, the reconciliation of the fact of a preexisting society and its legal tradition with the fact of Crown sovereignty). With a difficult case it becomes clear that neither rule nor situation can intelligibly be said to exist outside the context of mutual encounter. Or, in other words, the relationship between rule and case cannot be simply referential, for this could account neither for the emergence of a new rule nor for the determination of the facts of the situation. Second, we see the progressive determination of the legal concept as its components are actualized into a new assemblage. If with attentive judgment we saw that the various actualized elements of the pure past of law entertain new and creative relationships (e.g., in *Griswold* the rights to privacy and association), this feature is far more striking when we consider that the concept as composite exists simply as the relationship between its parts. Put another way, in both schemes there is an experience and a duration of judgment, wherein a new rule is created piece by piece as its various elements or components are actualized into unprecedented relationships.

  2. *Law and time.* As Deleuze and Guattari write, philosophical time is "a grandiose time of coexistence that does not exclude the before and after but superimposes them in a stratigraphic order. It is an infinite becoming of philosophy that crosscuts its history without being confused with it" (*WP*, 59). Our concept of the pure past of the law (see Chapter 7) has made an explicit case for this kind of legal time: a coexistence of all of the past of law creatively actualized in new situations. The same applies here. It is true that legal concepts cannot emerge haphazardly; their appearance must have been prepared by earlier concepts. Obviously, Lamer's concept of aboriginal title in *Delgamuukw* could not have been created before the series of immediately preceding cases around section 35(1), for these pro-

vide the necessary elements of the decision. But the creation of a legal concept does not conform to a historical succession in that a judgment would automatically follow from its historically contemporary elements of law. Instead, we see that the entire past of the law coexists for a judge who can cite and renew its relevant elements. Law, like philosophy, takes place in this time of becoming where all the past of the law (virtually) coexists with itself, and where components migrate (are actualized) from one judgment to another.

3. *Nonvoluntarism.* With the necessary precautions, we can see the judge as a kind of "spiritual automaton."[22] What Spinoza means by this term is that the connections made by an adequate idea are necessary, automatic, and universal; they are not dependent on the particularity of the individual thinking them (as in imagination), nor is thinking—the activity of drawing connections and conclusions—voluntary and discretionary. What a judicial automaton might mean for us, and unfortunately we cannot fully develop this thought,[23] is that given the exigencies of the case or encounter at hand, a particular judge is led necessarily from one component to the other. In calling the judge an automaton, we do not mean that judgments are universally arrived at or that one specific component necessarily leads to another specific component for *all* judges; of course, different judges link components together differently. Instead, what we wish to stress is that insofar as one component necessarily leads to another on a particular occasion of decision, there is no room left for understanding judgment on the basis of voluntarism or final causes (the old word for activism). For a particular judge, one component will imply another component—which is another way to attack the myth of the voluntary, undetermined judge who picks out rules at will, as though at leisure. Thus, for instance, when Lamer considers the component of common law occupation, he is compelled to connect it with, and adapt it to, other components, given the sui generis standing of aboriginal title. The legal concept is, in this sense, autopoietic. "[It] is not formed but posits itself in itself—it is a self-positing. . . . What depends on a free creative activity is also that which, independently and necessarily, posits itself in itself: the most subjective will be the most objective" (*WP*, 11).[24] When Deleuze likens the philosopher to the automaton, there is no implication of universality. Quite the contrary. The singular concept is created insofar as a philosopher is compelled by force of thought to link components in *this* manner.

Philosophers do not choose to create; they are led by their thought to create. Equally, when a judge is creating a legal concept, there is no occasion for willfulness; in fact, willfulness is an illusion dispelled by an adequate understanding of judgment. Never would judicial freedom be so complete as when the judge is led to establish certain connections between components in the creation of a concept.

Duration in Spinoza

Whereas in the last two sections I focused on *What Is Philosophy* to uncover a Spinozist inspiration for its philosophy of the concept, in the next two sections I turn to *Spinoza: Practical Philosophy* to see Deleuze discover an effective theory of time, that is, of duration in its Bergsonian sense, in Spinoza. For reasons that will become apparent, this is not an obvious move (neither in the sense of being easily reconcilable with Spinoza's theses on time, nor in the sense of being especially explicit in Deleuze), and it will be detailed in two steps. The first is Deleuze's characterization of Spinoza's concept of affect [*affectus*] as the continuous flow or passage registering variations of a mode's power. The second is Deleuze's original interpretation of the formation of adequate ideas (what Spinoza calls common notions) through a process of ongoing experimentation. Next, I take these two insights (only in reverse order) to contribute to my theory of law. First, I connect the theory of the formation of adequate ideas to Deleuze's concept of the problem to argue that adjudication becomes adequate (or powerful or joyful in Spinoza's terms) only once it is aware that the cause of an (attentive) judgment lies in the creation or determination of a problem. Second, I combine the concept of affect with a reading of *Delgamuukw* to see how adjudication exists in a continuum of becoming more or less adequate, that is, with a greater or lesser appreciation and affirmation of its conditions and capacities.

I start with the observation that if Bergson and Spinoza can be said to share a number of conclusions, albeit established through different procedures (such as the critique of mechanism, finalism, and the negative; the prioritization of ontology; the sense of Christ; and the doctrine of intuition),[25] they appear irreconcilable precisely on what is closest to Bergson: time and time as duration.[26] To quickly evidence this opposition, I cite three basic theses of Spinoza that are, on the face of it, incommensurable with Bergsonism.

1. *Substance as eternal.* A fundamental criticism that Spinoza makes in the *Ethics* is that to define substance as an indefinite or infinite duration is to confuse divine with modal nature. Substance is atemporal; it is eternal in the sense that its existence "follows solely from the definition of an eternal thing" (*E*, ID8). Because its existence follows solely from its definition or essence, substance is outside time.

2. *Duration as determined and determinable.* For Spinoza, duration is the continuation of the existence of a mode from a beginning onward. The birth, life, and death of a mode are strictly determined by causal relations that are, in principle, fully determinable by scientific investigation. Novelty and unforeseeability, just like possibility and contingency, are illusions stemming from human limitation and can be, in principle but not in fact, overcome (*E*, IIP30).

3. *Time as illusory.* In the *Ethics*, Spinoza makes a distinction between duration and time. Duration relates to the real existence of things and is apprehended under the aspect of necessity. Time, by contrast, is "a product of the imagination" and registers the way we are affected by moving bodies (*E*, IIP44S). Spinoza gives the following example: A boy sees Peter in the morning, Paul at noon, and Simon in the evening. From these experiences he constructs a temporal chain of association such that when he next sees Peter, he will anticipate Paul and Simon in the future, and having seen Paul, he will regard Peter as past and expect Simon in the future. If this chain is broken (e.g., Paul before Peter), the boy's imagination will waiver and he will regard future appearances as contingent. With the term *time*, therefore, Spinoza indicates subjective associations that are inadequate, illusory, and variable. If the determination of duration involves our power of science and intellect, time involves our impotence and uncertainty.

At three different levels, therefore, Spinoza seems unamenable to a Bergsonian (or for that matter, Deleuzian) conception of time: Substance is atemporal (and not time itself, as in *The Two Sources of Morality and Religion*); duration is strictly calculable (and not unforeseeable, as in *Creative Evolution*); and the experience of time is illusory (and not the fundamental psychical fact, as in *Time and Free Will*). How, then, can we locate a Bergsonian concept of duration in Spinoza?

Maybe we can find a clue in Deleuze's obsession with Spinoza's famous Scholium from Book III of the *Ethics* that announces that we do not yet know what a body can do.[27] But we must be clear in what ways this statement is, on the one hand, a denial of (one aspect of) duration, and how, through Deleuze's treatment, it is also a confirmation of (another aspect of) duration. We start with the denial.

> Nobody as yet has determined the limits of the body's capabilities: that is, nobody as yet has learned from experience what the body can and cannot do, without being determined by mind, solely from the laws of its nature insofar as it is considered as corporeal. For nobody as yet knows the structure of the body so accurately as to explain all its functions. . . . Hence it follows that when men say that this or that action of the body arises from the mind which has command over the body, they do not know what they are saying . . . [and] they are ignorant of the true causes of that action and are not concerned to discover it. (*E*, IIIP2S)

Here, to support his theory of mind-body parallelism, Spinoza undertakes an a posteriori critique of the dominant Cartesian picture of the control and primacy of the mind over the body.[28] Spinoza's tone and procedure (as is so often the case in the Scholia)[29] is aggressive and ironic: The Cartesians pretend that the mind governs the body, but far from knowing what the mind can do, nobody has even a true sense of the capacities of the body.[30] As Deleuze puts it, "It is a matter of showing that the body surpasses the knowledge we have of it, and that thought likewise surpasses the consciousness that we have of it" (*SPP*, 18). Thus, from a modal perspective, not only are there plenty of things a body can do that we cannot explain (e.g., the actions of sleepwalkers, architecture, and the unimaginable complexity of the body itself), but a forteriori, these things could never be explained by a facile recourse to the mind's control over the body.

The point of Spinoza's "we do not yet know . . ." thesis is used to debunk Cartesianism on two fronts: first, that the mind controls the body, and second, that we know everything there is to know about the body (and the mind). But we must acknowledge that Spinoza's thesis does not affirm novelty and unforeseeability, as though the body's (and mind's) capacities were in principle unknowable in advance. Indeed, it is an indirect denial of a central requirement of Bergsonian duration, especially as developed in *Creative Evolution*: that time is unforeseeable and creative. Spinoza's claim is rather that "nobody *as yet* has learned from experience what the body can and cannot do"; there is no reason why scientific investigation will not clear up one apparent mystery after another and explain, for instance, how sleepwalkers do what they do without recourse to a pseudo-explanation of the mind's relinquished control. This Scholium has a purely critical, ironic function; it does not permit us to discover an affirmation of contingency and creativity.[31]

Why then does Deleuze make such a big deal out of it? In answer we must cover the basics of Spinoza's theory of (modal) power in connection with Deleuze's original interpretation of the process by which adequate ideas are formed.[32] For Spinoza, the power of a mode (a finite individual made up of parts under a characteristic relation) corresponds, on the one hand, to its ability [*aptus*] to affect other modes, and, on the other hand, to its capacity to be affected. Modal power corresponds to the power to act and to be acted upon; it is at once "a production and a sensibility."[33] Those things or encounters that dispose us to be affected in more ways, or those that make us capable of affecting other modes in more ways, are advantageous and desirable; they are conducive to develop our capacities and powers (*E*, IVP38).

Seeing how our existence is always determined by this or that external mode, our capacity to be affected is correspondingly also always exercised, filled up with affections. But it is filled up "either by affections produced by external things (called passive affections), or by affections explained by the mode's own essence (called active affections)" (*EPS*, 93, translation modified). If we suffer affections [*affectio*] that we neither determine nor understand, we experience a separation from our powers and become sad; if, on the other hand, we experience affections of which we are the cause or of which we know the cause, we experience a connection to our powers and become joyful. Existence, in this sense, is an effort to experience a maximum of active affections; it is an effort to convert as many of our passive or passional affects into active ones; it is an effort to pursue activity as our own and only ethical task.

But all this is difficult to do. A mode is constantly besieged by encounters it does not wish to and cannot understand, encounters that destroy, bewilder, and sadden it. To counter or correct this situation, human modes come up with all kinds of illusions and superstitions (not the least of which are the illusions of final causes and of a providential God) so as to feel that they are in charge and understand. Sadly, these only compound the problem and further involve our impotence and inactivity. What, then, is a limited and finite mode to do? It must carve out, as best it can, a space of relationships that enables it to persevere in its being and, hopefully, to enhance its powers and potentials. In Spinozist terms, an individual must try to cultivate a life that compounds its own characteristic relations with other relations common to, and not destructive of, it (*E*, IVP39).

When this happens, when one body fruitfully compounds its relations with another, an idea is formed that Spinoza calls a common notion (*E*, IIP40S2). Unlike an imaginary or superstitious idea, a common notion is an adequate idea that expresses a true (and not an imagined or spurious) composition or agreement between bodies. A common notion is necessarily an adequate idea, for it comprehends what is common between bodies and what causes them to enter into a particular composition (*E*, IIP38–39). In this sense, they put us in connection with our powers. On the one hand, equipped with common notions, we have a basis to actively select and engage those encounters that agree (compose) with us; on the other hand, we have a principle to understand the causes of those encounters that do not agree (decompose) with us, and either avoid them or at least understand their necessity and their overall harmony (*E*, VP6). Once in possession of common notions, we are on track for an ethical life of adequate ideas, activity, and joy.

But how, in concrete fact, do we come into possession of common notions? How do we form them? At this point Deleuze's interpretation of Spinoza is original, for he argues that the order of presentation of the common notions in the *Ethics* is the reverse of its lived, modal genesis.[34] Deleuze's point is that although Book II of the *Ethics* may make it seem as though we are in full possession of the common notions (*E*, IIP37–40), Books IV and V show that, in fact, we acquire them through a long, often painful process of experimentation. There is, in other words, a practical formation of the common notions.

A thing being good to the extent that it agrees with our nature, the joyful affection itself induces us to form the corresponding common notion. The first common notions we form are thus the least universal, those, that is, that apply to our body and to another that agrees directly with our own and affects it with joy. If we consider the order in which common notions are formed, we must begin from the least universal; for the most universal, applying to bodies opposed to our own, have no *inductive principle* in the affections we experience. (*EPS*, 282)

We can finally pick up our earlier thread, for there are several keys to this passage that, taken together, unlock a concept of duration in Spinoza. First, the process whereby we form common notions is experimental; our first common notions are not acquired by a priori universal reasoning but are gained through a direct experience that affects our own body and enhances its relations. "We can know by reasoning that the power of action is the sole expression of our essence, the sole affirmation of our power of being affect. But this knowledge remains abstract. We do not know what this power is, or how we may acquire or discover it. And we will certainly never know this, if we do not try to become active" (*EPS*, 226). As Adam was the first to find out, but as we all do eventually, certain things compound with our characteristic relations and other things do not, and, unfortunately, there is no way to figure out which does which except through experimentation. This is a paradox of Spinozism, "to have rediscovered the concrete force of empiricism in applying it in support of a new rationalism, one of the most rigorous versions ever conceived"—universal (indeed, divine) freedom and truth are discovered only at the end of a long-lived process of experimentation (*EPS*, 149).

Second, this experimentation brings us directly to our famous phrase: We do not yet know what a body can do. No mode can know, and no modal history can fully tell, what will and what will not compound with its own relations. Given that there is an infinity of relations with which we can compound, and given that there is an infinity of assemblages we can create, we will always be discovering new powers and new weaknesses through experimentation. "It is a long affair of experimentation . . . you do not know beforehand what good or bad you are capable of; you do not know beforehand what a body or a mind can do, in a given encounter, a given arrangement, a given combination" (*SPP*, 125). Thus, although in principle (with or in the Idea of God) all the powers of body and mind can be adequately known through their causes, they are, in fact, subject to limitless and, for finite modes, novel discovery.

Third, through a positive encounter the individual mode is affected with joy, for it experiences an affection that composes with it and connects it to its powers. For Spinoza, it is fundamental that the experience of a composition, the discovery of a power, and the formation of an adequate idea (all these things go together) always provoke an affect [*affectus*] of joy. By contrast, the experience of a decomposition, the forfeiture of a power, and the formation of an inadequate idea always provoke an affect of sadness. It is precisely this affective dimension of the formation of common notions that is the centerpiece of Deleuze's interpretation; it is thanks to the initial experience of a joyful passion that we are encouraged to find out more and other common notions and eventually to organize our lives in such a way as to experience a maximum of these and, correspondingly, a maximum of joy. It is this affective experience that instigates a leap into activity; it is a joyful incitement to the individual mode to establish those relations and ideas that will simultaneously empower and delight it, that will fill its power (its capacity to be affected) with power, adequacy, and joy.

Every mode, therefore, spends its life in ongoing experimentation, a process that sometimes suffuses it with joy, other times with sadness. This is nothing other than to say that a mode is a kind of qualitative multiplicity, that it lives in a continuous flow of time and experience that is both real and psychical. "From one state to another, from one image or idea to another, there are transitions, passages that are experienced, *durations through which we pass to a greater or a lesser perfection*" (*SPP*, 48, emphasis added). Or, as Deleuze specifies in connection with the experience of sadness:

In [sadness, the passage to lesser perfection] there is something that does not come down to the privation of a greater perfection, nor to the comparison of two states of perfection. In sadness there is something irreducible, something that is neither negative nor extrinsic: a *passage* that is experienced and is real. A duration.... *Far from denying the existence of duration, Spinoza defines the continual variations of existence by duration.* (*SPP*, 39, emphasis added)

We can combine the two senses of duration. Spinozist duration is the continuation of the existence of a thing from a beginning onward. Through the course of its existence a thing is obliged to experiment and discover those things and relations that best agree with it. As we have seen, this process of experimentation is affect-infused: With a good encounter, we experience joy; with a bad encounter we experience sadness. This is where Bergsonian duration comes in. Every encounter in Spinoza stands for a *transition* or *passage* that increases or decreases, expands or restricts, our powers and existence; accompanying these transitions, registering them as it were, are affects of joy and sadness. As Spinoza and Deleuze tell us, what is at stake in this transition is not any kind of intellectualist comparison that the mind would make between its past and present states: as though it were to feel sadness and loss at the forfeiture, or joy and gain at the acquisition, of its powers (see *CC*, 139). Instead, the variations in our powers have an *intrinsic affective dimension*, a flow of feeling irreducible to any comparison or judgment of discrete past and present states (*E*, III, General Definition of Emotions). A finite mode at once exists in a continuous variation of its power given the encounters it experiences, and these variations of power find a continuous psychical expression in an affective flow of becoming joyful and becoming sad.

These modal transitions satisfy the two central requirements of Bergson's conception of duration (especially its early psychological formulation) as it is summed up by the term *continuous multiplicity*.[35] This term is handy, because each of its words relates a demand that, taken together, constitutes the sui generis reality of time as duration. First, duration is not reducible to division and comparative analysis in its experience, or to division and calculation in its study; it is, rather, a continuous and indivisible flow. Second, as Henri Gouhier points out, Bergson's definition of duration [*durée*] seems to fly in the face of what it means to endure [*durer*]. To endure conventionally means to "continue to be, to persist in being"; however, Gouhier notes that Bergson effects a shift in our understanding of that word, one that may, in fact, best realize it.[36] Bergson realized the sense in which to endure means to change for the reason that existence occurs within an irreversible dimension of time and experience. In these conditions, to endure cannot mean to be unvarying and resistant to change, but instead to be "multiple" and subject to inevitable change. We can now see how the term *continuous multiplicity* defines duration: To endure is to be in continuous variation; existence in time (duration) is at once continuous and multiple.

Jumping back to Spinoza, we can bring out a latent concept of duration by showing how Spinoza satisfies its two components: continuity and multiplicity. First, with respect to continuity we have seen that a mode experiences its existence as a real and affective flow or passage of empowerment and impotence, of joy and sadness, over the course of its encounters. Second, a mode is multiple (i.e., it changes continuously in time) because if it is to endure—if it is not to be decomposed by bad encounters—it must experiment with and discover relations that compound with it. If it is to last, the mode must by necessity change. A mode's development is ongoing; indeed, it is total. As Spinoza observes, we would not believe that we were once helpless children were it not for the fact that we see every adult was at first a child (*E*, IVP39S). This wonder at childhood is instructive, for what could be more illustrative of continuous multiplicity than that of a mode that starts off powerless, at the mercy of world and passion, and develops over time (i.e., through encounters, affections, and affects) into someone almost incapable of recognizing their origins, so complete has been the change. This is not to say that the life of a mode is an unimpeded progress. Spinoza will constantly remind us that most people never cease being childish and that we can never totally escape a condition of childhood. The existence of any finite mode has its ups and downs, and these constant and continual variations of power occur in time *as* a becoming. In this respect too, Spinoza can be seen to concur: to endure is to change. In other words, Spinoza's definition of duration as the continuation in existence anticipates the Bergsonian lesson: By the very fact of enduring, a finite thing is in continual variation; or, more directly, every mode is a continuous multiplicity.

Delgamuukw II: The Creation of Problems as the Power of Adjudication

Early in *A Thousand Plateaus* we see the little phrase "a sad image of thought" (*TP*, 16). Now, we could take this as just another way of saying that the dominant (dogmatic, or as they say, arborescent) image of thought is lame or regrettable. Or we could take this as a precise Spinozist claim to say that (dogmatic) thought can and has been separated from its capacities, that it only has inadequate ideas which fail to understand either the world or itself, and consequently that it feels its own powerlessness as sadness.

What is, in its most basic sense, an inadequate idea for Spinoza? It is an idea that fails to understand the order and connection of things; it is an idea that cannot comprehend the true cause of something.[37] A sad image of thought would imply a thought unable to properly grasp its own cause, such that what it thinks or imagines about itself fails to capture how it actually happens.[38] As such, thought would be impotent to comprehend itself (never mind the world)—a depressing thought to be sure.

If a sad image holds inadequate ideas about the causes of (or conditions for) thought, what might an adequate idea be? What could we identify as the cause of thought? For Deleuze, as I said in Chapter 4, the answer has to do with philosophy's critical vocation: The condition for an authentic (philosophical) thought is a break with opinion (*doxa*). Thought reveals itself to be dogmatic (inadequate, powerless, sad) if it is satisfied to say or believe that it is thinking when it is in fact engaged in the exchange and verification of opinion. ("There are things one cannot do or even say, believe, feel, think, unless one is weak, enslaved, impotent" [*EPS*, 269].) According to Deleuze, nowhere does thought reveal itself to be so sad as in its confusion as to what problems (and solutions) are, insofar as it confuses its highest opportunity in the pursuit of degrading, not to mention enslaving, exercises.

> *We are led to believe* that problems are given ready-made, and that they disappear in the responses of the solution. . . . *We are led to believe* that the activity of thinking . . . begins only with the search for solutions. . . . This *belief* probably has the same origin as the other postulates of the dogmatic image: *puerile* examples taken out of context and arbitrarily erected into models. According to this *infantile prejudice* [*préjugé infantile*], the master sets a problem, our task is to solve it, and the result is accredited true or false by a powerful authority. *It is also a social prejudice with the visible interest of maintaining us in an infantile state* [*de nous maintenir enfants*]*, which calls upon us to solve problems that come from elsewhere,* consoling or distracting us by telling us that we have won simply by being able to respond: the problem as obstacle and the respondent as Hercules. Such is the origin of the grotesque image of culture that we find in examinations and government referenda as well as in newspaper competitions (where everyone is called upon to choose according to his or her taste, on condition that this taste coincides with that of everyone else). Be yourselves—it being understood that this self must be that of others. As if we would not remain slaves so long as we do not control the problems themselves, so long as we do not possess *a right to problems* [*d'un droit aux problèmes*], to a participation in and management of the problems. (*DR*, 158, emphasis added, translation modified)[39]

Depending on one's taste, this passage has a kind of Kantian or Spinozist flavor to it (no doubt both). First, there are strong evocations of Kant's "What Is Enlightenment?" in that participation in this dogmatic sham of a "problem" worsens or deepens our self-incurred immaturity (*Unmündigkeit*). But at the same time, in content and tone, this passage feels like a fiery Scholium. A favorite theme of Deleuze's in Spinoza is the critique of the perfection and happiness of childhood (ontogenetically as babies, phylogenetically as Adamic).[40] Children, for Spinoza, cannot be joyful, for they are filled with inadequate ideas, ideas that place them at the mercy of their passions and of haphazard encounters. Sadly, this is not a condition we grow out of, for we are kept in immaturity (superstition and intolerance, sadness) by tyrants who are also immature and sad (this is, if I can put it this way, the basic problem of the *Theological-Political Treatise*). These Spinozist insights animate the passage. To conceive of problems on the model of question and answer is to become childish; it is the mark of inadequacy to convert the condition of thought (the invention of problems) into its ruination (the circulation of opinion to preestablished questions). By neutralizing the potentials of problems, dogmatism separates thought from what it can do.

And with dangerous consequences. Thought becomes limited to giving appropriate answers to acceptable questions. Deleuze's repetition of the phrase "we are led to believe" flags the link between the disempowerment of thought and despotism. Like Spinoza who revealed the mutual support between superstition and despotism, Deleuze also draws a link between a conception of the problem along the lines of an already solved question and the authority that sets the problem, poses the question, and sanctions the answer. As with Spinoza, where "[men] fight for their servitude as if for salvation," we too provide answers to questions that enslave us not by their content but by their readiness to conceive of thought on a model that makes it inadequate (unable to realize its true cause and condition), impotent (separated from its powers), and sad (unaware of the joys of its proper exercise and trapped in despotism).[41]

At the end of the passage there is another important, potentially Spinozist, phrase: "so long as we do not possess *a right to problems*." A right, or the rights of an individual, means for Spinoza all that the individual can do. "The right of the individual is coextensive with its determinate power."[42] If we take Deleuze's term *right* in this Spinozist sense (i.e., as coextensive with power), then a right to problems has two implications in accordance with the two meanings of power. On the one hand, a power (as in *potestas* or *pouvoir*) over problems is a right to create, control, and dispose them—that is, not to have them handed down to us, not to be locked into despotism by function of degraded problems. But more important, and grounding that need for the control over problems, is that a right to problems designates the right to our capacities or powers (as in *potentia* or *puissance*) of thought. If, for Deleuze, a problem is the condition or cause of thought, and if thought's fundamental capacity is its ability to create problems, then to understand what a problem is and does is to have an adequate idea of thought itself. A right to problems is a power to think; or rather, it is an empowerment of thought, a simultaneous affection (an adequate idea) and affect (a joy) of thought.

It is rewarding to compare Deleuze's remarks on power and problems with the way he redraws the distinction between the political left and right.

> I don't think that people on the Right are deluded, they're no more stupid than anyone else, *but their method is to oppose movement*. It's the same as the opposition to Bergson in philosophy, all that's the same. Embracing movement, or blocking it: politically, two completely different methods of negotiation. For the Left, this means a new way of talking. The point is not to convince but to be clear. *Being clear is to set out the "facts," not only of a situation but of a problem. To make visible things that would otherwise remain hidden.* . . . The Right refuses these questions. If these questions are well grounded, then by determining the facts we express a problem that the Right wants to hide. Because once the problem has been stated, it can no longer be gotten rid of, and the Right will have to change its way of speaking. So the job of the Left, whether in or out of power, is to discover the sort of problem that the Right wants to hide at all costs. (*N*, 127, emphasis added, translation modified)

If the left were to be defined by voluntarism, by the changing of the world according to a plan, nothing could be more foreign to Deleuze.[43] But in this passage Deleuze proposes a new criterion by which to understand what the left, as well as the right, means. Foremost, the right and left do not represent political positions; rather, these terms contrast an inadequate idea with an adequate idea (and, as a *consequence*, they contrast an inadequate practice with an adequate practice). Leftism is a practice possible only with an affirmation that our situation or condition *is* movement. Our powers of practice are unlocked by coming to terms with this situation and affirming its necessity. The right may attempt to block movement, and the right might also pass judgment from its perspective of the denial of movement,[44] but the left is, first and foremost, an affirmation of movement and a capacity for practice from within movement.

Given this condition, thought must create problems in order to become aware of the novel variations wrought by movement. As Deleuze says, the creation of *new* problems is the only way to get at the facts—that is, to achieve clear vision or appreciation—of the situation. To see a new situation (to be a seer in Deleuze's sense), one must effectively construct a perspective or problem for that situation. Old ways of seeing will not do; by definition they cannot appreciate the demands and potentials of a new situation. As we will see, this means that the left gains its powers or rights of thought when it realizes its problem-creating capacity; and it gains its power or rights of practice when it forces attention to problems by uncovering their reality and calling attention to the new situation.

Deleuze's characterization of the political left is indebted to Spinoza: Practice without metaphysics is nonsense; only a proper metaphysical sensibility can rightly conceive and judge actions.[45] But, as Deleuze seems to suggest, his remarks are also deeply Bergsonian. In a wonderful text, Bergson tells of his astonishment to learn that he is read to recommend change: "Because the permanence of substance was, in my eyes, a continuity of change, it has been said that my doctrine was a justification of instability. One might just as well imagine that the bacteriologist recommends microbic diseases to us when he shows us microbes everywhere" (*CM*, 88). And he continues that

> *the philosopher who finds mobility everywhere is the only one who cannot recommend it, since he sees it as inevitable.* . . . If he has any common sense at all, [this philosopher], like everyone else, will consider necessary a permanence of what is. He will say that institutions should furnish a relatively invariable framework for the diversity and mobility of individual designs. And he will understand perhaps better than other people the role of these institutions. (*CM*, 88, emphasis added)

On the surface, these remarks extolling the permanence and invariability of institutions do not seem particularly left-leaning. But I would say that they are just what Deleuze has in mind. The left must not recommend change (for then it collapses into finalism and possibilism—it misunderstands the nature of change); it must affirm the reality of movement. Only within this understanding can the value and actions of institutions be appraised. In this view, a left-leaning analysis of the institution of adjudication would immediately agree to the need for (inattentive) judgments that enact permanence in the predictable repetition of rules; at the same time, however, this analysis would also be sensitive to the need for (attentive) judgments able to create new problems and concepts that respond to *and* construct the novel encounters that mobility ceaselessly generates.

At this point we can revisit *Delgamuukw* with three guiding intuitions. First, if for Spinoza an adequate idea apprehends causes, for Deleuze an adequate idea of thought recognizes its cause in a problem and an encounter that forces a break with opinion. To deny thought its inspiration in problems—that is, to base problems on a model of opinion and propositional exchange—is to make it insipid and sad. Second, ethics or practice is a matter of affirming the necessity of movement and, in so doing, of uncovering new and necessary problems that become unavoidable by virtue of being stated. We must be open to and aware of the potential for new, invigorating, and necessary problems; otherwise, we resign ourselves to an inadequate grasp of our (factual and metaphysical) situation and, consequently, to an ineffective, powerless practice. Third, we must come to terms with Deleuze's enigmatic and underdeveloped statement in the *Abécédaire* that to be leftist—that is, to affirm the necessity of movement as a horizon for effective practice—is "first of all a question of *perception*" (*ABC*, G). I take this to mean that practice must be made sensitive or sensible to encounters.

The initial *Delgamuukw* trial in British Columbia (1991), presided over by British Columbia Chief Justice Allan McEachern, caused a political sensation and an academic scandal. Politically, it was significant because it decided that aboriginal title did not exist in law and that the province was under no obligation to cede land or to even enter into negotiations with aboriginal peoples. Academically, the decision was condemned as racist. In his decision McEachern represented the Gitksan and Wet'suwet'en peoples as warlike, illiterate, primitive, and lawless. "The plaintiffs' ancestors had no written language, no horses or wheeled vehicles, slavery and starvation was [*sic*] not uncommon, and there is no doubt, to quote Hobbs [*sic*] that aboriginal life in the territory was, at best, 'nasty, brutish and short.'"[46] This assessment is legally significant because it undercuts the plaintiffs' attempt to demonstrate control and occupation of the territories in question.

I cite these remarks not to criticize their ethnocentrism (this has been done elsewhere)[47] but to discuss the reaction of the Supreme Court of Canada. Perhaps surprisingly, the Court had none. It showed restraint and said that "unless there is a 'palpable and overriding error,' appellate courts should not substitute their own findings of fact for those of the trial judge" (*Delgamuukw*, ¶¶78, 90–91). Indeed, insofar as it passes over them in silence, the Court corroborates the findings at trial and accepts the characterization of the plaintiffs' society. In the Court's view, to substitute its own specific findings of fact—for example, to argue that the plaintiffs were civilized, that their rules were regular enough to be called laws, and so on—would compromise the integrity and autonomy of the trial process; such substitution would be activist and inappropriate.

The Court did, however, overturn the trial decision precisely on the question of evidence. Rather than dispute specific findings or conclusions, the Court uncovered a problem of which the trial judge was unaware and revealed the trial decision to be flawed. In a nutshell, the Court held that the trial decision was insensitive to the sui generis nature of evidence in aboriginal rights cases and that evidentiary rules were not accordingly adapted.

Appellate intervention is warranted by the failure of a trial court to appreciate the evidentiary difficulties inherent in adjudicating aboriginal claims when, first, applying the rules of evidence and, second, interpreting the evidence before it. . . . "[A] court should approach the rules of evidence, and interpret the evidence that exists, with a consciousness of the special nature of aboriginal claims, and of the evidentiary difficulties in proving a right which originates in times where there were no written records of the practices, customs and traditions engaged in. The courts must not undervalue the evidence presented by aboriginal claimants simply because that evidence does not conform precisely with the evidentiary standards that would be applied in, for example, a private law torts case." (*Delgamuukw*, ¶¶80–81, in part citing *Van der Peet*, ¶68)

I have spoken at length of the problem. What is it here? Chief Justice Lamer says that the justification for this special approach to aboriginal evidence lies in the nature of aboriginal rights. In the next paragraph he says that these rights aim at "reconciliation" and at "bridging of aboriginal and non-aboriginal cultures." As with the concept of aboriginal title, the modification of evidentiary standards is another expression and determination of the problem of reconciliation posed by aboriginal rights. Aboriginal evidence is like a problem within a broader problem (of reconciliation), and specific measures of inclusion and adaptation must be taken to resolve it.

The Court specifies an encounter and lays out a problem. First, there is an encounter with aboriginal evidence in that it does not conform to the normal common law of admissibility, and, strictly speaking, it would not count as evidence at all. Second, there is the problem of reconciliation: If aboriginal rights are to be given effect in court—that is, if reconciliation is to be honored—then the evidence argued from must be recognized on the same footing as conventional evidence. The question of evidence is a further uncovering of the motivating problem of aboriginal rights. Put in this way, the common law becomes sensitive to an encounter and frames it within a broader problem that, once stated, courts cannot avoid or dismiss; the rules of evidence will have to be adapted in order for aboriginal peoples to get a fair hearing.

I can cite a few specific instances where the trial judge was insensitive to the sui generis status of aboriginal evidence. Or, in other words, I can indicate in what ways the trial judge (McEachern) simultaneously failed to perceive the encounter before the court and failed to give expression to the problem of aboriginal rights.

First, the oral histories used by the plaintiffs to establish the boundaries of the claimed territory were systematically undervalued. On first appearance, many features of oral histories militate against their admission or, at best, put them at a disadvantage compared to conventional historical documents. For example, they consist of out-of-court statements inadmissible as hearsay; moreover, they are seen as expressions of cultural values tangential to fact finding (*Delgamuukw*, ¶86). Nevertheless, realizing the importance of the oral histories to the plaintiffs' case, the trial judge did admit them. It is telling, however, that McEachern admitted them not on the basis of their sui generis status; instead, he found a common law rule to provide for their inclusion.[48] Rather than admit a unique situation and proceed accordingly, he found a way to subsume this evidence under a ready-made rule.

Despite including them as evidence, McEachern accorded no independent weight to the oral histories. Citing reasons that oral histories were not "literally true" and that they confounded "what is fact and what is belief," and citing the fact that the verifying group is small and also involved in the dispute, he held that these histories were confined to providing "*confirmatory* proof of early presence in the territory."[49]

At the Supreme Court of Canada, Lamer makes two criticisms of the trial judge's fact-finding premises. First, he finds that the trial judge's decision does not address the specific oral histories before him and that he "based his decision on some general concerns with the use of oral histories as evidence in aboriginal rights cases" (*Delgamuukw*, ¶98). Second, he argues that if the trial judge's reservations about the value of oral histories were followed, "the oral histories of aboriginal peoples would be consistently and systematically undervalued by the Canadian legal system" (*Delgamuukw*, ¶98). Thus, because the trial judge was insensitive to the encounter posed by aboriginal evidence and because he failed to coordinate this encounter with the problem of reconciliation, he was unable to evaluate the specific evidence before the court, disqualifying it through general reservations.

The trial judge also discounted the "recollections of aboriginal life" provided by members of the plaintiffs' community. He said that they did not go back far enough in time and thus failed to demonstrate the requisite continuity between past and present necessary for occupation. But Lamer counters, "The trial judge expected too much of the oral history of the appellants. He expected that evidence to provide definitive and precise evidence of pre-contact aboriginal activities on the territory in question" (*Delgamuukw*, ¶101). This is an "impossible burden to meet" and such an inappropriately stringent demand would dismiss all evidence of this kind.

A final example of the trial judge's insensitivity to aboriginal evidence concerns the territorial affidavits filed by the plaintiff chiefs. These are declarations of the territorial holdings of the Gitksan and Wet'suwet'en houses, often made on behalf of deceased persons. Because these declarations are a form of hearsay, the plaintiffs attempted to get them recognized under the reputation exception to the hearsay rule.[50] The trial judge refused and gave the following three reasons: First, he questioned whether the declarations could amount to a reputation, seeing as they were confined to the community; second, he challenged the reliability of the affidavits, given that their content was under dispute; third, he disputed the objectivity of the information in the statements, given that they were under contemporary discussion. Lamer responds point by point: First, given that reputation is established by circulating oral histories within a community, it cannot be disqualified for being confined to that community; second, given that land claims are almost always under dispute, and hence in litigation, an affidavit cannot be dismissed simply because its content is contested; third, given that the affidavits exist as oral history, they must be in contemporary discussion or otherwise forgotten, and so cannot be discounted on that ground. In short, Lamer repeats that without the recognition of its sui generis character, aboriginal evidence is consistently undervalued, thereby placing an impossible demand on aboriginal peoples who would claim their rights in court.

Changing the terms, we might say that Lamer reproaches McEachern's sad image of law. If aboriginal jurisprudence is set into motion by an encounter with the sui generis nature of aboriginal rights (its sui generis title, its sui generis evidence), and if the motivating problem of this jurisprudence is to promote and clarify the manner in which reconciliation is to take place, then in a quite literal sense McEachern's judgment separates law from its potential and capacity. This judgment is inadequate in the strong sense; it is unaware of its cause in an encounter and, consequently, impotent in its practice.

How is it that McEachern severs law from its powers? How does he make it sad? First, he does not perceive the sui generis encounter before the court and cannot help but judge it by the ready-made standards of the common law; second, and as a direct consequence, he cannot pose or uncover the problem of reconciliation that animates aboriginal rights, the very problem that finds its determinate expression in Lamer's sensitive handling of aboriginal title and aboriginal evidence (as actualizations of that problem).

Returning to Deleuze and Spinoza, we can say that law exists in duration, in transitions of becoming inadequate and powerless (sad) in the trial decision and becoming adequate and powerful (joyful) in the appellate decision. But how does the law become powerful and attain its powers? By experimentation. In Deleuze's reading of Spinoza we saw that a mode is not, at first, equipped with the tools (the common notions) to make it powerful and joyful; it must instead acquire these through experimentation, by allowing itself to be affected by those things that enhance its powers and encourage the formulation of common notions. In *Delgamuukw* we touched on this process: The rules of evidence must be adapted in case- and situation-specific fashion. Or, in Spinozist terms, the common law must allow itself to be affected by the encounter. When we ask what the law can do, when we inquire about its powers, we are in effect asking how it allows itself to be affected in an encounter. As we have seen with McEachern, a law that cannot allow itself to be affected and to join with the affecting body is an impotent and inadequate law. Adequacy in law, therefore, is a practice of experimentally allowing the law to be affected by an encounter.

We can return to the previous examples. Lamer repeatedly recommends specific modifications of standard rules of evidence so as to include aboriginal evidence. First, oral evidence is not to be disqualified as hearsay or restricted to a confirmatory role. On a "case-by-case" basis, oral histories are to be admitted and evaluated as evidence in order to establish the historical use and occupation of the land (*Delgamuukw*, ¶¶87 and 94). Second, the continuity rule that common law requires continuity between present and past occupation is to be relaxed when dealing with aboriginal title. Instead, oral histories and testimony can seek to demonstrate that current occupation of the land has presovereign origins (*Delgamuukw*, ¶¶101 and 152). Third, as we have already seen, the reputation exception to the hearsay rule is amended to account for the peculiar conditions of territorial affidavits (*Delgamuukw*, ¶106). Fourth, the exclusivity rule of occupation requiring exclusive possession at the time of sovereignty is adapted to account for the context of aboriginal society (e.g., if two communities shared hunting grounds or if nomadic tribes had acknowledged rights of passage) (*Delgamuukw*, ¶156). We could multiply examples, but the point remains that an adequate judgment at common law experiments with an encounter (not, I caution, with just any case) and combines the unique features of that case to its own adapted rules. Only by allowing itself to be affected by the case, by joining its powers with it, can an adequate judgment be given for an encounter at law. Or, another Spinozist way of putting it, only if a common law judgment can express through the modification of its concepts its cause in an encounter can it be adequate.

Taking the necessary precautions, we could call this judgment leftist. Remember that for Deleuze the left has nothing to do with the realization of certain political protocols but is tantamount to embracing movement. In this same way, the Supreme Court's *Delgamuukw* decision is not of the left because it upholds minority rights or advances multiculturalism. Instead, it is leftist in its acknowledgment of movement (i.e., the recognition of sui generis encounters), and, with that acknowledgment, it is able to construct an effective adjudicative problem. Deleuze says that "being open [to movement] *is setting out the 'facts,'* not merely of a situation but of a problem. Making visible things that would otherwise remain hidden."

Or, as he says, without adequate problems "one may speak in this connection of *a real inability to get at the facts* [*impuissance à informer*]" (*N*, 127, emphasis added).

Word for word, this is the accomplishment of Lamer's judgment. Only by being sensitive to (by perceiving—remember, the left is a matter of perception [*ABC*, G]) the encounter and only by uncovering the problem of aboriginal rights are the facts of the case set out. The construction of a problem enables an appreciation of the situation, a view of the facts: If aboriginal evidence is discounted, then the boundaries of the occupied territory, not to mention the nature of the attachment with the land, could not be made apparent (or, more strongly, could not exist). The Supreme Court does not overturn the trial decision for its superficial findings of evidence; rather, its criticism is that the trial judge is insensitive to movement (to encounters and problems) and has no means to find the facts of the case. In the Court's language, there is not a specific but a "palpable and overriding error" in the factual findings of the trial decision (*Delgamuukw*, ¶78). Thus, negatively put, without the construction of a problem, there is an inability to get at the facts; positively put, an encounter shocks the law and initiates the uncovering of a problem that will establish the facts of the situation. Only by experimenting with common law concepts—by recreating them through a problem—can the basic facts of an encountered case be resolved.

No doubt this experimentation must be prudent. As Lamer stresses, the common law must accommodate the aboriginal perspective, but "this accommodation must be done in a manner which does not strain 'the Canadian legal and constitutional structure'" (*Delgamuukw*, ¶82, citing *Van der Peet*, ¶49). As experimental and open to modification as it may be, the common law cannot allow itself to be adapted to the point of dissolution. What this limit might be is unclear. In matters of aboriginal title, the limit might be tested by a claim for self-government, wherein the issue is not merely to incorporate aboriginal law into the common law to demonstrate occupation but to supersede the common law altogether within that territory.[51] Because these limits cannot be determined in a general way but must be specified in the context of an encounter, we will not pursue the question but raise it as a problem for further investigation. The limits of and the need for prudence can be judged only by the problems to which they are internal (see *TP*, 250).

Although the theme of prudence is not one usually associated with Deleuze, it is one of his most recurrent themes. For example, with respect to Spinozist experimentation, Deleuze writes, "No one knows ahead of time the affects one is capable of; it is a long affair of experimentation, *requiring a lasting prudence*, a Spinozian wisdom that implies the construction of a plane of immanence or consistency" (*SPP*, 125, emphasis added). And the call to prudence is found in several chapters of *A Thousand Plateaus* (most notably in the political ones), where experimentation risks turning into alternative twin terrors: either toward fascism and the dangerous self-assurance of "marginals" (*TP*, 227–229),[52] or toward a morbid abolition, a line of death (*TP*, 160–161, 229–231, 250, 270).[53]

Caution is stressed time and again in Deleuze's writings on experimentation, and it should come as no surprise that a philosopher who spent his life developing concepts such as movement and deterritorialization should be acutely aware of their dangers. As with Bergson's statement that a philosopher who sees movement everywhere cannot be taken to recommend it, and that, in fact, this philosopher knows best how to take it up and how to limit it (i.e., how to work with it), Deleuze too cannot be said to recommend experimentation to judges. He says only that an adequate institution of adjudication is necessarily experimental, and, in this way, he can acknowledge creativity while simultaneously exhorting prudence.

Immanence and Expression

As the virtual is to the reading of Bergson, or as the eternal return is to the reading of Nietzsche, immanence is the darling concept of Deleuze's reading of Spinoza. In these final two sections I continue the analysis of Deleuze's reading of Spinoza (as simultaneously commentator and original philosopher), this time tracking the concept of immanence. Afterwards, I use this concept to guide my summation.

Rather than address immanence head-on, I propose to examine the concept of expression as developed in two different texts of Deleuze's in order to state the problem and stakes of a philosophy of immanence. In the first text, *Expressionism in Philosophy: Spinoza*, Deleuze raises the hitherto unnoticed term *expression* from Spinoza's *Ethics* to the status of a concept that unfolds an unprecedented philosophy of immanence. In the second text, *Cinema 1: The Movement-Image*, expression resurfaces but without mention of Spinoza and this time in service of Deleuze's concept of the "plane of immanence." In observing this repetition of expression within *Cinema 1*, I propose three contributions. First, and as a kind of philological or detective work, I simply reveal the fact of its recurrence. Indeed, it seems remarkable that given the tremendous achievement of raising the term *expression* from near imperceptibility in Spinoza to the status of that philosophy's organizing concept, Deleuze would choose to embed it just as completely, just as silently, but just as powerfully in his reading of Bergson in *Cinema 1*. Second, I draw attention to Deleuze's powerful mixing of the genres of commentary and philosophy. This enables us to see how a concept that is developed through strict, meticulously textual commentary can be repeated in another context that simultaneously preserves the integrity of that concept (and context) while putting it to a different, creative use. Third, by showing the repetition of expression in these two texts, I achieve a perspective from which to notice the differences between Spinoza's concept of immanence as Deleuze formulates it and Deleuze's own concept of the plane of immanence. Given that in the commentary on Spinoza expression is in service of a concept of immanence, whereas in *Cinema 1* expression is in the service of a concept of the plane of immanence, I am able to contrast these two concepts according to the different use of expression. I argue that Deleuze's use of expression in *Cinema 1* represents the ideal limit toward which his interpretation of Spinoza tends but, given the nature of that primary text, cannot fully realize. As such, it is in connection with the Bergson of *Cinema 1* that expression becomes unfettered, free, and at the height of its powers—that it becomes, in other words, a concept in service of a properly Deleuzian philosophy of immanence.

I begin with the reading of Spinoza. Expression is the main concept Deleuze develops in his *Expressionism in Philosophy: Spinoza*. The development of this concept is a perfect example of Deleuze's practice of philosophical portraiture, given that the one concept he takes to bind together all of Spinoza's thought (ontological, epistemological, practical, and political) is nowhere defined or raised to an explicit level by Spinoza.[54] The term *expression* is used forty-six times in the *Ethics* and always indirectly at that; it never appears as a noun (*expressio*) but is used only as a verb (*exprimere*, together with its derivatives).[55]

Expression, according to Deleuze, takes on its fundamental importance in its use and operation in the *Ethics*. For this reason we cannot consider the concept on its own but can only grasp it in its operation (*EPS*, 19). To start, we identify its two fundamental uses, noting how it cuts straight to the heart of fundamental problems of Spinozism.

1. *Expression and univocity.* "By God I mean an absolutely infinite being, that is, substance consisting of infinite attributes, each of which *expresses* eternal and infinite essence" (*E*, ID6, emphasis added). Attributes are the essential forms of the single substance (God) that expresses itself though them. God, therefore, is expressive, and there is a constitution of substance in and by its expression in the attributes. Now the attributes, which are the infinite forms of being, re-express themselves in the modes whose essence they constitute (*E*, IIP25C). For example, human beings are modes and, inasmuch as they are mind and body, imply two of God's attributes: thought and extension (*E*, IIP1–2). We have, then, a kind of expressive triad: Substance expresses itself through attributes, which are both infinite in number and infinite in kind, and these attributes are themselves implied in the modifications of substance whose essence they constitute. What is radical about this scheme is that the attributes are forms common to God and to the modes (*E*, IIP38–39). This is Spinoza's thesis of univocity: The same attributes are predicated of God who expresses himself through them as of a mode that implies them. Contrary to the history of both positive and negative theology, God does not possess his attributes in an eminent, mysterious, or extraordinary fashion but does so just as the modes do.[56] As Deleuze says, "Attributes are not abstracted from particular things, still less transferred to God analogically. Attributes are reached directly as forms of being common to creatures and to God, common to modes and to substance" (*EPS*, 46).

2. *Expression and power.* According to Deleuze, expression also has a fundamental epistemological and practical role in the *Ethics*. For Spinoza, an inadequate idea, one that stems from the imagination, is inexpressive because it indicates only the state of our own body and how it feels itself to be affected (*E*, IIP16). It expresses nothing about the external body affecting us, nor does it explain our essence or power. An adequate idea, by contrast, is expressive in three simultaneous ways. First, it expresses the efficient cause of the existence of something (another mode); second, it expresses the formal cause of the essence of that same something (God);

and third, it expresses our powers of comprehension (our own essence). If we recall Spinoza's thesis of univocity, this means nothing less than that to have an adequate idea is to have that idea in the same form that God has it (*E*, IIP47). To express an adequate idea is, from a speculative viewpoint, to participate in the power and knowledge of God; from a practical viewpoint, it is to experience (a moment of) beatitude, that is, a participation in the practical power and contentment of God (*E*, VP27).

In these two admittedly terse summaries we can see what Deleuze is driving at through his reading of expression, univocity, and power: a philosophy of immanence. He says as much in his later reflections on the text added to the English translation.

> What interested me most in Spinoza wasn't his substance, but the composition of finite modes. I consider this one of the most original aspects of my book. That is: the hope of making substance turn on finite modes, or at least in seeing in substance a *plane of immanence* in which finite modes operate, already appears in this book. What I needed was both (1) the expressive character of particular individuals, and (2) an immanence of being. (*EPS*, 11)

What the term *expression* affords Deleuze—and its exclusively verbal form in the *Ethics* only invites and facilitates this reading—is the opportunity to characterize an active, genetic, and above all constructivist substance that expresses itself without reserve in or as a nature of finite modes with which it shares all its form of being. On the one hand, univocity eliminates all trace of transcendence (i.e., eminence and analogy) by sharing in common the forms of being between substance and modes; on the other hand, adequate ideas enable finite modes to participate in and express powers of knowledge and joy hitherto restricted to the transcendent divine. If indeed Deleuze distorts or differentially repeats Spinoza's text with his concept of expression, he does so not to depart from it but rather to use what is otherwise an unremarkable item to reveal the innermost operation and most urgent aspect of a philosophy: immanence.

Without a doubt, expression is in service of establishing univocal relations between modes and substance that result in a philosophy of immanence; but is this the same as saying that it works toward a concept of a *plane* of immanence? Nowhere, except in the last chapter of *Spinoza: Practical Philosophy* (which we will come to), does Deleuze mention the plane of immanence in his commentaries on Spinoza. Why is that?

Perhaps there is a clue in the quoted reflections (offered, probably, in the late 1980s when *Expressionism* was being translated into English), in which Deleuze confides his hope or aspiration to read Spinoza according to the *two* criteria denoted by a plane of immanence: (1) the expressive character of individuals; and (2) an immanence of being.

Are these met? To my mind, the first is fully satisfied. Modes, as degrees of power or essence of substance, are expressive and imply substance by virtue of the forms of being (attributes) that they share in common. But the second is another matter, and, in *Difference and Repetition*, we find a unique instance where Deleuze is critical of Spinoza precisely on the grounds that his philosophy of immanence is incomplete or indefinite.

> Nevertheless, there still remains a difference between substance and the modes: *Spinoza's substance appears independent of the modes, while the modes are dependent on substance*, but as though on something other than themselves. Substance must itself be said *of* the modes and only *of* the modes. Such a condition can be satisfied only at the price of a more general categorical reversal according to which being is said of becoming. (*DR*, 40, emphasis added)

I take the criteria for this criticism of Spinoza's incomplete immanence to be Deleuze's philosophy of time. As we have seen, substance in Spinoza is eternal, which means that its existence necessarily follows from its essence or definition. Although it is true that substance expresses itself in its attributes (and, consequently, in the modes), it does not follow that substance could be said to depend on the modes. Modes, by contrast, explicitly depend on substance for both their essence and their existence (*E*, IP25). In the theory of substance, therefore, we see firsthand that curious phenomenon that so often marks Spinoza studies: the fact of sound yet opposite interpretations. On the one hand, substance is expressed without reserve in a modalized universe (the total immanence of the *Deus sive natura* formula, God = Nature);[57] on the other hand, the eternity of substance makes it, by definition, independent of a modalized universe (thus not entirely immanent to it, able to exist without and outside it). Deleuze's criticism, I note, might also register this ambivalence—"Substance *appears* independent of the modes [*la substance spinoziste apparaît indépendante des modes*]"—as though Spinoza's commitment to immanence, his chief contribution according to Deleuze, is, in the last analysis, undecidable. (Then again, it might not: Deleuze could be taken as saying that Spinozist substance manifests itself independently of the modes—it all depends on how the word *appears* is taken.)

That Deleuze's criticism has for its basis his philosophy of time is corroborated in its last line: "Such a condition [complete univocity or immanence, wherein substance and mode have *exactly* the same sense] can be satisfied only at the price of a more general categorical reversal according to which *being is said of becoming*." Pure univocity is tied directly to a theory of time. Now it is no coincidence that the chapter in Deleuze's commentaries on Spinoza that most forcefully pushes a reading of being-as-becoming is the same place where the plane of immanence makes its appearance (*SPP*, 122–130). Here, as was his express wish in the translator's preface to *Expressionism*, Deleuze switches his emphasis from substance to modal nature, where "what is involved is no longer the affirmation of a single substance, but rather the laying out of a *common plane of immanence* on which all bodies, all minds, and all individuals are situated" (*SPP*, 122). In this chapter, exclusive attention is given to modal nature and to the practice of living. To live, according to this reading, means to carve out a system of relations and commonalities with other modes in order to persevere in existence and develop one's capacities. In this ("ethological") view, beings are defined by what they can do and discover their powers through the course of experimentation.[58] With nothing above or beyond it, nature is the infinite place or space of modal existence wherein individuals compose and decompose their relations; it is a plane of immanence without "supplementary dimension," whether theological or teleological (*SPP*, 128). Nature is obviously not independent of the modes but is constituted only in and by their movements. And, insofar as nature or the plane of immanence is nothing other than "a process of composition," or a "composition of speeds and slownesses," we can affirm of this universe that its being is becoming, that its being is constituted solely through the movement and becoming of the modes themselves (*SPP*, 123, 128). In Deleuze's reading, heavy on the *natura* of the *Deus sive natura* equation, univocal substance is modalized as the being of becoming.

But this last, wonderful chapter of *Spinoza: Practical Philosophy* has the feel of an experiment rather than a straight commentary; it is more like a reading *with*, instead of a reading *of*, Spinoza. For example, it never once directly cites from Spinoza, and it has extended remarks on Freud, the biological sciences, and reader reactions to Spinoza. And yet, it is as though only by taking off from Spinoza—using him as a gust or a broom—can Deleuze create the concept of the plane of immanence, for only then are its two criteria—the expressiveness of individuals and the immanence of being—fully realized. It is with this guiding intuition that I turn to Deleuze's reading of Bergson in *Cinema 1* to see how concepts begun with Spinoza acquire a new development and potential.

I am mainly concerned with the first chapter of *Cinema 1*, "Theses of Movement." Deleuze begins by stating a famous insight of Bergson: "Movement is distinct from the space covered" (*C1*, 1). This means that movement cannot be reconstituted by positions in space succeeding each other over abstract time; instead, it occurs in a concrete and continuous duration.[59] Movement always implicates a duration; or, in other words, a movement in space is inseparable from a change in duration. Bergson, therefore, establishes a preliminary opposition and critique: Real movement resists all attempts to reconstitute it by adding together spatial positions and abstract time.

Movement is indissociable from duration. And given that duration is defined as continuous qualitative change, it means that a movement is (and effects) qualitative change. In a word, a movement is a becoming. Deleuze offers the following formulation: "Each time there is a translation of parts in space, there is also a *qualitative change in a whole [un tout]*" (*C1*, 8, emphasis added). And he gives the following example. I am starving at point A and move to point B to eat. "When I have reached B and had something to eat, what has changed is not only my state, but the state of the whole which encompassed B, A, and all that was between them" (*C1*, 8). Here it is important to note two qualifications made by Deleuze: first, that it is *a* whole, that is, a limited whole; and second, in his example, that *the* whole is circumscribed to include only that which is between A and B. If we emphasize these qualifications, and if we take Deleuze to say only that the movement of the parts changes a delimited or artificially closed whole, then these statements are fully compatible with Spinoza: In nature there is a translation or exchange of parts between modes that transforms *a* whole. A starving mode can be moved to eat; in so doing, a movement modifies the state of a whole as encompassed by the affected modes. And, not only that, but insofar as all modes are connected on a plane of nature, the translation affects, however infinitesimally, all the modes of the whole.

But this agreement with Spinoza is only apparent, for there lies a decisive difference in the concept of the whole, and especially what change in the whole means. Change, for Spinoza, is a function of the rearrangement of parts between relatively closed sets (finite modes) that takes place within an absolutely closed set (Nature as a whole). A finite mode is a relatively stable collection of parts, and, insofar as it perseveres, it is a more or less closed set. Nature as a whole, on the other hand, is the set of all sets and is absolutely closed: "the whole of Nature as one individual whose parts—that is, all the constituent bodies—vary in infinite ways without any change in the individual as a whole" (*E*, IIL7S). Finite modes, the parts of this total set, shuffle around, but the whole of nature that contains them—the mediate infinite mode, Spinoza's famous "face of the universe [*facies totius universi*]" that varies "in infinite ways, yet remains always the same" (*L*, Letter 64)—is an invariant, closed set. And so although there appears to be continuous and irreversible change (transformation) from the limited perspective of the experience of finite modes, there is, from the perspective of the bigger picture, only a rearrangement of parts (translation) at the level of an unchanging whole.

As I have said, for Spinoza modes are relatively closed sets within an absolutely closed set. In his own philosophy, Bergson, in part, accepts this identification for the finite modes.[60] Life, as Bergson argues in *Creative Evolution*, endeavors to establish closed sets. "Life nevertheless manifests a search for individuality, as if it strove to constitute systems naturally isolated, naturally closed" (*CE*, 15). An organism is a perfect example. It is a more or less closed set or system of parts. With closed sets comes a spatial conception of movement, such that movement occurs between parts and alters their respective position without qualitative modification. The tendency of life to form closed systems, along with its corollary spatial movement, renders change a calculable displacement of parts over abstract (ineffective) time. Correcting my earlier statement, Bergson does not oppose closed sets and their spatial conception of time as an illusion or as a degradation of duration; rather, he says that closed sets and spatial time represent one tendency of life, one direction toward which it aspires.

There is, however, another half of movement. The tendency of a mode to close on itself—to form a closed set and to generate correspondingly spatial movement—is never fully achieved. As Bergson first discovered with the study of consciousness, and then again with the study of evolution, a mode exists only "insofar as it open[s] itself upon a whole, by coinciding with the opening up of a whole" (*C1*, 10). As Deleuze observes, in comparing an individual organism to the universe, Bergson appears to repeat the most ancient simile. But this is not at all the case.

For, if the living being is a whole and, therefore, comparable to the whole of the universe, this is not because it is a microcosm as closed as the whole is assumed to be, but, on the contrary, *because it is open upon a world, and the world, the universe is itself the Open.* (*C1*, 10, emphasis added)

There are two interdependent claims in this complex passage: first, that the mode is open upon a whole and, second, that this whole is itself open (and third, as we will see, that the opening of the mode upon a whole *is* the opening of the whole itself). But before distinguishing these points, we can ask, What does it mean to be open? Quite literally, not to be closed. Whether it pertains to the mode or to the whole, to be open means not to be a closed set. Consequently, the kind of movement that defines the open cannot be the kind of movement that defines closed sets, that is, spatial displacements of parts calculated over abstract time. The movement of the open is a concrete duration, a movement that expresses continuous qualitative change. This kind of movement, for both mode and whole, is a becoming.

Now, more specifically, what does an open whole or universe mean? On this point, not only is the difference between Spinoza and Bergson instructive, but for Deleuze it is opportune: It opens up new potential for the concepts of expression and immanence. For Spinoza, the whole indicates the total set that contains all subsets. The concept of the open whole directly contradicts Spinoza on two points. First, the whole is not a set because the whole's movement is continuous, hence without parts. The universe endures as a concrete duration, one not made up of parts that change position over (abstract) time (*C1*, 10). Second, the whole is not given because it constantly gives rise to the new. As Bergson says, "The duration of the universe must therefore be one with the latitude of creation which can find place in it" (*CE*, 340). This means, as Deleuze specifies, that whenever we are confronted with a duration, "we may conclude that there exists somewhere a whole which is changing, and which is open somewhere" (*C1*, 9). By virtue of the unceasing creativity that finds a place within it, the whole is neither givable and closed (as it is in Spinoza), nor nongivable and meaningless (as it is in Kant); instead, the whole is nongivable "because it is the Open, and because its nature is to change constantly, or to give rise to something new, in short, to endure" (*C1*, 9). The open whole is not a set, a collection of sets, or a totality. Instead, the movement that defines the whole—and thus the whole itself—*is* duration, it *is* becoming.

At this point, I can reintroduce the concept of expression. In *Expressionism*, Deleuze took a barely noticeable term from Spinoza and raised it to the role of the central operator of Spinozism: Each level (substance, attributes, modes) engages the others by a relation of expression—substance is expressed by the attributes, which are implied and re-expressed by the modes. In *Cinema 1*, we can see a doubly analogous use of expression. First, as in the previous reading of Spinoza, its presence is implicit, embedded, and strictly verbal.[61] But just because the term does not draw attention to itself, we cannot conclude that it is not a technical, if tacit, adaptation of an already developed concept. Second, its function is homologous to Spinoza's usage but, as my parentheses indicate, to different effect: Substance or the whole immanently and univocally (and *creatively*) expresses itself in the modes. In short, I hope to show a differential repetition of expression, one in service of a pure immanence wherein becoming can be fully affirmed of being.

I have said that the whole is open, but what of the modes and their tendency to constitute closed sets? According to Bergson, a set cannot fully close and any attempt to close it will be artificial; it will always participate in the whole. But this does not mean that a mode will join ever bigger sets (this would lead us straight to Spinoza's position); rather, it means that it will participate in the *openness* of the whole, in the movement or duration of qualitative change. A mode is prevented from closing not because it enters into larger sets but because its movement is qualitative, continuous, without parts, and creative. Qualitative movement or duration is not superadded to the mode and its parts, as though movement meant a mere change in the location of parts over time. This is what spatial time amounts to and, as such, always works within a set. Real movement, by contrast, *is* the mode itself; the mode *is* its qualitative and continuous change over time (*C1*, 27–28). The movement of the mode is its very being. Movement itself, therefore, prevents a set from closing and keeps it connected to the openness of the whole (*C1*, 10).

As Bergson writes, "[Things or modes] show on the surface, by their changes of situation, the profound changes that are being accomplished within the whole" (*CE*, 302). By virtue of its movement, not only is the mode open and not only is it creative, but also the movement of the mode expresses the creativity and openness of the whole. Modal movement coincides with the change of the whole; indeed, the whole is open (the whole is in continuous creation) *because* the movement of the modes is durational. There is a veritable constitution of the whole by the movement of the modes.

Changing the phrase, we can say that the open whole expresses itself only in and by the movement of the modes. Or, that the modes are the expression of the openness of the whole. Movement, as Deleuze puts it, "*expresses* something more profound, which is the change in duration or in the whole" (*C1*, 8, emphasis added). Over and over in *Cinema 1* (and in the summaries given of it in *Cinema 2*) Deleuze uses the term *expresses* to indicate this relationship between the modes and the whole, or rather, between the movement of the modes and the open whole it expresses. Expression works like it does in *Expressionism* but with a crucial difference: The modes still express substance (or the whole), but they do so creatively, such that, in a strict sense, the whole is created through its modal expression.[62]

We have seen that movement has two sides or faces. They are not opposed; one is not preferred to the other. They are, as Deleuze says, the "two aspects" of movement.

> On the one hand, that which happens [*se passe*] between objects or parts; on the other hand that which *expresses* the duration or the whole. . . . We can therefore say that movement relates the objects of a closed system to open duration, and duration to the objects of the system which it forces to open up. Movement relates the objects between which it is established to the changing whole which it *expresses*, and vice versa. Through movement the whole is divided up into objects, and objects are re-united in the whole, and indeed between the two "the whole" changes. (*C1*, 11, emphasis added)

There is not sometimes closed and sometimes open movement; these are two aspects of one and the same movement. In fact, it is movement that establishes an exchange between closed sets and the open whole, converting one into the other.[63] By moving, a closed system is opened up; parts "[lose] their contours" in qualitative becoming (*C1*, 11). In this sense, a mode expresses the open whole; no longer a set, no longer given, the moving mode (the movement of the mode) both constitutes and coincides with the openness and creativity of the whole. At the same time, movement occurs by rearranging parts within partially closed sets. This kind of movement is spatial in that the relative position of parts is varied. Thus the whole divides into parts or objects, which, by their very movement, reintegrate themselves into the whole as an expression of its openness, continuity, and creativity. There are indeed closed sets, but there is simultaneously movement that crisscrosses them and connects them to the openness of the whole. Movement always has two sides: one in relation to the objects whose position varies (spatial movement); and one in relation to a whole, through which it expresses absolute change (*C2*, 34).

Why is Deleuze's consistent use of expression significant? Because, to my mind, the reading of Bergson in *Cinema 1* pushes the concept past its limitation in the Spinoza commentaries. With Bergson, there is no eternal substance that may or may not reserve itself from the modes and put immanence and univocity into jeopardy. The whole is not supplementary to what transpires upon it, and the whole does not preexist its movements. There is only modal movement and its constructive expression of the whole.[64] Contrary to the eternal and necessary existence of substance, the life and evolution of the open whole is expressed without reserve in and by the modes. The open whole has, by definition, no other being (it is immanent) or sense (it is univocal) than the becoming expressed by modal movement.

We can finally turn to the concept of the plane of immanence. Recall that in his reflections on *Expressionism*, Deleuze spelled out the two requirements for a plane of immanence: first, the expressive character of particular individuals; and second, an immanence of being. The reading of Bergson in *Cinema 1* satisfies both. First, modes are expressive of a whole that opens them out of their closed sets; second, being is immanent insofar as it is not eternal (a substance independent of its modes, its expressions) but is becoming itself (an open whole *as* the movement modes). In *Cinema 2*, Deleuze sums up these requirements in a line: Each modal movement "expresses the whole that changes, as a function of the objects between which movement is established" (*C2*, 35). The modes are expressive and the whole is strictly immanent to their movement.

In a fascinating text from *Cinema 1*, Deleuze acknowledges the mix of Bergson and Spinoza that goes into the creation of a concept of the plane of immanence.

> Now, of course, closed systems, finite sets, are cut from this universe or on this plane; it makes them possible by the exteriority of its parts. But it is not one itself. It is a set, but an infinite set. The *plane of immanence* is the movement (*the face of movement*) which is established between the parts of each system and between one system and another, which crosses them all, stirs them all up together and subjects them all to the condition which prevents them from being absolutely closed. (*C1*, 59, emphasis added, translation modified)

The Bergsonian debt is unmistakable and repeats the earlier point that movement establishes a circulation between the parts of a closed set and the changing whole expressed in movement. The plane of immanence is another word for the movement that prevents the modes from closing and that expresses the whole.

But is there not also a less obvious acknowledgment, this time to Spinoza, with the parenthetical phrase "the face of movement"? Is this not an acknowledgment that at once reveals the limitations of certain elements of Spinoza and shows how these same elements, when repeated in different contexts, can become powerful new concepts? The reference Deleuze makes is to Spinoza's face of the whole universe (*facies totius universi*). For Spinoza, this face is the total set of the modes of nature, which includes the laws of motion and rest and the finite modes. These laws are the permanent feature of nature that govern all change but do not change. That is why Spinoza can say that "although varying in infinite ways," the face of the universe "remains always the same" (*L*, Letter 64).

In the context of *Cinema 1*, Deleuze affirms in Spinoza's face of the universe the conception of a one-all nature, an infinite plane on which modes interact, compose, and decompose. However, within this new context, two of its features must be rejected: first, that the whole is unvarying and, second, that the interaction of modes is a calculable displacement of parts over abstract time. But neither of these reservations prevents Deleuze from combining, as he does, the concept of a total plane or face of nature (Spinoza's insight) with a conception of movement as duration (Bergson's insight). In the combination of these two insights—call them components—a new concept is created: the plane of immanence. With this concept, Deleuze achieves a height of immanence: by their movement, individual modes are expressive of the open whole that keeps them from closing off, and this open whole is itself engendered by modal movement. By combining elements of Bergson and Spinoza and by deftly mixing commentary with original philosophy, Deleuze creates a concept of the plane of immanence beyond the limited immanence of Spinoza, one that is expressive, constructive, and creative.

Summation: The Image of Law

In his remarkable politico-intellectual biography, Phillipe Soulez claims that Bergson is unique as a political philosopher insofar as he is a theorist of the creative and not of the given as a political principle. Although Bergson does occasionally argue and urge from the perspective of the given (especially against idealists like Kant and Plato, or even Durkheim, who variously repress or forget our bestial origins in their accounts of the social), he always makes a point of reminding us that the tendency toward the given (toward bare repetition and calculable change) represents only one expression of sociopolitical life, the other being creative.[65]

In *The Two Sources of Morality and Religion*, Bergson borrows from Spinoza to restate this point. "We might say, by distorting the sense of Spinoza's terms, that it is to get back to naturing nature that we break away from natured nature" (*Two Sources*, 58, translation modified). I take it that in *Two Sources* Bergson argues that society is not only biologically created but also expresses the creativity *of* biology (life). But what is the distortion of Spinoza to which he refers? It maps revealingly onto the shift we tracked in Deleuze between *Expressionism* and *Cinema 1*. In its Spinozist usage, *natura naturans* (naturing nature) corresponds to substance and cause, and *natura naturata* (natured nature) corresponds to mode and effect; naturing nature is conceived in and through itself, and natured nature is conceived only through naturing nature (*E*, IP29S). Although "God is or equals Nature" (*Deus sive natura*), it is the separation of these two terms as cause and effect, as engendering and engendered, that for Deleuze represents the minimal yet maximal difference between Spinoza's philosophy of immanence and his own concept of the plane of immanence. In Spinoza's view, there is an enduring split between active (and eternal) and passive (and durational) being that ascribes preeminence and some kind of minimal transcendence to substance; in Deleuze's view, this split is replaced by an equality between two halves or tendencies of movement, one that engenders openness and creativity and one that engenders closure and predictability.

However, and as we have so often seen, in Bergson we find Deleuze *avant la lettre*, this time anticipating not only his criticism but also his reworking of Spinoza: There is in truth no real or eminent division between *naturans* and *naturata*, and these terms should instead designate two tendencies: opening and closing. A still persistent way to misread Bergson is to identify the creative potentialities of life and society as an outside by which life and society are inspired or to which they aspire—a kind of dual-world Bergsonism. But throughout his work, Bergson insists that there is *only* life (as in *Creative Evolution*), that there is *only* society (as in *The Two Sources of Morality and Religion*)—that is, that there is no completely open and creative life or society, or a completely closed and conservative life or society; there is only an ongoing process of opening and closing. Life and society, in other words, simultaneously express an opening and a closing in all their manifestations. In a nutshell, Bergson anticipates the concept of the plane of immanence: Life and society tend toward the formation of stable, closed sets whose movement amounts to the calculable rearrangement of parts, all the while expressing through this movement the openness and creativity of the whole.

I will return to the plane of immanence, but first I must situate it within the overall argument. If I can identify the thrust of Bergson's political philosophy as the introduction of creativity as a political principle, then my attempt to theorize creativity as an *adjudicative* principle follows his example. I began by examining three dogmatic theorists of adjudication, each of whom imagines judgment to be subsumptive. These theorists, I argued, variously sought to secure the conditions under which subsumption could be performed with the consequence that creativity was excluded and placed outside the proper exercise of judgment. In contrast to this tradition, I proposed three different ways to appreciate creativity as an inherent capacity of judgment. First, I radicalized Holmes's pragmatism to claim that if the needs and desires of a society are the basis of adjudication, and if these needs constantly change by virtue of being in time, then adjudication will be unavoidably creative insofar as it applies rules according to a criterion that continuously changes. Second, using Bergson, I combined the concepts of the encounter and the pure past to develop a concept of attentive judgment as simultaneously inventive of the case and of the rule by which it adjudicates. Third, with Spinoza and Deleuze I suggested that judges create legal concepts just as philosophers do by combining components, and then I proceeded to argue that when faced with an encounter, the relationship between the concepts and problems of law becomes mutually and creatively determinative.

From a practical point of view I have sought to push the question of creativity in adjudication beyond good (say, in legal pragmatism and realism) and evil (say, in critics of pragmatism and realism, but more fundamentally, in dogmatism). In this respect, I have cited Bergson's indignant surprise that he is taken as an advocate of change rather than as a theorist of its necessity, and also Deleuze's reconfiguration of the political left to mean openness to movement (what, in a different context, he calls "being equal to the event" [*WP*, 159]). But most important is Spinoza, whose ethical project is intended to create an awareness of the necessity of our situation and thereby to alter our emotions toward it. This ethical reasoning underlies my entire approach: to see that judgment is, under certain conditions, necessarily creative, and thereby to undermine evaluation of this fact as either good or evil. How creativity is or is not exercised can certainly give rise to good or bad judgments (as I have tried to show with the example of *Delgamuukw*), but, given the conditions of adjudication, criticism or praise of its creativity per se is senseless—it is a fact of judgment and must be affirmed if adjudication is to be understood and practiced properly.

In these closing arguments, I revisit the concept of the plane of immanence to reinforce the ties between my Bergsonian and Spinozist analyses and also to pose an unresolved problem. First, it is no stretch to identify law (especially the common law) as a plane of immanence, which is to say that it is simultaneously expressive of open and closed movement. Consider the Bergsonian scheme. In attentive judgment various virtual elements of the law (precedents, statutory and constitutional law, etc.) move into, or are actualized within, a new judgment. On the one hand, these elements crystallize together as a closed set within the judgment, which, on analysis, can be isolated and identified in their origin. In this sense, the movement that adjudication initiates exemplifies a spatial or closed tendency: The parts remain discrete; in almost every case we could have predicted which rules would have been chosen; and once set, together they establish a more or less closed, autonomous set. On the other hand, the judgment is doubly expressive of an open whole. First, in actualizing an element from the pure past of law, the whole finds itself expressed insofar as this element is selected from a particular tension and organization of the pure past. Second, even if we could have isolated the individually actualized rules of a judgment, together and by virtue of their composition, they express something new. An attentive judgment is not the sum of its parts; instead, it actualizes them in new, unexpected circumstances that encompass not only the novel fact-situation but also the hitherto unprecedented composition of the rules themselves.

For all the reasons I have considered, an attentive judgment is a creative judgment and the movement of the parts of law that it initiates is inventive, and, as such, expresses the open whole of law. With every new judgment the law grows and expands, and over time it locally constructs a plane of immanence with ever more parts able to be actualized in ever more judgments. The legal plane of immanence increases its dimensions with or by those individuals it cuts across and stirs together (see *TP*, 254). The judge, therefore, is at the border between two kinds of movements, simultaneously enacting a closed, spatial displacement of parts and expressing a creative, open whole.

The concept of the plane of immanence represents two further directions for research into jurisprudence informed by Deleuze. First, it provides another perspective to see or to make apparent the creative capacity of judgment. Throughout this book, my focus has been on what one might call the experience (or, taking precautions, the phenomenology) of judgment. My conceptual persona has been the judge, and I have examined various processes occurring at the intersection of perception and memory. Now, however, with the concept of a plane of immanence, another perspective or register is opened that takes as its level of analysis the whole of law, that is, the totality of rules (and conventions and customs, etc.). By surveying the whole of the plane of law, this kind of analysis could, first, see the movements and recombinations of the parts of law as expressive of the creativity of the whole and, second, appreciate the role of the judge as the basic propagator of this plane insofar as he or she takes parts of law from past contexts in order to reinstate them in new ones (indeed, we could think of this as the corollary processes of judicial deterritorialization and reterritorialization).

The second potential value of the concept of the plane of immanence is to connect jurisprudence to Deleuze's broader corpus insufficiently discussed in this book (especially his collaborations with Guattari). This represents one way to make these works available to an analysis of institutions and jurisprudence. One possible direction for research centers on the concept of lines of flight (*lignes de fuite*). According to the present analysis of the plane of immanence, we see that law flows or leaks in and out of judgment, in each movement it affects. Indeed, Deleuze's repeated statements on this concept of the line of flight open both a theoretical and an empirical research direction. "We think any society is defined not so much by its contradictions as by its lines of flight, it flees [*fuit*] all over the place, and it's very interesting to try and follow the lines of flight as they take shape" (*N*, 171, translation modified; see also *TP*, 216). Law also can be defined by its lines of flight—it is a plane of immanence constituted by a ceaseless lifting up and setting down of its parts. Where this concept might prove especially valuable is in initiating research into specific lines of flight whose movements constitute the legal plane of immanence: to track, for example, a particular concept of contract law (e.g., consideration) as it finds itself repeated in various contexts, modified by various components. In this way we might develop another method or model that raises the problem of the creativity of judgment to the level of a fact, or better, to the level of an image.

REFERENCE MATTER

Notes

PART I

1. Patton, "Deleuze and Democratic Politics," 50. See also Patton, *Deleuze and the Political*, 1; and Smith, "Deleuze and the Liberal Tradition," 300.
2. We must be careful not to confuse what Deleuze characterizes as the dogmatic image of thought with Kant's treatment of rational dogmatism. Unless expressly indicated otherwise, *dogmatic* signals the Deleuzian, not the Kantian critique.
3. Deleuze, "On Nietzsche," 139.

CHAPTER 1

1. Hart, "American Jurisprudence," 123.
2. Hart, "Problems of the Philosophy of Law," 106.
3. On the intellectual, institutional, and personal relationship between Hart and J. L. Austin, see Lacey, *Life of H. L. A. Hart*, especially 209–242.
4. Cited in Lacey, *Life of H. L. A. Hart*, 222.
5. For its part, pragmatism too has encouraged the substitution of the question "What is law?" with the problem "How does law work?" See Rorty, *Philosophy and Social Hope*, 104–105, 111; and Posner, *Problems of Jurisprudence*, 222.
6. Austin, *Province of Jurisprudence*, 193–194, 29.
7. In "Jhering's Heaven of Concepts," Hart claims that Austin represents the "English *Aufklärung* so far as law is concerned" (p. 271).
8. See Coleman, "Legal Positivism," 239–240.
9. See Hart, "Problems of the Philosophy of Law," 93–94.
10. Hart targets both Austin and Holmes with this criticism. It should be added that for Hart, the internal perspective does not replace the external. The internal perspective is only an alternative attitude that (most) subjects adopt.
11. See what Rawls calls the "summary view" of rules in his "Two Concepts of Rules," 34–35, 43–45.
12. Heidegger, *Kant and the Problem of Metaphysics*, §5.
13. Nancy, "Lapsus Judicii," 156, emphasis added.

14. Nancy, "Lapsus Judicii," 155–156, emphasis added. Compare with William James: "A sensation is rather like a client who has given his case to a lawyer and then has passively to listen in the courtroom to whatever account of his affairs, pleasant or unpleasant, the lawyer finds it most expedient to give" (*Pragmatism*, 119).

15. Heidegger, *Kant and the Problem of Metaphysics*, §18. In fact, Heidegger complained of much more than this, connecting the superficial formulation of schematism to his criticism of the whole juridical formulation of the *Critique* and especially the *quaestio juris* of the first Deduction.

16. Heidegger, *Kant and the Problem of Metaphysics*, §23.

17. Hart, "Problems of the Philosophy of Law," 114–116.

18. I do not propose incompatibility between a Kantian and a Wittgensteinian approach to this passage (or to Hart generally), especially given Wittgenstein's quasi-transcendental remarks with respect to criteria and judgment. Given that I will not pursue Wittgenstein, I merely mean to emphasize terminology and problems strongly associated with Kant. See Wittgenstein, *Philosophical Investigations*, §§90 and 242; and Cavell, *Must We Mean What We Say?* 1–72.

19. For a contemporary example of formalism, see Richard Delgado's attempt to fix certain racial terms as invariably insulting and therefore actionable. Matsuda et al., *Words That Wound*, 107.

20. The early pages of Stanley Cavell's *Claim of Reason* on criteria and judgment, to my mind, make a point similar to Hart's notion of the open texture of law (which is in itself perhaps unsurprising, given their shared indebtedness to ordinary language philosophy): "The work of the judge, in [difficult cases], must be to decide the identity of the case in question, i.e., decide whether established criteria, if any apply to it, i.e., *decide the question and the criteria of the question simultaneously*" (p. 12, emphasis added). This seems to me a statement of the kind of subsumption I have been developing in Hart with Kant. Cavell continues to say that this process of simultaneously determining the case and criteria is one that blurs the distinction between rule applying and rule creating: "In reaching his decision, the judge is obliged, in faithfulness to his office, to be open to and to provide arguments of an institutionally recognizable character; and the point of such argument is to allow, if possible, a natural extension of the body of law, which is neither merely applying existent law nor simply making new law" (*Claim of Reason*, 13).

21. See also Hart's "Positivism and the Separation of Law and Morals," 62–64.

CHAPTER 2

1. That Dworkin is indebted to Kant is undeniable and explicit. It is perhaps most apparent in his defense of the principled, deontological nature of law and judgment in light of classical and contemporary pragmatism and realism. But the particular source to which I trace his Kantianism is unacknowledged by Dworkin

and, as far as I can tell, by commentary. My claim is obviously not that he is ungenerous in his attribution but that his theory of adjudication takes its power from a coherent, powerful, yet tacit reworking of reflective judgments of teleology.

2. Deleuze, *Kant's Critical Philosophy*, 60.
3. Dworkin, *Taking Rights Seriously*, 22–30.
4. Nietzsche, *Will to Power*, §630.
5. Deleuze, *Kant's Critical Philosophy*, 60.
6. I am surprised to see Dworkin's theory of judgment described as aesthetic in the Kantian sense by Dworkin's commentators. In his *Justice and Judgment*, Alessandro Ferrera calls Dworkin's theory of law an aesthetic model of normative validity because aesthetic judgments are "controversial and undemonstrable" (pp. 72, 76). This identification seems incorrect. For Kant, aesthetic judgments are defined as strictly nonconceptual (and principles are obviously conceptual); purposiveness in aesthetic judgments is purely formal, that is, an indeterminate, free accord between the imagination and understanding (*CJ*, §§7–8). I do not dispute Ferrera's identification of reflective judgment in Dworkin's philosophy of law; my disagreement is with his specification of *aesthetic* reflective judgments instead of *teleological* reflective judgments.
7. Thanks to this use of reflective judgment, Dworkin escapes entangled questions of legal philosophy about the original intention of lawmakers and judges in the formation of laws. See Dworkin, "Comment."
8. This is precisely the approach that Duncan Kennedy adopts in his critique of Dworkin, arguing through an empirical case study of American private law that law is not a coherent whole but an aggregate of incompatible principles. See Kennedy, "Forms and Substance." See also Posner, *Problems of Jurisprudence*, 23; and Frankenberg, "Down by Law," 392–393.
9. Teleological reflective judgment also informs Dworkin's later writings: "Judges may not read their own convictions into the Constitution. They may not read the abstract moral clauses as expressing any particular moral judgment, no matter how much that judgment appeals to them, unless they find it consistent in principle with the structural design of the Constitution as a whole, and also with the dominant lines of past constitutional interpretation by other judges. They must regard themselves as partners with other officials, past and future, who together elaborate a cohere constitutional morality, and they must take care to see that what they contribute fits with the rest" (Dworkin, *Freedom's Law*, 10). Here we see both the presumption of integrity with respect to the Constitution and also an insistence particular to reflective judgment that we cannot interpret any part (clause) outside its presumed whole.
10. As I will show in Part 2 (Chapters 5 and 7), subsumption in Dworkin reappears after, or rather by virtue of, the substantial detour through reflective judgment.
11. Deleuze, *Kant's Critical Philosophy*, 62. See also *DR*, 169.

CHAPTER 3

1. Bernstein, "Retrieval of the Democratic Ethos," 1140. See also Hutchings, *Kant, Critique, and Politics*, 72–77.
2. Badiou, *Ethics*, 8; Douzinas, "Human Rights," 219–221.
3. See Wellmer, *Endgames*, 85. For Habermas, see "Alternative Way Out."
4. Kant, *Metaphysics of Morals*, 387–389.
5. Legal norms are, for Habermas, the fundamental type of action norm for modern artificial (i.e., detraditional) societies that can no longer count on the integrative powers of a shared and unreflective substantial ethical life.
6. Habermas, "Remarks on Legitimation," 117. Also, *BFN*, 127.
7. As one commentator has pointed out, *Between Facts and Norms* is itself a massive argument for an institutional solution as to how communicative power might be transformed into, and protected by, administrative power. See Scheuerman, "Between Radicalism and Resignation," 78–79.
8. Habermas, "Kant's Idea of Perpetual Peace," 190.
9. Benhabib, *Rights of Others*, 43. It is in this specific sense—that sovereignty and human rights are co-original—that we can interpret Habermas's call for constitutional patriotism (*Verfassungspatriotismus*). See Habermas, *Between Facts and Norms*, app. 2, 500; and Borradori, *Philosophy in a Time of Terror*, 73–81.
10. For a nearly analogous point, see Derrida, "Laws of Reflection," 16–19, 22.
11. Habermas is careful to distinguish law from morality: Positive law provides a motivational structure (facticity) absent from moral law. Moral discourses *in the law* are moral because they assume a universal audience. For a detailed account of this relationship, see Rehg, "Against Subordination."
12. In what follows, I move almost indiscriminately between Günther's and Habermas's theories of adjudication. *Between Facts and Norms* is deeply indebted to Günther (in fact, it could be argued that Günther's *Sense of Appropriateness* initiated a substantial turn in Habermas's thought by separating out the two moments of justification and application, which I explain at length). This is plainly indicated in the book's preface: "I [Habermas] am indebted to Klaus Günther's legal expertise for so much instruction that I almost hesitate to relieve him of responsibility for my mistakes" (*BFN*, xliii). More substantially, when Habermas outlines his theory of adjudication, it exactly replicates Günther's scheme (*BFN*, 162). Moreover, in his main treatment of application (*BFN*, ch. 5), it is expressly Günther's theory of appropriateness that is adopted as Habermas's own. For these reasons, I cannot concur with Jacques Lenoble's identification that "Habermas's theory of legal judgment (his 'theory of adjudication') relies entirely on a procedural version of Dworkin's coherence theory" ("Law and Undecidability," 63).
13. Wellmer, *Persistence of Modernity*, 130. Wellmer's essay is intriguing from our perspective because it tries to develop a situation-sensitive concept of practical judgment and action while tenuously remaining within the tradition of discourse

ethics. There are, however, crucial points where our interpretations diverge (especially around his conception of law/legitimacy as set against morality/validity and his conception of appropriate action and situational appreciation as the negation of nongeneralizable maxims).

14. Günther, "Normative Conception of Coherence," 156.
15. Günther, *Sense of Appropriateness*, 33, emphasis added.
16. Günther, *Sense of Appropriateness*, 34.
17. Günther, *Sense of Appropriateness*, 35, emphasis added.
18. Günther, *Sense of Appropriateness*, 40.
19. Günther, *Sense of Appropriateness*, 53.
20. Günther, "Normative Conception of Coherence," 163.
21. In the original translation of Günther's text ("Normative Conception of Coherence," 163), there is no interpolated "subtly."
22. Here, I note Habermas's closeness to Dworkin's concept of integrity in that an application of any one norm affects, however minimally, the totality of norms that must complement it.
23. Günther is strict on the following: Norms at the level of justification do not collide because practical reason is noncontradictory. They *apparently* collide in concrete situations where one norm must be suspended in favor of another. For example, we have the two following justified maxims: "Promises ought to be kept," and "In case of emergency you ought to help your friend." Prima facie they do not conflict, but say I had accepted a dinner party invitation, and just before I leave, my friend falls ill. We have a conflict. For reasons we won't go into, application discourses determine that the second maxim is appropriate and appropriately suspends the first. See Günther, "Normative Conception of Coherence," 158–159, 161–162; and Günther, *Sense of Appropriateness*, 207–219.
24. Günther, "Normative Conception of Coherence," 158–159.
25. Originally in Günther, "Normative Conception of Coherence," 163.
26. Günther, "Normative Conception of Coherence," 163.
27. A fascinating text in relation to the problems of justification and application is Habermas's *Future of Human Nature* (delivered at a philosophy of law colloquium organized by Dworkin and Nagel). Here, Habermas takes a stand against the use of genetic technologies insofar as they precipitate an unprecedented instrumentalization of the other. What is tricky, however, is that he admits that certain genetic selections and modifications must be permitted to prevent debilitating diseases and suffering. This makes it difficult to draw a clear line between prevention and eugenics. How does he propose to solve this difficulty? *By projective speech acts*. What we must do is adopt a communicative attitude toward the embryo, such that this embryo could hypothetically and in advance consent to the genetic intervention and affirm the clinical (and not instrumental) attitude of the persons intervening. "The presumption of informed consent transforms egocentric action into

communicative action . . . what solely matters here is not the ontological status of the embryo but the clinical attitude of the first person toward another person—however virtual—who, for some time in the future, may encounter him in the role of a second person" (*Future of Human Nature*, 52). Here, the justification discourse establishes and absorbs a dialogue with a future interlocutor who affirms the genetic intervention made in his or her case (astonishingly, this consent can include the destruction of the embryo—a euthanasia assumed counterfactually by means of dialogue before dialogue is ontogenetically possible [*Future of Human Nature*, 43]).

PART 2

CHAPTER 4

1. Deleuze, *Empiricism and Subjectivity*, 46.
2. Deleuze, *Empiricism and Subjectivity*, 45. If we go back slightly earlier to Deleuze's first acknowledged publication, we find the same opposition at play (Deleuze, "Instincts and Institutions," 19–21). For Deleuze's later reflections on this concept of institutions, see *Negotiations*, 169.
3. Unless expressly indicated with brackets, the ellipses in the *Abécédaire* signal pauses and hesitations, not my textual amendments.
4. The only exception I am aware of is a passing reference in Deleuze and Guattari, *What Is Philosophy*, 72.
5. I cite and work with the English definition of jurisprudence rather than the French for several reasons. First, in this book I try to create a concept of adjudication within an Anglo-American institutional context. Second, on the rare occasions that Deleuze discusses jurisprudence, he does not specify or elaborate its institutional context. His discussions of jurisprudence focus on its opposition to law and rights and attempt to elaborate certain of his own concepts, such as singularity and creativity, within the context of law. Third, the English and French definitions of jurisprudence overlap extensively, only the English is more expansive and explicitly connects it to the principles and philosophy of law (which suits us perfectly). The French definition, taken from the *Petit Larousse*, reads: "Ensemble des décisions de justice qui interprètent la loi ou comblent un vide juridique. (Elle constitute une source du droit.) *Faire jurisprudence*: faire autorité et servir d'exemple dans un cas déterminé; créer un précédent." With respect to this definition, the *ensemble des décisions* is covered by the English *case law*—with the difference being that in common law precedents are binding *rules*, whereas they are not in civil law. The notion of a juridical void is common to both the English and the French traditions (and will be critically addressed in Chapter 6). And although the phrase *faire jurisprudence* has no precise equivalent in English (especially given its creative or inventive element), it could be said to be a meditation on what it means for a judge to "do jurisprudence," that is, to cite, use, and create law.

6. "Jurisprudence," in Garner, *Black's Law Dictionary*.

7. I take common law to indicate the body of law derived from judicial decisions and not from statutes or constitutions. The contrast Deleuze appears to establish between common and civil law systems parallels what he and Claire Parnet describe as the "Superiority of Anglo-American Literature": "The English and the Americans do not have the same way of beginning again as the French. French beginning again is the *tabula rasa*, the search for a primary certainty as a point of origin, always the point of anchor. The other way of beginning again, on the other hand, is to take up the interrupted line, to join a segment to the broken line. . . . What is interesting is the middle. . . . One begins again through the middle" (Deleuze and Parnet, *Dialogues*, 39). To reflect these distinctions of literature in the context of law, we have the following from *What Is Philosophy*: "English law is a law of custom and convention, as the French is of contract (deductive system) and the German of institution (organic totality)" (p. 106).

8. For an extended analysis of the requirements of political philosophy from within the difficult and technical idiom of *What Is Philosophy*, see Patton, "Utopian Political Philosophy."

9. Deleuze, "Preface to Jean-Clet Martin's *Variations*," 361–363.

10. Deleuze and Guattari, *Anti-Oedipus*, 180.

11. Of course, appellate courts choose which cases they review, but the fact remains that these cases first occur outside any decision by a court. Appellate courts merely narrow the field of accidental cases.

12. The concept of the encounter is also developed in Deleuze's readings of Spinoza (*SPP*, 30–43), Bergson (*B*, 94–95), and Nietzsche (*Nietzsche and Philosophy*, 44), but it finds its most sustained analysis in *Proust and Signs*.

13. On this issue, Deleuze is joined by American legal pragmatism. As Holmes observes, "The law only ends with a theory, but begins with a concrete case" ("Holdsworth's English Law," 287). Or as Cardozo writes, "What Professor Dewey says of problems of morals is true [in] large measure, of the deepest problems of the law; the situations which they present, so far as they are real problems, are almost always unique" (*Growth of Law*, 215–216). And again Cardozo, who approvingly cites François Gény, "The [legal] process is set in motion by some concrete situation . . . [the judge] decides in view of particular cases, and with reference to problems absolutely concrete" (*NJP*, 156). Although in Chapter 6 I demarcate the differences between a Deleuzian jurisprudence and legal pragmatism, on this preliminary but important point the two concur.

14. See Zourabichvili, *Deleuze*, 16.

15. See Marrati, "Against the Doxa."

16. Descartes, *Discourse on Method*, 29. "The first [maxim] was never to accept anything as true if I did not have evident knowledge of its truth."

17. We might say that the exceptions to this tradition (of recognition as the

image of thought of philosophy) are those that Deleuze chose as the subjects for his monographs: Bergson, Nietzsche, Proust, Spinoza. I revisit this question in the next two chapters. See Deleuze, "On Nietzsche," 139.

18. When Deleuze calls the image preconceptual, he does not mean that it is intuitive, as in prediscursive or prelinguistic. He means that the image does not belong to the defined order of philosophical concepts that it launches or inspires. The image is, as he puts it in *What Is Philosophy*, "pre-philosophical" (*WP*, 40).

19. Aristotle, *Metaphysics*, 1038a15–20. For the differences of Aristotle's accounts of division and definition in the *Topics*, *Categories*, and *Metaphysics*, see Granger, "Aristotle."

20. I note that *Cinema 1* (pp. 3–8) has a more thorough analysis of the shift from ancient to modern scientific explanation than *Difference and Repetition*. For my purpose, however, the latter is more relevant in that it addresses the question of law.

21. We could say that for Deleuze law separates a thing from what it can do: Law confines a thing, or at least our appreciation of a thing, to its own conception of change (a statement that ties law to the problem of *ressentiment*, the separation of a thing from its powers). See Deleuze, *Nietzsche and Philosophy*, 58–59.

22. Kant also calls this concept the "transcendental object = x of all possible experience" (A103–110, A253).

23. See Deleuze, *Negotiations*, 145; and Deleuze, "Bergson's Conception of Difference," 36.

24. For a rigorous discussion of this point, see Lebrun, "Le transcendantal."

25. See Zourabichvili, *Deleuze*, 48.

26. Kant, *Prolegomena*, 10.

27. "Most thought-provoking in our thought-provoking time is that we are still not thinking [*Das Bedenklichste in unserer bedenklichen Zeit ist, dass wir noch nicht denken*]" (Heidegger, *What Is Called Thinking*, 6).

28. Contemporary social and political theorists as diverse as Arendt, Cavell, Derrida, Lyotard, Wellmer, Habermas, and Caygill have turned to the *Critique of Judgment* as a rich source of insight for questions of political judgment and singularity. Deleuze also repeatedly praises Kant's discussion of the sublime both as an encounter and for the indeterminate accord of the faculties it reveals (and which all the *Critiques*, in fact, presuppose). See Deleuze, "On Four Poetic Formulas That Might Summarize the Kantian Philosophy," in *CC*, 27–35; and Deleuze, "Idea of Genesis."

29. For these reasons, it does not seem to me that the characterization of the problem as an encounter is inconsistent with Deleuze's statement in *Difference and Repetition* that "all begins with sensibility . . . that, in an encounter, what forces sensation and that which can only be sensed are one and the same thing, whereas in other cases the two instances are distinct" (*DR*, 144–145). In Chapter 8, I will

revisit this complicated concept of the problem as subrepresentative and I will also address Deleuze's remarks that political sensibility is a matter of perception.

30. From the *Critique*, see the preface to the second edition: "[The *Critique*] is a treatise on the *method*, not a system of the science itself; but it catalogs the entire outline of the science of metaphysics, both in respect of its boundaries and in respect of its entire internal structure. For pure speculative reason has this peculiarity about it, that it can and should measure its own capacity according to the different ways for choosing the objects of its thinking, and also *completely enumerate the manifold ways of putting problems before itself*, so as to catalog the entire preliminary sketch of a whole system of metaphysics" (Bxxiii, emphasis added). And, from the famous 1798 letter to Christian Garve: "The antinomy of pure reason—'the world has a beginning; it has no beginning, and so on,' right up to the fourth: 'there is freedom in nature, versus there is no freedom, only the necessity of nature'—that is what first aroused me from my dogmatic slumber and drove me to the critique of reason itself, in order to resolve the scandal of ostensible contradiction of reason itself" (Kant, *Philosophical Correspondence*, 252).

31. In this too, Deleuze is deeply Bergsonian. See, for example, Bergson's horror of conversation and its intellectualist persona, the *homo loquax*, content to voice an opinion on all subjects scientific and metaphysical (*CM*, 85).

32. Marrati, "Against the Doxa," 215.

33. "The criticism that must be addressed to this image of thought is precisely that it has based its supposed principle upon extrapolation from certain facts, particularly insignificant facts such as Recognition, everyday banality in person" (*DR*, 135).

34. Mengue, and Patton following him, call "doxalogical" the plane wherein opinions are exchanged and criticized toward a "solidarity and consensus regarding what is to be one here and now" (Mengue, *Deleuze*, 52; Patton, "Deleuze and Democratic Politics," 55).

35. On the opposition between problem and proposition, see Lebrun, "Le transcendantal," 227–228.

36. This concept of philosophical participation and authentication organizes *What Is Philosophy* and is another instance of Deleuze's Platonism: Some claimants to philosophy are legitimated, others excluded. In this sense, Deleuze dispatches communication using the same method that long ago dispatched sophism. See *DR*, 60–63; *CC*, 136; and especially, *Logic of Sense*, 253–256.

37. For the definition of *ressentiment* as the separation of a thing from what it can do, see Deleuze, *Nietzsche and Philosophy*, 57–58; and *SPP*, 24.

38. Deleuze, "We Invented the Ritornello," 380; and "The best one can say about discussions is that they take things no farther, since the participants never talk about the same thing" (*WP*, 28).

39. Habermas, "America and the World," 118.

40. Habermas, "America and the World," 119–120; see also Habermas, "Kant's Idea of Perpetual Peace," 181; Kant, *Metaphysics of Morals*, 455, 483; and Kant, *Toward Perpetual Peace*, 322.
41. Habermas, "America and the World," 120, emphasis added.
42. Patton, "Utopian Political Philosophy," 42.
43. Patton, "Utopian Political Philosophy," 46.
44. Patton, "Utopian Political Philosophy," 48.
45. Patton, "Deleuze and Democratic Politics," 59.

CHAPTER 5

1. To sum up these three points, Bergson cites a wonderful text of T. H. Huxley: "If the fundamental proposition of evolution is true, that the entire world, living and not living, is the result of the mutual interaction, according to definite laws, of the forces possessed by the molecules of which the primitive nebulosity of the universe was composed, it is no less certain that the existing world lay, potentially, in the cosmic vapor, and that a sufficient intellect could, from a knowledge of the properties of the molecules of that vapor, have predicted, say the state of the Fauna of Great Britain in 1869" (*CE*, 38).
2. Deleuze, "Bergson's Conception of Difference," 33. Internal difference is also a critique of the shared assumption made by mechanism and finalism that difference and determination are exterior to being, either in a mechanical cause or a plan.
3. Deleuze, "Bergson's Conception of Difference," 33, emphasis added.
4. Ansell-Pearson, "Bergson and Creative Evolution/Involution," 153. For the argument that for Bergson the essence of life is the tendency to change (as expressed by the concept of the *élan vital*), see Marrati, "Time, Life, Concepts." The concept of life as a tendency to change is precisely what Bergson, in a 1915 letter to Harald Höffding, reproaches the biological sciences for failing to appreciate: "The essential argument I make against mechanism in biology is that it fails to explain how life unravels a *history* [*déroule une* histoire], that is to say a succession without repetition, where each moment is *unique* and carries within itself the representation of the whole of the past" (Bergson, *Mélanges*, 1149).
5. Deleuze, "Cours inédit de Gilles Deleuze," 211.
6. For this, see Ansell-Pearson, *Philosophy*, 70–96; and Durie, "Creativity and Life."
7. With the noteworthy exception of White, *Justice Oliver Wendell Holmes*, 151–152.
8. Alschuler, *Law Without Values*, 52–83.
9. Holmes, "Reflections," 6.
10. Holmes, "Law and the Court," 296.
11. *Buck v. Bell*, 274 U.S. 200 (1927). This judgment was infamous enough to be read at length in Stanley Kramer's film *Judgment at Nuremberg* (1961) in defense of a Nazi war criminal.

12. I will not take up the vexed question of Holmes's pragmatism for the reason that my aim is to read Holmes through Bergson without direct attention to American philosophical pragmatism. But on Holmes's pragmatism, see Grey, "Holmes and Legal Pragmatism." Nevertheless, Holmes's letters do show that he read Bergson.

13. Holmes, "Holmes to Pollock," 17.

14. In his biography of Holmes, White claims that "the bulk of *The Common Law* is devoted to a highly purposive reading of historical cases." Thus, and I agree here with White, Holmes will take a particular theoretical conclusion as to the essence of a branch of law—for instance, objective standards of liability for torts—and narrate the history of that branch as the realization of this idea. This is what I call historicism—the reading of historical growth as if it were directed toward a present goal or conclusion. I disagree with White, as will be made clear shortly, in his claim that the evolutionary strain of Holmes's thought endeavored to reconcile "a historicist attitude toward the past with an interest in deriving general organizing principles around which knowledge could be synthesized." In my reading, such a historicism was precisely what the evolutionist metaphor sought to overcome: an evolutionary conception of time proper to the becoming of law. See White, *Justice Oliver Wendell Holmes*, 154, 149.

15. Holmes, "Law in Science," 217–218.

16. For Bergson's statements on the finalistic character of all historical inquiry, see *CE*, 51–53; Bergson, *Two Sources*, 262; but especially *CM*, 20–26. Deleuze, for his part, strongly adhered to the distinction between becoming and history, calling history only the set of more or less negative preconditions necessary for an event to come into being and always narrated retrospectively (*ABC*, G; *WP*, 96).

17. Holmes, "Letter to Harold Laski." And, in a speech: "The law has got to be stated over again; and I venture to say that in fifty years we shall have it in a form of which no man could have dreamed fifty years ago" (Holmes, "Use of Law Schools," 42).

18. Alschuler, *Law Without Values*, 8–10, 60–61; *LE*, 160.

19. Holmes, "Holdsworth's English Law," 285.

20. Posner, "Introduction," 240.

21. Holmes, "Path of Law," 181, emphasis added.

22. Holmes, "Holdsworth's English Law," 285–286; Holmes, "Introduction to the General Survey," 299; Holmes, "Ideals and Doubts," 303.

23. Holmes, "Introduction to the General Survey," 300. Or again: "I confess that such a development as that fills me with interest, not only for itself, but as an illustration of what you see all through the law—the paucity of original ideas in man, and the slow, coating way in which he works along from rudimentary beginnings to the complex and artificial conceptions of civilized life. It is like the niggardly uninventiveness of nature in its other manifestations, with its few smells or colors or types, its short list of elements, working along in the same slow way from

compound to compound until the dramatic impressiveness of the most intricate compositions, which we call organic life" (Holmes, "Law in Science," 215–216).

24. Holmes, "John Marshall," 267.
25. *Southern Pacific Co. v. Jensen*, 244 U.S. 205 (1916).
26. *Riggs v. Palmer*, 115 N.Y. 506, 22 N.E. 188 (1889).
27. *McLoughlin v. O'Brian* (1983), 1 A.C. 410, reversing (1981), Q.B. 599.
28. They are: "(1) No one has a moral right to compensation except for physical injury. (2) People have a moral right to compensation for emotional injury suffered at the scene of an accident against anyone whose carelessness caused the accident but have no right to compensation for emotional injury suffered later. (3) People should recover compensation for emotional injury when a practice of requiring compensation in their circumstances would diminish the overall costs of accidents or otherwise make the community richer in the long run. (4) People have a moral right to compensation for any injury, emotional or physical, that is the direct consequence of careless conduct, no matter how unlikely or unforeseeable it is that that conduct would result in that injury. (5) People have a moral right to compensation for emotional or physical injury that is the consequence of careless conduct, but only if that injury was reasonably foreseeable by the person who acted carelessly. (6) People have a moral right to compensation for reasonably foreseeable injury but not in circumstances when recognizing such a right would impose massive and destructive financial burdens on people who have been careless out of proportion to their moral fault" (*LE*, 240–241).
29. See Hart's characterization of Dworkin: "[The judge] must always suppose that for every conceivable case there is some solution which is already law before he decides the case and which awaits his discovery.... [According to Dworkin,] to make sense of what they do, judges must believe that there is some single theory, however complex, and some single solution for the instant case derivable from it, which is uniquely correct" (Hart, "American Jurisprudence," 138, 139).
30. I do not imply that for Dworkin judges are intransigent, refuse revision, or fail to suffer natural hesitation. In fact, Dworkin devotes fine pages to the issue of persuasion and reason giving (*LE*, 144–147). Nevertheless, Dworkin repeatedly maintains that there is a best solution to the case at hand, and, given that Hercules is always on the mark, the full range of possible principles can be considered only out of thoroughness.
31. Günther, "Normative Conception of Coherence," 163.

CHAPTER 6

1. Bergson's last work (*The Two Sources of Morality and Religion*, 1932) fully takes up political problems; however, its discussion of law is negligible. I also mention that Bergson had active political responsibilities during the Great War, acting as a French emissary to President Wilson and, subsequently, working to help

establish the League of Nations. See Soulez, *Bergson politique*; and Soulez and Worms, *Bergson*.

2. Gadamer, *Truth and Method*, 26; Rose, *Dialectic of Nihilism*, 87–108.

3. Hardt, *Gilles Deleuze*, 24.

4. Alliez et al., "The Contemporary," 135.

5. For James, who never seemed to run out of superlatives for Bergson, see *A Pluralistic Universe*, 223–274; and for Dewey, see "Preface," xii. Turning to the contemporary scene, Rorty's *Consequences of Pragmatism* mentions Bergson only once (and dismissively at that) (pp. 213–214). And Dickstein's recent collection, *The Revival of Pragmatism*, raises Bergson only in connection to his friendship with James.

6. Posner, *Cardozo*, 118.

7. *Ostrowe v. Lee*, 256 N.Y. 36, 175 N.E. 505 (1931).

8. Posner, *Problems of Jurisprudence*, 465. Posner identifies the "needs of the present" as the "standards by which we justify old rules" (*Cardozo*, 27).

9. Grey, "Freestanding Legal Pragmatism," 256.

10. Marrati, "Mysticism."

11. Marrati, *Deleuze*, 332.

12. Bergson's radical formula, according to Deleuze, goes further than Husserl's neo-Kantian statement that "all consciousness is consciousness *of* something," with the claim that "all consciousness *is* something"; that is, it is an image (*C1*, 56).

13. This praise is far removed from *Difference and Repetition*, where Bergson does not even make the short list (Duns Scotus, Spinoza, and Nietzsche) of the great thinkers of immanence (*DR*, 35–42).

14. Holmes's letters outline a theory of the subject and universe remarkably suggestive of Bergson's account: "I often say over to myself the verse 'O God, be merciful to me a fool,' the fallacy of which to my mind (you [Pollock] won't agree with me) is in the 'me,' that it looks on man as a little God over against the universe, instead of as a cosmic ganglion, a momentary intersection of what humanly speaking we call streams of energy, such as gives white light at one point and the power of making syllogisms at another, but always an unseverable part of the unimaginable, in which we live and move and have our being, no more needing its mercy than my little toe needs mine" (Holmes, "Letter to Pollock").

15. See Goldschmidt's lecture course on Bergson that picks up Hyppolite's suggestion of "a transcendental field in which the conditions for subjectivity would appear and in which the subject would be constituted by this field" ("Cours," 77). And, with reference to Sartre's *Transcendence of the Ego* (and not Hyppolite, Goldschmidt, or even Bergson), Deleuze's last essay develops a concept of a transcendental field without a subject perfectly consistent with his interpretation of *Matter and Memory* (Deleuze, "Immanence," 26–27).

16. For a discussion of Bergson's theory of perception in light of contemporary neurophysiology, see Connolly, *Neuropolitics*, 26–49.

17. Worms, "*Matter*," 92.

18. Llewellyn, *Bramble Bush*, 35, emphasis added. A little later, Llewellyn restates the point: "The defendant's auto was a Buick painted pale magenta. He is married. His wife was in the back seat, an irritable, somewhat faded blonde. She was attempting back-seat driving when the accident occurred. He had turned around to make objection. In the process the car swerved and hit the plaintiff. . . . The road was smooth and concrete. It had been put in by the McCarthy Road Work Company. How many of these facts are important to the decision? How many of these facts are, as we say, legally relevant?" (*Bramble Bush*, 47).

19. White, *Tort Law*, 96.

20. *Palsgraf v. Long Island Railroad Co.*, 248 N.Y. 339, 162 N.E. 99 (1928), at 340–341.

21. *Palsgraf*, at 345.

22. Posner, *Cardozo*, 37, emphasis added.

23. Andrews, in dissent and in support of the overruled principle of proximate cause, writes that it is a category "of convenience, of public policy, or a rough sense of justice, the law arbitrarily declines to trace a series of events beyond a certain point. That is not logic, it is practical politics. Take our rule as to fires. Sparks from my burning haystack set on fire my house and my neighbor's. I may recover from a negligent railroad. He may not. Yet the wrongful act as directly harmed the one as the other. We may regret that the line was drawn just where it was, but drawn somewhere it had to be" (*Palsgraf*, at 352).

24. This information comes from Posner, *Cardozo*, 33–37.

25. Posner, *Cardozo*, 47.

26. This includes the chapter "Memory as Virtual Coexistence" in *Bergsonism*, the "second synthesis of time" in *Difference and Repetition*, and the "Crystals of Time" chapter in *Cinema 2*.

27. Deleuze's *Bergsonism* has a different (but obviously related) set of four paradoxes (pp. 61–62). The organization of *Cinema 2* is more complex in that it develops the concept of the "crystal of time" (pp. 68–83) and proceeds to relate the paradoxes of preexistence and coexistence (pp. 98–100).

28. Bergson states, "Pure memory interests no part of my body. No doubt, it will beget sensations as it materializes, but at that very moment it will cease to be a memory and pass into the state of a present thing, something actually lived" (*MM*, 139).

29. Deleuze argues that it is in a strictly ontological sense that there is a "being of the past" (*DR*, 80).

30. The line comes from Proust, *Time Regained*, 906.

31. In *Difference and Repetition* Deleuze claims that the whole theory of the

pure past is set against a psychological understanding of time; indeed, Bergson's theory of the pure past is a monumental effort to reclaim a temporality "without psychological existence" and without reduction to representation (*DR*, 314n5).

32. Deleuze draws this notion of the past in general—a stand-in term for the virtual past—from Bergson's *Mind-Energy* [*L'énergie spirituelle*] (1919), but it is fully consistent with *Matter and Memory*: "What past? A [pure] past that has no date and can have none; it is the past in general, it cannot be any past in particular" (Bergson, *Mind-Energy*, 166).

33. Deleuze, "Bergson," 29–30.

34. It may appear as though my identification of transcendental arguments is fast and loose: first the encounter (transcendental empiricism in Chapter 4), now the pure past. I will develop at length the relation between the pure past and the encounter (especially with the concept of attentive judgment in Chapter 7), but I can clear up a potential confusion here by stating that for Deleuze the pure past is the transcendental condition for *all* experience insofar as it is the ground of time and the passing present, and the encounter is the transcendental condition for thought and experience irreducible to dogmatism.

35. *Southern Pacific Co. v. Jensen*, 244 U.S. 205, 221 (1916). Both Holmes and Deleuze take the terms *molar* and *molecular* from the French sociologist Gabriel Tarde.

36. Posner, "Pragmatic Adjudication," 250–251.

37. Scalia, *Matter of Interpretation*, 8–9.

38. Breyer and Scalia, "Constitutional Relevance."

39. Scalia, *Matter of Interpretation*, 13.

40. French, "Time in the Law."

41. French, "Time in the Law," 673–674. Although it is not a criticism I undertake, note that French's forms of time are devoted to the measure of movement. Eternal time is a measure of transcendence, cyclical time measures natural cycles, industrial time measures clock units, and saturated time measures our overloaded demands. In short, she lacks a conception of time as it might be freed from the measurement of movement (say, as in Kant, Bergson, or Deleuze); or, in other words, her notion of time lacks a temporality in and of itself.

42. French, "Time in the Law," 672.

43. French, "Time in the Law," 747, emphasis added.

44. French, "Time in the Law," 695.

45. To evidence this sterile antinomy, we need only cite Scalia's criticism of the living constitution: "My theory of what I do when I interpret the American Constitution, I try to understand what it meant, what it was understood by the society to mean when it was adopted. And I don't think it changes since then. . . . What's another approach to interpretation of the Constitution? Well, 60 years or so ago we adopted, first in the Eighth Amendment area—cruel and

unusual punishment—the notion that the Constitution is not static: it doesn't mean what the people voted for when it was ratified. Rather, it *changes*, from era to era, to comport with—and this is a quote from our cases—the evolving standards of decency that mark the progress of a maturing society. *I detest that phrase, because I'm afraid societies don't always mature, sometimes they rot. What makes you think that human progress is one upwardly inclined plane . . . ?* It seems to me that the purpose of the Bill of Rights was to prevent change not to encourage it and have it written into the Constitution" (Breyer and Scalia, "Constitutional Relevance"). Thus Scalia reproaches the living constitution (and its specific temporality) precisely on the ground of preference, arguing that ours is a society in decline and that we ought to return to healthier times.

46. Mullarkey, *Bergson*, 48.

47. The dreamer is Bergson's persona for the most expanded or dilated tension of the virtual (see *MM*, 155).

CHAPTER 7

1. Deleuze, *Kant's Critical Philosophy*, 58.

2. This is originally Kierkegaard's claim from *Repetition* (1843), which Carl Schmitt repeats in his *Political Theology*, 15.

3. Strictly speaking, the term *actual* is inappropriate with respect to Dworkin, but I use it for simplicity's sake. For Deleuze and Bergson the actual is always linked to the virtual. In truth, Dworkin's rules are either "possible" or "real," but either way they are *given* in the fashion I outlined in Chapter 5. By "actual" I mean that for Dworkin rules are given, identified, and assigned a purpose and a place within a teleological interpretation. It is only in my discussion of Dworkin that my use of this term carries this meaning.

4. Smith, "Deleuze and the Liberal Tradition," 312–313. Also, see Deleuze, *What Is Philosophy*: "It is Kant who finally turns the philosopher into the Judge at the same time that reason becomes a tribunal; but is this the legislative power of a determining judge, or the judicial power, the jurisprudence, of a reflecting judge? These are two quite different conceptual personae" (*WP*, 72).

5. See *DR*, 165, and especially Deleuze's short essay "Idea of Genesis."

6. In what follows, I use the term *reflective judgment* to indicate those judgments that propose a reflective principle of the finality of nature in order to perform its function, namely, to think the particular as contained under the universal.

7. I note the exception of John Protevi's "Organism as the Judgment of God." See also his forthcoming *Bodies Politic*, especially ch. 3.

8. "A hidden structure necessary for forms, a secret signifier necessary for subjects . . . It exists only in a supplementary dimension to that to which it gives rise ($n + 1$). This makes it a teleological plan(e) [*plan*], a design, a mental principle" (*TP*, 265–266). See also *SPP*, 128.

9. I thank Melanie White for coining the "LwO."

10. Nietzsche, *Genealogy of Morality*, II, §12, emphasis added.

11. Not all readers appreciate how Bergson moved beyond the psychological time that characterizes his early work. See, for example, Kolakowski, *Bergson*, 3.

12. For example, Bergson, *Time and Free Will*, 80; *CE*, 59; *B*, 42–43.

13. As Deleuze claims, "All these points are themselves virtual" (*B*, 100).

14. On this tricky question of rotation and translation I have greatly benefited from conversation with Melanie White.

15. *CL*, 50–76, and elsewhere. For the previous decisions, see *Palsgraf v. Long Island Railroad Co.*, at 344.

16. They are: to replace a subsumptive conception of judgment with a connective one (this chapter) and to see adjudication as positively problem-creating (Chapter 8).

17. Holmes, "Learning and Science," 139.

18. *Palsgraf*, at 344.

19. As connected with this rule, Cardozo cites *Munsey v. Webb*, 231 U.S. 150, 156 (1913); *Condran v. Park & Tilford*, 213 N.Y. 341, 345 (1915); and *Robert v. U.S.E.F. Corp.*, 240 N.Y. 474, 477 (1925).

20. *MM*, 19, 38 (translation modified), and 42; all emphases are mine. Deleuze also is aware of Bergson's peculiar use of the term *choice* and in *Bergsonism* singles it out with quotation marks (*B*, 52).

21. Like the kind that Judith Shklar uses to attack Bergson in "Bergson and the Politics of Intuition." For Shklar, meaningful decision depends centrally on a conception of uncoerced "choice," wherein "freedom depends on the number of genuine alternatives of action open to the individual, not on the possibility of creating a new, future self out of nothing" (p. 325). Incidentally, Bergson anticipated and criticized this weak concept of choice (*CM*, 19).

22. In a fascinating aside in an essay roughly contemporary with the *Concept of Law*, Hart says the following: "It may well be that 'choice', 'discretion', and 'judicial legislation' fail to do justice to the *phenomenology of considered decision*: its felt involuntary or even inevitable character which often marks the termination of deliberation on conflicting considerations. Very often the decision to include a new case in the scope of a rule or to exclude it is guided by the sense that this is the 'natural' continuation of a line of decisions or carries out the 'spirit' of a rule" (Hart, "Problems of the Philosophy of Law," 108, emphasis added). Unfortunately, Hart left this line of thought underdeveloped. It would be worthwhile to ask why, given these misgivings, he persisted in using the concept of choice. My guess is that Hart's remark is closely related to Wittgenstein's observations on rule following in *Philosophical Investigations*, especially §§217–219: "When I obey a rule, I do not choose. I obey the rule blindly." It may very well be that, read alongside Wittgenstein, Hart's observations on judicial choice could be supplemented to

make valuable interventions into debates about judicial activism, creativity, and decision. But this is for another day.

23. Deleuze, "Bergson," 25.

24. Bergson, *Mind-Energy*, 177, emphasis added.

25. Bergson will, in fact, collapse the difference between motor and intellectual representations and claim that our most general ideas and concepts—for instance, the categories of the understanding—are born from, and first of all serve, the material exigencies of life (*CE*, 226–227). On this point, see Deleuze's "Third Commentary on Bergson": "Automatic or habitual recognition (the cow recognizes grass, I recognize my friend Peter)" (*C2*, 44).

26. Holmes, "Path of Law," 168, emphasis added.

27. Holmes, "Law in Science," 223.

28. Holmes, "Law in Science," 223.

29. This is the concluding sentence to Bergson's second (1910) introduction.

30. See Deleuze's first synthesis of time (*DR*, 70–79) and also his later reflections on this text in *Negotiations*: "I like some passages in *Difference and Repetition*, those on tiredness and contemplation, for instance, because in spite of appearances they're living experiences" (*N*, 7). On this matter, Bergson also devotes fine pages to the necessity of habits in *The Two Sources of Morality and Religion*, and, in fact, claims that they constitute an enduring foundation of social and political life (*Two Sources*, 27).

31. In my initial attempt at a philosophy of law with Deleuze, I did not sufficiently emphasize the value and necessity of habits and inattentive perception for adjudication. I thank Bill Connolly for pointing this out. See Lefebvre, "New Image of Law," 112–115.

32. Holmes, "Law in Science," 230–231, emphasis added, and 232. And elsewhere: "It is revolting to have no better reason for a rule of law than that so it was laid down in the time of Henry IV. It is still more revolting if the grounds upon which it was laid down have vanished long since, and the rule simply persists from blind imitation of the past" (Holmes, "Path of Law," 187). For Cardozo's commentary on these remarks, see Cardozo, "Mr. Justice Holmes," 83–85.

33. Once again, neither Bergson nor Deleuze uses this term. Respectively, they use attentive perception and attentive recognition.

34. Cardozo, *Growth of Law*, 212–213.

35. Arendt especially admires this aspect of the *Critique of Judgment*, claiming that nowhere else does Kant attend to judgments of particular existents. "For judgment of the particular—*this* is beautiful, *this* is ugly; *this* is right, *this* is wrong—has no place in Kant's moral philosophy" (Arendt, *Lectures*, 15).

36. In his entry on beauty, Caygill shows us that "judgments of the beautiful are defined negatively in the *Critique of Judgment* according to the table of the categories as: (quality) that which 'pleases apart from any interest' (§5); (quantity) that which 'pleases universally' without a concept (§9); (relation) the 'form of

finality in an object . . . perceived in it apart from the representation of an end'; and (modality) the object of a 'necessary delight' 'apart from a concept' (§22)" (Caygill, *Kant Dictionary*, 92).

37. On Deleuze's concept of constructivism, see *What Is Philosophy*, 7, 35–36.

38. See Deleuze, "Actual and the Virtual," 148. This short draft was posthumously published. It is especially helpful in that its first two pages are dedicated to an elaboration of Bergson's circuit diagram.

39. Proust, *Swann's Way*, 47.

40. Proust, *Swann's Way*, 46.

41. Proust, *Swann's Way*, 46.

42. As Deleuze says, "The flavor of the madeleine has, in its volume, imprisoned and enveloped Combray. . . . This is the characteristic of involuntary memory: it internalizes the context, it makes the past context inseparable from the present sensation" (*PS*, 59).

43. Proust, *Swann's Way*, 46, emphasis added.

44. *Griswold v. Connecticut*, 381 U.S. 479 (1965), at 482.

45. Thus in *Pierce v. Society of Sisters*, 268 U.S. 510 (1925), the right to educate one's children as one chooses is covered under the First Amendment; and in *Meyer v. Nebraska*, 262 U.S. 390 (1923), the right to learn German or any other foreign language in a private school was upheld using the First Amendment.

46. *Griswold*, at 483.

47. *Griswold*, at 483.

48. *Griswold*, at 486.

49. Although I won't go into it, the concurrent opinion written by Justice Goldberg (joined by Chief Justice Brennan) takes the seldom used Ninth Amendment ("Rights retained by the people") route.

50. *Griswold*, at 482.

51. *Griswold*, at 484, emphasis added.

52. *Griswold*, at 484.

53. Justice Black (joined by Justice Stewart): "I have expressed the view many times that the First Amendment freedom, for example have suffered from *a failure of the courts to stick to the simple language of the First Amendment in construing it*, instead of invoking multitudes of words substituted for those the Framers use. . . . I like my privacy as well as the next one, but I am nevertheless compelled to admit that government has a right to invade it unless prohibited by some specific constitutional provision" (*Griswold*, at 509, emphasis added).

54. Kafka, *The Trial*, 213.

PART 3

1. Readings of this nature often try to sniff out Hegelianism in Deleuze and claim that his total aversion to Hegel is only a symptom of their dangerous prox-

imity. See, for example, Zizek, *Organs Without Bodies*, and Malabou, "Who's Afraid," 135–136.

2. I have tried to undertake this task elsewhere by emphasizing Spinoza's *Theological-Political Treatise*, in "We Do Not Yet Know." See also Belaief, *Spinoza's Philosophy of Law*.

3. *Delgamuukw v. British Columbia*, [1997] 3 S.C.R. 1010. Cited in text by paragraph reference.

4. Paul Patton's *Deleuze and the Political* ends with an extended discussion of the Australian High Court's decision in *Mabo v. Queensland*, A.L.R., 107 (1992).

CHAPTER 8

1. The only (indirect) corroboration I find for my suggestion that Deleuze and Guattari's philosophy of the concept is based on Spinoza's physics is their claim that "the pre-Socratics treat physical elements like concepts" (*WP*, 91). I make a similar, if reverse, claim: Deleuze and Guattari treat concepts like physical elements.

2. I use the term *characteristic relation* to indicate those relations between the parts of the individual characteristic of it, even if Spinoza's use is rather more technical. For Spinoza, a mode's essence, which is eternal, passes into existence when an infinity of extensive parts is determined from without to come under and express the relation characteristic of its essence (*E*, IIIP7).

3. I use Patton's example of Hobbes and the social contract rather than Deleuze's example of Leibniz and other minds because, frankly, I find it much clearer. See Patton, *Deleuze and the Political*, 12.

4. "It is like the bird as event. The concept is defined by the inseparability of a finite number of heterogeneous components traversed by a point of absolute survey [*survol*] at infinite speed" (*WP*, 21).

5. I discuss the evental status (as singular assemblages of parts) of Spinoza's modes in my "We Do Not Yet Know," 65. Hampshire also makes this point, if in different terms, in his *Spinoza and Spinozism*, 185.

6. Deleuze also calls a concept a multiplicity in *DR*, 182, and in Deleuze and Parnet, *Dialogues*, 144. Also, see the preface to *Dialogues*: "In a multiplicity what counts are not the terms or the elements but what there is 'between,' the between, a set of relations which are not separable from each other" (p. viii).

7. Patton, *Deleuze and the Political*, 12. Also, consider: "This is really what the creation of concepts means: to connect internal, inseparable components *to the point of closure or saturation* so that we can no longer add or withdraw a component without changing the nature of the concept; *to connect the concept with another in such a way that the nature of other connections will change* [*changeraient leur nature*]" (*WP*, 90, emphasis added). To my mind, this passage reveals what is at stake in Deleuze's philosophy of the concept, what I can tersely put as an attempt

to combine a Spinozist conception of perfection [*perfectus*] (concepts make no reference to anything other than themselves; they cannot be judged as lacking or incomplete except by virtue of an inappropriate mode of thinking, comparison, or judgment—see the preface to Book IV of the *Ethics*) with a Bergsonian conception of internal multiplicity (a concept may be perfect and complete in itself, yet this does not prevent a subsequent philosophy from reconfiguring its components, an ongoing activity that turns the history of philosophy into a continuous becoming).

8. Hence the reason that Deleuze is, to my mind, inassimilable to any approach of internal critique: He doesn't believe in it; he doesn't think it's possible. Either you preserve, and perhaps enhance, the characteristic relations of the thinker you comment on (as he does in his own commentaries), or else you criticize externally; that is, you modify the concepts of a writer by introducing components foreign to them. It is an interesting and open question whether deconstruction—or any philosophical perspective strongly committed to internal criticism—would be amenable to this kind of approach, or even if it would make sense for it.

9. I thank Kirsten Anker for her help on aboriginal rights and title.

10. In what follows I omit discussion of the *Delgamuukw* appeal at the provincial level (1993). For my purposes little would be gained by its inclusion, which, in the main, confirms the trial findings.

11. *Delgamuukw v. The Queen* (1991), 79 D.L.R. (4th) 185 (B.C.S.C.), at ¶87.

12. In *Guerin v. Canada* ([1984] 2 S.C.R. 335), Justice Dickson concludes that aboriginal interest cannot be described as a beneficial interest, or a personal interest, or a usufructuary right (even if all these contain, as he puts it, "a core of truth"), and ends up, famously, calling it "sui generis" (¶382). In *R. v. Sparrow* ([1990] 1 S.C.R. 1075), Dickson goes on that, "courts must be careful to avoid the application of traditional common law concepts of property as they develop their understanding of what the reasons for judgment in *Guerin* referred to as the '*sui generis*' nature of aboriginal rights" (¶1112). Finally, in *Paul v. Canadian Pacific Ltd.* ([1988] 2 S.C.R. 654), the Court puzzles that "the inescapable conclusion from the Court's analysis of Indian title up to this point is that the Indian interest in land is truly *sui generis*. It is more than the right to enjoyment and occupancy although . . . it is difficult to describe what more in traditional property law terminology" (¶678).

13. For this dimension, see the Royal Proclamation of 1763 and its interpretation by the Privy Council in *St. Catherine's Milling and Lumber Co. v. The Queen* (1888), 14 A.C. 46 (P.C.), and *Canadian Pacific Ltd.*, at ¶677.

14. *Guerin*, at ¶376; cited in *Delgamuukw*, at ¶114.

15. Or, as Lamer states in *R. v. Van der Peet* ([1996] 2 S.C.R. 507), aboriginal rights are a "form of intersocietal law that evolved from long-standing practices linking the various communities" (¶42). For a specifically Deleuzian analysis of this

feature of contemporary aboriginal jurisprudence, see Patton, *Deleuze and the Political*, 125–131, especially 129. Focusing on the concept of the "apparatus of capture" from Deleuze and Guattari's *A Thousand Plateaus* (pp. 424–473), Patton elaborates how the Australian High Court's *Mabo v. Queensland* ([1992] A.L.R. 107) "opens up a smooth space in between indigenous and colonial law," one that can undermine the colonial legal capture of aboriginal territory, insofar as it has the potential to provoke "a becoming-indigenous of the common law to the extent that it now protects a property right derived from indigenous law; and a becoming-common law of indigenous law to the extent that it now acquires the authority along with the jurisprudential limits of the common law doctrine of native title."

16. For an insightful discussion of the "problem" of reconciliation from a Deleuzian perspective, see Patton, "Event of Colonization." By understanding a Deleuzian problem to mean "a virtual structure whose nature is never entirely captured in any given specification or determination of its conditions" (p. 113), Patton takes the problem of reconciliation in a more basic sense than the one we examine in *Delgamuukw*. Rather than assume that it necessarily implies the reconciliation of preexisting aboriginal societies with the *sovereignty* of the Crown, Patton argues that the real, fundamental problem of reconciliation is to determine "the conditions of co-existence of different peoples" (p. 117). The determination of the problem as one of legal incorporation (say, by declaring that all aboriginal title is usufruct and depends on the goodwill of the Sovereign) represents merely one possible working-out of the (colonial) encounter between two peoples. And even if the problem has taken the form of incorporation, it is not resolved and settled once and for all. To the contrary, contemporary aboriginal jurisprudence represents an ongoing reconsideration—or as Deleuze would have it, a counteractualization—of the conditions of its problem. "Contemporary efforts to undo the legal and political institutions of internal colonization in countries with captive Indigenous populations may be understood as attempts to return to the original conditions of the problem. They seek to 'problematize' existing solutions to the problem of colonial society in order to arrive at new ones" (p. 115). Taking the Australian High Court's 1992 *Mabo* decision, Patton explores how the Court reverses the long-standing solution for denying indigenous land rights (declaration of *terra nullius* and subsequent appropriation) by "re-problematizing" the hypothesis that frames the colonial encounter as one between a civilized rights-bearing people and a rights-less people too low on the civilizational scale to enjoy property. In other words, the High Court redetermined the problem of reconciliation precisely by questioning "whether the colonial encounter need to have taken the form of the imposition of sovereignty at all" (p. 116). I do not take Patton's analysis to be at odds with my own, only to stress a different dimension. He uses the concept of the problem to argue that the actual forms taken by the colonial problem are nonnecessary and also to provide a perspective to resist and challenge them; in the pres-

ent analysis, on the other hand, I use the concept of the problem to analyze the formulation and logic of a particular legal decision.

17. Of course, a concept of aboriginal title cannot solve the whole problem; it is only one element of reconciliation. The problem of reconciliation will find as many expressions as there are aboriginal rights able to give a concrete sense to it.

18. I cannot follow Deleuze and claim that problems are the transcendental condition for *all* adjudication (as he says, they are the condition for *all* thought). In fact, the overwhelming majority of judgments are *unproblematic*—they simply call up a recollected rule to treat the situation. Problems, and the creation of problems, are the condition only for what I call attentive judgment.

19. See Llewellyn's exhortation to his first-year law students: "Everything, everything, everything, big or small, a judge may say in an opinion, is to be read with primary reference to the particular dispute, the particular question before him. You are not to think that the words mean what they might if they stood alone" (*Bramble Bush*, 41).

20. See, for example, Hadley Arkes's fine account ("Lochner v. New York") of *Lochner v. New York* (1905) in which he tries to give back to this notorious case its forgotten or repressed problem (along with its credibility).

21. On this point, see McNeil, "Meaning of Aboriginal Title."

22. Spinoza, "Treatise on the Emendation of the Intellect," in his *Complete Works*, 24.

23. Were we to develop this further, the relevant text would no doubt be Spinoza's critique of Descartes on the question of judgment (*E*, IIP49S). Spinoza argues that will and intellect are the same thing and denies an independent and indeterminate faculty of judgment able to affirm or reject ideas at its discretion. To have an idea is to affirm that idea, and the automaton, unable to resist the power of adequate affirmations, is free from the illusion of an indeterminate will or power of judgment. Needless to say, this text goes a long way in criticizing the notion of the activist judge able, apparently, to suspend legal reasoning and conclusion in favor of extrinsic interest.

24. In a lecture, Deleuze brings this motif of "the most subjective as the most objective" to bear directly on the term *spiritual automaton*: "We are, [Spinoza] says, spiritual automata, that is to say it is less we who have the ideas than the ideas which are affirmed in us" (Deleuze, *Spinoza, 24/01/1978*, available at http://www.webdeleuze.com).

25. See Zac, "Les thèmes spinozistes."

26. In his correspondence, Bergson expresses a feeling of being simultaneously close to and remote from Spinoza. See in particular his letter dated July 7, 1928, to Vladimir Jankélévitch, where he notes his surprise that he always felt at home reading Spinoza, even while considering his own work the "opposite of Spinozism." Cited in Trotignon, "Bergson et Spinoza," 6.

27. The places and uses to which Deleuze puts this phrase are too many to enumerate. But perhaps his most sustained uses are found in *SPP*, 122–130; *EPS*, 217–234; and especially *TP*, 256–260, and elsewhere.

28. For its most famous expression, see Descartes's Sixth Meditation.

29. Although Deleuze is credited with defining the many distinctive styles of the *Ethics* (the Propositions and their apparatus as smooth and scholarly; the Scholia, Prefaces, and Appendices as ostensive and polemical; and the inimitable Book V as a style onto itself) (*CC*, 138–151), an early, elegant statement to the same effect can be found in Bergson (*CM*, 113).

30. "When Spinoza says that we do not even know what a body can do, this is practically a war cry. He adds that we speak of consciousness, mind, soul, of the power of the soul over the body; we chatter away about these things, but do not even know what bodies can do" (*EPS*, 255). I also note that, although Spinoza's main target in the Scholium is Descartes, in a late letter he makes use of exactly the same argument against belief in miracles: We do not know enough about nature to say that something defies its laws, that is, a miracle (*L*, Letter 75, to Oldenburgh).

31. If it is true that Deleuze does use this Scholium toward theorizing creativity or nongivenness ("*Not even God* can say in advance whether two borderlines will string together or form a multiplicity" [*TP*, 250, emphasis added]), he never implies that this is Spinoza's position.

32. What follows is an all too condensed summary of this major theme, one that has received tremendous treatment in contemporary Spinoza scholarship. The key (English-language or translated) references are to Negri, *Savage Anomaly*; Balibar, *Spinoza and Politics*; Gatens, and Lloyd, *Collective Imaginings*; and, as a sort of sampling of the topic, Montag and Stolze, *New Spinoza*.

33. Hardt, *Gilles Deleuze*, 72.

34. I note that Deleuze's reading is contested within Spinoza studies. Pierre Macherey has found Deleuze's claim to be problematic in that it proposes joyful passions as able to truly reveal common notions. Michael Hardt, on the other hand, recommends its appreciation of the practical constitution of knowledge. See Macherey, "Encounter with Spinoza," 152–157; and Hardt, *Gilles Deleuze*, 95–107.

35. Bergson, *Time and Free Will*, 122. I covered this same concept, but for difference reasons, in Chapter 5 under the name "internal difference."

36. Gouhier, "Introduction," xxii.

37. See, for example, Chapter 1 ("Of Prophecy") of Spinoza, *Theological-Political Treatise*. Also, Chapter 3 ("Of the Vocation of the Hebrews"): "All worthy objects of desire can be classified under one of these three general headings: 1. To know things through their primary causes" (p. 417).

38. I note the connection between the therapeutic powers of adequate ideas

in Spinoza and Freud. In both cases a sad individual is cured (or starts on a cure) by acknowledging the real *causes* of their thought or psychic state. See Yirmiyahu Yovel's essay "Spinoza and Freud: Self-Knowledge as Emancipation" in his *Spinoza and Other Heretics*, 136–167.

39. For a *very* similar statement from Bergson ("philosophy [as] a jigsaw puzzle where the problem is to construct with the pieces society gives us the design it is unwilling to show us"), see *CM*, 50.

40. "No one has been more forceful than Spinoza in opposing the theological tradition of a perfect and happy Adam" (*SPP*, 20).

41. Spinoza, *Theological-Political Treatise*, 389–390.

42. Spinoza, *Theological-Political Treatise*, 527.

43. According to Deleuze, both the traditional political right and left are based on a fundamental misunderstanding. The right denies the powers of becoming in its attempt to block movement and preserve the status quo; and the left denatures the virtual in its representation of change as the realization of a possible plan. Zourabichvili, "Deleuze et le possible."

44. Thus, when the perspective of the denial of movement is taken for granted ("Royal Science"), the thought and practices of the left ("Nomad Science") appear as a "prescientific or parascientific or subscientific agency" (*TP*, 367). Criticism of the Nomad leveled by the Royal reveals yet another way to approach the misunderstandings and illusions surrounding the accusation of judicial activism. Recriminations of judicial activism are possible when one position committed to blocking movement designates as activist one that affirms and works with movement. Because the first position denies the reality and necessity of movement, it assumes that a position open to it must be one that recommends and affects it, rather than accepts and affirms it (and thus it appears as activist: parascientific or prescientific).

45. See Hampshire, *Spinoza and Spinozism*, 93. Given the tradition with which we are dealing, we should not be too hasty to confine metaphysics to a narrowly discursive and cognitive definition at the expense of its perceptive and affective registers. Only recall Spinoza's extraordinary line in Book V: "We *feel* and *experience* that we are eternal" (*E*, VP23S, emphasis added). Perhaps Deleuze is at his most Spinozist when he emphasizes the themes of vision, clarity, perception, and dwelling with respect to metaphysical awareness and practice.

46. *Delgamuukw*, 1991, p. 13.

47. See Mills, *Eagle*, 14–33; and Asch, "Errors in *Delgamuukw*."

48. This rule is the exception that statements made by deceased persons could be admitted without being disqualified as hearsay (*Delgamuukw*, ¶95).

49. *Delgamuukw*, 1991, p. 13, emphasis added. Cited in *Delgamuukw*, 1997, ¶¶96–97.

50. Hearsay evidence is usually inadmissible on the grounds that it cannot be

cross-examined and is not made under oath (hence it is potentially unreliable). This exception guarantees reliability on the basis of a person's reputation for truthfulness in the community.

51. The question of aboriginal self-government was a major issue at trial, and McEachern chose to interpret (and deny) it as a demand by the plaintiffs for legal sovereignty over the territory and its inhabitants (aboriginals and nonaboriginals alike). In the Supreme Court appeal, the claim for self-government for jurisdiction was underplayed and did not enter seriously into the judgment. Whether or not it is an encounter that the common law could handle is reserved for another day.

52. See also the text explicitly signed by Deleuze in Deleuze and Parnet, *Dialogues*, 138–139.

53. These remarks from Deleuze and Guattari's *A Thousand Plateaus* could prepare study on laws that participate in lines of death, or in developing a concept of judicial activism internal to a Deleuzian analysis (reckless experimentation or deterritorialization of a legal tradition, inventing encounters where there are none, etc.).

54. Which is why, I take it, expression is not listed as an entry in Deleuze's "Index of the Main Concepts of the *Ethics*" (*SPP*, 44–109). Nor does it appear in any English-language index of Spinoza's works.

55. I am grateful to Macherey's "Encounter with Spinoza" for this count (p. 144).

56. For an excellent summary of these traditions to which Spinoza responds, see Laclau, "Names of God."

57. Deleuze advances this interpretation as forcefully as possible in *Expressionism in Philosophy*. For example: "What is expressed has no existence outside its expressions; each expression is, as it were, the existence of what is expressed" (*EPS*, 42).

58. For an extended analysis of the concept of ethology, see Gatens and Lloyd, *Collective Imaginings*, 100–107; and Gatens, "Through a Spinozist Lens." Deleuze's concept of ethology must be distinguished from one perhaps more familiar to English-speaking readers, namely, J. S. Mill's ethology as developed in his *System of Logic* (1843). On this, see M. White, "Liberal Character."

59. According to the terms in previous sections, movement is an internal difference (Chapter 5) or a continuous multiplicity (earlier in this chapter).

60. To avoid confusing changes in vocabulary, I use the term *mode* to refer to finite individuals in both Spinoza and Bergson.

61. In his discussion of the affection-image Deleuze does use *expression* as a noun, but this context is far removed from our present discussion (*C1*, 66).

62. Or, as Deleuze puts it in another context, "Multiplicity, which replaces the one no less than the multiple, is the true substantive, substance itself" (*DR*, 182).

63. Marrati, *Deleuze*, 252.

64. Minus the specific reading of *Cinema 1*, this is perhaps what Eric Alliez is getting at when he remarks, "What is it in Deleuze which exceeds Spinozism as a historical formation? Answer: Deleuze will project a *Spinoza beyond Spinoza* by basing his entire philosophy on the great wager stated in the equation: Expression = Constructivism" (Alliez, "The Contemporary," 123).

65. Soulez, *Bergson politique*, 279–281.

Cases Cited

CANADA

Delgamuukw v. The Queen (1991), 79 D.L.R. (4th) 185 (B.C.S.C.)
Delgamuukw v. British Columbia, [1997] 3 S.C.R. 1010
Guerin v. Canada, [1984] 2 S.C.R. 335
Paul v. Canadian Pacific Ltd., [1988] 2 S.C.R. 654
R. v. Sparrow, [1990] 1 S.C.R. 1075
R. v. Van der Peet, [1996] 2 S.C.R. 507
St. Catherine's Milling and Lumber Co. v. The Queen (1888), 14 A.C. 46 (P.C.)

UNITED STATES

Buck v. Bell, 274 U.S. 200 (1927)
Griswold v. Connecticut, 381 U.S. 479 (1965)
Ostrowe v. Lee, 256 N.Y. 36, 175 N.E. 505 (1931)
Palsgraf v. Long Island Railroad Co., 248 N.Y. 339, 162 N.E. 99 (1928)
Riggs v. Palmer, 115 N.Y. 506, 22 N.E. 188 (1889)
Southern Pacific Co. v. Jensen, 244 U.S. 205 (1916)

Bibliography

Alliez, Eric, Eliot Albert, Keith Ansell-Pearson, Amalia Boyer, David Toews, and Alberto Toscano. "The Contemporary: A Roundtable Discussion." *Pli* 8 (1999): 119–137.

Alschuler, Albert W. *Law Without Values: The Life, Work, and Legacy of Justice Holmes.* Chicago: University of Chicago Press, 2000.

Ansell-Pearson, Keith. "Bergson and Creative Evolution/Involution." In *The New Bergson*, edited by John Mullarkey, 146–167. Manchester, U.K.: Manchester University Press, 1999.

———. *Philosophy and the Adventure of the Virtual: Bergson and the Time of Life.* London: Routledge, 2002.

Arendt, Hannah. *Lectures on Kant's Political Philosophy.* Chicago: University of Chicago Press, 1992.

Aristotle. *Metaphysics*, translated by Jonathan Barnes. Princeton, NJ: Princeton University Press, 1984.

Arkes, Hadley. "*Lochner v. New York* and the Cast of Our Laws." In *Great Cases in Constitutional Law*, edited by Robert P. George, 94–129. Princeton, NJ: Princeton University Press, 2000.

Asch, Michael. "Errors in *Delgamuukw*: An Anthropological Perspective." In *Aboriginal Title in British Columbia: Delgamuukw v. the Queen*, edited by Frank Cassidy, 221–243. Lantzville, Canada: Oolichan Books and the Institute for Research on Public Policy, 1992.

Austin, John. *The Province of Jurisprudence Determined.* New York: Hackett, 1998 [1832].

Badiou, Alain. *Ethics: An Essay on the Understanding of Evil*, translated by Peter Hallward. London: Verso, 2001. Originally published in French in 1993.

Balibar, Etienne. *Spinoza and Politics*, translated by Peter Snowdon. New York: Verso, 1998. Originally published in French in 1985.

Belaief, Gail. *Spinoza's Philosophy of Law.* Hague: Mouton, 1971.

Benhabib, Seyla. *The Rights of Others: Aliens, Residents, and Citizens.* Cambridge, U.K.: Cambridge University Press, 2004.

Bergson, Henri. *Creative Evolution*, translated by Arthur Mitchell. New York: Dover, 1998. Originally published in French in 1907.

———. *The Creative Mind: An Introduction to Metaphysics*, translated by Mabelle L. Andison. New York: Citadel Press, 1974. Originally published in French in 1938.

———. *Duration and Simultaneity*, edited by Robin Durie. Manchester: Clinamen Press, 1999. Originally published in French in 1922.

———. *Matter and Memory*, translated by N. M. Paul and W. S. Palmer. New York: Zone Books, 1988. Originally published in French in 1896.

———. *Mélanges*. Paris: PUF, 1972.

———. *Mind-Energy*, translated by H. Wildon Carr. New York: Henry Holt, 1920. Originally published in French in 1919.

———. *Time and Free Will: An Essay on the Immediate Date of Consciousness*, translated by F. L. Pogson. New York: Dover, 2001. Originally published in French in 1889.

———. *The Two Sources of Morality and Religion*, translated by R. Ashley Audra and Cloudesley Brereton. Notre Dame, IN: University of Notre Dame, 1977. Originally published in French in 1932.

Bernstein, Richard. "The Retrieval of the Democratic Ethos." *Cardozo Law Review* 17 (1996): 1127–1146.

Borradori, Giovanna. *Philosophy in a Time of Terror: Dialogues with Jürgen Habermas and Jacques Derrida*. Chicago: University of Chicago Press, 2003.

Breyer, Stephen, and Antonin Scalia. "Constitutional Relevance of Foreign Court Decisions." *C-SPAN*, January 13, 2005.

Cardozo, Benjamin N. *The Growth of Law*. New York: Fallon, 1947. Originally published in 1924.

———. "Mr. Justice Holmes." In *Selected Writings of Benjamin Nathan Cardozo*, 77–86. New York: Fallon, 1947. Essay originally published in 1931.

———. *The Nature of the Judicial Process*. New York: Fallon, 1947. Originally published in 1921.

Cavell, Stanley. *The Claim of Reason: Wittgenstein, Skepticism, Morality, and Tragedy*, 2nd ed. Oxford, U.K.: Oxford University Press, 1999.

———. *Must We Mean What We Say?* 2nd ed. Cambridge, U.K.: Cambridge University Press, 2002.

Caygill, Howard. *A Kant Dictionary*. Oxford: Blackwell, 1995.

Coleman, Jules. "Legal Positivism." In *Encyclopedia of Philosophy*, edited by Donald Borchert, 237–245. New York: Macmillan, 2005.

Connolly, William. *Neuropolitics: Thinking, Culture, Speed*. Minneapolis: University of Minnesota Press, 2002.

Deleuze, Gilles. *L'Abécédaire de Gilles Deleuze, avec Claire Parnet*. Paris: DVD Editions Montparnasse, 2004.

———. "The Actual and the Virtual." In *Dialogues II*, 148–152. New York: Columbia University Press, 2002.

———. "Bergson, 1859–1941." In *Desert Islands and Other Texts: 1953–1974*, edited by David Lapoujade, 22–31. Los Angeles: Semiotext(e), 2004. Essay originally published in 1956.

———. *Bergsonism*, translated by Hugh Tomlinson and Barbara Habberjam. New York: Zone Books, 1991. Originally published in French in 1966.

———. "Bergson's Conception of Difference." In *Desert Islands and Other Texts: 1953–1974*, edited by David Lapoujade, 32–51. Los Angeles: Semiotext(e), 2004. Essay originally published in 1956.

———. *Cinema 1: The Movement-Image*, translated by Hugh Tomlinson and Barbara Habberjam. Minneapolis: University of Minnesota Press, 1986. Originally published in French in 1983.

———. *Cinema 2: The Time-Image*, translated by Hugh Tomlinson and Robert Galeta. Minneapolis: University of Minnesota Press, 1989. Originally published in French in 1985.

———. "Coldness and Cruelty." In *Masochism: An Interpretation of Coldness and Cruelty*, by G. Deleuze, 8–138. New York: Zone Books, 1989. Originally published in French in 1967.

———. "Cours inédit de Gilles Deleuze sur le chapitre III de *L'Evolution Créatrice*." In *Annales bergsoniennes II*, edited by Frédéric Worms, 151–188. Paris: PUF, 2004.

———. *Difference and Repetition*, translated by Paul Patton. New York: Columbia University Press, 1994. Originally published in French in 1968.

———. *Empiricism and Subjectivity: An Essay on Hume's Theory of Human Nature*, translated by Constantin Boundas. New York: Columbia University Press, 1991. Originally published in French in 1953.

———. *Essays Critical and Clinical*, translated by Daniel W. Smith and Michael A. Greco. Minneapolis: University of Minnesota Press, 1997. Originally published in French in 1993.

———. *Expressionism in Philosophy: Spinoza*, translated by Martin Joughin. New York: Zone Books, 1992. Originally published in French in 1968.

———. "The Idea of Genesis in Kant's Esthetics." In *Desert Islands and Other Texts: 1953–1974*, edited by David Lapoujade, 56–70. Los Angeles: Semiotext(e), 2004. Essay originally published in 1963.

———. "Immanence: A Life." In *Pure Immanence: Essays on A Life*, 25–33. New York: Zone Books, 2001. Essay originally published in 1995.

———. "Instincts and Institutions." In *Desert Islands and Other Texts: 1953–1974*, edited by David Lapoujade, 19–21. Los Angeles: Semiotext(e), 2004. Essay originally published in 1953.

———. *Kant's Critical Philosophy: The Doctrine of the Faculties*, translated by

Hugh Tomlinson and Barbara Habberjam. Minneapolis: University of Minnesota Press, 1984. Originally published in French in 1963.

———. *The Logic of Sense*, translated by Mark Lesser. New York: Columbia University Press, 1990. Originally published in French in 1969.

———. *Negotiations, 1972–1990*, translated by Martin Joughin. New York: Columbia University Press, 1995. Originally published in French in 1990.

———. *Nietzsche and Philosophy*, translated by Hugh Tomlinson. New York: Columbia University Press, 1983. Originally published in French in 1962.

———. "On Nietzsche and the Image of Thought." In *Desert Islands and Other Texts: 1953–1974*, edited by David Lapoujade, 135–142. Los Angeles: Semiotext(e), 2004. Interview originally published in 1968.

———. "Preface to Jean-Clet Martin's *Variations: la philosophie de Gilles Deleuze.*" In *Two Regimes of Madness: Texts and Interviews 1975–1995*, edited by David Lapoujade, 361–363. Los Angeles: Semiotext(e), 2006. Originally appeared in French in 1993.

———. *Proust and Signs*, translated by Richard Howard. Minneapolis: University of Minnesota Press, 2000. Originally published in French in 1970.

———. *Spinoza: Practical Philosophy*, translated by Robert Hurley. San Francisco: City Lights Books, 1988. Originally published in French in 1970.

———. "We Invented the Ritornello." In *Two Regimes of Madness: Texts and Interviews 1975–1995*, edited by David Lapoujade, 377–381. Los Angeles: Semiotext(e), 2006. Interview originally published in 1991.

Deleuze, Gilles, and Félix Guattari. *Anti-Oedipus, Capitalism, and Schizophrenia*, translated by Robert Hurley, Mark Seem, and Helen R. Lane. Minneapolis: University of Minnesota Press, 1977. Originally published in French in 1972.

———. *A Thousand Plateaus: Capitalism, and Schizophrenia*, translated by Brian Massumi. Minneapolis: University of Minnesota Press, 1987. Originally published in French in 1980.

———. *What Is Philosophy?* translated by Hugh Tomlinson and Graham Burchell. New York: Columbia University Press, 1994. Originally published in French in 1991.

Deleuze, Gilles, and Claire Parnet. *Dialogues*, translated by Hugh Tomlinson and Barbara Habberjam. London: Athlone, 1987. Originally published in French in 1977.

Derrida, Jacques. "The Laws of Reflection: Nelson Mandela, in Admiration." In *For Nelson Mandela*, edited by Jacques Derrida and Mustapha Tlili, 11–42. New York: Seaver, 1987.

Descartes, René. *Discourse on Method*, translated by John Cottingham, Robert Stoothoff, and Dugald Murdoch. Cambridge, U.K.: Cambridge University Press, 1988 [1637].

Dewey, John. "Preface." In *A Contribution to a Bibliography of Henri Bergson*. New York: Columbia University, 1912.
Dickstein, Morris, ed. *The Revival of Pragmatism: New Essays on Social Thought, Law, and Culture*. Durham, NC: Duke University Press, 1998.
Douzinas, Costas. "Human Rights and Postmodern Utopia." *Law and Critique* 11(2) (2000): 219–240.
Durie, Robin. "Creativity and Life." *Review of Metaphysics* 56 (December 2002): 357–383.
Dworkin, Ronald. "Comment." In *A Matter of Interpretation: Federal Courts and the Law*, edited by Amy Guttman, 115–128. Princeton, NJ: Princeton University Press, 1997.
———. *Freedom's Law: The Moral Reading of the American Constitution*. Cambridge, MA: Harvard University Press, 1996.
———. *Law's Empire*. Cambridge, MA: Belknap Press of Harvard University Press, 1986.
———. *Taking Rights Seriously*. Cambridge, MA: Harvard University Press, 1977.
Ferrera, Alessandro. *Justice and Judgment*. London: Sage, 1999.
Frankenberg, Gunter. "Down by Law: Irony, Seriousness, and Reason." *Northwestern University Law Review* 83 (1988): 360–397.
French, Rebecca R. "Time in the Law." *University of Colorado Law Review* 72 (2001): 663–748.
Gadamer, Hans-Georg. *Truth and Method*, translated by Joel Weinsheimer and Donald G. Marshall. New York: Continuum, 1975. Originally published in German in 1960.
Garner, Bryan A., ed. *Black's Law Dictionary*, 8th ed. St. Paul, MN: Thomson, 2004.
Gatens, Moira. "Through a Spinozist Lens: Ethology, Difference, Power." In *Deleuze: A Critical Reader*, edited by Paul Patton, 139–161. Oxford: Blackwell, 1996.
Gatens, Moira, and Genevieve Lloyd. *Collective Imaginings: Spinoza, Past and Present*. London: Routledge, 1999.
Goldschmidt, Victor. "Cours." In *Annales bergsoniennes I*, edited by Frédéric Worms, 73–128. Paris: PUF, 2002.
Gouhier, Henri. "Introduction." In *Oeuvres: Henri Bergson*, edited by André Robinet, vii–xxx. Paris: PUF, 1959.
Granger, Hebert. "Aristotle on Genus and Differentia." *Journal of the History of Philosophy* 22 (1984): 1–24.
Grey, Thomas C. "Freestanding Legal Pragmatism." In *The Revival of Pragmatism: New Essays on Social Thought, Law, and Culture*, edited by Morris Dickstein, 254–274. Durham, NC: Duke University Press, 1998.

———. "Holmes and Legal Pragmatism." *Stanford Law Review* 41(4) (1989): 787–870.

Günther, Klaus. "A Normative Conception of Coherence for a Discursive Theory of Legal Justification." *Ratio Juris* 2(2) (1989): 155–166.

———. *The Sense of Appropriateness: Application Discourses in Morality and Law*, translated by John Farrell. Albany, NY: SUNY Press, 1993. Originally published in German in 1988.

Habermas, Jürgen. "An Alternative Way Out of the Philosophy of the Subject: Communicative Versus Subject-Centered Reason." In *The Philosophical Discourse of Modernity: Twelve Lectures*, 294–326. Cambridge, MA: MIT Press, 1987. Originally published in German in 1985.

———. "America and the World: A Conversation with Jürgen Habermas." *Logos* 3(3) (2004): 101–122.

———. *Between Facts and Norms: Contributions to a Discourse Theory of Law and Democracy*, translated by William Rehg. Cambridge, MA: MIT Press, 1998. Originally published in German in 1992.

———. *The Future of Human Nature*, translated by Hella Beister, William Rehg, and Max Pensky. Cambridge, MA: Polity, 2003.

———. "Kant's Idea of Perpetual Peace: At Two Hundred Years' Remove." In *The Inclusion of the Other: Studies in Political Theory*, edited by Ciaran Cronin and Pablo De Greiff, 165–202. Cambridge, MA: MIT Press, 1998. Originally published in German in 1996.

———. "Remarks on Legitimation Through Human Rights." In *The Postnational Constellation*, edited by Max Pensky, 113–130. Cambridge, MA: MIT Press, 2001. Originally published in German in 1998.

Hampshire, Stuart. *Spinoza and Spinozism*. Oxford, U.K.: Oxford University Press, 2005.

Hardt, Michael. *Gilles Deleuze: An Apprenticeship in Philosophy*. Minneapolis: University of Minnesota Press, 1993.

Hart, H. L. A. "American Jurisprudence Through English Eyes: The Nightmare and the Noble Dream." In *Essays in Jurisprudence*, 123–144. Oxford, U.K.: Oxford University Press, 1983. Essay originally published in 1977.

———. *The Concept of Law*. Oxford, U.K.: Oxford University Press, 1961.

———. "Jhering's Heaven of Concepts and Modern Analytical Jurisprudence." In *Essays in Jurisprudence*, 265–277. Oxford, U.K.: Oxford University Press, 1983. Essay originally published in 1970.

———. "Positivism and the Separation of Law and Morals." In *Essays in Jurisprudence*, 49–87. Oxford, U.K.: Oxford University Press, 1983. Essay originally published in 1958.

———. "Problems of the Philosophy of Law." In *Essays in Jurisprudence*, 88–120.

Oxford, U.K.: Oxford University Press, 1983. Essay originally published in 1977.

Heidegger, Martin. *Kant and the Problem of Metaphysics*, translated by Richard Taft, 4th ed. Indianapolis: Indiana University Press, 1990. Originally published in German in 1973.

———. *What Is Called Thinking?* translated by J. Glenn Gray. New York: Harper and Row, 1962. Originally published in German in 1954.

Holmes, Oliver Wendell. *The Common Law*. New York: Dover, 1991. Originally published in 1881.

———. "Holdsworth's English Law." In *Collected Legal Papers*, 285–290. New York: Harcourt Brace, 1920. Essay originally published in 1909.

———. "Holmes to Pollock, April 10th, 1881." In *Holmes-Pollock Letters: The Correspondence of Mr. Justice Holmes and Sir Frederick Pollock, 1874–1932*, edited by Mark de Wolfe. Cambridge, MA: Harvard University Press, 1941.

———. "Ideals and Doubts." In *Collected Legal Papers*, 303–307. New York: Harcourt Brace, 1920. Essay originally published in 1915.

———. "Introduction to the General Survey." In *Collected Legal Papers*, 298–302. New York: Harcourt Brace, 1920. Essay originally published in 1913.

———. "John Marshall." In *Collected Legal Papers*, 266–271. New York: Harcourt Brace, 1920. Speech originally published in 1913.

———. "Law and the Court: Speech at a Dinner of the Harvard Law School Association of New York on February 15, 1913." In *Collected Legal Papers*, 291–297. New York: Harcourt, 1920. Speech originally published in 1913.

———. "Law in Science and Science in Law." In *Collected Legal Papers*, 210–243. New York: Harcourt Brace, 1920. Address originally published in 1889.

———. "Learning and Science." In *Collected Legal Papers*, 138–140. New York: Harcourt Brace, 1920. Speech originally published in 1913.

———. "Letter to Harold Laski, March 11, 1922." In *The Essential Holmes*, edited by Richard A. Posner, 56. Chicago: University of Chicago Press, 1992.

———. "Letter to Pollock, April 2nd, 1926." In *The Essential Holmes*, edited by Richard A. Posner, 43. Chicago: University of Chicago Press, 1992.

———. "The Path of Law." In *Collected Legal Papers*, 167–202. New York: Harcourt Brace, 1920. Essay originally published in 1897.

———. "Reflections on the Past and Future: Remarks at a Dinner of the Alpha Phi Club, Cambridge, September 27, 1912." In *The Essential Holmes*, edited by Richard A. Posner, 4–6. Chicago: University of Chicago Press, 1992.

———. "The Use of Law Schools: Oration Before the Harvard Law School Association, at Cambridge, November 5, 1886, on the 250th Anniversary of Harvard University." In *Collected Legal Papers*, 35–48. New York: Harcourt Brace, 1920. Speech originally published in 1913.

Hutchings, Kimberly. *Kant, Critique, and Politics*. London: Routledge, 1996.
James, William. *A Pluralistic Universe*. Lincoln: University of Nebraska Press, 1996 [1909].
———. *Pragmatism*. Cambridge, MA: Harvard University Press, 1978 [1907].
Kafka, Franz. *The Trial*, translated by Breon Mitchell. New York: Schocken, 1998 [1925].
Kant, Immanuel. *Critique of Judgment*, translated by Werner S. Pluhar. Indianapolis: Hackett, 1987 [1790].
———. *Critique of Pure Reason*, translated by Paul Guyer and Allan Wood. Cambridge, U.K.: Cambridge University Press, 1998 [1781/1787].
———. *The Metaphysics of Morals*, translated by Mary Gregor. Cambridge, U.K.: Cambridge University Press, 1996 [1797].
———. *Philosophical Correspondence 1759–1799*, edited by Arnulf Zweig. Chicago: University of Chicago Press, 1967.
———. *Prolegomena to Any Future Metaphysics*, translated by Gary Hatfield. Cambridge, U.K.: Cambridge University Press, 1997 [1783].
———. *Toward Perpetual Peace*, translated by Mary Gregor. Cambridge, U.K.: Cambridge University Press, 1996 [1795].
———. "What Is Enlightenment?" In *Practical Philosophy*, edited by Mary Gregor, 15–22. Cambridge, U.K.: Cambridge University Press, 1996 [1784].
Kennedy, Duncan. "Forms and Substance in Private Law Adjudication." *Harvard Law Review* 89 (1976): 1685–1778.
Kolakowski, Leszek. *Bergson*. Oxford, U.K.: Oxford University Press, 1985.
Lacey, Nicola. *A Life of H. L. A. Hart: The Nightmare and the Noble Dream*. Oxford, U.K.: Oxford University Press, 2004.
Laclau, Ernesto. "On the Names of God." In *Political Theologies: Public Religions in a Post-Secular World*, edited by Hent de Vries and Lawrence E. Sullivan, 137–147. New York: Fordham University Press, 2006.
Lebrun, Gérard. "Le transcendantal et son image." In *Gilles Deleuze: une vie philosophique*, edited by Eric Alliez, 207–232. Paris: Institute Synthélabo, 1998.
Lefebvre, Alexandre. "Critique of Teleology in Kant and Dworkin: The Law without Organs (LwO)." *Philosophy and Social Criticism* 33(2) (2007): 179–201.
———. "Habermas and Deleuze on Law and Adjudication." *Law and Critique* 17(3) (2006): 389–414.
———. "A New Image of Law: Deleuze and Jurisprudence." *Telos* 130 (2005): 103–126.
———. "We Do Not Yet Know What the Law Can Do." *Contemporary Political Theory* 5(1) (2006): 52–67.
Lenoble, Jacques. "Law and Undecidability: Toward a New Vision of the Proce-

duralization of Law." In *Habermas on Law and Democracy: Critical Exchanges*, edited by Michel Rosenfeld and Andrew Arato, 37–81. Berkeley: University of California Press, 1998.

Llewellyn, Karl N. *The Bramble Bush: On Our Law and Its Study*, 2nd ed. New York: Oceana, 1960.

Macherey, Pierre. "The Encounter with Spinoza." In *Deleuze: A Critical Reader*, edited by Paul Patton, 139–161. Oxford, U.K.: Blackwell, 1996.

Malabou, Catherine. "Who's Afraid of Hegelian Wolves?" In *Deleuze: A Critical Reader*, edited by Paul Patton, 114–138. Oxford, U.K.: Blackwell, 1996.

Marrati, Paola. "Against the Doxa: Politics of Immanence and Becoming-Minoritarian." In *Micropolitics of Media Culture: Reading the Rhizomes of Deleuze and Guattari*, edited by Patricia Pisters and Catherine M. Lord, 205–220. Amsterdam: Amsterdam University Press, 2001.

———. *Deleuze: cinéma et philosophie*. Paris: PUF, 2004.

———. "Mysticism and the Foundation of the Open Society: Bergsonian Politics." In *Political Theologies: Public Religion in a Post-Secular World*, edited by Hent de Vries and Lawrence E. Sullivan, 591–601. New York: Fordham University Press, 2006.

———. "Time, Life, Concepts: The Newness of Bergson." *Modern Language Notes* 120(5) (2005): 1099–1111.

Matsuda, Mary J., Charles Lawrence, Richard Delgado, and Kimberlè Williams Crenshaw. *Words That Wound: Critical Race Theory, Assaultive Speech, and the First Amendment*. Boulder, CO: Westview, 1993.

McNeil, Kent. "The Meaning of Aboriginal Title." In *Aboriginal and Treaty Rights in Canada: Essays on Law, Equity, and Respect for Difference*, edited by Michael Asch, 135–154. Vancouver, Canada: UBC Press, 1997.

Mengue, Phillipe. *Deleuze et la question de la démocratie*. Paris: L'Harmattan, 2003.

Mills, Antonia. *Eagle Down Is Our Law: Wet'suwet'en Law, Feasts, and Land Claims*. Vancouver, Canada: UBC Press, 1997.

Montag, Warren, and Ted Stolze, eds. *The New Spinoza*. Minneapolis: University of Minnesota Press, 1997.

Mullarkey, John. *Bergson and Philosophy*. Notre Dame, IN: University of Notre Dame Press, 2000.

Nancy, Jean-Luc. "Lapsus Judicii." In *A Finite Thinking*, edited by Simon Sparks, 152–171. Stanford, CA: Stanford University Press, 2003. Originally published in French in 1985.

Negri, Antonio. *The Savage Anomaly: The Power of Spinoza's Metaphysics and Politics*, translated by Michael Hardt. Minneapolis: University of Minnesota Press, 1991. Originally published in Italian in 1981.

Nietzsche, Friedrich. *On the Genealogy of Morality*, translated by Carol Diethe; edited by Keith Ansell-Pearson. Cambridge, U.K.: Cambridge University Press, 1994 [1887].
———. *The Will to Power*, translated by Walter Kaufmann and R. J. Hollingdale; edited by Walter Kaufmann. New York: Vintage, 1968.
Patton, Paul. "Deleuze and Democratic Politics." In *Radical Democracy: Politics Between Abundance and Lack*, edited by Lasse Thomassen and Lars Tønder, 50–65. Manchester, U.K.: Manchester University Press, 2005.
———. *Deleuze and the Political*. London: Routledge, 2000.
———. "The Event of Colonization." In *Deleuze and the Contemporary World*, edited by Ian Buchanan and Adrian Parr, 104–108. Edinburgh: Edinburgh University Press, 2006.
———. "Utopian Political Philosophy: Deleuze and Rawls." *Deleuze Studies* 1(1) (2007): 41–59.
Posner, Richard A. *Cardozo: A Study in Reputation*. Chicago: University of Chicago Press, 1990.
———. "Introduction." In *The Essential Holmes*, edited by Richard A. Posner, ix–xxxi. Chicago: University of Chicago Press, 1992.
———. "Pragmatic Adjudication." In *The Revival of Pragmatism: New Essays on Social Thought, Law, and Culture*, edited by Morris Dickstein, 235–253. Durham, NC: Duke University Press, 1998.
———. *The Problems of Jurisprudence*. Cambridge, MA: Harvard University Press, 1990.
Protevi, John. *Bodies Politic: A Dynamic Systems Approach to Affective Cognition in Social Context*. Minneapolis: University of Minnesota Press, 2009 (in press).
———. "The Organism as the Judgment of God: Aristotle, Kant, and Deleuze on Nature (That Is, on Biology, Theology, and Politics)." In *Deleuze and Religion*, edited by Mary Bryden, 30–41. London: Routledge, 2001.
Proust, Marcel. *Swann's Way*, translated by Lydia Davis. New York: Penguin, 2002 [1913].
———. *Time Regained*, translated by C. K. Scott Moncrieff. New York: Random House, 1981 [1926].
Rawls, John. "Two Concepts of Rules." In *Collected Papers*, edited by Samuel Freeman, 20–46. Cambridge, MA: Harvard University Press, 1999. Essay originally published in 1955.
Rehg, William. "Against Subordination: Morality, Discourse, and Decision in the Legal Theory of Jürgen Habermas." In *Habermas on Law and Democracy: Critical Exchanges*, edited by Michel Rosenfeld and Andrew Arato, 257–271. Berkeley: University of California Press, 1998.
Rorty, Richard. *Consequences of Pragmatism*. Minneapolis: University of Minnesota Press, 1982.

———. *Philosophy and Social Hope*. New York: Penguin, 1999.
Rose, Gillian. *Dialectic of Nihilism: Post-Structuralism and Law*. Oxford, U.K.: Basil Blackwell, 1984.
Scalia, Antonin. *A Matter of Interpretation: Federal Courts and the Law*. Princeton, NJ: Princeton University Press, 1997.
Scheuerman, William E. "Between Radicalism and Resignation: Democratic Theory in Habermas's *Between Facts and Norms*." In *Discourse and Democracy: Essays on Habermas's Between Facts and Norms*, edited by René Von Schomberg and Kenneth Baynes, 61–85. New York: SUNY Press, 2002.
Schmitt, Carl. *Political Theology*, translated by George Schwab. Cambridge, MA: MIT Press, 1985. Originally published in German in 1922.
Shklar, Judith. "Bergson and the Politics of Intuition." In *Political Thought and Political Thinkers*, edited by Stanley Hoffmann, 317–338. Chicago: University of Chicago Press, 1998. Essay originally published in 1958.
Smith, Daniel W. "Deleuze and the Liberal Tradition: Normativity, Freedom, and Judgement." *Economy and Society* 32(2) (2003): 299–324.
Soulez, Phillipe. *Bergson politique*. Paris: PUF, 1989.
Soulez, Phillipe, and Frédéric Worms. *Bergson*. Paris: PUF, 2002.
Spinoza, Baruch. *Complete Works*, translated by Samuel Shirley. Indianapolis, IN: Hackett, 2002.
———. *The Ethics*, translated by Samuel Shirley. Indianapolis, IN: Hackett, 2002 [1677].
———. *The Letters*, translated by Samuel Shirley. Indianapolis, IN: Hackett, 2002.
———. *Theological-Political Treatise*, translated by Samuel Shirley. Indianapolis, IN: Hackett, 2002 [1670].
Trotignon, Pierre. "Bergson et Spinoza." In *Spinoza au XXe siècle*, edited by Olivier Bloch, 3–12. Paris: PUF, 1993.
Wellmer, Albrecht. *Endgames: The Irreconcilable Nature of Modernity—Essays and Lectures*, translated by David Midgley. Cambridge, MA: MIT Press, 1998. Originally published in German in 1993.
———. *The Persistence of Modernity: Essays on Aesthetics, Ethics, and Postmodernism*, translated by David Midgley. Cambridge, MA: Polity, 1991. Originally published in German in 1986.
White, G. Edward. *Justice Oliver Wendell Holmes: Law and the Inner Self*. Oxford, U.K.: Oxford University Press, 1993.
———. *Tort Law in America: An Intellectual History*. Oxford, U.K.: Oxford University Press, 1985.
White, Melanie. "The Liberal Character of Ethological Governance." *Economy and Society* 34(3) (2005): 475–493.

Wittgenstein, Ludwig. *Philosophical Investigations*, translated by G. E. M. Anscombe, 3rd ed. Oxford: Blackwell, 2001.

Worms, Frédéric. "*Matter and Memory* on Mind and Body." In *The New Bergson*, edited by John Mullarkey, 88–98. Manchester, U.K.: Manchester University Press, 1999.

Yovel, Yirmiyahu. *Spinoza and Other Heretics: The Adventures of Immanence*. Princeton, NJ: Princeton University Press, 1989.

Zac, Sylvain. "Les thèmes spinozistes dans la philosophie de Bergson." *Les Études Bergsonniennes* 8 (1969): 123–158.

Zizek, Slavoj. *Organs Without Bodies: On Deleuze and Consequences*. London: Routledge, 2003.

Zourabichvili, François. *Deleuze: Une philosophie de l'événement*. Paris: PUF, 2004. Originally published in French in 1994.

———. "Deleuze et le possible (de l'involontarisme en politique)." In *Gilles Deleuze: une vie philosophique*, edited by Eric Alliez, 335–358. Paris: Institute Synthelabo, 1998.

Index

Adjudication, 1, 2, 5, 163, 165, 197, 230; creativity in, 101, 103, 106, 194–95, 213–14, 253; Dworkin, 23–25, 27, 28, 31–32, 35, 109–11, 151; Habermas, 37, 43, 44, 47–48, 111–13, 262*n*12; Hart, 7, 15, 18–21, 161; Holmes, 90–91, 97–98, 101, 103–4, 106; pragmatism, 115–16, 138–42; subsumption, 3, 49, 65, 171–2; time, 108–13, 143–47, 152. *See also* Attentive judgment; Case; Inattentive judgment; Judgment

Alliez, Eric, 115, 285*n*64

Andrews, William, 125, 272*n*23. See also *Palsgraf*

Antinomy: Bergson, 92; Dworkin, 23–24; Kant, 76–77, 267*n*40

Arendt, Hannah, 276*n*35

Aristotle, 62–64

Attentive judgment, 180–84, 186–87, 189–91, 193–95, 215–16, 253–54, 281*m*8. *See also* Inattentive judgment; Encounter; Judgment; Perception

Austin, J. L., 7, 8, 259*n*3

Austin, John, 8–12, 160, 259*nn*7, 9

Badiou, Alain, 51

Benhabib, Seyla, 40

Bergson, Henri: actualization of the virtual past, 143, 145, 153–57, 188–89; "all is given," 99, 107–13; attentive perception, 181–82, 185–86; choice, 158, 160–62, 275*nn*20, 21; cone of time, 136–37, 147; creativity, 89, 91, 251; critique of mechanism, 91–92, 98; critique of psychology (associationism), 129–30, 132, 146, 272*n*31; Deleuze, 51–52, 90, 93–94, 119, 120–21, 162, 175, 186, 197, 230, 239, 265*m*7, 267*n*31, 278*n*7; differentiation of life, 94–96, 105, 107; critique of dogmatism, 59–60; duration, 89, 94, 219, 220, 225; Dworkin, 109–13; encounter, 59–60, 96, 105–6, 165, 167–68, 176–77, 181, 185, 186–87; critique of finalism, 91–92, 95, 269*m*6; image, 117–23, 130, 145, 193, 271*m*2; image of thought, 89–91, 117, 120–21; inattentive perception, 165–68, 174; internal difference, 92–94, 105; judgment, 163, 167, 169–70, 183–84, 190, 194; Kant, 122, 177; law, 51, 97, 114–15, 270*m*1; memory, 135–37, 140–41, 144, 153, 162–64, 167–68; movement, 118, 122, 229, 238, 244–51, 273*n*41; perception, 121–23, 127–28, 140–41; pragmatism, 92, 115–17, 141, 153, 160–61, 163–64, 193, 271*n*5; precision in philosophy, 162, 186; problem, 75, 95–96, 106, 212; pure past, 127, 129, 131–32, 135, 144, 152, 158; retrospective illusion, 109, 112–13; Spinoza, 218, 251–52, 281*n*26, 282*n*29

Black, Hugo, 277*n*53

Body without Organs (BwO), 149–51. *See also* Law without Organs

Breyer, Stephen, 138

Cardozo, Benjamin, 115–16, 137–38, 147, 165, 172, 174, 265*m*3; *Palsgraf*, 124–26, 157, 159

302   Index

Case: composite of memory and perception, 127, 141, 145–48, 157–60, 170, 172, 174; as encounter, 58–59, 72, 85, 178, 191, 193, 208–11; as image, 123–24, 126, 145, 157–58, 171; as singularity, 56–57, 83–84; subsumption of, 3, 5–7, 13–14, 16–17, 65, 103, 110, 112–13, 150–52. *See also* Adjudication

Cavell, Stanley, 260*n*20

Caygill, Howard, 276*n*36

Concept: conceptual difference, 63–64; creation of concepts, 81, 201, 203–7, 209–12, 278*nn*1, 7; creation of legal concepts, 213–18

Cone of Time, 136, 147, 163

Constitution, US, 139, 191–94, 261*n*9, 273*n*45

Creativity: adjudication, 18–19, 100–103, 138, 194–95, 211, 213–15; creation of concepts, 41, 204–7, 215–18, 250–51, 278*n*7; judgment, 181–87, 190–91; jurisprudence, 54–56, 84–85; new image of thought, 89–90; and problems, 75–77, 95–96, 212–13, 228–30; suppression of, 20, 42, 48, 59–60, 67, 78, 81, 86, 92, 98, 110, 112, 150–51; time, 66, 91, 97, 116, 188, 216–17, 246–49. *See also* Attentive judgment

Deconstruction, 279*n*8

Deleuze, Gilles: Bergson, 51–52, 74, 75, 93–94, 114, 117, 119, 120–21, 155, 162; Body without Organs, 149–51; critique of communication, 41–42, 77–82, 86–87; concept of the concept, 201, 203–7, 278*nn*1, 7; concept of difference, 62–64; dogmatic image of thought, 2–3, 59, 60–62, 69, 78–79, 168, 266*n*8; encounter, 58–59, 72–77, 175–76, 180, 205–7, 266*n*29; experimentation, 235, 238; expression, 238, 239–41, 247–48; human rights, 55–56, 82–87; immanence, 119, 238, 241–43, 249–51; judgment, 62, 64–65, 70–72, 143, 149–52, 167, 195, 197; jurisprudence, 54–59, 83–84, 264*n*5; Kant, 1–2, 35–36, 68–75, 77, 177, 266*n*28, 274*n*4; law, 1–2, 53, 66–68, 265*n*7; the Left, 229–31, 236–37, 283*n*43; movement, 229, 244, 246–48; new image of thought, 88, 90, 117, 120–21; open whole, 152, 246, 248–49; as Platonic, 60, 78, 267*n*36; problem, 75–77, 80–82, 95, 212, 227–230; prudence, 238; repetition, 66–68, 188, 194; *ressentiment*, 81–82, 86, 266*n*21; Spinoza, 198, 201, 217–18, 220–22, 224, 243–44, 283*n*45; time, 66, 110, 127–37, 141, 216–17, 218, 242–43; transcendental philosophy, 61, 72–74, 212, 273*n*34

Delgado, Richard, 260*n*19

Delgamuukw v. British Columbia, 198–99, 207–8, 218, 231, 253; aboriginal title, 214–16; as an encounter, 209–11, 233, 235–36; evaluation of evidence, 232–37; reconciliation, 210–12, 232, 280*n*16, 281*n*17. *See also* Lamer

Descartes, René, 60, 61, 220, 281*n*23, 282*nn*28, 30

Dewey, John, 115, 265*n*13

Dogmatism: critique by Deleuze, 60–62, 73–74, 77–78, 81–82, 86, 88–91, 117, 120, 151, 186, 226–28; dogmatic image of law, 1, 3, 52, 53, 88, 107, 113, 235; dogmatic image of thought, 2, 3, 68–69, 71, 79, 168, 252, 259*n*2; in law and judgment, 59, 62, 67, 70

Douglas, William, 192, 193

Doxa (opinion), 41–42, 60–61, 78–82, 86, 88, 90, 120, 227

Durkheim, Emile, 251

Dworkin, Ronald: Bergson, 109–113; chain novel, 33–35, 151; Hercules, 107–8, 110–11, 150–51, 270*n*30; integrity, 22, 28, 30–33, 35, 108, 151, 263*n*21; Kant, 2–3, 5, 22, 25, 27–28, 31, 32, 35, 49, 260*n*1, 261*n*6; law with organs, 35, 148–52; purpose in law,

25–28; reflective judgment, 23, 24, 28, 30, 31, 32–33, 34–35, 36, 49, 88, 261*n*7; rules contrasted with principles, 23–26; subsumption, 23, 24, 25, 49; teleology, 27–28, 31, 32, 35, 261*n*9

Encounter: attentive judgment, 167, 174–75, 182–84, 187–91, 193–95, 216, 230–31; Bergson, 96, 165, 167, 168, 176–77, 181, 185, 186–87; case as, 59, 85, 236–37; Deleuze, 58–60, 71–77, 165, 176–77, 180, 207, 231, 265*n*12, 266*nn*28, 29, 273*n*34; *Delgamuukw* as, 209–11, 233, 235–36; Spinoza, 203, 204, 206, 221–25, 228; suppression, 59–60, 62, 65, 67, 69, 70–71, 86
Ethology, 243, 284*n*58
Evolution, 94–96, 104–5, 246, 268*n*1, 269*n*14
Ewald, François, 56
Experimentation: common notions, 218, 222–24, 282*n*34; judgment, 181–83, 190, 235–38. *See also* the Left; Prudence
Expression, 198, 238–41, 246, 247, 248, 249, 284*nn*54, 75

Ferrera, Alessandro, 261*n*6
French, Rebecca, 139–40, 273*n*41
Freud, Sigmund, 153, 243, 282*n*38

Gadamer, Hans-Georg, 114
Geophilosophy, 85
Goldschmidt, Victor, 271*n*15
Gouhier, Henri, 225
Grey, Thomas, 116
Griswold v. Connecticut, 191–95, 216
Guattari, Félix, 38, 56, 84, 198, 201, 202, 203, 204, 205, 207, 216, 255, 278*n*1, 284*n*53
Guerin v. Canada, 209, 279*n*12
Günther, Klaus, 42–44, 46–48, 111, 262*n*12, 263*n*23

Habermas, Jürgen: application discourses, 37, 42–49, 263*n*27; Deleuze, 41–2, 48, 78–83; Günther, 262*n*12; human rights, 39–41, 82–83; Kant, 2–3, 5, 37–38, 40, 45, 49, 82; perfect norms, 43–46, 48, 108, 112, 113; retrospective temporality, 37, 45–48, 108, 111–13
Hardt, Michael, 114, 282*n*34
Hart, H. L. A.: adjudication, 15, 18–21; critique of Austin, 8–12, 259*n*10; and choice, 7, 19–21, 159–61, 275*n*22; internal perspective, 10–12, 16; Kant, 2–3, 5, 8, 9, 13, 17–20, 49, 260*n*20; schematism, 6–7, 14–17, 88
Heidegger, Martin, 12, 14, 74, 260*n*15
Hobbes, Thomas, 203–205
Holmes, Oliver Wendell, 8, 32, 90–91, 157, 173, 271*n*14; creativity in adjudication, 100, 102–3, 158; deodand, 103–4; desire, 98, 101, 115; differentiation of law, 97, 105–7; duration in, 97, 102; eugenics, 96–97; evolution, 104–6; finalism, 98–100, 116, 269*n*14; interstitial legislator, 137–38; pragmatism, 97, 252, 265*n*13, 269*n*12
Human rights, 37, 39–40, 42, 828–3, 262*n*9; critique by Deleuze, 54–57, 77, 83–87
Hume, David, 53–54
Huxley, T. H., 261*n*1

Image, 175–76, 180–81; Bergsonian image, 117–22, 127, 130, 135–36, 160–61, 167–70, 184, 193; case as image, 123–24, 126, 145, 157–58, 171; dogmatic image of law, 1–3, 5, 49, 88, 107–8, 113, 235; dogmatic image of thought, 2–3, 60–62, 68–71, 73, 78–79, 92, 226–27, 265*n*17; new image of thought, 88–91, 97, 100, 120–21
Inattentive judgment, 143, 167–73, 175, 176, 179, 182, 184, 186, 190, 191, 195, 210. *See also* Attentive judgment; Encounter; Judgment; Perception

James, William, 115, 260*n*14, 271*n*5

Judgment, 137, 161, 281*n*23; attentive judgment, 180–84, 186*n*7, 189–91, 193–95, 215–16, 253–54, 281*n*18; creativity, 101–2, 106–7, 213, 255; Deleuze, 1, 143, 149–52, 197; determinative judgment, 22–25, 141; dogmatism of, 62, 64–65, 70–72, 151; inattentive judgment, 143, 167–73, 175, 176, 179, 182, 184, 186, 190, 191, 195, 210; Kant, 2, 7, 13–15, 20, 40, 45, 69–70, 177, 276*n*36; reflective judgment, 22–23, 26–30, 32, 34, 36, 148–50, 152, 261*n*6; retrospective illusion, 48, 112–13; schematism, 6–7, 14, 16, 260*n*15; subsumption, 3, 5, 14, 16, 49, 65, 140, 160, 163, 169–72, 252, 260*n*20; teleology, 27, 31, 33, 35, 115, 149, 261*n*9; time, 101–2, 109, 144, 153, 157–58. *See also* Adjudication

Judicial activism, 116, 138, 217, 283*n*44, 284*n*53

Jurisprudence, 51–52, 155, 166, 264*n*5; analytical, 10, 58; Deleuze, 54–59, 83–87, 150; Hart, 5, 8, 9, 18–19

Kafka, Franz, 194

Kant, Immanuel, 5, 8, 17–18, 20, 37, 45, 76–77, 121, 144, 160, 247, 267*n*30; beauty, 177, 276*n*35; Deleuze, 1–2, 61, 68–71, 73, 77, 134, 149, 177, 227; dogmatism of, 68–72; law, 38, 68, 82, 274*n*4; reflective judgment, 22, 26–27, 32, 35, 148–49, 261*n*6; schematism, 6–7, 14, 16, 260*n*15; sublime, 74–75, 266*n*28; subsumption, 12–15, 49; teleology, 27, 30, 33; transcendental deduction, 29, 69–70

Kennedy, Duncan, 261*n*8

Lamer, Antonio, 209–11, 214–17, 232–37. *See also* *Delgamuukw*

Langdell, Christopher Columbus, 98

Law without Organs (LwO), 150, 152. *See also* Body without Organs

Left, the, 229–31, 236–37, 253, 283*nn*43, 44

Llewellyn, Karl, 8, 123–24, 272*n*18, 281*n*19

Locke, John, 54

Mabo v. Queensland, 279*n*15, 280*n*16

Macherey, Pierre, 282*n*34

Marrati, Paola, 117

McEachern, Allan, 231, 233, 235, 284*n*51

Memory: attentive judgment, 180–84, 187, 189–90, 193; Bergson, 116, 127, 132, 140, 153, 161, 185, 189; habit and recollection memory, 162–66; inattentive judgment, 167, 169, 170, 173; law, 144–47, 158–59, 164, 171–72, 19; pure past, 135–36, 154–57. *See also* Virtual

Nancy, Jean-Luc, 13–14

Nietzsche, Friedrich, 25, 102, 151, 153, 238, 266*n*17, 271*n*13

Open whole, 152, 246–49, 251, 254

Palsgraf v. Long Island Railroad Co, 124–26, 145, 157–59, 165

Paradoxes of time, 126–37, 141, 147, 153

Parnet, Claire, 265*n*7

Patton, Paul, 84, 85, 203, 205, 267*n*34, 279–80*n*15, 280*n*16

Perception, 121–22; attentive perception, 167, 179, 181–82; choice, 160–61; inattentive perception, 167–70, 174–76; memory, 127, 132, 140, 164, 166–67, 180–86; perceiving cases, 123–26, 141, 146–47, 158, 170–72; politics, 231, 237

Plane of immanence, 119, 130, 198, 238–39, 241–44, 249–55

Plato, 60, 61, 78, 86, 88, 251, 267*n*36

Posner, Richard, 102, 115–16, 124, 126, 137

Pragmatism: Bergson, 92, 98, 115–17, 141, 153, 160, 163–64, 193, 271*n*5; legal pragmatism, 97, 123–24, 126, 137–42, 164, 252–53, 260*n*1, 265*n*13, 269*n*12, 259*n*5; ontological pragmatism,

116–17, 130–31; perception, 121–22, 146, 177
Problem: creation of, 75–77, 209–10, 212–13, 229–31, 237, 267*n*30; as encounter, 75–77, 165, 174, 266*n*29; and evolution, 95–96; Holmes, 105–7; jurisprudence, 56–58, 84–87, 216; and philosophies of communication, 42, 48, 78–82; reconciliation in *Delgamuukw*, 210–12, 232–35, 280*n*16, 281*n*17; right to problems, 227–29, 283*n*39; as transcendental, 81, 212–13, 281*n*18
Proust, Marcel, 58–59, 132, 187–88, 266*n*17
Prudence, 237–38

R. v. Sparrow, 214, 279*n*12
R. v. Van der Peet, 214, 232, 279*n*15
Rehg, William, 46–47
Repetition: denied by dogmatism, 65–69, 114, 173; differential, 74, 101, 188, 194, 206; of the pure past, 135–37, 147, 159
Riggs v. Palmer, 111, 148
Rorty, Richard, 259*n*5, 271*n*5
Rose, Gillian, 114

Sartre, Jean-Paul, 271*n*15
Scalia, Antonin, 138, 139, 273*n*45
Shklar, Judith, 275*n*21
Soulez, Phillipe, 251

Spinoza, Baruch, 205, 253, 278*n*2, 283*n*45; adequate idea, 222, 226–29, 281*n*23; encounter, 203, 204, 206, 221–25, 228; expression in, 239–41, 247; face of the universe, 245, 250; immanence, 119, 238–39, 242–43, 250–52, 271*n*13; joy and sadness, 221–28, 235, 282*n*38; parallelism, 203; physics, 201–3, 206–7, 278*n*1; power, 221–26, 228–29, 240–41; spiritual automaton, 217, 281*n*24; time and duration, 204, 218–21, 223–26, 235–36; "what can a body do?" 220–23, 282*n*30
Stare decisis, 171

Tarde, Gabriel, 273*n*35
Time. *See* Bergson, Creativity, Deleuze, Memory, Virtual
Transcendental empiricism, 72, 273*n*34. *See also* Encounter
Twelve Angry Men, 178–80

Virtual, 127, 132–37, 141–42, 153–57, 185, 273*n*32; and judgment, 143–48, 182, 186, 189

Wellmer, Albrecht, 262*n*13
White, Edward, 269*n*4
Wittgenstein, Ludwig, 7, 8, 17, 260*n*8, 275*n*22

Cultural Memory | *in the Present*

Samira Haj, *Reconfiguring Islamic Tradition: Reform, Rationality, and Modernity*

Marcel Detienne, *Comparing the Incomparable*

Diane Perpich, *The Ethics of Emmanuel Levinas*

François Delaporte, *Anatomy of the Passions*

René Girard, *Mimesis and Theory: Essays on Literature and Criticism, 1959-2005*

Richard Baxstrom, *Wrecking Balls, Ruins, Reform: The Experience of Place and the Problem of Belief in Urban Malaysia*

Jennifer L. Culbert, *Capital Punishment and the Problem of Judgment*

Samantha Frost, *Lessons from a Materialist Thinker: Hobbesian Reflections on Ethics and Politics*

Regina Mara Schwartz, *When God Left the World: Sacramental Poetics at the Dawn of Secularism*

Gil Anidjar, *Semites: Race, Religion, Literature*

Ranjana Khanna, *Algeria Cuts: Women and Representation, 1830 to the Present*

Esther Peeren, *Intersubjectivities and Popular Culture: Bakhtin and Beyond*

Eyal Peretz, *Becoming Visionary: Brian De Palma's Cinematic Education of the Senses*

Diana Sorensen, *A Turbulent Decade Remembered: Scenes from the Latin American Sixties*

Hubert Damisch, *A Childhood Memory by Piero della Francesca*

Dana Hollander, *Exemplarity and Chosenness: Rosenzweig and Derrida on the Nation of Philosophy*

Asja Szafraniec, *Beckett, Derrida, and the Event of Literature*

Sara Guyer, *Romanticism After Auschwitz*

Alison Ross, *The Aesthetic Paths of Philosophy: Presentation in Kant, Heidegger, Lacoue-Labarthe, and Nancy*

Gerhard Richter, *Thought-Images: Frankfurt School Writers' Reflections from Damaged Life*

Bella Brodzki, *Can These Bones Live? Translation, Survival, and Cultural Memory*

Rodolphe Gasché, *The Honor of Thinking: Critique, Theory, Philosophy*

Brigitte Peucker, *The Material Image: Art and the Real in Film*

Natalie Melas, *All the Difference in the World: Postcoloniality and the Ends of Comparison*

Jonathan Culler, *The Literary in Theory*

Michael G. Levine, *The Belated Witness: Literature, Testimony, and the Question of Holocaust Survival*

Jennifer A. Jordan, *Structures of Memory: Understanding German Change in Berlin and Beyond*

Christoph Menke, *Reflections of Equality*

Marlène Zarader, *The Unthought Debt: Heidegger and the Hebraic Heritage*

Jan Assmann, *Religion and Cultural Memory: Ten Studies*

David Scott and Charles Hirschkind, *Powers of the Secular Modern: Talal Asad and His Interlocutors*

Gyanendra Pandey, *Routine Violence: Nations, Fragments, Histories*

James Siegel, *Naming the Witch*

J. M. Bernstein, *Against Voluptuous Bodies: Late Modernism and the Meaning of Painting*

Theodore W. Jennings, Jr., *Reading Derrida / Thinking Paul: On Justice*

Richard Rorty and Eduardo Mendieta, *Take Care of Freedom and Truth Will Take Care of Itself: Interviews with Richard Rorty*

Jacques Derrida, *Paper Machine*

Renaud Barbaras, *Desire and Distance: Introduction to a Phenomenology of Perception*

Jill Bennett, *Empathic Vision: Affect, Trauma, and Contemporary Art*

Ban Wang, *Illuminations from the Past: Trauma, Memory, and History in Modern China*

James Phillips, *Heidegger's Volk: Between National Socialism and Poetry*

Frank Ankersmit, *Sublime Historical Experience*

István Rév, *Retroactive Justice: Prehistory of Post-Communism*

Paola Marrati, *Genesis and Trace: Derrida Reading Husserl and Heidegger*

Krzysztof Ziarek, *The Force of Art*

Marie-José Mondzain, *Image, Icon, Economy: The Byzantine Origins of the Contemporary Imaginary*

Cecilia Sjöholm, *The Antigone Complex: Ethics and the Invention of Feminine Desire*

Jacques Derrida and Elisabeth Roudinesco, *For What Tomorrow . . . : A Dialogue*

Elisabeth Weber, *Questioning Judaism: Interviews by Elisabeth Weber*

Jacques Derrida and Catherine Malabou, *Counterpath: Traveling with Jacques Derrida*

Martin Seel, *Aesthetics of Appearing*

Nanette Salomon, *Shifting Priorities: Gender and Genre in Seventeenth-Century Dutch Painting*

Jacob Taubes, *The Political Theology of Paul*

Jean-Luc Marion, *The Crossing of the Visible*

Eric Michaud, *The Cult of Art in Nazi Germany*

Anne Freadman, *The Machinery of Talk: Charles Peirce and the Sign Hypothesis*

Stanley Cavell, *Emerson's Transcendental Etudes*

Stuart McLean, *The Event and Its Terrors: Ireland, Famine, Modernity*

Beate Rössler, ed., *Privacies: Philosophical Evaluations*

Bernard Faure, *Double Exposure: Cutting Across Buddhist and Western Discourses*

Alessia Ricciardi, *The Ends of Mourning: Psychoanalysis, Literature, Film*

Alain Badiou, *Saint Paul: The Foundation of Universalism*

Gil Anidjar, *The Jew, the Arab: A History of the Enemy*

Jonathan Culler and Kevin Lamb, eds., *Just Being Difficult? Academic Writing in the Public Arena*

Jean-Luc Nancy, *A Finite Thinking*, edited by Simon Sparks

Theodor W. Adorno, *Can One Live after Auschwitz? A Philosophical Reader*, edited by Rolf Tiedemann

Patricia Pisters, *The Matrix of Visual Culture: Working with Deleuze in Film Theory*

Andreas Huyssen, *Present Pasts: Urban Palimpsests and the Politics of Memory*

Talal Asad, *Formations of the Secular: Christianity, Islam, Modernity*

Dorothea von Mücke, *The Rise of the Fantastic Tale*

Marc Redfield, *The Politics of Aesthetics: Nationalism, Gender, Romanticism*

Emmanuel Levinas, *On Escape*

Dan Zahavi, *Husserl's Phenomenology*

Rodolphe Gasché, *The Idea of Form: Rethinking Kant's Aesthetics*

Michael Naas, *Taking on the Tradition: Jacques Derrida and the Legacies of Deconstruction*

Herlinde Pauer-Studer, ed., *Constructions of Practical Reason: Interviews on Moral and Political Philosophy*

Jean-Luc Marion, *Being Given That: Toward a Phenomenology of Givenness*

Theodor W. Adorno and Max Horkheimer, *Dialectic of Enlightenment*

Ian Balfour, *The Rhetoric of Romantic Prophecy*

Martin Stokhof, *World and Life as One: Ethics and Ontology in Wittgenstein's Early Thought*

Gianni Vattimo, *Nietzsche: An Introduction*

Jacques Derrida, *Negotiations: Interventions and Interviews, 1971-1998*, ed. Elizabeth Rottenberg

Brett Levinson, *The Ends of Literature: The Latin American "Boom" in the Neoliberal Marketplace*

Timothy J. Reiss, *Against Autonomy: Cultural Instruments, Mutualities, and the Fictive Imagination*

Hent de Vries and Samuel Weber, eds., *Religion and Media*

Niklas Luhmann, *Theories of Distinction: Re-Describing the Descriptions of Modernity*, ed. and introd. William Rasch

Johannes Fabian, *Anthropology with an Attitude: Critical Essays*

Michel Henry, *I Am the Truth: Toward a Philosophy of Christianity*

Gil Anidjar, *"Our Place in Al-Andalus": Kabbalah, Philosophy, Literature in Arab-Jewish Letters*

Hélène Cixous and Jacques Derrida, *Veils*

F. R. Ankersmit, *Historical Representation*

F. R. Ankersmit, *Political Representation*

Elissa Marder, *Dead Time: Temporal Disorders in the Wake of Modernity (Baudelaire and Flaubert)*

Reinhart Koselleck, *The Practice of Conceptual History: Timing History, Spacing Concepts*

Niklas Luhmann, *The Reality of the Mass Media*

Hubert Damisch, *A Theory of /Cloud/: Toward a History of Painting*

Jean-Luc Nancy, *The Speculative Remark: (One of Hegel's bon mots)*

Jean-François Lyotard, *Soundproof Room: Malraux's Anti-Aesthetics*

Jan Patočka, *Plato and Europe*

Hubert Damisch, *Skyline: The Narcissistic City*

Isabel Hoving, *In Praise of New Travelers: Reading Caribbean Migrant Women Writers*

Richard Rand, ed., *Futures: Of Jacques Derrida*

William Rasch, *Niklas Luhmann's Modernity: The Paradoxes of Differentiation*

Jacques Derrida and Anne Dufourmantelle, *Of Hospitality*

Jean-François Lyotard, *The Confession of Augustine*

Kaja Silverman, *World Spectators*

Samuel Weber, *Institution and Interpretation: Expanded Edition*

Jeffrey S. Librett, *The Rhetoric of Cultural Dialogue: Jews and Germans in the Epoch of Emancipation*

Ulrich Baer, *Remnants of Song: Trauma and the Experience of Modernity in Charles Baudelaire and Paul Celan*

Samuel C. Wheeler III, *Deconstruction as Analytic Philosophy*

David S. Ferris, *Silent Urns: Romanticism, Hellenism, Modernity*

Rodolphe Gasché, *Of Minimal Things: Studies on the Notion of Relation*

Sarah Winter, *Freud and the Institution of Psychoanalytic Knowledge*

Samuel Weber, *The Legend of Freud: Expanded Edition*

Aris Fioretos, ed., *The Solid Letter: Readings of Friedrich Hölderlin*

J. Hillis Miller / Manuel Asensi, *Black Holes / J. Hillis Miller; or, Boustrophedonic Reading*

Miryam Sas, *Fault Lines: Cultural Memory and Japanese Surrealism*

Peter Schwenger, *Fantasm and Fiction: On Textual Envisioning*

Didier Maleuvre, *Museum Memories: History, Technology, Art*

Jacques Derrida, *Monolingualism of the Other; or, The Prosthesis of Origin*

Andrew Baruch Wachtel, *Making a Nation, Breaking a Nation: Literature and Cultural Politics in Yugoslavia*

Niklas Luhmann, *Love as Passion: The Codification of Intimacy*

Mieke Bal, ed., *The Practice of Cultural Analysis: Exposing Interdisciplinary Interpretation*

Jacques Derrida and Gianni Vattimo, eds., *Religion*